1979
YEARBOOK
of Jehovah's Witnesses
Containing Report for the Service Year
of 1978
Also Daily Texts and Comments

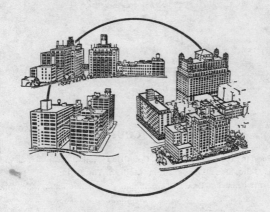

Corporate Publishers
**WATCH TOWER BIBLE AND TRACT SOCIETY
OF PENNSYLVANIA**
**WATCHTOWER BIBLE AND TRACT SOCIETY
OF NEW YORK, INC.**
INTERNATIONAL BIBLE STUDENTS ASSOCIATION
124 Columbia Heights
Brooklyn, N.Y. 11201, U.S.A.

Branch offices appear on last page

Made in the United States of America

*Jehovah's Witnesses
find great delight in
serving the Sovereign
Lord Jehovah
under their Leader,
Jesus Christ.
—Isa. 55:4.*

—————◆—————

INDEX OF COUNTRIES

1979
YEARBOOK
of Jehovah's Witnesses

We live in a restless and mixed-up world. With each passing day people observe and experience things that add to their anxieties. Many are bewildered. They do not know what to do or where to turn to get relief from the pressures and problems of life. They see governments in turmoil. Economic problems go unsolved and inflation plagues many lands. Pollution is causing all kinds of health problems. Morally, there is a serious breakdown. Religious paradoxes and hypocrisy abound. Despite the "leadership" of many prominent individuals in government, business, science, religion, social activity and other fields, the world is in a mess.

With all the publicized talk that comes from leaders who wield authority in this world, it is timely to ask: Is there anyone among them who really knows the right way to go? Can there be found among the leaders of thought in the world anyone to whom people can turn to get satisfying answers to their vital questions, or to find a sure hope for the future? Whom can the people follow with assurance that they will not be disappointed? Is there a leader who can bring them out of their confused and bedarkened state and provide the direction they so sorely need at this time?

It is not at all presumptuous for us to say that there is a leader in whom people can place their full confidence. A little time is required for one to learn the facts so as to be convinced of this and to identify that leader unerringly. There is an abundance of evidence to support his claims and credentials if one will just take the necessary time and be patient enough to examine it. Really, that is asking so little if it means getting set straight and gaining the present and future benefits that come from following this leader. He has already done so much for those who have willingly chosen to follow him. Individuals who are not yet benefiting from his leadership still have an opportunity to take their stand on his side. If you have not yet made this decision, are you interested in doing so?

The situation today calls for someone altogether different from any of the multiplicity of imperfect human leaders who are failing to cope with mankind's growing problems. There is an urgent need for a leader who can unify people from among all nations and who possesses qualifications to solve whatever problems need attention. It surprises many persons when they are told that such a leader has been actively on the scene for some time now. He has not come into this position by virtue of his being elected as the people's choice. Primarily he occupies his office by reason of God's appointment. About whom are we talking? Let's briefly review a little history.

FOLLOWING OUR GOD-APPOINTED LEADER

Nineteen hundred years ago a group of close associates were given some unusual counsel by their leader about greatness. It was most appropriate since 10 of them had become indignant over a question involving prominence that had been requested for two other members of the group. Using an example, he said to them: "You know that the rulers of the nations lord it over them and the great men wield authority over them. This is not the way among you; but whoever wants to become great among you must be your minister, and whoever wants to be first among you must be your slave." (Matt. 20:25-27) The speaker on that occasion was none other than Jesus Christ. He had already demonstrated his greatness by what he taught and the way he ministered to others. Previously, he had been telling his followers about the trials and kind of death awaiting him. The 12 men to whom he was speaking were his apostles. Two of them were brothers whose mother had asked that they be given positions at the right- and left-hand side of Jesus in his kingdom.—Matt. 20:17-24.

Not only was Jesus the recognized leader of those 12 apostles and other disciples who followed him, but he was destined to become a ruler, yes, a king sitting upon a throne, in the kingdom of God. (Matt. 23:10; 25:31-34) In pointing out what greatness involves, Jesus used himself as an example, tying in a twofold reason for his coming to this earth. Note his words: "Just as the Son of man came, not to be ministered to, but to minister and to give his soul a ransom in exchange for many." (Matt. 20:28) Being sent from heaven, Jesus came to serve his Father, to do His will, at the same time ministering in a way that would benefit the world of mankind.

In order to accomplish his mission, it was necessary for Jesus Christ to leave the realm above, divest himself of heavenly glory and humbly accept an earthly assignment, where tests and trials would serve to perfect his obedience. According to the Scriptures, "he emptied himself and took a slave's form and came to be in the likeness of men. More than that, when he found himself in fashion as a man, he humbled himself and became obedient as far as death, yes, death on a torture stake." (Phil. 2:7, 8) It certainly took great humility on his part to serve God in this way. No other human has ever given up anything that comes near to comparing with what Jesus Christ gave up in order to please God.

In 'taking a slave's form' Jesus came to minister or to serve. He did not waste time or procrastinate in carrying out his assigned work. Following his baptism in the Jordan River he was anointed with God's holy spirit. Under its impulse he was led into the wilderness, where he no doubt meditated on the course ahead of him. (Ps. 19:14) During his 40-day period in the wilderness he successfully resisted the Devil's temptations. (Matt. 4:1-10) Shortly thereafter Jesus embarked on an intensive work of preaching and teaching. There was no ambiguity about his message. Matthew's account reads: "From that time on Jesus commenced preaching and saying: 'Repent, you people, for the kingdom of the heavens has drawn near.'" (Matt. 4:17) He did not limit his activity to any one location, such as his hometown of Nazareth where he had been brought up. At a synagogue meeting in Nazareth, Jesus read his commission from Isaiah 61:1, 2. He left that town shortly thereafter to spend some time elsewhere in Galilee touring cities and villages, preaching the good news of the Kingdom and teaching, as well as performing miraculous cures. Multitudes were attracted to hear his words and seek relief from their infirmities. Observing their condition Jesus knew there was a need for more workers because the harvest was great. (Matt. 9:35-38) He saw to it that those workers were provided by training his apostles and disciples to go forth with the same message of hope that he was proclaiming. Due to the urgency of the time, they were not to be burdened down with an excess of personal effects; just the essentials would suffice.—Matt. 10:5-10; Luke 10:1, 2.

When the time came for him to "give his soul a ransom in exchange for many" he did not hold back but displayed his greatness by willingly submitting to a sacrificial death. (Mark 10:45) He was falsely accused of being a criminal blasphemer. Laying down his life in this way was not easy but was a real test of faith and devotion. This is evident from his prayer: "My Father, if it is possible, let this cup pass away from me. Yet, not as I will, but as you will." (Matt. 26:39) His faithfulness until death glorified his Father's name, proved his own integrity and worthiness to be exalted to God's right hand and has resulted in the greatest benefits for the entire human family.

There have been many individuals down through the corridors of time who have tried to make a name for themselves in history as human leaders. But none can compare with Jesus Christ. He excels them all in greatness. Jesus stands alone as the one whom God has appointed as a leader, not just for the fleshly descendants of Abraham but for all national groups, that is, members of all races of mankind who choose to follow him. (Isa. 55:4) While the first ones to follow him in the first century of our Common Era were from among the fleshly nation of Israel, in due time people from among the Gentiles or non-Jewish nations accepted him and became his disciples.

In our time there are hundreds of millions of people who profess to be followers of Jesus Christ. But where is the proof that they are really such? As recorded at Matthew 16:24, Jesus said: "If anyone wants to come after me, let him disown himself and pick up his torture stake and continually follow me." Are the hundreds of millions of adherents to Christendom's churches doing that? Are they proving themselves his disciples by bearing righteous fruit and making known the truth concerning his kingdom? Christendom's own leaders admit that they are not.

In striking contrast, Jehovah's Witnesses recognize and publicly acknowledge Jesus Christ as their leader and model, whose steps they are determined to follow closely. (1 Pet. 2:21) They are obeying his command to preach the good news of the Kingdom in all the world for a witness, doing so in over 200 lands. They are also making disciples by teaching people all the things that Jesus Christ commanded should be observed. The fact that 95,052 new disciples were baptized during the 1978 service year gives evidence of their determination to fulfill the commission to preach the Kingdom good news and teach others right down to the conclusion of the system of things. (Matt. 28:19, 20) Are you one of such disciples? If not, would you be interested in becoming a dedicated follower of Jesus Christ, even as hundreds of thousands of others have because of being taught and helped by zealous servants of Jehovah God?

Jehovah's Witnesses in these modern times are doing all they can to make disciples while there is yet time. They realize they must continue their God-given work of spreading the message from God's Word without letup. As to the extent to which this must be done, they have taken to heart the direction provided by their leader, Jesus Christ. Toward the end of the 40-day period following his resurrection, Jesus assembled with some of his disciples at a prearranged meeting on the

Mount of Olives on "the day that he was taken up." On that occasion he made it plain that their work would extend far beyond Jerusalem, Judea and Samaria, in fact, "to the most distant part of the earth." (Acts 1:1-9) Hence, Jehovah's Witnesses today are convinced, even as those early disciples of Jesus were, that their Christian activity must be carried out on a global scale, to the fullest extent possible. The 1978 Service Year Report of Jehovah's Witnesses set out on pages 24-31 in this *Yearbook* is clear evidence that this and other commands given by Jesus Christ are being carried out today.

SOCIETIES AND CORPORATIONS
USED IN CHRISTIAN ACTIVITY

In order to carry on the global Kingdom-preaching and disciple-making work properly, a number of religious corporations and associations have been formed. The principal purpose for establishing these various organizations is in line with what is set out in the articles of incorporation of the Watch Tower Bible and Tract Society of Pennsylvania (organized in the year 1884), namely, "to preach the gospel of God's kingdom under Christ Jesus unto all nations as a witness to the name, word and supremacy of Almighty God JEHOVAH" and to employ such means as are necessary to accomplish that purpose.

The officers of all such corporations or associations are Jehovah's Christian witnesses, dedicated servants of Jehovah God and disciples of Jesus Christ. They all perform any legal duties incumbent upon them freely, and without monetary consideration, all as unto Jehovah.—Col. 3:23, 24.

So that the religious activity of Jehovah's Witnesses may be carried on as smoothly as possible, the Watch Tower Bible and Tract Society of Pennsylvania has established branches in all parts of the world. There are 98 branch offices that care for the interests of God's people in all the lands where the "good news" is now being proclaimed. The facilities in a number of these branches include printing plants where Bibles, books, magazines and other publications are produced for use by Jehovah's Witnesses and for distribution world wide for the benefit of truth seekers.

This year saw the introduction of the highly efficient offset printing process on a large scale. It made possible the publishing of the Society's first multicolored publication *My Book of Bible Stories*.

As part of its chartered purposes, the Watch Tower Society also sends out ministers and other representatives, such as missionaries, special pioneers and traveling overseers, into domestic and foreign fields. This has involved an expenditure of $14,914,756.03 this past year in all parts of the world. Voluntary contributions on the part of Jehovah's Witnesses have made this possible and we are thankful to our heavenly Father for his spirit in moving the hearts of those who have shared their material resources and thus 'honored Jehovah with their valuable things.'—Prov. 3:9.

WATCH TOWER'S VENTURE INTO COMPUTER OPERATIONS

The year 1978 saw considerable progress in the Society's venture into computer operations. Why was this step taken? Because of the trend throughout the printing industry. Less and less equipment is being manufactured for printing by means of typesetting that involves the use of hot metal. So the Society has no alternative but to move into computer operation if it is to keep on publishing books and magazines. To this end, a meeting was held in Wiesbaden, Federal Republic of Germany, late in 1977 at which coordinators and other representatives from 17 branches directly interested in this major step met with representatives from the Brooklyn headquarters. The first of such computer systems was installed in Brooklyn in July 1978. It will be used for program development in three principal areas: (1) bookkeeping and records (2) magazine distribution (3) publishing. While these applications will be used first in Brooklyn, their design includes extension in the future to other branches.

BETHEL FAMILIES AROUND THE WORLD

Bethel means "House of God" and aptly identifies the residence of devoted men and women who care for the various activities at the branch locations around the world. The members of each Bethel family have unique privileges of sacred service. They are able to spend their full time at assigned duties that serve the interests of the Kingdom in all parts of the earth. They render a variety of services. Whether they have duties to perform in the Bethel home, care for work at the various offices, work in the factory producing the literature, or serve on one of the Society's farms where food is produced for the Bethel family, they view all these assignments as essential. By close cooperation, members of the Bethel family are able to accomplish a tremendous amount of work in getting the Kingdom message out in printed form to all parts of the world. For example, during the past year they shared in producing a total of 70,576,240 Bibles, books and booklets and 422,285,935 *Watchtower* and *Awake!* magazines. Millions of other pieces of printed matter including tracts, programs, handbills, and so forth, were also produced.

The largest group serving in this way is located in the United States. At the Brooklyn headquarters there are 1,825 members in the Bethel family, and, together with the 646 serving at Watchtower Farms, we now have a total of 2,471. Earth wide there are upward of 3,000 who enjoy this special privilege of Bethel service. All of them share in preaching the good news of the Kingdom in association with the congregations to which they are assigned.

VARIOUS SCHOOLS IN OPERATION WORLD WIDE

The Society's charter provides for the establishment of private Bible schools and classes.

The Watchtower Bible School of Gilead has been used ever since 1943 to train and equip dedicated and qualified men and women for missionary service. This past year, 53 graduated from the school and were sent to assignments in 25 lands. At the present time Gilead graduates are serving in more than 120 different lands in various parts of the earth. They are doing a wonderful work and their efforts have been richly blessed.

In Brooklyn, starting in December 1977, the first class of the new school for Branch Committee members began. During the year four classes were held. Others will follow in the 1979 service year. The course provides units of instruction on Scriptural subjects, organizational matters and practical training in the home, offices and factory. The entire program has been prepared to help those attending to fulfill the many responsibilities involved in caring for the work in their assigned territories. It has been most encouraging and upbuilding to them, and their wives who could be present, to be in association with the brothers at the Brooklyn headquarters. Their reports and experiences about the work in their own lands have been greatly appreciated by members of the Bethel family in Brooklyn and at Watchtower Farms.

A big responsibility rests on the congregation elders who are charged with paying attention to themselves and to all the flock over which the holy spirit has appointed them overseers. (Acts 20:28) Arrangements were made during the year for them to receive special instruction at the Kingdom Ministry School. Many new elders have been appointed within the last few years and they see the need to learn from more experienced elders as they cooperate with one another. The Denmark branch wrote: "This 15-hour course was just what was needed. Fine material was presented in an effective way with many questions drawing out the thoughts and insight of the elders on various points."

Since the 1977 district assemblies, many have been looking forward to the benefits of the Pioneer Service School. During the year thousands of regular and special pioneers, missionaries and wives of traveling overseers have greatly benefited from the course. It has proved to be a tremendous source of encouragement to those who have attended the school, and they feel rejuvenated spiritually, determined to press on as more effective servants in preaching and teaching the good news of the Kingdom.

Since the course allows for those in the class to engage in actual field witnessing, some interesting experiences take place. In Colombia one group of 22 students obtained three subscriptions, placed 95 magazines and 124 books and started 30 home Bible studies. They themselves were amazed with the results when territory is covered thoroughly.

One 73-year-old pioneer in Jamaica said: "I had been thinking about giving up pioneering since I felt I could no longer manage it. The school has brought new life to me." All of those who have gone to the school are now in a position to put their training to good use in territory where there is a greater need.

In all the 42,255 congregations of Jehovah's Witnesses the Theocratic School is conducted. Those enrolled are given regular assignments to present. All in the congregation are encouraged to keep up with the Bible reading program week by week. The benefits of this school are reflected in the improved ability our brothers now have to converse with others on Bible topics and to conduct home Bible studies more effectively. Also, the school has helped qualified male Christians to handle service meeting assignments and has trained many of them as public speakers.

In addition to these schools, some of the larger branches conduct a school for new members of the Bethel family. The instruction in all these educational arrangements is based on God's Word. By making personal application of the things learned, individuals who are taught in the various schools are able to make their advancement manifest.—1 Tim. 4:15, 16.

FAITH MANIFEST BY WORKS

Throughout the world Jehovah's Witnesses find that their taking in knowledge of the Bible increases their faith; they are strengthened by attending the regular weekly meetings of the congregation. Besides the Theocratic School there is a weekly service meeting and congregation book studies, as well as a public Bible lecture and the *Watchtower* study, all of which provide excellent material for consideration. These meetings build up the spirituality of God's people, help them to cope with the problems of life and to live in accord with Scriptural principles, while also encouraging all associated to have a regular share in witnessing to others.

During the year Jehovah's Witnesses spent 307,272,-262 hours in the field service, endeavoring to help others. In addition to giving a witness concerning the Kingdom, their commission is to make disciples, actually teaching people the basic Bible truths that will enable them to come out of Babylon the Great, separate themselves from the world and take a firm stand on the side of the truth. (John 18:37) Service campaigns that received excellent support world wide included the tract distributions and placing the *Blood* booklet. Two fine tracts were used to good advantage. One dealt with the subject "The Family—Can It Survive?" while the other asked the interesting question

"Why Are We Here?" These subjects provided a good basis for introducing the message at the doors, and for then developing a fine discussion wherever possible. Often literature was placed that led to home Bible studies.

Use of Bible literature by Jehovah's Witnesses is helping them to reach many individuals with the truth. For example, in a new territory to which special pioneers were assigned, a report from Colombia says: "We want to let you know that the preaching work here in El Bordo has been accepted readily and in six weeks the four of us have placed 1,067 books. We are already conducting 18 home Bible studies. My 10-year-old son has placed 68 books and is conducting two studies. With the help of the nearby congregation in Pasto, we were able to get six benches and we have started to have meetings. Last Sunday there were 35 persons in attendance. We believe that, with Jehovah's blessing, we will be able to start a congregation."

Our brothers in Portugal are very happy to have a variety of Bible aids to use in their Bible study work, as indicated in this report: "How wonderful to have a publication for any type of person we meet! The *Youth* book has a strong appeal to teen-agers, and one young special pioneer brother placed 199 copies at high schools during a recent campaign. Above all, we rejoice to see more and more people seriously studying the Bible with us as the number of home Bible studies has been over 16,000 for the last two months."

The special campaign with the booklet *Jehovah's Witnesses and the Question of Blood* produced excellent results. It served to acquaint doctors, nurses, hospital administrators, judges and lawyers with the position of Jehovah's Witnesses. Many letters were received at the Society's headquarters, as well as at the branch offices, in which people expressed their appreciation for the fine Scriptural explanation presented in the booklet. It has enabled individuals in these professional fields to recognize the Scriptural and reasonable position taken by Jehovah's Witnesses on this vital issue.

AUXILIARY PIONEER SERVICE

It has been observed that the ranks of the auxiliary pioneers have shown a fine increase in many countries throughout the world. Those unable to arrange their affairs to share in the regular pioneer service have found that they can continuously or at different times of the year share in the auxiliary pioneer work. Quite a number of elders and ministerial servants have been in a position to share in the auxiliary pioneer service, thus providing a fine example for others in the congregation. They have been able to spend more time with publishers in the field, especially with some of the younger ones.

'THEY WILL FIGHT AGAINST YOU'

During the year our brothers have found great comfort in the yeartext taken from Jeremiah 1:19: "And they will be certain to fight against you, but they will not prevail against you, for 'I am with you,' is the utterance of Jehovah, 'to deliver you.'" Time and again Christians have placed their confidence in these reassuring words, especially in lands where there has been opposition to the Kingdom work and our brothers have come under great pressure and have suffered from violent persecution. There are more than 40 countries where an official ban or other restrictions have been imposed on the Christian worship and activity of Jehovah's Witnesses. In all these lands our brothers demonstrate a victorious faith and willingly continue to endure the harassments, indignities, detentions and other forms of persecution because they follow Jesus Christ as their Leader and do good to people.—Matt. 24:9; 1 Pet. 3:16, 17.

In one African country the brothers find it extremely difficult and dangerous to meet together. Nevertheless, they remember the admonition at Hebrews 10:24, 25 and have found ways of coming together in worship. According to a report, "curfews in some places allow only two to six hours per day for freedom to move away from one's home. This has posed big problems, especially in congregations where the brothers are scattered."

In another African land our brothers are confined to certain areas where 'their movements are greatly restricted; they are not allowed to leave the camps even to get needed provisions.'

In still another land the brothers are not allowed to receive literature from outside the country, although the spiritual food is somehow provided by our heavenly Father to sustain the brothers. In one African land 5 percent of the brothers have spent time in prison. Some are still there. A number have experienced tortures and three have been killed. (John 16:2) Jesus indicated that such things would befall some of his followers as a test of their faith and integrity. But, as in his own case, such faithfulness would work out to God's glory and praise.—1 Pet. 1:6-8.

In addition to the official opposition that Jehovah's Witnesses experience, we must not overlook what the Scriptures foretold about domestic opposition in divided households. Many of our brothers have to endure opposition from unbelieving members of their own families. In many cases the fine conduct of the believer serves to win over an opposer. (Matt. 10:34-38; 1 Pet. 3:1, 2) There has been opposition, but it has not stopped Jehovah's Witnesses from worshiping God. Truly, our brothers have appreciated the truthfulness of the 1978 yeartext at Jeremiah 1:19.

"VICTORIOUS FAITH" INTERNATIONAL CONVENTIONS OF JEHOVAH'S WITNESSES

When the December 1, 1976, issue of *The Watchtower* first announced that plans were being made for the international conventions to be held in 1978, it said: "God's Word clearly states that the 'scene of this world is changing.' (1 Cor. 7:31) Despite the increasing uncertainty and tension as the present system of things nears its end, the activity of God's people must move ahead in having the 'everlasting good news' declared in all the earth. (Rev. 14:6) Therefore, if it be Jehovah's will, a series of international conventions will be held during the year 1978." By the end of the service year most of the international conventions that were planned for the northern hemisphere had become part of our modern-day history.

In reviewing some of the highlights of the "Victorious Faith" International Conventions it is evident that this was the big event of the year, another milestone in the forward movement of Jehovah's visible organization. The lives of all of those who had the privilege of attending were certainly enriched by what they were able to see, hear and experience. As we are told at Proverbs 10:22: "The blessing of Jehovah—that is what makes rich, and he adds no pain with it." For the abundant outpouring of Jehovah's blessings we are certainly thankful.

FIVE-DAY PROGRAM GREATLY APPRECIATED

Many expressions of appreciation have been received for the timely and practical program that was arranged. The brothers felt that the information that was presented really came to grips with the problems of life and that what was served at these spiritual feasts was truly food at the proper time. (Matt. 24:45) There was something for everyone. Whether they were overseers, young people, married couples or little children, all received information that they felt was especially applicable in their lives.

The information on the first day's program was particularly helpful to elders in the congregation, encouraging them to carry on as men and to pay attention to the flock as well as do the work of evangelizers. One brother who appreciated the points that were emphasized said: "The repeated reminders to us elders of our responsibilities was the highlight of this convention."

Many who have been contemplating taking the step into the full-time service appreciated the second day's talks on pioneering and Bethel service. Quite a number acted on the information by filling out applications to take up these branches of full-time service. The parts on that afternoon's program enthused the brothers in preparation for the special witnessing that was to be engaged in during the convention. The brothers appreciated the Scriptural reasons that were given to show why we must work hard in our preaching activity, stay clean as bearers of Jehovah's vessels and continue to walk by faith as we work together with God in the worldwide field.

The third afternoon focused attention on the youth in the organization, encouraging them to be examples in faith. There was a most enthusiastic response to the release of the new publication *My Book of Bible Stories*. It was certainly heartwarming to observe the reaction of many of the younger ones when they received their personal copies of the book at the time of its release. Many began reading it immediately and others clutched copies to their bosoms, indicating that they really treasured this new publication.

On the fourth day the talks dealing with marriage and making family life happy were very well received. Regarding the release of the book *Making Your Family Life Happy*, one individual said: "Families today are under much pressure. We are very happy to hear so much information designed to help families deal with these pressing problems."

Then on the final day came faith-strengthening talks that were climaxed in the morning session by the release of the cassette tapes entitled "The Good News According to John." Many were excited about the possibilities of using this tape recording in different ways to help the infirm and incapacitated as well as those who have difficulty in reading. The public talk on the subject "Jesus Christ—Victorious King with Whom Nations Must Reckon" incorporated a fine explanation of Psalm 45. The audience was impressed with the fact that the day of reckoning for all nations is near, but that those who are on the side of the warrior-king, Jesus Christ, need have no dread of that time of reckoning, providing they have the approval of this victorious king and his heavenly Father, Jehovah.

There were four dramas presented on the convention program, each one of them containing powerful points that were easily understood and that should be applied. Regarding the drama dealing with Lot and his escape from the doomed cities of the plain, one conventioner observed: "This drama emphasized how important it is to separate ourselves from any strong attachment to this system that has materialistic pursuits as its goal."

SPECIAL CONVENTION WITNESSING

Prior to the series of conventions an insert in *Our Kingdom Service* built up enthusiasm for the special witnessing featured on the third morning of the convention. In most of the cities where this was carried on, an attractive yellow and blue plastic service kit was prepared for use by the conventioners. Each service kit contained copies of the new brochure entitled "Jehovah's Witnesses in the Twentieth Century," which was released at the convention on the preceding afternoon. The kit also included current copies of *The Watchtower* and *Awake!* and the special handbills that were used to invite the public to attend the convention sessions and the public lecture.

It was observed that the majority of the brothers attending the conventions participated in this special witnessing campaign. In one city about 75 percent of Thursday's attendance participated in the field service on Friday, which meant that 32,000 publishers were in the field that morning. One observer commented that in downtown Seattle, Washington (U.S.A.), it looked like a sea of dandelions Friday morning because of all the yellow service kits that were visible. In Honolulu, Hawaii, the brothers reported that the entire city was thoroughly covered as a result of the two conventions held there. In Dublin, Ireland, activity at the convention was closed down for most of Friday morning to allow everyone to participate in the special witnessing activity. The same thing was done at one of the conventions in Japan. It was marvelous to see the enthusiasm and spirit displayed by the brothers who shared in this special effort to reach the public with the Kingdom message. Fine publicity was given to the special convention witnessing. In several cities reporters from local newspapers accompanied the brothers as they went from house to house. Later, they wrote interesting stories that appeared in the local press.

CONVENTION PROGRAM HIGHLIGHTS
ROLE OF JESUS CHRIST

On the final afternoon the talk entitled "Did We Get the Sense of It?" reviewed the convention program. Judging by the enthusiastic response of the brothers, it was evident that the conventioners did grasp the meaning of the timely material that was presented. This included an appreciation for the role of Jesus Christ as a world conqueror and victorious king, the one whom Jehovah's Witnesses recognize as their Leader and whom Jehovah God has appointed as head of the Christian congregation.

In the keynote address on the first morning the speaker had said: "What a grand privilege to be united with the Supreme Sovereign of all the universe through his Son, Jesus Christ, the One whose blood 'cleanses us from all sin'! . . . Will you thus magnify the name of Jehovah and the kingdom of his Son, Jesus Christ? So doing, you too may succeed gloriously as world conquerors by faith."

On the second afternoon the "Declaration of Our Faith" expressed the determination of the conventioners by saying: "We know we must give proof of our faith in Jesus Christ as our Ransomer and Head and King, . . ." (See pages 256-258.)

In harmony with the talk on the final morning, "To Whom Shall We Go but Jesus Christ?" Jehovah's Witnesses feel like Peter when he answered the question that the Master asked him: "You do not want to go also, do you?" The apostle Peter said: "Lord, whom shall we go away to? You have sayings of everlasting life." Truly there is no other leader to whom we can turn.—John 6:67, 68.

In the public lecture a high point was reached when the speaker asked: "Are we joining in with the psalmist and saying for everybody to hear: 'My works are concerning a king'? We have no reason to be ashamed of this king, God's own anointed one. So our principal 'works' should be speaking, teaching and preaching about this royal Messiah. We are working mainly in behalf of his Kingdom interests, not in behalf of any of the worldly kingdoms that are nearing their disastrous end. We are stirred to use our tongues in advertising God's kingdom and his anointed King."

OTHER INTERESTING ASPECTS
OF THE CONVENTIONS

In some lands international conventions were held for the first time. This was true of Portugal. Up until 1974 Jehovah's people could have no assemblies in that country and so congregational meetings had to be held in small groups in private homes, and even so, the brothers were often troubled by the police. There were similar problems in the preaching work when some of the brothers were arrested and tried in courts. But this year, for the very first time in Portugal, public advertising of the convention's main talk was carried out. It was quite an experience for the brothers to form such a big assembly organization and put on a five-day program.

A similar situation has obtained in Spain, and this year for the first time an international convention of Jehovah's Witnesses was held on Spanish soil. As the brothers in Spain explained: "In 1973 it was impossible to obtain permission for such a convention. Since then there have been many changes in Spain, resulting in greater freedom of expression. Thus a search was started in 1977 to find a suitable location to bring together some 50,000 people."

The brothers in Spain certainly have reason to rejoice over the 54,000 that attended the convention in that country. They received fine publicity in the press and over television, resulting in a countrywide witness being given.

Two international conventions were also held in Greece, a country where our brothers have suffered from restrictions for many years. The attendance of 28,417 at the conventions in Athens and Thessalonica brought great rejoicing to the brothers in Greece. It was a source of encouragement to have foreign delegates visiting them on these occasions.

For the first time, the brothers in Italy had more than 100,000 in attendance at the international conventions, which were held in Milan and Rome. All together 111,320 were present, thus giving a tremendous witness in that Catholic country. *La Nota* devoted a full page to the Milan convention, making the comment that it was the greatest non-Catholic assembly held in Milan for many centuries. The article went on to describe the brothers at the convention as orderly, quiet, precise, clean and organized. It also said that they were holding their convention in absolute serenity. The following week, while many persons in Rome were mourning the death of Pope Paul VI, Jehovah's Witnesses held their convention in that city and received widespread publicity due to so many reporters being in Rome that week.

Over in the Orient four conventions were held in Japan with a peak attendance of 78,136. In order to get to the convention in Osaka, more than 800 brothers from Okinawa endured a very rough sea voyage that required 64 hours rather than the usual 35. They missed the first day's sessions due to the delay caused by a typhoon. The same storm drenched the brothers at the first day's sessions in Osaka, but the audience just stayed right on through the program.

Of the total number baptized at 71 conventions held in the northern hemisphere it is interesting to note that nearly 34 percent were immersed in the four countries of Portugal, Spain, Italy and Japan. Apparently there are still many to be helped in these lands before the four figurative winds of destruction described in Revelation, chapter seven, are released.

It was certainly stimulating to hear from so many of the missionaries serving in foreign fields as well as to have the privilege of meeting with them in the convention cities where this was arranged. In some places there were only a few present, while at the larger conventions there were sizable groups that came together. The largest missionary meetings were in Montreal, Canada, and Munich, Federal Republic of Germany. It was delightful for all present to enjoy a special meal together and to hear from those who have been faithfully serving in their missionary assignments. Many have spent 10, 20, 30 and more years in these special fields. Some from earlier classes of Gilead School have grown old in their assignments but are continuing on in faith, thus setting a fine example of endurance. Without exception the missionaries wanted to express their thanks to all the brothers whose contributions during the year made it possible for them to attend an international convention in their native country and visit with family members and friends. So through this report we are pleased to convey to Jehovah's Witnesses throughout the world the thanks and appreciation of these missionaries for such generosity.

CHART SHOWING ATTENDANCE FIGURES AND THE NUMBER BAPTIZED AT CONVENTION CITIES

The following chart shows the attendance at the public meeting and the number baptized at each convention city. At a number of these conventions, sessions were conducted in various languages. For example, in Montreal, Canada, sessions were conducted simultaneously in Arabic, French, Greek, Italian, Portuguese and Spanish as well as English. The Montreal convention was also outstanding in that the largest number attended the public talk in that city when compared with all other "Victorious Faith" International Conventions held to this writing. It was the largest convention ever held in Canada and had a tremendous effect, not only on the people in the city of Montreal, but also on the Province of Quebec.

LOCATION	ATTENDANCE	BAPTIZED
ALASKA, Anchorage	2,519	27
AUSTRIA, Vienna	14,359	203
BARBADOS, Bridgetown	6,142	45
BELGIUM, Brussels	23,567	289
BRITISH ISLES, Sheffield (first)	19,651	81
Sheffield (second)	16,842	50
London (first)	31,190	154
London (second)	30,272	97
Edinburgh	12,621	82
CANADA, Montreal	80,008	831
Winnipeg	16,164	93
Vancouver	22,819	165
Edmonton	21,599	137
DENMARK, Copenhagen	16,912	107
FINLAND, Helsinki	16,345	211
FRANCE, Marseilles	12,371	203
Lille	10,957	130
Nantes	10,197	171
Paris	28,827	445
Toulouse	9,365	127
Grenoble	11,702	133
GERMANY, Munich	58,559	647
Düsseldorf	50,186	427
GREECE, Athens	19,407	167
Thessalonica	9,010	132
GUADELOUPE, Pointe-à-Pitre	6,274	74
HAWAII, Honolulu (first)	8,730	67
Honolulu (second)	8,815	54
HONG KONG	1,321	30
IRELAND, Dublin	4,437	37
ITALY, Milan	45,880	1,080
Rome	65,440	1,208
JAPAN, Nagoya	10,282	238
Osaka	31,785	629
Sapporo	8,099	205
Tokyo	27,041	586
KOREA, Taegu	5,845	78
Seoul (first)	8,673	187
Seoul (second)	11,884	193
Taejon	5,169	73
LEEWARD ISLANDS, Antigua	1,717	35
MARTINIQUE, Fort-de-France	2,888	21
NETHERLANDS, Rotterdam	35,361	122
PHILIPPINES, Manila	35,684	305
PORTUGAL, Lisbon	37,567	1,130

LOCATION	ATTENDANCE	BAPTIZED
PUERTO RICO, San Juan (first)	9,963	123
San Juan (second)	9,045	111
San Juan (third)	13,259	118
SPAIN, Barcelona	54,283	1,356
SWEDEN, Stockholm	25,338	248
TAIWAN, Taipei	1,603	22
UNITED STATES		
Irving, Texas (Spanish)	16,682	162
Milwaukee, Wisconsin	50,143	330
New Orleans, Louisiana (first)	36,006	209
Washington, D.C.	52,302	306
Lakeland, Florida (Spanish)	7,725	90
New Orleans, Louisiana (second)	34,015	203
Pontiac, Michigan	58,410	301
Los Angeles, California (first)	47,243	249
Philadelphia, Pennsylvania	41,965	238
St. Louis, Missouri	33,776	249
Houston, Texas	58,430	468
Los Angeles, California (second)	41,406	290
New York, New York	71,566	487
San Francisco, California	50,820	274
Cincinnati, Ohio	40,729	315
Monroe, New York (French)	1,969	28
Pittsburgh, Pennsylvania	36,996	279
Seattle, Washington	46,391	326
Los Angeles, California (Spanish)	28,905	416
Elmont, New York (Spanish)	24,012	319
TOTALS	1,807,465	19,023

The series of "Victorious Faith" International Conventions that began with the first ones held from June 14 to 18 in the United States continued during September and October in Southeast Asia, and then from the latter part of November through January (1979) in Central and South America, the South Pacific and in several countries on the African continent.

WORLDWIDE SERVICE ACTIVITY

When we consider the service that has been accomplished during the 1978 service year, it gives us cause for gratitude. (Ps. 32:11) The activities of Jehovah's Witnesses in the worldwide field are set out on the accompanying chart. At the conclusion of the alphabetical list of countries, you will find that a number of lands are grouped together. This is due to the severe opposition and other problems that exist in such places. Difficult conditions are being encountered in other countries too, but the dangers are such in the 16 countries whose reports are combined that it is not advisable to list them separately. In all parts of the world there are problems of one kind or another, including opposition, persecution, economic hardships and other trials. As with the apostles and early disciples, Jehovah's servants today have been able to persevere in giving the worldwide witness because of the help and strength that God supplies. (Acts 26:22; 1 Pet. 4:11) They find much joy in thus serving despite the various trials that must be endured.—Jas. 1:2-4.

Reports have been received from 205 lands and islands of the sea. The decrease in the total number of countries lies in the fact that reports from several of them are now combined with those of other branches. For example, last year such places as Manus Island, New Britain, New Guinea, New Ireland and the North Solomons were listed separately. This year they are all included in the report from Papua New Guinea since they now form one country. Abu Dhabi, Dubai and Sharja are shown now as United Arab Emirates. Bequia, Carriacou and Tobago are now part of St. Vincent, Grenada and Trinidad respectively. And Bhutan now reports with India.

There has been an overall 1.4-percent decrease in the number of Kingdom publishers. This has had a bearing on the decline in other features of the work as far as the totals are concerned. There are individual countries where increases continue, whereas other lands show a leveling off or a drop in activity. While 95,052 new ones were baptized in expression of their faith, thus declaring themselves to be disciples of Jesus Christ, this has not resulted in a proportionate increase in the number of Kingdom publishers. On the contrary, there were 2,086,698, on the average, who shared in making known the "good news" compared with 2,117,194 the year before. The peak number of publishers came to 2,182,341, which is also below that of last year. It is obvious that for one reason or another a number did not share in giving a witness each month, and others became inactive.

How should we view this situation? There is certainly no need to become unduly disturbed and lose our spiritual balance. As with all other things, Christians let God's Word adjust their thinking and set things straight in their minds. Jehovah always provides them with needed direction in his own time and way. He never forsakes his people. (1 Ki. 8:57; Ps. 94:14) During this new service year, we will confidently look to him, praying for his guidance and working to retrieve any who have strayed. (Matt. 18:12-14) If there are those in our congregations who have slacked their hand,

1978 SERVICE YEAR REPORT OF

Letter and number following each country's name indicates the country's

Country	Population	1978 Peak Pubs.	Ratio, One Publisher to:	1978 Av. Pubs.	% Inc. over 1977
Afghanistan (G-24)	17,000,000	3	5,666,667	3	-40*
Alaska (A-49)	404,615	1,146	353	1,087	-7*
Algeria (H-17)	17,800,000	26	684,615	17	
American Samoa (N-40)	30,000	73	411	64	3
Andorra (F-17)	28,737	81	355	66	-6*
Anguilla (J-10)	6,524	13	502	11	-8*
Antigua (J-10)	70,794	187	379	171	-10*
Argentina (P-9)	25,050,000	32,977	760	31,713	9
Aruba (K-9)	62,577	311	201	292	-12*
Australia (M-31)	14,212,900	28,635	496	27,864	-1*
Austria (E-18)	7,511,000	12,730	590	12,504	1
Azores (G-14)	264,400	294	899	275	8
Bahamas (H-8)	215,000	473	455	428	-8*
Bahrain (H-23)	216,000	6	36,000	3	50
Bangladesh (B-28)	85,000,000	4	21,250,000	3	200
Barbados (J-10)	254,000	1,238	205	1,141	-6*
Belgium (E-17)	9,772,413	18,588	526	17,706	-3*
Belize (J-7)	142,000	568	250	530	-2*
Benin (K-17)	2,700,000	1,304	2,071	1,106	13
Bermuda (G-9)	60,000	210	286	202	-4*
Bolivia (N-9)	4,687,718	2,395	1,957	2,278	2
Bonaire (K-9)	8,460	30	282	26	-10*
Botswana (O-19)	720,000	295	2,441	268	8
Brazil (M-11)	117,250,000	106,197	1,104	101,929	-1*
British Isles (D-16)	54,504,300	76,242	715	73,859	-2*
Brunei (F-30)	170,000	5	34,000	4	New
Burma (B-29)	31,170,000	914	34,103	884	8
Burundi (L-20)	4,000,000	161	24,845	128	-12*
Cameroon (L-18)	6,700,000	12,056	556	11,025	-4*
Canada (D-4)	23,388,100	61,836	378	60,540	-1*
Canary Islands (H-15)	1,519,794	1,258	1,208	1,174	1
Cape Verde Rep. (J-14)	350,000	96	3,646	90	32
Cayman Islands (J-8)	15,600	29	538	24	41
Central Afr. Emp. (K-19)	2,200,000	939	2,343	797	-10*
Chad (J-19)	4,117,000	154	26,734	127	-3*
Chile (P-9)	10,857,128	15,501	700	14,703	-4*
Colombia (L-8)	25,894,289	15,200	1,704	14,856	-5*
Congo (L-18)	1,400,000	1,071	1,307	892	-32*
Cook Islands (P-41)	18,068	54	335	49	-4*
Costa Rica (K-7)	2,070,560	5,090	407	4,842	
Curaçao (K-9)	158,882	755	210	717	4
Cyprus (G-20)	500,000	905	552	864	4
Denmark (D-18)	5,105,423	13,689	373	13,081	-3*
Djibouti (K-21)	101,000	3	33,667	2	-50*
Dominica (J-10)	70,302	191	368	176	-6*
Dominican Rep. (J-9)	4,977,701	6,444	772	6,129	-3*
Ecuador (N-8)	6,797,299	5,417	1,255	5,043	-7*
El Salvador (J-7)	4,440,188	6,017	738	5,693	-1*
Equatorial Guinea (L-18)	300,000	16	18,750	14	-13*
Ethiopia (K-21)	27,500,000	1,593	17,263	1,466	-19*
Faroe Islands (C-16)	41,806	71	589	64	-4*
Fiji (N-38)	588,068	634	928	610	3
Finland (B-20)	4,743,100	12,728	373	12,480	-1*
France (E-17)	53,223,000	66,778	797	64,167	-1*
French Guiana (K-11)	45,000	250	180	233	7

JEHOVAH'S WITNESSES WORLD WIDE

location on endsheet maps. Nos. 1-25 front and nos. 26-50 back endsheet.

1977 Av. Pubs.	1978 No. Bptzd.	Av. Pio. Pubs.	No. of Congs.	Total Hours	Av. Bible Studies	Memorial Atten- dance
5			1	423	1	10
1,164	55	99	22	185,571	542	2,785
17	3	1	3	1,434	16	52
62	4	8	1	13,967	60	170
70		3	1	6,220	29	129
12		2	1	2,951	10	16
189	38	12	4	29,074	128	458
29,111	858	846	615	3,376,755	21,907	59,268
332	12	6	5	37,137	184	875
28,078	1,365	1,551	530	4,441,012	11,082	57,960
12,349	530	562	215	1,888,866	6,000	22,612
254	15	26	12	55,426	260	745
463	30	17	9	61,591	379	1,368
2				125	1	
1			1	762	3	
1,220	66	35	16	128,535	593	2,667
18,180	813	663	280	2,509,062	6,394	37,328
542	13	44	14	100,685	442	1,952
975	13	10	71	92,365	390	2,627
210	1	11	4	34,291	150	432
2,240	275	366	64	658,581	2,644	9,495
29	1	4	1	7,637	35	110
249	16	23	12	58,418	268	726
102,503	6,643	4,185	2,012	12,997,190	66,433	292,565
75,136	2,944	3,526	1,125	10,184,446	31,734	150,715
		1		690	10	14
816	50	169	59	283,871	752	2,174
146	26	16	5	29,641	155	187
11,449	396	18	426	738,979	6,425	18,382
60,940	2,501	3,076	1,035	8,523,719	24,839	120,060
1,163	44	90	31	217,118	756	2,945
68	30	16	4	33,757	220	237
17		2	1	4,208	29	102
887	36	47	47	118,535	519	2,227
131	17	28	11	51,004	200	546
15,339	945	868	280	2,211,154	13,678	44,444
15,696	540	878	273	2,531,462	14,980	65,012
1,305	12	22	43	59,420	383	1,602
51	4	5	2	9,057	37	171
4,832	258	205	110	683,755	3,502	13,247
691	40	49	8	142,215	902	1,857
830	14	44	13	116,024	288	1,462
13,426	262	588	234	1,599,269	3,752	22,148
4			1	85	1	4
188	1	19	8	38,509	101	467
6,324	291	475	112	1,181,239	7,268	19,912
5,400	327	406	105	984,986	5,288	22,708
5,768	472	333	133	1,000,331	5,883	21,285
16			1	925	23	
1,811	84	101	50	258,154	1,545	4,316
67		14	4	15,217	32	109
590	24	73	24	135,805	618	2,124
12,592	438	737	251	1,714,560	5,146	20,986
64,546	3,474	2,158	1,188	8,961,433	32,398	131,053
218	16	13	3	45,133	296	598

Country	Population	1978 Peak Pubs.	Ratio, One Publisher to:	1978 Av. Pubs.	% Inc. over 1977
Gabon (L-18)	520,000	364	1,429	330	8
Gambia (K-15)	493,000	14	35,214	13	30
Germany, F. R. (E-18)	59,660,000	99,632	599	96,738	-1*
Ghana (K-17)	10,304,683	22,167	465	20,924	-3*
Gibraltar (G-16)	29,278	87	337	82	1
Gilbert Islands (L-39)	54,500	5	10,900	2	
Greece (F-19)	9,000,000	18,738	480	18,620	
Greenland (A-12)	49,148	76	647	64	-16*
Grenada (K-10)	109,000	305	357	282	-8*
Guadeloupe (J-10)	324,000	2,619	124	2,537	
Guam (G-36)	98,580	146	675	115	13
Guatemala (J-7)	6,000,000	5,176	1,159	4,974	-2*
Guinea (K-15)	5,143,284	259	19,858	205	-2*
Guinea-Bissau (K-15)	517,000	1	517,000	1	-67*
Guyana (K-10)	800,000	1,260	635	1,214	-9*
Haiti (J-9)	5,000,000	3,368	1,485	3,199	-6*
Hawaii (K-45)	851,824	4,613	185	4,458	-4*
Honduras (K-7)	3,438,388	3,166	1,086	2,978	-5*
Hong Kong (C-31)	4,600,000	760	6,053	723	13
Iceland (B-15)	222,470	133	1,673	125	-13*
India (J-25)	625,000,000	4,750	131,579	4,506	-1*
Iran (G-23)	32,000,000	69	463,768	58	18
Iraq (G-22)	9,498,362	20	474,918	19	19
Ireland (D-16)	4,580,000	1,784	2,567	1,738	
Israel (G-21)	4,825,000	244	19,775	236	-6*
Italy (F-18)	56,324,727	71,796	785	69,252	8
Ivory Coast (K-16)	6,670,000	1,216	5,485	1,173	
Jamaica (J-8)	2,109,400	6,520	324	6,240	-1*
Japan (B-36)	113,361,230	45,314	2,502	43,776	9
Jordan (H-21)	2,560,000	71	36,056	47	-13*
Kenya (L-21)	14,400,000	1,989	7,240	1,948	1
Korea (B-35)	37,091,000	26,286	1,411	25,264	-9*
Kosrae (J-38)	3,989	22	181	19	6
Kuwait (H-22)	990,000	28	35,357	25	47
Lebanon (G-21)	3,213,000	1,768	1,817	1,699	2
Lesotho (P-20)	1,181,900	630	1,876	571	1
Liberia (K-16)	1,400,000	1,119	1,251	1,000	2
Libya (H-19)	2,440,000	14	174,286	6	100
Liechtenstein (E-18)	24,715	28	883	23	21
Luxembourg (E-17)	423,500	861	492	838	5
Macao (C-31)	375,000	11	34,091	9	13
Madagascar (N-22)	9,000,000	878	10,251	829	2
Madeira (G-15)	262,800	326	806	313	8
Malaysia (E-28)	13,341,000	471	28,325	454	5
Mali (J-17)	5,000,000	36	138,889	34	10
Malta (G-18)	320,000	86	3,721	79	5
Malvinas Islands (R-10)	2,089	6	348	4	33
Marquesas Islands (P-45)	5,419	4	1,355	3	50
Marshall Islands (J-39)	25,044	168	149	148	-14*
Martinique (J-10)	330,000	1,073	308	1,049	
Mauritania (J-16)	1,500,000	1	1,500,000	1	
Mauritius (N-23)	894,100	380	2,353	367	4
Mayotte (N-22)	32,607	1	32,607	1	-50*
Mexico (H-5)	66,943,976	95,374	702	92,649	3
Montserrat (J-10)	12,335	23	536	21	11

1977 Av. Pubs.	1978 No. Bptzd.	Av. Pio. Pubs.	No. of Congs.	Total Hours	Av. Bible Studies	Memorial Attendance
306	12	14	17	40,266	299	786
10		4	1	5,525	19	34
97,760	2,748	2,898	1,412	12,057,576	31,338	163,114
21,531	1,021	1,209	442	3,514,973	19,019	59,443
81	2	5	1	11,424	24	123
2			1	136	5	50
18,712	382	744	450	2,585,537	6,141	31,815
76	1	17	8	16,018	36	114
305	12	24	7	51,748	225	832
2,535	133	55	36	322,628	1,827	5,805
102	6	20	1	27,524	96	355
5,079	305	287	90	827,232	4,257	15,568
210	10	62	15	102,748	454	782
3		1	1	441	9	4
1,327	54	144	32	258,267	1,110	3,358
3,407	212	218	73	605,036	3,867	10,777
4,653	185	602	59	989,978	3,917	11,191
3,149	180	270	64	657,529	3,833	15,446
640	98	136	9	242,394	943	1,579
144	4	10	3	21,276	75	317
4,535	338	568	270	1,077,680	3,174	11,418
49	4	16	1	24,322	113	176
16	3	1	1	1,129	6	47
1,745	77	285	67	489,282	764	3,296
250	13	12	5	34,428	105	409
63,896	5,429	3,995	1,270	12,272,071	45,628	151,413
1,168	62	93	43	247,891	1,604	4,140
6,277	191	226	165	844,957	4,437	15,024
40,176	4,715	10,666	1,018	15,910,201	59,363	101,941
54	2	2	1	6,447	32	118
1,929	181	275	88	587,383	2,091	5,061
27,655	1,162	2,018	499	3,903,225	13,889	49,545
18		4	1	5,059	35	89
17	3		1	1,925	14	91
1,663	43	81	45	258,558	981	3,381
568	29	49	30	113,356	424	2,089
979	41	104	30	245,786	1,256	3,014
3				378	2	8
19		2	1	3,385	14	57
799	50	56	19	146,351	527	1,868
8		5	1	6,713	19	27
811	77	45	29	141,321	1,055	3,441
289	15	19	8	53,803	272	747
433	42	54	18	124,380	674	1,010
31	3	11	1	19,907	117	52
75	5	6	1	13,261	55	285
3		2	1	336	8	15
2		3	1	2,081	1	8
173	3	23	3	35,163	197	596
1,048	59	32	17	145,728	796	2,644
1				177	3	
353	11	19	7	59,315	280	929
2				66	1	
89,606	4,785	6,738	3,717	15,422,261	82,034	380,164
19	1	2	1	3,512	26	87

Country	Population	1978 Peak Pubs.	Ratio, One Pub- lisher to:	1978 Av. Pubs.	% Inc. over 1977*
Morocco (G-16)	18,884,000	168	112,405	146	-10*
Nepal (A-27)	13,000,000	17	764,706	16	14
Netherlands (D-17)	13,935,964	27,332	510	26,545	-4*
Nevis (J-10)	11,230	52	216	31	-30*
New Caledonia (N-36)	138,000	402	343	372	1
Newfoundland (E-10)	530,000	1,098	483	1,052	-3*
New Hebrides (N-37)	103,954	49	2,122	45	-6*
New Zealand (R-35)	3,107,000	6,844	454	6,520	-1*
Nicaragua (K-7)	2,295,046	3,338	688	3,246	-1*
Niger (J-18)	2,870,000	58	49,483	47	-11*
Nigeria (K-18)	79,758,969	97,056	822	91,656	-8*
Niue (O-40)	3,881	14	277	11	-21*
Norway (C-18)	4,064,000	7,014	579	6,808	-2*
Okinawa (D-34)	1,229,950	885	1,390	859	
Pakistan (H-24)	72,850,000	197	369,797	184	2
Palau (G-33)	12,674	30	422	29	-3*
Panama (K-8)	1,742,500	2,963	588	2,879	-2*
Papua New Guinea (K-34)	2,811,537	1,404	2,003	1,365	-2*
Paraguay (O-10)	2,646,000	1,555	1,702	1,464	2
Peru (M-8)	16,000,000	12,925	1,238	11,992	
Philippines (E-32)	45,000,000	64,986	692	60,676	-7*
Ponape (J-37)	19,262	73	264	67	-13*
Portugal (F-16)	9,137,000	19,976	457	19,281	3
Puerto Rico (J-9)	3,319,200	16,381	203	15,853	-3*
Réunion (O-23)	488,300	532	918	510	1
Rhodesia (N-20)	6,856,300	12,077	568	11,357	-2*
Rodrigues (N-24)	27,600	11	2,509	10	-23*
Rwanda (L-20)	4,650,000	118	39,407	103	66
St. Eustatius (J-10)	1,335	6	223	5	67
St. Helena (N-16)	5,058	94	54	89	-3*
St. Kitts (J-10)	35,135	144	244	115	-14*
St. Lucia (J-10)	107,000	267	401	240	-11*
St. Martin (J-10)	10,423	59	177	48	-6*
St. Pierre & Miquelon (E-10)	6,200	5	1,240	5	67
St. Vincent (J-10)	105,000	153	686	136	-11*
Saipan (F-36)	14,335	17	843	16	-20*
San Marino (F-18)	19,621	69	284	64	12
São Tomé (L-18)	72,480	5	14,496	4	100
Saudi Arabia (J-22)	7,200,000	28	257,143	20	300
Senegal (K-15)	5,000,000	347	14,409	328	2
Seychelles (M-23)	63,000	49	1,286	39	-15*
Sierra Leone (K-15)	3,002,426	1,041	2,884	895	-18*
Solomon Islands (L-36)	210,000	547	384	487	-7*
South Africa (P-19)	26,228,000	28,105	933	26,196	-4*
South-West Africa (N-18)	850,000	295	2,881	263	-9*
Spain (F-16)	35,588,939	38,983	913	37,380	3
Sri Lanka (C-26)	14,200,000	564	25,177	547	2
Sudan (K-20)	18,000,000	89	202,247	80	-10*
Surinam (K-10)	375,000	879	427	854	-4*
Swaziland (O-20)	493,728	740	667	612	2
Sweden (C-19)	8,277,665	16,568	500	16,277	
Switzerland (E-18)	6,292,000	10,118	622	9,858	
Syria (G-21)	6,895,000	169	40,799	153	-10*
Tahiti (Q-43)	131,963	460	287	437	8
Taiwan (D-33)	16,800,000	1,044	16,092	962	-3*

1977 Av. Pubs.	1978 No. Bptzd.	Av. Pio. Pubs.	No. of Congs.	Total Hours	Av. Bible Studies	Memorial Attendance
162	9	8	3	23,092	87	288
14		1	1	1,317	7	
27,776	686	1,488	290	3,964,594	8,410	45,801
44		2	1	5,764	13	86
370	17	12	7	48,562	279	958
1,086	15	92	33	182,186	413	1,980
48	2	5	3	9,232	61	114
6,606	252	349	116	945,050	3,010	14,315
3,282	292	272	68	644,829	3,822	12,080
53	3	21	6	34,705	76	119
99,163	3,182	4,447	2,107	13,767,805	61,970	240,814
14			1	1,061	12	101
6,982	106	183	198	703,649	1,841	12,206
859	34	147	21	263,948	984	1,952
181	11	30	6	53,543	186	441
30	3	10	1	16,677	116	118
2,927	121	221	68	574,168	3,389	11,454
1,396	73	113	82	257,645	1,165	4,808
1,439	169	133	47	282,725	1,047	3,829
12,011	1,200	1,382	276	2,697,143	13,033	45,647
65,381	2,279	5,815	2,008	9,716,980	24,461	172,005
77	2	9	1	16,306	46	213
18,708	1,735	750	368	2,586,827	14,943	49,135
16,402	817	501	229	2,344,499	10,114	44,354
503	35	21	10	80,184	348	1,408
11,592	332	612	521	1,798,806	7,350	27,591
13			1	804	3	42
62	33	28	7	56,476	215	502
3	1	2		4,746	15	27
92	3	1	2	8,356	33	178
133	2	8	2	19,384	100	309
271	6	14	5	34,884	209	679
51	3	3	1	7,157	44	144
3	1	2	1	2,110	4	12
152	6	13	4	27,392	80	320
20		5	1	7,779	30	34
57	1	4	1	10,761	34	119
2			1	316	5	18
5				1,183	6	53
322	20	53	8	103,154	418	810
46	2	3	1	7,154	34	118
1,095	28	218	40	362,236	1,690	3,564
524	9	73	30	118,175	443	2,092
27,149	1,290	1,549	855	4,370,450	16,649	67,017
288	25	16	11	47,063	231	676
36,242	2,657	2,589	704	6,922,694	25,665	80,555
535	57	89	17	160,494	562	1,622
89	3	9	2	19,913	96	202
886	36	79	12	167,316	663	2,126
601	39	31	28	118,553	472	1,388
16,212	515	1,013	305	2,339,370	7,240	27,307
9,873	338	288	224	1,295,854	5,729	19,326
170	2	7	6	21,202	73	335
404	19	35	12	73,114	372	1,084
987	42	127	48	212,391	671	2,442

Country	Population	1978 Peak Pubs.	Ratio, One Publisher to:	1978 Av. Pubs.	% Inc. over 1977
Tanzania (M-20)	16,000,000	1,469	10,892	1,401	3
Thailand (C-29)	44,272,693	736	60,153	720	
Togo (K-17)	2,371,100	2,660	891	2,145	-11*
Tokelau Isls. (N-40)	1,600	6	267	4	-20*
Tonga (O-39)	90,128	23	3,919	20	-5*
Trinidad (K-10)	1,098,200	3,020	364	2,875	-1*
Truk (H-36)	31,600	39	810	36	6
Tunisia (G-18)	6,000,000	52	115,385	48	7
Turkey (G-21)	42,000,000	839	50,060	822	-1*
Turks & Caicos Isls. (H-9)	6,000	19	316	17	6
Tuvalu Isls. (L-39)	10,000	3	3,333	2	-33*
Uganda (L-20)	11,750,000	148	79,392	127	-9*
U. Arab Emirates (H-23)	210,000	33	6,364	12	-43*
U.S. of America (G-6)	216,030,000	535,737	403	513,673	-3*
Upper Volta (K-16)	5,258,141	100	52,581	87	26
Uruguay (P-10)	2,763,964	4,503	614	4,149	-5*
Venezuela (K-9)	13,565,000	13,815	982	13,332	
Virgin Is. (Brit.) (J-9)	11,000	80	138	75	6
Virgin Is. (U.S.) (J-10)	80,000	467	171	450	-1*
West Berlin (E-18)	1,985,000	5,174	384	5,095	-2*
Western Samoa (N-40)	151,983	139	1,093	127	-3*
Yap (F-34)	7,869	43	183	40	8
Zaire (L-19)	25,000,000	19,512	1,281	18,114	
Zambia (N-20)	5,700,000	56,517	101	52,617	
189 Countries		1,963,671		1,881,625	-1.5*
† 16 Other Countries		218,670		205,073	-1.0*
GRAND TOTAL (205 countries)		2,182,341		2,086,698	-1.4*

* Percentage of decrease
† Work banned and reports are incomplete

efforts should be made, especially by those who are undershepherds, to encourage them kindly by word and, above all, by setting a good example.—Heb. 12:12, 13; 1 Cor. 11:1.

At the same time, we will have in mind the scriptures that forewarn us of what to expect. Some will stumble and fall away or become unfruitful for various reasons. (Matt. 13:18-22) Furthermore, as shown at Revelation 3:15, 16, the Lord Jesus Christ, who knows the spiritual condition of each one who professes to be his follower, does not tolerate lukewarmness. He advises any who are in that state now to rectify their condition if they are to please him. And just as some deviated from the truth in the first century, it is not surprising that the same thing happens today. Jehovah knows those who belong to him. (2 Tim. 2:18, 19) Warning examples of what befell the Israelites as they were about to enter

1977 Av. Pubs.	1978 No. Bptzd.	Av. Pio. Pubs.	No. of Congs.	Total Hours	Av. Bible Studies	Memorial Attendance
1,358	57	137	76	303,581	1,145	3,681
723	33	114	28	193,149	581	1,621
2,418	6	190	71	422,670	2,221	9,544
5			1	269	12	19
21		3	1	4,155	18	49
2,915	148	203	44	481,979	2,426	7,278
34	1	8	1	14,978	60	188
45	3	1	1	4,320	26	73
832	19	37	11	137,386	464	1,407
16	2	1	3	5,126	32	86
3			1	450	5	21
139	3	12	9	31,710	153	375
21				517	2	10
530,374	20,471	28,192	7,445	72,065,793	263,156	1,264,420
69	25	26	5	45,564	228	396
4,377	317	310	90	744,104	3,774	11,767
13,810	746	785	176	2,252,248	12,527	48,013
71	1	2	3	7,934	50	235
453	20	14	9	56,475	304	1,316
5,196	76	150	63	626,857	1,622	7,565
131	4	20	3	36,757	148	404
37	2	10	1	17,088	94	203
18,153	1,600	2,307	679	4,948,915	27,328	79,726
52,629	1,608	1,934	1,198	7,161,452	49,394	191,591
1,910,129	88,361	111,902	38,281	290,208,128	1,161,941	4,765,033
207,065	6,691	3,487	3,974	17,064,134	95,143	330,798
2,117,194	95,052	115,389	42,255	307,272,262	1,257,084	5,095,831

MEMORIAL PARTAKERS WORLD WIDE: 9,762

the Promised Land should keep us individually from becoming overconfident. (1 Cor. 10:12) The seriousness of this matter is emphasized in the fact that 29,893 were disfellowshiped last year. There is no question that our faith is being tested today. Jehovah will retain in his favor and service only those who are clean, yes, the ones striving to meet all the Scriptural requirements and prove themselves fit to be entrusted with the "good news."—Mic. 6:8; 2 Cor. 6:17–7:1; 1 Thess. 2:4.

In view of the 307,272,262 hours spent in Kingdom service, it is apparent that millions of persons have had opportunity to receive a witness. To aid individuals to learn of God's purposes Jehovah's Witnesses placed 25,580,648 books—607,899 more than in 1977—and 15,107,899 booklets, as well as 216,709,937 *Watchtower* and *Awake!* magazines in addition to 1,496,766 subscriptions for these two journals. To emphasize that Jehovah's Witnesses are not just interested in arousing interest in the Kingdom message and placing Bible literature, they made 130,177,724 return visits and conducted 1,257,084 home Bible studies. Their aim in this is to make disciples by teaching responsive people 'all the things that Christ commanded.' (Matt. 28:19, 20) All such diligent efforts contributed toward giving a thorough witness to the most distant part of the earth. —Acts 1:8.

It is indeed a cause for rejoicing that we have again had over five million attend the Memorial of Christ's death. Actually 5,095,831 were present and 9,762 partook of the emblems when this most important event was observed on March 23, 1978. How clearly this indicates that we have much to do in helping millions of righthearted persons to become regularly associated with the 42,255 congregations throughout the world!

Down through the years Jehovah has richly blessed the activities of his people. The following chart helps one to appreciate the progress that has been made during the past 60 years, showing the activity at 10-year intervals.

KINGDOM-PREACHING ACTIVITY AT 10-YEAR INTERVALS

Year	Countries Reporting	Average Publishers	Hours of Service	Books & Bklts. Distributed	Magazines Distributed
1918	14	3,868	19,116	359,384	13,140
1928	32	23,988	2,866,164	20,412,192	1,381,107
1938	52	47,143	10,572,086	26,772,882	6,933,307
1948	96	230,532	49,832,205	17,031,901	11,380,767
1958	175	717,088	110,390,944	16,038,445	86,498,251
1968	200	1,155,826	208,666,762	21,674,179	157,511,892
1978	205	2,086,698	307,272,262	40,688,547	216,709,937

Looking ahead, the faithful remnant will continue to demonstrate that they "keep following the Lamb [Jesus Christ] no matter where he goes." (Rev. 14:4) The "great crowd" who associate with them will do likewise. Unitedly they will all continue to obey their Leader, Jesus Christ, and to fulfill their twofold commission of preaching 'this good news of the kingdom in all the inhabited earth for a witness,' and of 'making disciples of people of all the nations,' knowing they have the full backing of Jehovah God and his Son. —Matt. 24:14; 28:19, 20.

ACTS OF JEHOVAH'S WITNESSES
IN MODERN TIMES

Fields of ripened grain, orchards filled with luscious fruit, productive vineyards—all of these are deeply satisfying. Especially does a bountiful harvest bring great delight to "the hardworking farmer." (2 Tim. 2:6) Industriously, he engages in the work of planting, watering and cultivating. Then he patiently waits for "the precious fruit of the earth."—Jas. 5:7.

Yes, the farmer must wait for "the living God" to give "rains from heaven and fruitful seasons." (Acts 14:14-17) Jehovah is "the One giving food to all flesh." (Ps. 136:25) God makes things grow.

The apostle Paul likened the activity of the Christian to a farmer's planting and watering of seed. Nourishing of the implanted word must be followed by patient waiting for God to make it grow by means of his holy spirit. (1 Cor. 3:5-9) Jehovah is pleased with such efforts and is glorified by spiritual fruit-bearing and proof of discipleship.—John 15:8.

On the following pages you can read about activities in various parts of God's worldwide field. For instance, you can "visit" Burma. The "good news" has been spread throughout that picturesque land, and this has been accomplished in the face of various problems.

Bible truth, as declared by Jehovah's people, has been known in Canada since about 1880. However, the clergy have opposed it intensely. From the stirring account presented in later pages you can 'look in on' true Christians in that country and observe their bearing of fruit to God's glory.

Herein you can also undertake a "voyage" to the Leeward Islands, once renowned for material treasures. You will learn how some of these islanders found much more precious spiritual riches.

Then you can "travel" to Peru, the ancient Land of the Incas. There, Jehovah's Witnesses have been sharing the "good news" with others in spite of hardships, including those associated with a devastating earthquake of relatively recent times. You can follow their activities in the towering Andes mountains, the vast Amazon jungle and other regions of Peru.

Too, you can "journey" to Africa and watch the planting of seeds of truth in Senegal and neighboring lands. It will be possible to observe how effective Kingdom witnessing has resulted in fine spiritual development in that part of Africa.

Indeed, Jehovah is having a great work done today. Moreover, God is being glorified by this fruit-bearing and disciple-making activity throughout the earth.

BURMA

Burma is a lush and picturesque land. It runs some 1,300 miles (2,100 kilometers) from north to south, from the lofty mountains of Tibet to the tropical waters of the Indian Ocean. From west to east, it extends 575 miles (925 kilometers) from the Bangladesh border to the Mekong River that separates Burma from Laos.

A horseshoe of mountains forms strong natural frontiers with Bangladesh and India in the northwest, with Tibet in the north, with China in the northeast, and with Laos and Thailand in the east and southeast. In total area, Burma covers 261,789 square miles (678,030 square kilometers). Hence, it is almost as large as England and France combined.

The exclamation of the psalmist seems so appropriate here in Burma: "How many your works are, O Jehovah! All of them in wisdom you have made. The earth is full of your productions." (Ps. 104:24) In the extreme north, snowcapped Hkakabo Razi, Burma's highest peak, towers 19,315 feet (5,887 meters) above sea level. Three mountain systems—the Western (or Arakan) Yoma, the Pegu Yoma and the Shan Plateau—divide three parallel river valleys, the Irrawaddy, the Sittang and the Salween.

HISTORY AND RELIGIONS

The Burmese chronicles begin with the foundation of Tagaung, in the upper reaches of the Irrawaddy, in 850 B.C.E., but the early history of Burma is obscure. The indigenous races of the country are of Mongolian stock, from which have come three main branches, the Tibeto-Burman, the Mon-Khmer and the Tai-Chinese. The migration of Burmese to this sunny southern land followed an earlier group, the Mons, who first blazed the trail, settled near the sea and achieved a high degree of culture. The Tai provided the last of the great migrations, coming from Yunnan in the thirteenth century. In the ninth century C.E., the Burmese proper settled in the dry zone of central Burma, and there one finds the sites of their ancient capitals—Pagan, Ava, Amarapura and Mandalay.

The hill areas of Burma, with their difficult terrain and poor communications, split the main races into numerous tribes having distinctive languages. Consequently, over 100 different hill peoples who are all Burmese nationals live in the Kachin, Kayah, Kawthule, Shan and Chin States. This leaves high concentrations of population in the delta and the dry zone.

By religion the Burmese proper, the Mons and the Shans, are predominantly Buddhist. But most of the Chins, Kachins and Karens are nominal Christians. And there are some animists among them too.

Burma is not well provided with surface land connections. The Burma Road in the east, connecting Burma and China, is very difficult and dangerous to travel. The Tamu Road in the west, joining India and Burma, is another difficult route. These roads now are used only by smugglers of commercial goods. Thus Burma is dependent on sea traffic and airlines.

THE "GOOD NEWS" REACHES BURMA

However, the message of God's kingdom has come into Burma in various ways. Now it has spread into all nooks and corners of the country.

It was in 1914 that the spark of Bible truth began to kindle Burmese interest in God's kingdom. In that year, two colporteurs, Hendry Carmichael and another brother, came to Burma from Madras, India. In the capital city, Rangoon, they placed some of the books and tracts written by C. T. Russell, the first president of the Watch Tower Society. Among those who took the literature, two persons showed unusual interest. In no time, they found themselves engrossed in reading the Watch Tower publications. They could easily see the truth explained in plain language, and it did not take them very long to sever their connections with Christendom.

In those days, no training was given to newly interested persons, as far as witnessing was concerned. So the new brothers, Bertram Oscar Marcelline and Vernon French, were left on their own. They witnessed only informally whenever their friends called on them.

ENDEAVORING TO MAINTAIN NEUTRALITY

At the beginning of 1918, the British government in Burma ordered all persons to register for military service. In obedience to the law, Brother Marcelline registered his name but made it clear that he was a conscientious objector and could not take part in any fighting. The result? Brother Marcelline recalls: "I was taken to the army headquarters and later allowed to go back to work. But I was told to come before a military tribunal for orders. I did that, but the tribunal said that I was not an 'ordained minister' and so could not be exempted from military service. They sent my case to the court for judgment. . . . Before the magistrate, I tried to prove that as a Christian I was neutral and could not join any side. It was all in vain. They

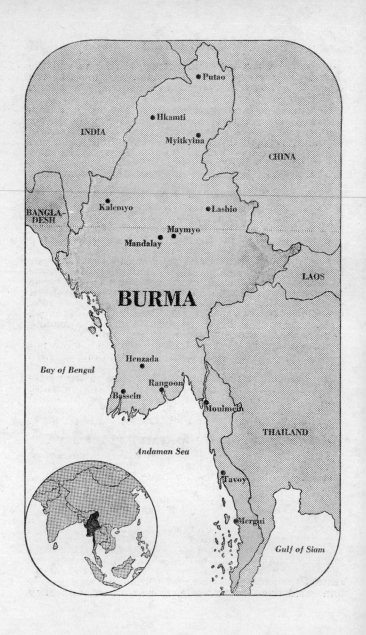

upheld the decision of the tribunal but added that I should be given some noncombatant work. I was sent back to my secular work and told to await further orders."—John 17:16.

In March 1918, while Brother Marcelline was at Maymyo, a summer resort of the government, the military authorities requested that he participate in military training, drilling with arms. He drilled, but without arms. His persistent refusal to drill with arms led to arrest and hard labor, such as breaking stones and building roads along with other prisoners. Every day two armed guards escorted Brother Marcelline for court-martial, but each time he was returned to his cell. At last, after a month, he was released.

EXPANDING THE WITNESS

From 1914 to 1927 very little preaching work was done here, except for incidental witnessing. However, Brothers French, Clay, Wooten and F. Trutwein and some interested persons would meet at Brother Marcelline's house. He tells us: "We used to open with prayer and then read *The Watch Tower and Herald of Christ's Presence,* ask questions and give comments. Then we would sing a hymn or so and close with a prayer. We had about 18 to 20 persons attending."

In 1926 the Watch Tower Bible and Tract Society of Pennsylvania opened a new branch office at Bombay, India. It had supervision over the Kingdom work in India, Afghanistan, Burma, Ceylon and Persia. At first, only correspondence was exchanged between the branch office and the small band of God's people in Rangoon, Burma.

In 1928, however, the Bombay branch sent George A. Wright to Burma. Till then, our work had been confined to only the city of Rangoon. But when Brother Wright came to Burma, he made an extensive tour of the country for some five months, distributing the Society's books *The Harp of God* and *Deliverance,* and volumes of *Studies in the Scriptures.* Undoubtedly by this means the seed of truth was sown. Also, contact was made with those who had shown interest earlier. So, it was not until 1928 that it was possible to make a serious attempt to expand the Kingdom work in Burma.

ZEALOUS COLPORTEURS LEND A HAND

In 1930 the Bombay branch sent to Burma two zealous colporteurs, Claude Goodman and Ronald Tippin, after completion of their assignment in Ceylon.

Brother Goodman says of their trip from Ceylon and efforts in Burma:

"Around these waters it is common for natives to travel 'deck' passage. This means taking your bedding roll and spreading it out on an assigned portion of deck, and that becomes your cabin for the duration of the journey. Ron and I secured a deck passage on one of the more exclusive lines running between England and Burma . . . I well recall lying on a half-inch thick mattress, sliding up and down on it with the roll of the ship until points of contact felt like raw flesh. I remember, too, the English officer who scornfully accused us of 'lowering British prestige' by traveling deck passage along with the natives. But we were not moved in any way, and thus Rangoon was reached.

"We had been given the address of a Brother Marcelline, who, along with Brothers French, Clay, Trutwein and Wooten, were the only interested persons then in Burma. It was now June of 1930. Here, as in Ceylon, no organized witnessing was being done. We set about encouraging these brothers to accompany us on Sunday mornings, and gradually they responded. I recall one of these brothers asking if he could do the witnessing work by proxy, by aiding us pioneers financially, and I remember Ron's reply, 'By all means, if you want to get into the new world by proxy also.'

"Ron and I repeated the practice developed in Ceylon of going to places outside Rangoon. Places visited were Pegu, Toungoo, Pyinmana, Mandalay, Maymyo, Hsipaw, Lashio, Shwebo, Mogok, Bhamo, Myitkyina, Magwe, Bassein, Moulmein, Akyab and others."

THEY FOUND THE TRUTH

An incident is of interest here. In his door-to-door witnessing Brother Tippin met a railway stationmaster, Mr. Sydney Coote, at Kemmendine, Rangoon, and placed with him a set of 10 books. Mr. Coote's eldest daughter recalls:

"That very night my dad read parts of *The Harp of God* and that same night he told my mother that this was the truth. Within a few days he realized that this was just the thing he had been searching for all his life. As a lad of 14 years he remembers asking his pastor to explain the Trinity to him. His reply to my dad was: 'Run away, Sonny. You are too young to bother about such things.' My dad ran away all right, but the Trinity doctrine still kept bothering him. When he read the Watch Tower publications, his problem was eventually solved. In a short time he had severed all connections with his church and did not have any trouble either, as they must have been glad to get rid of someone who was always asking them Bible questions that they could not and would not answer. It did not take my mother long to recognize the ring of truth. So, today I am very thankful to Jehovah God that both my father and mother became Jehovah's Witnesses and brought their four children up to love and serve God."

At that time there was no book like *"Make Sure of All Things; Hold Fast to What Is Fine."* But Brother Coote made one of his own along similar lines. He called it "Where Is It?" All the doctrines were listed, and whenever he came across a scripture he thought could be used, he would enter it under the appropriate heading in his book.

Brother Coote next wrote to the Society's India branch, asking if there were other Witnesses in Burma. He was sent a list with a few names and addresses. Upon receipt of this, he wrote to each one, inviting them to come and spend a day with him, as he was very anxious to find out how the preaching work was being carried on. About five or six brothers visited him and they had a small gathering. Although no door-to-door witnessing was being done in Burma, Brother Coote wrote to all his relatives and sent them our literature.

When Brother Coote's Roman Catholic sister, Mrs. Daisy D'Souza, received from him the booklet *The Kingdom, the Hope of the World,* she "devoured" its contents hungrily. She wrote to her brother for more books and a Bible. In no time, a big package of literature arrived. She went through the publications from cover to cover, one book after another, staying awake till the early hours of the morning to read them. This was it! She had found the truth! Mrs. D'Souza set off alone from house to house. She also sent her children to all her neighbors with booklets. This did not go unnoticed by her husband. Though terribly opposed at first, he started thinking: "What makes her read those books till 2 a.m.? There must be something in them." He was a railway refreshment-room manager and used to finish his work at about 11:30 p.m. One night, he remarked to his wife: "What you are reading must be very interesting to keep you up so late. Why don't you read to me?" Sister D'Souza did not need a second invitation. After that, she kept reading to him nightly. Soon they separated themselves from the Catholic Church.

After some time the parish priest called, trying to get them to return to the Church. But by this time, Sister D'Souza was well armed with the "sword of the spirit." (Eph. 6:17) So, using the Roman Catholic Bible, she proved to him how wrong the doctrines of the Catholic Church were. The priest said: "I know there is no such place as hell or purgatory. But if I don't teach people these doctrines, how am I going to make them come to church?"

"If you are an honest man and a Christian, you will teach the people the truth about God and not represent him as a fiend," replied Sister D'Souza. At that, the cleric rose in a flurry and stumped out of the room. As he was leaving, he said: "After telling people these things for years, how do you expect me to tell them something different now?"

"If you were a true Christian you surely would," retorted Sister D'Souza. Finally, he warned her to leave his flock alone.

One Sunday morning this priest collected all the Watch Tower publications he could get from his flock, along with some books he had borrowed from Brother D'Souza, and made a bonfire outside his church. But this did not discourage the D'Souza family; they continued spreading the Word of God.

TOURING BURMA WITH THE KINGDOM MESSAGE

Meanwhile, Brothers Goodman and Tippin kept on touring Burma, placing literature and spreading the good news of God's kingdom. Listen as Brother Goodman relates one of his tour experiences:

"We were informed that a *Watch Tower* subscriber had moved into the area of the Namtu silver and lead mines (Northern Shan States). The only way to get there was by company railway from a nearby town. I wrote asking for permission to use this line and was turned down, being told that we were not wanted there. But in those days we did not easily take No for an answer. So when I got to Lashio, I made inquiries and found that there was a jungle track from Lashio to Namtu, and that a taxi driver was willing to make the trip. So, on the next day I loaded many cartons of books in his auto and we set off.

"Namtu was a smelting town tucked away in the mountains, with the ore brought from the pithead several miles away. I took refuge in the government rest house and from there worked the town. Placements were many. At last, the town was finished, but I had not yet contacted the subscriber who lived in Bawdwin, the pithead. Nor was there any way to get there but by the company railway. So, I decided to place my case before the managing director himself after witnessing to him.

"He obviously knew nothing of my having been denied entry. The man was a burly Australian and, when I openly related my story (I still see the twinkle in his eyes as I told him of coming in by jungle track), he promptly left the guests he was entertaining and took me in his car to the mines office. There he introduced me to his private secretary, a Roman Catholic and the one responsible for previously preventing my entry. I can still see his jaw drop when hearing my name. He was instructed: 'I want you to make Mr. Goodman the guest of the company. He may go anywhere he wishes and you are to put a special train at his disposal and provide accommodations and meals so long as he is on the company lands.' So I was called 'Sir' and was asked when I wanted my special train and how long I wished to stay in each place—all that by the man who had tried to prevent the message from reaching the people."

By about January 1931, the brothers had covered Burma to a certain extent and were ready to move on to Singapore. Ronald Tippin went ahead, but Claude Goodman went by a coastal steamer so that he could work Tavoy and Mergui on his way south.

OTHERS CARRY ON

The preliminary work by Witnesses George Wright, Claude Goodman and Ronald Tippin was continued by Ewart Francis, who came from India in 1933. By then our work was getting well organized in Rangoon, Martaban and Mandalay. However, Brother Francis was called back to India and was replaced in 1934 by Randall Hopley and Clarence Taylor. Brother Hopley then had Brother J. F. Rutherford's recorded lectures, which were even broadcast for a few weeks over the local radio station. To meet the need for Burmese literature, in 1934 the booklets *The Kingdom, the Hope of the World* and *Escape to the Kingdom* were translated and sent to press. Other publications were to follow in Burmese and Karen.

Witness Hopley concentrated first on the city of Rangoon. While witnessing on a street there, he placed some literature with a young Greek working in a restaurant. This man quickly grasped Bible truth and wanted to know more. Hence, he wrote to the Bombay branch office and ordered some books. At the same time, he remarked in his letter: "Why don't you send someone to preach this good message to the people here? As far as I know, I am the only one here who knows anything about it." Immediately, the branch wrote to the Rangoon Congregation, asking that someone call on him. Association with the brothers made this young Greek, Basil Tsatos, a stalwart Christian. After some time, he served as a congregation servant (presiding overseer) in the Rangoon Congregation.

In the years 1935 and 1936, the brothers concentrated on the Karens, Anglo-Burmese and Anglo-Indians, for they seemed more responsive to the message of God's kingdom. It should be noted that most of the Karens are members of the sects of Christendom. While Clarence Taylor worked in Pyinmana, Randall Hopley concentrated on Mandalay and other northern towns. By this time the message was penetrating toward northern Burma.

Incidentally, Burma then was a province under the Indian government; it was not treated as a separate country. So, all field service figures were included with India's report till 1937, and no record is available to indicate how many Burmese Witnesses were reporting in those years.

A CHANGE IN BRANCH SUPERVISION

In 1938 a change took place in the supervision of the Kingdom-preaching activity in Burma. Till the beginning of that year, the Watch Tower Society's branch office in India was supervising the work in Burma. Then the Australian branch was given this responsibility. So, in 1938 the pioneers from India returned to that country, and pioneers from Australia took care of 'watering' the seeds that had been sown here. As those brothers and the Kingdom publishers in Burma faithfully did their part, God gave the increase.—1 Cor. 3:6.

For a short time, Brother S. Keltie cared for Kingdom activity in Burma. But he had to return to Australia. So, Frank Dewar looked after the work here from March to July 1938.

NEW PIONEERS ARRIVE

The 1938 service year ended with 25 congregation publishers reporting in Burma's three congregations. Meanwhile, Hector Oates and Fred Paton from Australia arrived in Rangoon to look after the work.

Downtown Rangoon is neatly laid out in parallel streets and rectangular blocks, with main and minor streets and even back alleys all systematically named and numbered. Toward the eastern edge of the city lies the large block of government buildings called the Secretariat. Around these are neatly paved streets lined with well-kept trees. In Rangoon there are long rows of uniform, four-storied flats side by side, running from street to street with no spaces between them. In the 1930's, Rangoon's transportation system included trams, buses, rickshaws and one-horse coaches.

In preparation for the arrival of Fred and Hector, Frank Dewar had rented an upstairs flat facing the Secretariat on Dalhousie Street in Rangoon. The new pioneers had brought a transcription machine, a set of some musical records, and recorded speeches by J. F. Rutherford, then the president of the Watch Tower Society. As soon as the pioneers had moved in, they set up the machine on the little front balcony, with the speaker directed toward the Secretariat. They put on an orchestral air, and in a few seconds, heads began to pop out of the many windows on every floor. Then Fred Paton put on one of the short recorded speeches by Brother Rutherford. It presented some plain, hard facts about this old system and the new one that God has promised. Quite a few clerks in the Secretariat were Baptists. Many others were Roman Catholics, and the big Catholic St. Mary's Cathedral lay at the other end of the Secretariat. So, you can imagine how startling that message was.

Eventually, Frank Dewar left Burma for Singapore. He recalls: "On July 14, 1938, I had my passport renewed at Rangoon, and shortly after that I said au revoir to Fred and Hector and went by rail and road down the coast of Burma, riding seven ferries between Tavoy and Mergui. I covered those towns, as well as smaller places, with the Kingdom message. From Mergui I got an overnight deck passage on a steamer to Victoria Point (now called Kawthaung), the small British official post at the extreme southern tip of Burma. After a night in the dak bungalow (a nice little cottage kept in most towns throughout the old Indian Empire for the convenience of traveling officials), I gave a sampan man a rupee to ferry me and my luggage over the mouth of the Pakchan River to the harbor entrance of Pinang."

SPREADING THE "GOOD NEWS"

Meanwhile, the Kingdom message was penetrating not only into many towns in Burma, but also into the hearts of sheeplike people. For instance, at this time Ruby Goff and her children accepted the truth. To Sister Goff minimum service was not satisfactory. So, she and her son, Desmond, joined the pioneer ranks.

They were the first local publishers to take up pioneer service.

With the Society's car and big sound-car van, the pioneers witnessed in Pegu, Nyaunglebin, Toungoo, Letpadan, Tharrawaddy, Prome and other places. They would park their car in the market area and start playing music for a short while and then play one of Brother Rutherford's talks. Hundreds of people at the market would hear the message and, of course, the majority would ignore it. However, almost in every case some people would come for literature.

As her territory, Sister Goff worked Insein, a town 10 miles (16 kilometers) from Rangoon. Insein has a strong settlement of Karen Baptists (who have a theological seminary there till this day), and these did not welcome the message that Sister Goff had for them. It was late one evening, after receiving a very bad reception all day, that she silently prayed, "Jehovah, please let me find just one sheep before I have to go home." At the very next house Sister Goff met a humble lady, Daw Hmwe Kyaing, a Karen Baptist. She took a Bible from Sister Goff and told her to come back on Saturday afternoon when her children would be home. That evening the woman told her two daughters that she thought Sister Ruby Goff was a little mad because she kept condemning all the other religions.

Sister Goff made the return visit and a Bible study was started with Daw Hmwe Kyaing and her daughters, Ma Chu May (now Daisy Ba Aye) and Ma Hnin May (now Lily Dewar). In no time, all three saw that this message was the truth. Later, the daughters became great assets in our translation work. Ma Hnin May joined Sister Goff in door-to-door activity and thus became the first Karen Witness.

One day, when Sister Goff was witnessing at the Thamaing railway station, she stopped a young man. He had been living most of his life as a hobo, illegally entering countries, stealing jewelry, joining circuses, participating in boxing matches, and so forth, without getting any satisfaction out of life. Since he was unable to contribute for literature, the sister kindly gave him a booklet and provided the local Kingdom Hall address. That was the turning point in his life. During a train ride, he read the booklet, and by the time he reached Rangoon station, he had concluded that this was the truth.

The very next day this young man, Cyril Gay, called on the Witnesses and asked them many questions. Witness Hector Oates played recorded sermons as answers to his questions. From that time onward, this former vagabond became a changed man and soon joined the pioneer ranks.

The pioneers continued to spread the "good news" into the districts. Once they rushed to Henzada in their sound car to witness to the delegates at a Baptist convention being held there. But the Baptists did not want to hear the message. With the help of a police officer, they managed to drive the brothers away. But the pioneers went to the marketplace and continued playing the records of J. F. Rutherford's lectures. Moreover, they placed much literature. But would this do any good?

Some time later, a group of Witnesses went to that area. While witnessing there, they called on a Karen man who rejected the literature, saying he did not need it, as he had his own handbook on the Bible that he and his family used in their prayers. When the brothers asked to see it, he brought out one of the Watch Tower Society's books.

In another instance, a man from Henzada went to Rangoon to search for the Witnesses. He found them doing magazine street work, offering our journals to passersby. How had he come to know about the Witnesses, and why was he looking for them?

During the earlier trip of the pioneers to Henzada, a Karen Catholic had taken some books from the brothers and returned to his village, Thinganain, about 12 miles (19 kilometers) from Henzada. He started reading the books there and quickly accepted their message as the truth. So he began to spread the "good news" in his village. But before he could contact the brothers, World War II started, and so he held meetings with whatever literature he had, conducting them in his own style. He used to gather his relatives together on Sundays, reading and translating the Society's publications for them into Karen. Soon, 12 of his relatives accepted the truth and cut themselves off from the Catholic Church. The local priest tried to get these persons back into his "fold," but they were firm in their stand for the truth. After the war, this man heard that there were some Witnesses in Rangoon. So he sent a man to contact them with a letter from him, although he did not know their address. But while personally inquiring about the Witnesses in Rangoon, the man accidentally met them on the street.

Thus the witnessing work done with the sound car and the playing of Brother Rutherford's recorded talks at market squares proved successful. This led to placing literature with interested persons, and certain ones embraced true Christianity.

THE FIRST BURMESE ASSEMBLY

In 1938, Burmese Witnesses were thrilled with the news that an assembly would be held in Rangoon from November 26 to 28, and that the branch overseer of Australia, Brother Alex MacGillivray, would be present. The pioneers in Singapore, Malaya and Siam (now Thailand) were invited to attend, and the assembly location was the City Hall, a palatial building with huge bronze doors.

It was like a small international assembly. Other delegates also came from Australia and Thailand. Among those present were Brothers J. E. Sewell and F. Dewar, from Thailand. Their journey to Rangoon was not an easy one. Starting at Bangkok, they traveled by train and bus to the village of Rahaeng. Regarding the rest of the trip, Brother Sewell says:

"We stayed [at Rahaeng] that night and crossed the Meping River in a large dugout canoe the next morning at daybreak. Then we began our long adventure of walking 50 miles [80 kilometers] across the mountain in virgin tropical jungle. A telephone line ran across the area and we followed that. (It linked Siam and Burma.) It was a dangerous trip to take— one we couldn't recommend to anyone.

"We were afraid of the wild animals in the jungle. For instance, tigers were reported in that region. We saw many monkeys, but no tigers, elephants or black bears. Some beautiful bantams live wild in that area and they would fly across our paths at times. After walking the first day, we felt very tired, and met up with two carriers. These men really were smugglers taking goods from one country to another. We could see that we would have difficulties ahead trying to get through this long walk and would not know where to sleep at night or how to protect ourselves anywhere. So we asked these two smugglers who were coming back from Burma with empty baskets (one on each end of a pole) if they would help us. For a small price each, they decided to do this. We put our things in their baskets and followed them. After sleeping one night on a platform in a tree and in a little village the next night, we finally reached Mae Sot, the border town of Siam. Crossing a river there, we were able to continue the journey on a little bus for a stretch of over 50 miles [80 kilometers]. This was over a very mountainous and craggy path. That night we stayed in a Karen village, where a gentleman took us in and gave us a place to sleep. Finally, we went on by bus for another 18 miles [29 kilometers] and caught a little river steamer that took us another 40 miles or so [about 65 kilometers] from Pa-an to Moulmein. There we crossed the estuary of the Salween River to Martaban, the terminus of the railway line. We then traveled by train to Rangoon. It took us a week to make this trip, but then we had a fine assembly in the City Hall of Rangoon."

Many brothers and interested persons from Mandalay, Martaban, Insein and other places also attended the assembly. The public talk was well advertised, and the hall was filled beyond its capacity, with 1,000 present in the 850-seat hall. The attendants tried to close the huge gates to keep out the further surging crowds and succeeded only after a third attempt. However, some enterprising young men came in through the smaller side doors. There were perhaps 1,000 outside that could not get in. The title of the talk and the extensive advertising could have been the reason for the record crowds. Brother MacGillivray, the branch overseer from Strathfield, Australia, delivered the discourse entitled "Universal War Near." Whatever may have been the reason for the success of the assembly, it certainly was a highlight in the history of Jehovah's people in Burma.

INTERFERENCE ENCOUNTERED

Toward the end of 1939 the Society's Strathfield branch office sent another pioneer, Mick Engel, to care for the Burma literature depot. By then the number of pioneers had increased in Burma, and Ma Hnin May (Lily) was one of them. Four local pioneers were declaring the Word of God shoulder to shoulder with the Australian pioneers. When the 1939 service year ended, there were 28 Witnesses reporting field service in three congregations in Burma.

With Kingdom proclamation gaining momentum, persecution reared its ugly head. Toward the end of 1940, the Anglican, Methodist, Roman Catholic and American Baptist clergymen in Burma pressured the British-raj to put a ban on our literature. But even before the order was received by the government authorities in Rangoon, the brothers had learned about it. How?

Two of our brothers who were working in the cable office had seen a telegram come through ordering all our literature in Burma to be banned and confiscated. Immediately, they informed Brother Mick Engel, and he saw to it that most of our literature was hidden in different places, including the homes of friendly Karens in Thamaing and other suburban areas.

In those days, a tremendous amount of war material was being sent from the United States to the Nationalist Chinese government under Chiang Kai-shek, for use in his war against the Japanese. These supplies were sent to Lashio, in northern Burma, then were transshipped over the winding, dangerous Burma Road to Chungking. Thousands of military trucks moved in unbroken lines from Rangoon on their way northward, laden with tires, fuel, ammunition and other war supplies. The brothers thought that they could get our literature on one of these trucks headed for Chungking, where it would be safe from confiscation. But this effort did not succeed.

Brother George Powell then decided to go to Singapore, obtain a vehicle there, return to Burma, load our literature on it and convey the publications to Chungking. Unfortunately, however, just before his arrival in Singapore an order had been issued there forbidding the taking out of any vehicles. Now what would happen to our publications? Would they be confiscated and destroyed?

Meanwhile, Brother Engel had approached a high U.S. official and had managed to get a letter of authority allowing us to transport our literature on the army trucks. Equipped with that letter, Mick Engel, Fred Paton and Hector Oates went to Lashio. When they called on the official controlling the huge convoy to China and asked him for space on those trucks, he nearly had a fit! "What?" he shouted. "How can I give you precious space in my trucks for your miserable tracts when I have absolutely no room for urgently needed military and medical supplies rotting here in the open, with the monsoon rains due to begin soon?"

Fred looked at him, paused, and reached into his briefcase and took out the letter from the high official in Rangoon. Handing it to the road controller, Fred remarked that it would be a very serious matter if the controller ignored the authorities in Rangoon and refused to help. Fred's argument proved overpowering. The road controller not only arranged for two tons of books to be transported, but placed a light truck, complete with driver and supplies, at the disposal of the brothers. Thus the two intrepid pioneers, Fred Paton and Hector Oates, went by truck to Chungking, where they distributed their consignment. In Chungking, they met Chiang Kai-shek and witnessed to him.

When the Japanese started to invade Burma, almost

all the Witnesses left the country. Mick Engel left for Australia and most of the Anglo-Indian and Anglo-Burman brothers went to India. Brother Coote and his two daughters trekked to India, but he died before reaching that country.

From August to October 1941, only 18 publishers were reporting field service in Burma, and there were no pioneers here by then. By November, all the Witnesses had left Burma except for three, Brother Cyril Gay and Sisters Ma Chu May and Ma Hnin May. They did only informal witnessing.

On March 8, 1942, Rangoon, the capital of Burma, fell to the Japanese forces. The fall of other towns took place rapidly thereafter. As for the British, it was a grim record of continued withdrawal. The Japanese could hardly have been more successful. In five months they overran a country larger than France and nearly as populous as Australia and Canada combined (at that time). By the end of May 1942, all Burma was in Japanese hands.

During the Japanese occupation, from 1942 to 1945, the work of declaring the "good news" practically came to a dead stop in Burma. Due to lack of publications, the three Witnesses here studied the same issues of *The Watchtower* over and over again. They used the *1942 Yearbook of Jehovah's Witnesses* for studying the daily Bible texts for more than four years.

Burma, however, was part of the Japanese empire only for a short period. Again bombing raids started, but this time by the British. Their planes dropped tons of bombs, destroying thousands of buildings and killing thousands upon thousands of people. By 1945 the war was over, and the British reoccupied Burma.

OUR WORK REESTABLISHED

Immediately after the war, the brothers and sisters who had fled to India started coming back to Burma. So, the witnessing work began afresh, and on April 20, 1946, a congregation was established once more in Rangoon, with eight publishers reporting field service. The Society's branch office in India directed the Kingdom-preaching work in Burma for some time after the war.

Brother R. W. Kirk, the first Gilead School graduate sent here, arrived early in 1947. That same year saw the first visit of the Society's third president, N. H. Knorr, and his secretary, M. G. Henschel. To coincide with that visit, a convention was arranged for the 19 Witnesses in the country.

Brothers Knorr and Henschel came from Siam by seaplane. It touched down on the other side of the Rangoon River on April 12, 1947, and by a motor launch they were then transported across the river to a pier where a bus was waiting to take them to the center of Rangoon. As they rode into the main part of the city, they could see how much devastation had been caused by the war. Temporary bamboo homes had been constructed along the roads and thousands of people were living in these improvised structures. As the visitors got to the center of the city, they found that the buildings were made of brick and were quite modern. But many were merely shells, as the interiors had been burned out.

Brother Knorr was to give his public address on Sunday morning at ten o'clock. The talk was well advertised by the 18 congregation publishers and one missionary then living in Rangoon. A motion-picture house, the New Excelsior Theatre, was the place chosen for the public talk. About an hour before the lecture, however, the theater manager suffered a heart attack and died. So his assistants quickly hung up a sign stating that, due to his death, the theater would be closed for the day. Nevertheless, the brothers prevailed upon those left in charge to permit the meeting to go on; so access was gained to the theater. It was a pleasant surprise to see 287 present.

Rangoon is a warm and humid city, and even at ten o'clock in the morning it does not take much exercise for one to perspire. Brother Knorr did not have tropical clothing and soon became soaked with perspiration while he delivered the public discourse. There was no ventilation on the platform, and the doors had been closed to keep out the heat. So he sweltered and found it quite novel to give a discourse and feel water running down his back and into his shoes. Why, at the end of the talk he had wet feet!

But that was just one way to get wet in Rangoon. Before going to an afternoon meeting at the newly built Kingdom Hall, the travelers reported to the airways office to check on their departure for Calcutta. It was the first day of *Thingyan* (the water festival), a religious celebration when the Buddhists throw water on one another. Brothers Knorr, Henschel, Kirk and Tsatos climbed into a jeep and got on their way downtown. The young people were out in full force on this first day of the festival, lining up on both sides of the streets where water hydrants were located. Every pedestrian and vehicle passing by was showered with water. Tin cans, buckets, pots, water guns and hoses were used to throw water on people. The report in *The Watchtower* says:

"The four of us were soaked before we got very far, but we would laugh and try to enjoy our plight every time we got drenched. We might as well have fallen into the Irrawaddy river, for that is how we looked by the time we got down to the airways office. And we were only getting a good start, for after our tickets were fixed up we had to return to the same part of the city whence we had come, to the Kingdom Hall.

"When we stepped from the jeep in front of the Kingdom Hall and let some of the water drip off our frames we found some of the brethren were already assembled at the Kingdom Hall, but they too had had similar experiences. However, they were familiar with the customs of the people and had brought with them in waterproof containers some changes of clothing. They changed their clothes and looked presentable. But as for the three speakers of the afternoon, Brothers Kirk, Knorr and Henschel, they looked as if they had just come in out of the rain. It was good that the brethren understood the position. The speakers went ahead giving the Scriptural advice and admonition. The only interruption was that about halfway through the meeting some bold young men ventured to the door of the hall and threw in a bucketful of water, hitting no one. The 37 brethren who attended the meeting enjoyed it very much."

During this trip, arrangements were made for the establishment of a branch office of the Society in Rangoon, beginning September 1, 1947. Also, plans were made to send more missionaries to Burma.

MORE AID FROM GILEAD

On July 4, 1947, the brothers assembled at the jetty to welcome Norman H. Barber, the second missionary to arrive in Burma. What a delightful surprise to see two brothers disembark instead of one! The unexpected arrival was an old associate. At Singapore, Brother Barber had met Frank Dewar, who had decided to accompany him to Burma.

At that time, Burma was seeking independence from Britain. After much negotiation, she became independent on January 4, 1948, at 4 a.m. Would this particularly affect our work? It did not, for the Burmese government promised freedom of worship.

Two more Gilead graduates, Brothers R. W. Richards and H. A. Smedstad, arrived on January 15, 1948, just 11 days after Burma had attained independence. As they landed, the immigration officers asked: "Where are your visas?" "We have no visas," was the answer. The brothers explained that they had left Canada (a self-governing dominion of the British Commonwealth of Nations) in November 1947, when Burma was part of the British Empire, and they had expected to arrive in this country before it became independent; so no visas were called for. However, the officers were unimpressed. Their country now was independent. "How can you enter Burma without a visa?" they insisted. After long deliberation, one of the officers relented. How relieved the new missionaries were! With that problem resolved, they were taken to the recently rented missionary home at 39 Signal Pagoda Road, Rangoon.

The missionaries were pleasantly surprised to find that the Burmese generally were approachable, friendly and hospitable. Even when a stranger called at their homes, often he was served tea and cake and made to feel welcome.

Speaking of food, the Burmese dread the odor from frying food, particularly when there is a sick person in the house. They claim that this odor can cause the death of an individual having any kind of sore and also that of a newborn baby and its mother. Fearing this, they close doors and windows, then cover the "odor allergic" person with a thick blanket, even in the hot summertime, till the odor has passed away. This is the reason why a Burmese housewife, when about to fry something in her own home, will loudly warn her neighbors.

The missionaries were unaware of this Burmese viewpoint. So, one day when they were frying something for their lunch, the Burmese lady who lived upstairs came down and angrily exclaimed: "Now look here! If you want to fry anything, tell us first and do it on the pavement. Do you hear?" The confused missionaries could not understand this until the local brothers explained the matter to them. Well, Brother Barber was frying fish out on the pavement one day, when, to his surprise, a number of children gathered around him with money in their hands. They were waiting patiently to buy the fish. It is common to see men frying and selling eatables on the pavements here in Burma.

A PERIOD OF UNREST

Not very long after Burma gained independence, various dissident groups and tribes rose up in armed rebellion against the newly established government. They went underground and played havoc with the government, as well as with the people. The dissidents blew up bridges and railway lines and caused much damage. Most of the insurgents were Karens and Kachins, converts to the American Baptist Mission. Every now and then, one would hear reports that passenger trains had been wrecked, towns looted and water pipelines blown up by the insurgents.

It was under such conditions that the Witnesses traveled from Maymyo to attend the district assembly held at Rangoon. On January 19, 1949, after the assembly, Frank Dewar went to Maymyo to help the small group there.

On February 4, 1949, the Burmese police arrested all suspected Karen nationals in Maymyo, sending them to the Mandalay jail, and later to the Shwebo jail. On February 6, the Burmese intelligence officers had the police arrest Brother Dewar who was staying in the home of a Karen Witness. They had suspected him of spying for the rebel Karens. After one night, however, the authorities released him.

In March, the Karen rebel forces attacked Maymyo and Mandalay. Bitter fighting ensued between the rebels and the Burmese government forces. For several nights people had to sleep in trenches while bullets whistled overhead. By March 7 the battle was over, with the Karen insurgents occupying both towns. The rebels captured many other towns and even came as far as Insein, 10 miles (16 kilometers) from Rangoon, the capital city. But their powerful thrust did not last long. The government forces regrouped and, being well equipped with modern arms, forced the insurgents back to the jungles. While this fighting was going on, our witnessing work was confined solely to Rangoon, Insein, Maymyo and Thinganain, with communications between the brothers completely cut off.

"THIS IS THE TRUTH"

In 1948, a Kingdom publisher obtained employment with the Burma Oil Company and was transferred to the oil field in Chauk. As soon as he and his family settled down there, they started witnessing on Sundays and holidays. While declaring the "good news" from house to house, they met a sheeplike Tamilian. The very same week that this man, M. C. Nathan, met the Witnesses he cut off all ties with the Catholic Church and, without delay, became a witness of Jehovah.

At the time, Brother Nathan's nephew was spending his school vacation with him and could not avoid hearing the Kingdom message as his uncle witnessed to his own family. Although the youth had considered becoming a Catholic priest, in time he admitted, "What uncle says is true." Whenever his uncle was not at home, he would pick up the Society's publications and read them. The message was so convincing that he said, "This is the truth." Accordingly, this young man, Maurice A. Raj, was baptized in the Irrawaddy River on December 24, 1949. In time, he began pioneering, and in 1963 he became a circuit overseer. Then, in 1966, Brother Raj was appointed both as the district and branch overseer.

ANOTHER HELPFUL VISIT

After the Karen insurrection, the village of Thinganain was wiped out by a ruthless gang of robbers. Not only did our brothers lose all their possessions, Bible literature and homes, but one of them was murdered. The rest were scattered and practically all contact with them was lost. Afterward, it was found that, because of the many hardships, all but four had died.

In 1951, after the government had restored order in the major areas of the country, we were able to reorganize our witnessing activities and good progress resulted. When the Society's president, N. H. Knorr, and his secretary, M. G. Henschel, had visited Burma in 1947, there were only 18 publishers and one Gilead School graduate in the country. Now, with this second visit scheduled to take place on April 10, 1951, Burma had a new peak of 94 publishers.

An assembly was arranged to coincide with the around-the-world trip of Brothers Knorr and Henschel. After a rousing welcome at the airport, our visitors were rushed off to the convention, which was already in session at the Kingdom Hall. A round of applause greeted them. Brother Henschel gave his talk first and was followed by Brother Knorr. Their discourses were translated into Burmese.

On Wednesday Brother Knorr spoke to 256 persons gathered at Rangoon's City Hall to hear the public lecture "Proclaim Liberty Throughout All the Land." Then, while Brother Henschel was speaking, Brother Knorr was taken to the government radio station in

Rangoon to give a 15-minute talk over the air. This program also was heard at the assembly hall. The convention itself continued the next day and ended with 90 persons attending the closing meeting.

During this visit Brother Knorr made arrangements for the newly appointed branch overseer, Robert W. Richards, to visit the brothers in the north where there were problems due to the insurgents. His visits proved very upbuilding and fruitful.

There had previously been a change in branch overseers when Robert W. Kirk (Burma's first branch overseer) had left this assignment to marry a pioneer sister, Claire D'Souza. In 1954 Sister Kirk was sent to Gilead's 22nd class, and that year Brother Kirk was reappointed as branch overseer. From 1955 to 1959, the Burma branch sent six more local pioneers to Gilead. Brother D. J. O'Neill and Sister Norma Barber graduated in 1956; a local Lushai special pioneer, Joyce Ralte, graduated in 1958; and Dorinda Smedstad, Georgianna Redmond and Doris Ba Aye (now Mrs. Maurice Raj) graduated in 1959.

In 1956, Burma was again on Brother Knorr's itinerary when he visited countries in the East. This time there were 268 persons present to hear him speak on the subject "Making All Mankind One Under Their Creator." After the public talk Brothers Knorr and Kirk rushed off by car to the Burma Broadcasting Station, where Brother Knorr was interviewed. Significantly, it was during this convention that he released the new Burmese *Watchtower*.

In speaking to the missionaries, Brother Knorr particularly emphasized the importance of learning the Burmese language. The missionaries admitted that they still were not fluent in Burmese. Impressed with his remarks, however, they set out in earnest to learn the language.

Naturally, the first thing the missionaries tried to learn was what to say at the doors in their house-to-house witnessing work. So they learned short Bible presentations and a conclusion, *Ta-ouk tamma,* meaning, "Each booklet four annas." When one missionary tried this out in the field, a householder looked confused and asked the woman standing next to her, "What is he saying?" "He says that he has eggs to sell," was the prompt reply. "How much is he charging for them?" asked the first woman. The other replied, "Twenty-five annas for an egg." Instead of saying *Ta-ouk,* the missionary had said *Ta-ook,* as though eggs were being sold.

It is really very difficult for foreigners to pronounce Burmese words correctly. If one is unable to pronounce each syllable accurately, the meaning may be just the opposite of what was intended. For example, "a new world" (*kaba-a'thit*) can become "a dead world" (*kaba-a'theyt*), if not pronounced correctly. So quite often after witnessing in the Burmese language the missionaries would be told by the householder: "Please speak in Burmese. I don't understand English."

ENCOURAGED BY ANOTHER VISITOR

Now let us turn our attention to the visit of another representative of the Watch Tower Society. It was at 5 p.m. on Sunday, December 30, 1956, that a plane carrying Brother F. W. Franz, then the Society's vice-president, landed at Mingaladon airport. What a joyous occasion it was as we traveled toward Rangoon by bus, singing Kingdom songs accompanied by Brother Franz playing his mouth organ! On our arrival at the Kingdom Hall, the *Watchtower* study was just ending. Promptly, Brother Franz was put on the program to give us a travelogue for more than an hour. A five-day assembly was to begin three days from then, but the 55 persons gathered at the Kingdom Hall felt as if it had already begun.

During his eight-day stay in Burma, Brother Franz had the pleasure of lodging at the missionary home with the five graduates of Gilead. He was surprised to learn that the New Year celebration was held even in Buddhist Burma. Yes, at midnight of Monday, December 31, with the twelfth and last stroke of the night watchman's iron, there was a chain reaction of firecrackers, the sounding of sirens and the blowing of whistles of vessels in the Rangoon River.

Delegates to the assembly came from an unusually wide area. Whole families traveled hundreds of miles on trains with hard wooden seats, not knowing when they would be delayed in view of the unsettled conditions then prevailing in the country. They arrived safely, however, and were glad to be in time for the convention. One delegate, who was due to deliver her baby about assembly time, came to Rangoon early and gave birth to her child. A few days later she was listening to the assembly talks with her baby in her arms.

On Saturday, 11 persons (a record number up to that time) symbolized their dedication to Jehovah God by submitting to water baptism at the Royal Lakes, where one can see the reflection of the Shwe Dagon Pagoda, its gold sheath gleaming in the sunshine. The baptism candidates were composed of four racial groups—six Tamilians, three Karens, one Anglo-Indian and one Gurkha.

Nearly all the discourses were translated from English into Burmese, and the baptism talk was partly translated into Tamil. A Tamil meeting on Saturday summarized the main talks of the assembly.

Until Thursday it appeared that F. W. Franz would be prevented from delivering the widely announced public talk "New World Peace in Our Time—Why?" But by the skillful maneuvering of the Almighty God, Jehovah, the way was cleared for the public event to go on as advertised. At 4 p.m. on Sunday, January 6, 1957, the public meeting was held at the Railway Institute Hall, with 237 persons present. After the talk, the film "The Happiness of the New World Society" was shown for the first time in Burma, and the hall was filled to overflowing. On Monday, at 10:30 p.m., Brother Franz said au revoir to us and flew to Bangkok.

The visit of F. W. Franz encouraged us very much. After the assembly the brothers returned to their homes well fed spiritually. Immediately after the convention, certain pioneers were sent to new territories to spread the Kingdom message. By then our work was going ahead well in Insein, Bassein, Maymyo, Taunggyi and other places.

PROGRESS IN THE "GOLDEN CITY"

Missionary Robert W. Richards and his wife, who was appointed as a special pioneer, were assigned to work in Mandalay, the second-largest city in Burma, with a population of 180,000. It was founded in 1857 C.E. by King Mindon. The Burmese often call it *Shweman,* meaning "Golden City." Why? Well, near Mandalay Hill King Mindon built a magnificent gold-gilded wooden palace surrounded by high, thick walls. Unfortunately, during World War II the palace was destroyed, but the square brick walls that guarded the palace still stand.

Another place of interest to the visitor to Burma is the nearly 1,000-foot- (300-meter-) high pagoda-crowned Mandalay Hill. Three covered stairways, marked at intervals by giant statues of Buddha, lead up to the top of the hill. From there a magnificent view of Mandalay and its environs can be enjoyed. Everything around the hill seems to speak of King Mindon, who built several pagodas here.

By far the most famous of these is the Kuthodaw Pagoda, lying just southeast of the hill. There one can see truly remarkable religious work. Inside the pagoda compound stand rows of small white pagodas. Each little pagoda covers an upright marble slab on which has been inscribed in Pali a portion of the Buddhist scriptures. The slabs are four or five feet high and three or four feet wide (about 1.5 by 1.2 meters). To inscribe one slab alone would require a great deal of painstaking work; yet there they stand by the hundreds. The grand total of these slabs is given as no fewer than 729. This remarkable work was performed at the order of King Mindon in 1857 C.E. He summoned 2,400 monks to the palace. They discussed and examined the Buddhist scriptures for five months and then had them inscribed on the 729 marble slabs.

In 1957, the first circuit assembly to be held outside Rangoon was scheduled in Mandalay. During that assembly only one person was baptized. He was the first Kachin to embrace true Christianity. Nobody knew at that time that through him many more Kachins would see the truth and would constitute six congregations and many isolated groups by 1978. This brother later became the presiding overseer of one of these Kachin congregations.

Incidentally, Mandalay has extremes of climate. During winter it gets very cold, but in summer it is unbearably hot and dry. In fact, some of the brothers who came to this assembly from other parts of the country were not able to bear the heat. So they would dampen their bed sheets with water before retiring and some would even sleep on wet mats. In the daytime the brothers' shirts would simply be soaked with perspiration. But in this city Brother Robert W. Richards, a Canadian, witnessed without any complaints, along with his wife and other local pioneers.

PERSEVERING ELSEWHERE

Meanwhile, Frank Dewar and his wife, Lily, worked very hard in Bassein and managed to establish a congregation there. Bassein is a coastal town in the south where many Karen Baptists live. There, as in Mandalay, the Baptist clergymen have firm control of their people. And, as in other places, their cry is: "Why don't you go and preach to the Buddhists? Why do you come taking away our sheep?" Frank Dewar was referred to in Bassein as "that white-faced sheep thief."

Whatever we might be called, however, Jehovah's Witnesses in Burma have kept on helping the people to flee from Babylon the Great, the world empire of false religion. But it is not very easy to go from house to house and village to village in the rurals of Burma. During the summer the brothers have to walk on hot and dusty pathways. They come home tired and covered with dust. During the monsoons, they return muddy after crossing flooded fields.

In the villages most of the houses are built with bamboo poles, the sides of these homes being covered with bamboo mats and the roofs with thatched grass. These houses are always built four to six feet (about 1 to 2 meters) above the ground. The floor is a sort of woven bamboo mat stretched tightly across bamboo "beams." Usually, the steps are made of bamboos or logs. At the steps one finds a water jar, with a can. Rainwater from the roof fills such vessels. The jar is kept there for people to wash their feet before entering the house. So when doing door-to-door witnessing work, a person washes his feet before entering the house. When leaving, he gets back into the dust or mud (depending on the season) and trudges on to the next house. Again he washes his feet before entering that home. And so it goes till the end of the day's witnessing.

Of course, in Rangoon a Witness would take a bus to his territory, where he would start climbing the stairs in four-story apartment buildings. In these there are from six to eight flats. When you ring the doorbell, someone looks through a peephole in the door. We cannot blame them for not readily opening the door, because very often impostors come to the door as friends, then enter the house and rob the occupants at gunpoint. So, many times we finish a whole block of flats and never get a chance to get into one home or present the Kingdom message.

Imagine yourself carrying on your shoulder a bag full of books and booklets in different languages (Rangoon is a cosmopolitan city), and two Bibles (one in English and the other in Burmese). Perspiring from head to foot, you can become quite exhausted. However, Jehovah's Witnesses are happy in Burma, as elsewhere, for the "sheep" are hearing the voice of the Great Shepherd, Jehovah.

In 1958 Brother Robert W. Richards and his wife were assigned to Kachin State. Their base of activities was the town of Bhamo, Northern Burma. Brother Richards tells us:

"The population of Bhamo consisted of Kachins, Karens, Chinese and a few Shans and Burmese. Scattered villages round about were populated mostly by Shans and Kachins. Of the latter, about half were of the Catholic and Baptist religions. The remainder were animists. Since my wife and I both had bicycles, we spent most of the first week visiting the villages near town. On Sunday we worked in town. Everywhere we were received with kindness. Many of the villagers kept chickens and, before we left their houses, they would bring us welcome gifts of chicken eggs.

"We arranged to call back the following week on those who showed interest, and we were totally unprepared for the reception we received. The villagers still were friendly, but told us firmly: 'Unless you bring a letter signed by the Ministerial Alliance, giving you permission to preach in this locality, we cannot discuss religion with you.' What a surprise! Already the clergy of Christendom were busy warning their flock not to listen to Jehovah's Witnesses. What should we do? Well, what would Jesus Christ have done in our place? . . . We kept on preaching.

"The Kachin Bible, which was widely circulated among at least the Kachin Baptists, contained the name Jehovah hundreds of times in the Hebrew Scriptures. What was the attitude of the clergy of Christendom toward this glorious name? Soon we had an opportunity to find out. I had established a Bible study with a retired army captain who spoke English well. Some of his family were churchgoers. One day the Kachin Baptist pastor visited their home and someone mustered up enough courage to ask him what he thought of Jehovah's Witnesses. His reply was shocking. He said, 'I would just as soon smell the smell of human dung as hear this name Jehovah!' "

Regarding a trip to the capital of Kachin State, Brother Richards writes:

"My wife and I arranged to make what was to be our last visit to Myitkyina, 115 miles [185 kilometers] northwest of Bhamo over a rough mountain road. It was a tiresome trip by overloaded jeep and took six hours. So we tried to get an early start.

"This particular morning everything seemed to go wrong. Instead of catching the first passenger jeep going out of town, we were able to go only on the third and were irritated at the loss of time. Little did we dream that the delay would save us from capture and kidnapping, if not worse. Unknown to travelers, insurgents were entrenched alongside a particularly wild section of the road some 60 miles [100 kilometers] from Bhamo. They seized the two cars that went ahead of us. Ours was next. Suddenly, though, the rebels themselves were taken by surprise when, entirely by chance, an army officer with a strong escort happened to pass by from the opposite direction. The insurgents fired on the leading truck, and several soldiers were killed and wounded. The following troops, however, drove back the rebels. A jeep carrying the wounded soldiers halted us and told us to wait some time until the road was cleared. This we did, and we finally arrived in Myitkyina late but safe. With grateful hearts, we thanked Jehovah God for that deliverance."

FRUITFULNESS IN THE CHIN HILLS AND VICINITY

Till 1959, the work of declaring the "good news" was concentrated among the Karens, Kachins and Mons. But in November 1960 we began witnessing in virgin territory—the Chin Hills, in the west, near the Indian border. How fruitful this territory proved to be! Now we have 20 congregations there. Maurice Raj, one of the special pioneers who went to this area, tells us:

"Tahan is located on a dusty plain at the foot of the Chin Hills. . . . At that time, it had a population of about 5,000 and was really a great sprawling village, inhabited mostly by Lushais who had come over from India and a few Chins from the hills. The Lushais belonged to various denominations of Christendom, and the Chins were Catholics and Baptists, while the remainder of the residents were animists.

"The Lushais and Chins are great readers of the Bible and they love to discuss religion. The very night we arrived in Tahan, about 40 persons gathered to discuss the Bible. How they learned about our arrival I do not know. But they were there, each one with his own Lushai Bible. They simply barraged us with questions, and we had to use interpreters, for they could not speak Burmese or English. These people would sit there and ask us questions till 11 p.m. or midnight. This went on for many days. . . .

"After some time the attendance at the nightly gathering decreased in number, leaving only a few genuine ones. I quickly turned the gatherings into regular meetings, five of them. They were held with the help of interpreters.

"In a month's time five persons were going out in the field service. The Society sent another special pioneer brother to work with me in Tahan. . . . As we walked to our territory, we would practice speaking to each other in the Lushai language. At the same time, we used to look for someone who could translate our presentations at the doors. One day we found a young boy herding cows and asked if he could speak in Burmese and would be our interpreter. He agreed to do this at once, and after a few houses, he started to witness by himself. (Two years later when I visited the Tahan Congregation as a circuit overseer, the presiding overseer, Brother James Xavier, my former pioneer partner, directed my attention to a young and lively publisher who looked familiar. He was the same boy who had been our interpreter.)

"After seven months, two special pioneer sisters were sent to Tahan and I was called back to Rangoon. Within a year the pioneers were speaking fluently in the Lushai language . . . The work went ahead very fast, a congregation was formed and a Kingdom Hall was built. It was the first Kingdom Hall to be constructed by the Witnesses in Burma. This congregation produced 13 Lushai special pioneers."

In 1960, Burma reached a peak of 201 Kingdom publishers, as a result of the growth in the Chin State. A record of 38 were immersed that year. The peak rose to 216 publishers in 1962.

In that same year, while the brothers were attending a circuit assembly at Moulmein, it was announced by radio that on March 2, 1962, a coup d'etat had taken place. Of course, we maintain Christian neutrality. But we wondered if the change of government would affect our work. Would this new government permit the bringing in of more missionaries? And would it allow our special pioneers to attend Gilead School? In 1961, the previous government had refused to allow two of our pioneers to go to Gilead. A second attempt to obtain passports also had failed. But what would now take place?

The new military government guaranteed freedom of worship. Their policy is that if religion does not interfere with political affairs, they will not interfere with religion. As they have requested, we have provided full information about our work.

"EVERLASTING GOOD NEWS"
ASSEMBLY OF JEHOVAH'S WITNESSES

What a thrill it was for Jehovah's Witnesses in Burma, a country then with little more than 200 Kingdom publishers, to host one of the Around-the-World conventions of God's people! We certainly looked forward to this "Everlasting Good News" Assembly, to be held at Rangoon in August 1963. Due to strict regulations governing the holding of meetings and the use of sound equipment, special police permits had to be obtained. Although these had been requested long in advance, the necessary permission had not been forthcoming. All angles of approach to the authorities had been exhausted. Then the branch overseer happened to mention the problem in a conversation with a friendly Buddhist who was printing the assembly programs. He offered his help, made the necessary contact and placed the required permits in our hands in time.

The assembly was held at the Rangoon City Hall. In arranging for the cafeteria, we encountered a problem peculiar to Burma, the one commonly referred to as "frying smell." As explained earlier, Burmese people strongly believe that the smell of food frying is injurious to health, particularly to that of sick people. Since many offices are located in adjoining sections of the City Hall, the brothers, while given permission to cook in the room reserved for that purpose, were earnestly requested by the staff not to make any "frying smell." This meant that some of our cooks had to start on the job before 4 a.m. in order to avoid any semblance of "frying smell" after 8 a.m. Otherwise, objections likely would have led to a closing down of the cafeteria. It is to the credit of the brothers that no difficulty of any kind arose with the City Hall neighbors. Incidentally, one City Hall employee said that ours was the first group ever permitted to cook on the premises.

That assembly was unforgettable. Never had we seen so many of our foreign brothers and sisters all at one time. Among our visitors were Brothers N. H. Knorr, F. W. Franz and Grant Suiter.

The assembly opened, on August 8, with an attendance of 310. At the conclusion of a moving talk that evening, Brother Suiter released the long-awaited Burmese edition of the book *From Paradise Lost to Paradise Regained*.

On Saturday, at 6 p.m., Brother Knorr delivered the public talk "When God Is King over All the Earth." To the joy of all the brothers, by then the attendance figures had climbed to a peak of 603. Since an estimated 100 of those present were foreign brothers, and about 200 were local publishers, some 300 of the public attended the lecture. That was excellent, indeed!

That evening a group of 10 missionaries serving in Burma enjoyed a meal with Brothers Knorr and Franz. After exchanging interesting experiences, the group listened intently as Brother Knorr gave pointed instructions to "keep working faithfully and keep building up your brothers." Clearly, he showed that whether the local organization could stand up under the fiery test of persecution would depend chiefly on how mature it would be at that time.

A notable discourse on the assembly's final day was "The World—God's Field of Work," given by F. W. Franz. After a short intermission, he brought the memorable assembly to a close with a two-hour talk and a final prayer.

FOREIGN MISSIONARIES DEPORTED

We reached a peak of 270 Kingdom proclaimers in 1965, and our work was making steady progress. But the month of May 1966 brought shocking news. The government informed the branch office that all our foreign missionaries were to leave the country by June 30, 1966. Of course, not only our missionaries, but also those of Christendom were ordered to depart by June 30. Later, it appeared that the reason for this action was that Christendom's missionaries were interfering in the political affairs of the country. Nothing could be done but to arrange for Brother Kirk to leave for England, to join his sick wife there, and for Brothers Barber and Richards, with their wives, to depart for India. Frank Dewar and his family left for Thailand.

Now what would happen to our work in Burma? All the foreign brothers had left. Would the local Witnesses be able to carry on the work?

Though the brothers were shocked, they were not discouraged. They knew that Jehovah God was with them. (1 Chron. 28:20) Quickly, the Society appointed Brother Maurice Raj as the branch overseer, and Brother Dunstan O'Neill took care of the circuit work. Yes, God's people in Burma functioned as usual. In fact, our work continued to move ahead, showing that Jehovah's hand is not short.—Isa. 59:1.

THE WORK EXPANDS

Toward the end of 1966 the branch office opened up the witnessing work in Myitkyina, the capital of Kachin State in Northern Burma. Most of the Kachin people belong to some denomination of Christendom, but her religions there, as elsewhere, had led the people into darkness. Most of her young people had joined the insurgents and were wreaking havoc in the jungle areas, blowing up bridges, wrecking passenger trains, and so forth. But some Kachin people, particularly the elderly ones, were looking for guidance elsewhere. It was the right time for us to declare to such people the message of God's kingdom.

Labang Gam, the Kachin special pioneer who went to Myitkyina, worked very hard. For the first few months, he witnessed from door to door from morning till evening. Before the clergy realized it, the town was soon flooded with our magazines, and everyone was talking about the Witnesses. Then waves of attack came. Every Sunday, in all the churches, sermons were given against Jehovah's Witnesses. People were told not to talk to the pioneer and not to accept literature from him. Nevertheless, the interest increased. In fact, it was too great for one pioneer; so another was sent to help him. When they could not care for all the increase, more pioneers were sent. In six months a congregation was formed. And in 1968 the Myitkyina Congregation built a Kingdom Hall.

Many publishers from the Myitkyina Congregation were appointed as special pioneers and were sent to Monhyin, Bhamo, Katha and Putao. The pioneers who went to Lashio had such success that a congregation was established there within a year's time. Witnesses there have also built a Kingdom Hall, one with bamboo mats and a grass roof. Now in Kachin State our work is carried on in nine different places. Though the interest is very great among the Kachin people in the interior, it has been impossible for us to send pioneers into those areas because of the rebels.

In December 1966, the branch overseer made an extensive tour, visiting all the congregations and isolated groups, as well as some new places. Many new special pioneers were appointed and were sent to virgin territories. As a result, our work continued to expand.

AIDED BY HARDWORKING ZONE OVERSEERS

Here it seems fitting to mention the zone overseers and how hard they have worked when visiting this branch. At one time the Burmese government did not allow tourists to come into the country. So one of the zone overseers, Ronald Jacka, had to come in with a transit visa that allowed him to stay here only 24 hours. He arrived at the Mingaladon airport at 7 p.m. and, after the usual formalities at the customs office, he got to the branch at 9 p.m. That night Brother Jacka started the work at 10 p.m. He and the branch overseer, Brother Raj, worked the whole night, neither of them getting a wink of sleep. At 5 o'clock in the morning, they left for the airport. The same thing happened when Brother T. H. Sanderson of India visited Burma as a zone overseer. Even though these visits were short, they were very much appreciated.

AN ASSEMBLY THAT WAS DIFFERENT

The 1969 "Peace on Earth" District Assembly was something different in that it was held, not in Rangoon as usual, but in Myitkyina. In Burma the majority of the people travel by train or steamer, and usually all of these are crowded, passengers often sitting on the roof. The Society arranged for special railway coaches for the journey to Myitkyina. The Burma Railway authorities were very cooperative, providing two coaches from Rangoon to Mandalay, where two more were added. Had it not been for this arrangement, it would have been almost impossible to travel the 722 miles (1,162 kilometers) from Rangoon to Myitkyina in the congested train for those two days and two nights.

Delegates from Lower Burma left Rangoon on Saturday and were met at the Mandalay station on Sunday morning by conventioners from Chin and Shan States. Since they were not to leave Mandalay until the late evening, house-to-house preaching work was scheduled.

At Mandalay and Mohnyin the Society arranged for the delegates to have food. Usually, when a train stops at a station near mealtime, passengers rush to the food stalls to buy something to eat. Often, though, many miss their meals because the food has been sold out. But the Witnesses received their food right in the coaches. How grateful they were to know that the food cost them only 80 pyas (12 cents, U.S.) per meal, whereas food packets sold at the stations cost at least kyat 2.00 (29 cents, U.S.)! In appreciation, one brother said: "How thankful I am to the Society for being considerate! If it were not for this arrangement, I would have spent about K20.00 [$2.86, U.S.] for my family of eight just for one meal. But now I have spent only K6.40 [$0.91, U.S.] and yet the food was good."

These traveling Christians were cared for, not only with physical food, but also with spiritual food. Eighty pioneers were assigned to give Bible talks on the train. A huge bamboo dome was constructed for the assembly. The main auditorium, which had no supporting center posts, was constructed with bamboos, except for the roof. Bamboo poles were first spiked into the ground at equal intervals opposite each other, and then the lighter and more agile men started climbing the poles in order to bend them. This climbing work had to be done very carefully and slowly. The bamboos bent toward each other and, as the tops met in the center, they were tied together. Bamboos also were used for tying. How? By slicing them very thin and soaking them in water they became useful ropes. The skill and speed of experienced hands in slicing bamboos really is astounding. Finally, the bamboo dome was roofed with grass thatches.

The cafeteria tables also were made with bamboo poles and mats. For that matter, bamboo poles split in half, with the partitions removed, served as troughs conveying water from a nearby well. During the assembly bamboos also were used as receptacles for water and soup.

The delegates were well rewarded, for never before had three new Burmese publications been released during an assembly. How glad the audience was to receive the books *"Things in Which It Is Impossible for God to Lie"* and *"Your Word Is a Lamp to My Foot,"* as well as the new songbook *"Singing and Accompanying Yourselves with Music in Your Hearts"!* Besides these Burmese releases, the delegates were blessed with five new English publications.

Three Bible dramas were presented. But how did we manage with the needed costumes? Well, it is really amazing how well local clothing can be converted into the ancient Israelite style of dress. The Lushai sarongs became very useful on this occasion. Each participant in the dramas brought his own costume. But the brother who was to portray the prophet Daniel forgot to bring his costume, including his gray beard! Something had to be done quickly!

The curtain was raised. The drama started. And there was aged Daniel. Those in the 'Dressing Department' had taken some cotton and two pieces of adhesive from the First-Aid Department. The pieces of tape were sewed together with the adhesive sides out. One side was placed on the face and the cotton was stuck onto the other side. To get the required color, powdered charcoal and ashes were mixed with cooking oil and this was rubbed onto the cotton. So, there was "Daniel"!

PROMOTING GREATER EXPANSION

During 1970 we tried to expand the work even more. The message of God's kingdom was not then being proclaimed in the Naga Hills, in the northwestern part of the country. So two special pioneers were sent to Hkamti in the month of April. They found many interested persons there. Why, in just one week five individuals were attending meetings!

But the rapid progress was short-lived. The government issued an order saying that the brothers must leave Hkamti Province (the Naga Hills) in 24 hours or be imprisoned. No reason was given for the order. The pioneers appealed, but to no avail; the officer concerned with the matter was determined that they should leave Hkamti. Traveling to and from Hkamti was done only by air, and there was no daily flight. So the brothers told the officer that they could not leave within 24 hours, for they had to wait for the next plane, which was not due within the time limit.

Still, the officer was determined that they should leave within 24 hours. "But how?" asked the brothers. "Make a bamboo raft and float on the river and go," was the firm reply. To travel on a raft for hundreds of miles on a rough river would be absolutely impossible. Yet, no amount of reasoning did any good. The special pioneers, Brothers Win Pe and Aung Naing, were in a great predicament, but Jehovah did not abandon them. Unexpectedly, an air force plane landed at the Hkamti airfield. So, the authorities put the brothers on that plane, giving them a free trip back to Myitkyina. Thereafter, the interested persons were helped through correspondence.

At that time, an unexpected problem flared up in Tiddim, Chin State. The Mizo rebels in India had crossed the border, had set fire to some places in Tiddim, and had then returned to their own country. Mizos are known as Lushais in Burma. So, many Lushais were suspected of being supporters of those foreign rebels. Lal Chhana and Chal Liana, two Lushai special pioneers in that town, were falsely accused of being agents for the rebels and were put in custody. They were released only after six months of detention. At the same time and for the same reason, B. T. Ruala and Vai Chunnunga, special pioneers in Khampat, were put in Tamu jail. They were released after six months without any charges filed against them.

FURTHER PROBLEMS ENCOUNTERED

Not long thereafter, the brothers in Vanna, Chin State, encountered opposition because of their stand as Christian neutrals. At election time, voting was mandatory. When the brothers refused to take part in politics because of their religious convictions and determination to keep free from the world, they were not allowed to do any house-to-house witnessing. (Jas. 1:27) Also, Witness children were expelled from school. At that, the branch overseer, accompanied by his wife, went to see and encourage the brothers in that area. From Rangoon to Kalemyo the trip was by plane, then by truck from there to Haka. Though this "bus" was meant for only 22 passengers, more than 50 were jammed inside, with another 10 persons or so on the roof. The journey took two days, even though it was only 112 miles (180 kilometers). Because of the weather, the roads were very muddy and slippery. The dangerous winding road takes one as high as 6,000 to 8,000 feet (1,800 to 2,400 meters) above sea level. From Haka the trip was completed on horseback and on foot to Vanna and Hmaika, where the trouble was taking place. Opportunity was afforded to speak to various local authorities and explain our neutral stand based on our religious faith. The brothers and sisters were encouraged by this visit and appreciated it very much. They are strong in faith and are determined to remain loyal to God.

When things "cooled off" somewhat and changes in local authority took place at Hkamti, we sent four other special pioneers there to help the interested persons. Within a few months, three groups had been formed, with 16 persons reporting field service.

The pioneers penetrated deep into the jungle, calling on all the villagers with the Kingdom message. This certainly irritated the clergymen of Christendom. With their cunning lips and lying ways, they poisoned the minds of the local authorities by falsely accusing the brothers of being agents of the insurgents. After much interrogation, the pioneers were ordered to leave the province within seven days. No amount of explanation helped. When the final day came, the pioneers went to the office of the Council of State to explain that there was no transportation available on that day and that they would have to stay for a day or two longer. But the authorities were determined that they should leave that very day, before sunset. So, Brothers S. Dewar, B. Mawia and Ba Yee, as well as Sister Z. Liani, had to take their belongings and depart from Hkamti immediately. They kept walking until they got to a village that night. However, the brothers and interested persons that they left behind still are strong in the truth and are regularly declaring the "good news."

COPING WITH PRINTING PROBLEMS

Our production of *Kinhmyozin* (the Burmese *Watchtower*) rapidly increased, until it reached 8,500 copies in the month of January 1967. Then the government put an end to the increase by allowing us to print only 5,000 copies monthly beginning with the May 1967 issue. To make matters worse, in April 1972 the authorities informed us that they would be able to give us only enough paper to print, not 5,000 copies, but a mere 3,000. That number of magazines would be too few for us. What could we do? Well, all that could be done was to take the matter to Jehovah God in prayer.

Maurice Raj, the branch overseer, asked for a special interview with the manager of Trade Corporation No. 9, and it was granted immediately. Brother Raj explained to the manager that the Watch Tower Society would be able to buy paper with foreign money, that is, with United States dollars. This was very appealing to him. "But," said Brother Raj, "we would be able to do this only if we could buy paper for 10,000 copies." The result? During the very next month we were able to print 10,000 copies. Why, since January 1975 we have had the privilege of printing two issues monthly— 20,000 copies every month!

It seems appropriate to explain how we do the printing here. Four copies of each issue to be printed must be typed and submitted to the Printers and Publishers Board for approval. It may take a week, or sometimes even a month, to get the permit. After receiving the printing permit, we apply for the permit to buy the paper. This takes another week or so. With that permission from the paper controllers' office, we go to the godown (a warehouse where paper is stocked) to buy paper. There we must line up for our turn to make a purchase.

After the issue is printed and before the magazines are brought to the branch office from the printing press, we have to send 17 copies to the Printers and Publishers Board, which checks to see whether the magazine agrees with the manuscript originally submitted. No deletion or addition is permitted. After receiving an "OK" certificate, we submit it, along with five copies of *The Watchtower*, to the paper controllers' office for them to check at the press to see whether the paper issued was, in fact, utilized for the purpose stated in our application. This procedure goes on for every issue, month after month.

ON THE ROAD WITH TRAVELING OVERSEERS

Especially after 1967 did our work begin progressing rapidly. Because of Jehovah's blessing upon Burmese Christians, including the special pioneers and the two traveling overseers, D. J. O'Neill and J. T. Xavier, within four years the number of Witnesses in Burma nearly doubled. In 1968, there was a 24-percent rise in publishers, during 1969, a 26-percent increase, in 1970 the number was up 18 percent, and for 1971 it rose 12 percent. Within those four years, 276 individuals symbolized their dedication to God by being immersed in water. Thus, in 1971 nearly half of the Witnesses in Burma had been baptized within the previous four years. We had arranged for three circuits by 1971, the third circuit overseer being Donald Dewar, the son of special pioneer Frank Dewar who had been deported in 1966.

It seems appropriate here to mention some of the difficulties experienced by circuit overseers. To visit fellow believers, they often travel in crowded trains, buses or boats. Sometimes they even ride on the roofs of the trains, buses or launches. In some places, rebels blow up bridges, or the roads are mined. In the Chin Hills, most of the traveling is done on foot. But this is not easy, for one must climb as high as 8,000 feet (2,400 meters) above sea level. To visit all the congregations in the mountains, the traveling overseers have to walk some 500 miles (800 kilometers). Also, they have to carry their own food, as well as utensils for cooking it along the way. Moreover, there are dangers from wild animals. To illustrate: While traveling alone from Tonzang to Tiddim, James Xavier encountered a group of baboons. When the biggest one stared at him, Brother Xavier was nearly scared to death. "I picked up a stick and shouted as loud as I could," he recalls. "When they moved a bit, I walked as fast as I could. Then it started raining very heavily. I was terribly cold and almost exhausted when I reached a village on the way. I found shelter from the rain in a very friendly Baptist pastor's house. While warming myself, I had a nice Bible discussion with him."

Donald Dewar had thought it best to walk the 42 miles (68 kilometers) from Haka to Leitak, Chin State, in a single day. Arising before dawn, he packed his food in a banana leaf and set out on the journey. Without resting very much along the way, he and the brother accompanying him kept walking fast, climbing up and down the mountains. The last three miles (5 kilometers) required a continual climb up a very steep, rocky mountain. With great difficulty and the help of his companion, Brother Dewar managed to finish the trip as planned, but he could hardly get up the next day.

Even bus travel is not easy in some places here. One day tragedy struck as a fully loaded bus was coming down the winding road from Mogok, where Burma's famous rubies are mined. Donald Dewar and many other passengers were sitting on the roof when the driver suddenly lost control of the vehicle and it met with an accident that proved fatal to some persons. On that occasion, Brother Dewar ended up in Mandalay with a broken leg.

But there can be other perils, too. James Xavier recalls: "As I was traveling in a truck [or bus] from Loikaw (Kayah State) to Taunggyi (Shan State), the vehicle suddenly was caught in cross fire between the government forces and the insurgents. We had to jump from the truck and take shelter under it till the fighting was over. Afterward, we transported the dead and wounded soldiers to a nearby hospital in Sisaing Village."

AIDED BY MEMBERS OF THE GOVERNING BODY

Visits by members of the Governing Body have been very helpful and encouraging. Especially have we been impressed by the way these brothers display humility and loving concern for God's people. For instance, when M. G. Henschel visited Burma from January 24 to 27, 1973, he mixed freely with the local brothers, and everyone admired his humility.

Brothers N. H. Knorr and F. W. Franz visited us in January 1975. Shortly before they were scheduled to speak at Gandhi Memorial Hall in Rangoon, it was learned that the authorities would not permit the holding of gatherings in public halls. Why? Because of trouble caused by radical students and some bad elements in connection with the funeral of the late United Nations Secretary-General, U Thant. So, the nearly 500 brothers and interested persons already gathered at the Gandhi Memorial Hall were asked to proceed to a nearby Kingdom Hall. Although the hall could accommodate only about 150 persons, 270 squeezed themselves inside to hear Brothers Knorr and Franz speak that evening. Over 200 individuals had to return home without hearing the visitors. However, during the next two days, more than 600 persons gathered in Eric Marcelline's yard, sitting under the trees in picnic style, but enjoying spiritual food. The local Witnesses put on a fine variety show for the visitors, and, in response, F. W. Franz played the mouth organ, while his traveling associates sang songs.

In March 1977, John Booth of the Governing Body visited Burma along with Brother and Sister Don Adams of the Brooklyn Bethel family. This also was a happy occasion for Jehovah's people in this country, and many came from Upper Burma to attend the assembly that coincided with the visit. That gathering was held on Zion Hill, Insein, about 10 miles (16 kilometers) from Rangoon. Once again, Burmese Witnesses arranged a very interesting show for the visitors.

The most recent zone visit by a member of the Governing Body was made by L. A. Swingle in January 1978. At an assembly in Okkalapa, 302 persons heard him give an encouraging talk that urged them to endure, as did God's prophet Jeremiah. During this visit, Brother Swingle also spoke at the dedication of our new Bethel home. His audience then numbered 248 persons. But suppose we tell you about the acquisition of this property.

ACQUIRING OUR NEW BETHEL HOME

One Sunday, after engaging in the field service, the branch coordinator visited a certain brother. In the course of conversation, it was mentioned that since his visit in 1962 N. H. Knorr had wanted us to find new branch and Bethel home facilities. Eager to be of help, the brother remarked that he knew of a very nice place quite near. So Brother Raj, the branch coordinator, followed him to the place and found it to be most suitable. It was a two-story building on a half acre of land. The structure had sufficient bedroom and office space, as well as an area that could be used as a Kingdom Hall. Also, the building was large enough for future expansion.

The next day the branch coordinator took other branch members to the building. His wife, Doris, was surprised to find the owner's wife to be a former school friend. Sister Raj soon was able to start a Bible study with the children. When Brother Raj offered to study with the parents, the mother said, "I will study but will never change my religion." The father did not care either way, as he was quite disappointed with the Catholic Church. So Brother Raj started a Bible study with them. After three months of study, they knew that this was the truth. They cleared their house of religious idols and stopped going to church. At the next district assembly they and their eldest son symbolized their dedication to Jehovah by undergoing water baptism. Thereafter, the deed to the house was officially registered in the name of Jehovah's Christian Witnesses. Hence, in January 1978 Brother Swingle was able to give the dedication talk for our branch office and Bethel home.

THE WORK KEEPS MOVING AHEAD

Despite setbacks, our work has kept moving ahead. The 1972 service year ended with 644 Kingdom publishers, representing a 7-percent increase. In 1974 we saw a 5-percent increase, with 762 reporting field service and 111 symbolizing their dedication to God by being baptized. During 1975 the Burmese brothers worked very hard and were blessed with a 14-percent increase. In that year, 108 were baptized and the peak of Kingdom publishers was 822. The 1976 service year ended with a publisher peak of 845. In October of that year, Brother and Sister Maurice Raj had the privilege of spending time at the Society's headquarters in Brooklyn, New York, during the branch coordinators' meetings held there.

During the 1977 service year there was a one-percent decrease in the number of this country's Kingdom proclaimers. That was the first time in the history of Jehovah's Witnesses in Burma that we had a decrease. Why did this occur?

Inflation seems to have been one reason. Prices of commodities have kept spiraling upward. For example, a pound of coffee was K7.00 ($1.00, U.S.) just a few years ago, but by early 1978 its cost had risen to K85.00 ($12.14). That is a 1,114-percent increase! Thus many Witnesses and interested persons have been very busy working 'to make ends meet,' and this seems to have caused some to lose appreciation of spiritual things.

Others, who had stopped smoking or chewing betel nut, have returned to their former unclean habits. From 1975 to 1977, 32 persons were disfellowshiped for these practices alone.

Some stopped associating with us because events did not develop as they expected in the year 1975. When their interest in God's promises cooled off, they succumbed to worldly interests. So, when the 1977 service year ended, we noted a one-percent decrease in the number of Burma's Kingdom publishers.

However, the majority of the brothers have not allowed themselves to fall into spiritual decline. They have kept themselves busy in sacred service and have received many blessings. The beginning of the 1978 service year again saw an increase in our witnessing activity throughout the field—a new peak of Kingdom publishers every month. In September 1977 there was a 4.3-percent increase. October saw a 5-percent rise; November, an 8-percent increase and December, an 11-percent growth, with 903 persons reporting field service that month. For the first time, we then passed the 900 mark. This required that we arrange for a fourth circuit in this country.

All kinds of people have been associating with Jehovah's servants here in Burma. For instance, T. Tamang, a staunch Yoga-practicing Hindu, became a Christian witness of Jehovah and has been an overseer for the last 20 years. Through his efforts, many Hindus have been helped to leave Babylon the Great, the world empire of false religion, and to become praisers of the true God, Jehovah.—Rev. 18:1-5.

LOOKING AHEAD

It was in 1914 that the spark of Bible truth penetrated into Burma. But it was not till 1926 that the Kingdom work was properly organized here. During the second world war, it came to a dead stop. But after that conflict our activity started all over again, with eight Kingdom publishers in 1946. Foreign missionaries first came to this country in 1947 and 1948, but they were deported in 1966. In the 32 years since 1946, we have progressed from 8 publishers to 903 in December 1977. During March 1978, a peak of 905 Kingdom proclaimers was reached here, and we were delighted that 2,174 persons gathered throughout Burma on March 23, 1978, to commemorate the death of Jesus Christ.

We know that God will certainly bring all sheeplike people into association with the Christian congregation before the final end comes for this wicked system of things. Jesus said: "This good news of the kingdom will be preached . . . and then the end will come." (Matt. 24:14) So, until God says that this work has been done, we will continue without wavering to advertise the King and Kingdom. And eagerly we wait to see what blessings the future will bring true Christians in Burma.

CANADA

The Iroquois Indians called it *Kanata,* meaning merely "a group of huts." You, however, may know it as the land of the fur trapper and the Eskimo, the moose and the polar bear—and, yes, the "Mounties," the red-coated Royal Canadian Mounted Police 'who always get their man.'

But present-day Canada is much more than that. This vast country covering 3,851,809 square miles (9,976,139 square kilometers) is the second largest in the world. It spans North America from the Atlantic Ocean on the east to the Pacific on the west. Southward lies the United States and to the north, the frigid waters of the Arctic.

Within the borders of Canada are the towering and majestic Rocky Mountains, thousands of sparkling lakes and rivers, and thundering waters of world-famous Niagara Falls. Also delighting the eye are extensive prairies with their seas of golden grain, and great forests of pine, spruce, maple, fir and birch.

This is "home" for 23,000,000 people. Because of a relatively liberal immigration policy, among Canada's populace are found Austrians, Dutch, Germans, Greeks, Hungarians, Italians, Jews, Latin Americans, Poles, Portuguese, Russians, Scandinavians, Spaniards, Ukrainians, West Indians and Yugoslavians. From Eastern lands have come Arabs, Chinese, East Indians, Filipinos, Japanese, Koreans and Pakistanis. Years ago, before the white man settled here, this land was the home of the Eskimo and of many colorful American Indian nations. Happily, a person can still meet some of these people, among them the Crees, Cayugas, Mohawks, Ojibways, Kutanais and Haidas.

In 1534 the French explorer Cartier came, and in 1604 the first permanent French colony was established in what is now eastern Canada. Late in the 1500's, the British first came to Newfoundland and the adjacent coasts. Later, the English spread out over what is now Nova Scotia, Quebec and Ontario. In 1763, Canada became part of the British Empire, though retaining both French and English as official languages. Confederation came in 1867 and equality of status as part of the British Commonwealth in 1931. Presently, Canada consists of 10 provinces and two territories.

The population is concentrated mainly within a narrow ribbon all along the border shared with the United States, the number of persons per square mile dropping quickly as one moves northward. Most of the land remains unsettled and undeveloped, perhaps only

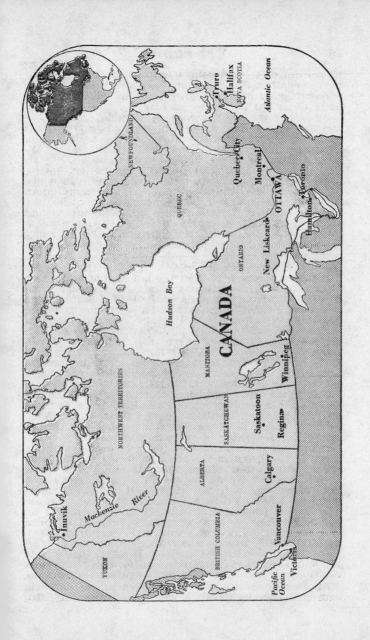

12 percent of it now being occupied by 90 percent of the population. In part, this is because of a severe winter climate in the northern regions, although summers there are pleasant and bright.

As you might imagine, with Canada's many immigrants came their interesting customs and various religions. Here you will find evidences of Buddhism, Islamism, Judaism and Hinduism. But the larger religious groups are the so-called Christian bodies. Roman Catholicism is the largest single denomination, having nearly 10,000,000 members, most of them in the Province of Quebec. The United Church claims more than 3,000,000 adherents, and the Anglicans another 2,500,000. Smaller Protestant bodies, such as Presbyterians and Baptists, as well as Orthodox Catholics, make up a large part of the remaining populace, although many people profess no religion at all.

A GLIMMER OF LIGHT IN THE EAST

It was in the year 1880, at the latest, that a glimmer of true spiritual light began shining in Canada. From earnest friends and relatives in the United States, some Canadians received literature and a heartening message about the restoration of all things by God's kingdom in the hands of the glorified Jesus Christ. (Acts 3:19-21; Rev. 21:1-5) One of these thought-provoking publications—*Food for Thinking Christians*, published in 1881—found ready acceptance here. How its forceful exposure of the doctrinal errors taught in Christendom's churches cleared away false religious cobwebs!

This "good news" was being proclaimed by Charles T. Russell and a small group of Bible Students with headquarters in Allegheny (now part of Pittsburgh), Pennsylvania, U.S.A. What was the caliber of the Canadians responding favorably to the Kingdom message? Well, genuine gratitude for Bible truth is evident in this letter from a man in Ontario (published in the January/February 1882 *Watch Tower*):

"Will you kindly advise me in regard to severing my connection with the church of which I am a member? I feel as though I should not attend, because it would be consenting to their teaching, which I do not now believe. I have not really believed it for a long time, but I knew no better way. Now, thank God, it is different. I remain yours in the hope of eternal life."

One of the earliest Canadian Bible Students was William Brookman, apparently a former clergyman. Under his direction, a class met regularly in Toronto.

Another Canadian to accept Bible truth at an early date was Thomas Baker, a sawmill operator of Elba,

Ontario, a small community about 50 miles (80 kilometers) northwest of Toronto. A very religious man, Baker had been the superintendent of the Anglican Sunday school. But his buzzing sawmill became a place that also buzzed with the grand news of God's kingdom. As his daughter Annie puts it: "Every customer who came in was given a tract or booklet or book. I don't think he missed anyone!"

Since Thomas Baker was so well known, his departure from the established church in the community raised plenty of questions. In fact, so many people asked about this that he published a booklet giving the reasons for his action. Baker died in 1906, and the funeral talk was delivered by a person to whom he himself had taught the truth of God's Word.

During the late 1880's, colporteurs (full-time Kingdom proclaimers) shared the "good news" with Caleb Crandell. He accepted Bible literature and entertained the visitors in his home at Crandell's Corners (now within Port Perry), Ontario. No study group was formed there at the time, but we know that Caleb made at least one trip to hear C. T. Russell speak at Massey Hall in Toronto. Crandell was delighted with what he saw and heard. His oft-told story went like this: Several clergymen, invited to the platform to ask questions, became quite annoyed when they were unable to contradict Russell's sound Biblical answers. Then they all tried to hurl queries at him at the same time. Russell quietly called them to order, asking that they conduct themselves as gentlemen and saying that he would gladly deal with every question. Crandell was impressed to see that the clerics could not refute Russell's Scriptural arguments. In time, they merely left the platform and disappeared into the crowd without further ado.

BIBLE TRUTH REACHES WESTERN CANADA

The light of truth was shining somewhat brightly in eastern Canada when a shaft of such light penetrated the spiritual darkness in western Canada. In 1889, William Flewwelling of Carberry, Manitoba, came into possession of "The Divine Plan of the Ages," the first volume of C. T. Russell's *Millennial Dawn* series (later called *Studies in the Scriptures*). Convinced that he had found the truth, Flewwelling shared it with others, especially after moving to Vancouver, British Columbia, in 1890. One man who listened with appreciation was Robert Pollock. Soon Bible study classes were being held in the Pollock home. To our knowledge, this was the first of such groups on Canada's west coast.

In later years, William Flewwelling helped to establish Bible study groups at Asquith (about 20 miles [32 kilometers] west of Saskatoon) and Wadena, Saskatchewan. Later in life (in 1934), he moved to Witchekan, Saskatchewan, and declared the "good news" throughout that part of the province. William died at Chitek Lake in 1945, but many of his relatives continue to carry on the Kingdom-preaching work he began in that area.

Of course, Bible truth reached western Canada by other means, too. In 1889, the same year Flewwelling first learned the truth, a well-meaning man threw a magazine onto a Canadian's bunk at a typically Western horse sales yard in Fargo, North Dakota. "Here, Mais," said the man. "This is something that will interest you!" Leslie Mais was there to sell a herd of horses raised at his homestead in Fort Qu' Appelle, Northwest Territories (now Saskatchewan). A member of the Church of England, he was an avid Bible reader and talked to others about what he read in the Scriptures. No wonder the man tossed that magazine onto his bunk! Well, Mais read through that *Watch Tower*, promptly became a subscriber and continued reading that journal until his death in 1924.

C. T. RUSSELL'S FIRST VISIT TO CANADA

By 1891, the number of Bible Students in the Toronto area was sufficient to hold the first one-day convention in that city. Then, for the first time, Pastor Russell visited fellow believers in this land. At the morning session on February 22, more than 400 persons listened as he spoke for over two hours. That afternoon about 700 were present for another two-hour talk by Brother Russell. In the evening, he addressed a congregation at the other end of Toronto, returning to the convention site before nine o'clock to participate in a question-and-answer session. It surely was a busy day!

OPPOSITION AS THE PACE QUICKENS

The pace of spreading the "good news" was quickening in this land. Early in 1891, a colporteur wrote: "While I have been in Canada but a short time, it has been my privilege to see an excellent interest awakened and the harvest work well started here. . . . There are over 5,000 DAWNS [volumes of *Millennial Dawn*] out in Ontario now, and the work is only well begun."

But this activity did not occur without clerical opposition. At least two of Christendom's ministers in Ontario publicly burned copies of *Millennial Dawn* and denounced Brother Russell, as well as distributers of the books.

During that period, the weekly Niagara Falls *Review* was carrying C. T. Russell's sermons. The newspaper's editor was Brother James E. Anger, who admitted: "I had [by 1892] succeeded in bringing upon myself a boycott from the hackmen, the Sabbath Desecrators, the hotel men, the R[oman] C[atholic] Church and the Protestant churches in town." He finally had to sell the newspaper. But Brother Anger's descendants are active witnesses of Jehovah to this day, and we can count some 20 spiritually prosperous Christian congregations in that part of the Niagara peninsula.

Despite clerical and other opposition in the early 1890's, some clergymen and former clerics were getting Scriptural matters straight in their minds. Moreover, they were seeing their responsibility to teach others the truth found in the Bible. One of these men, John L. Lawson, wrote to Brother Russell in 1892, saying:

"The Lord has been preparing me for years for these Millennial truths. In 1874 I left [resigned from] the Primitive Methodist ministry in England, where I had been for nine years . . . Since then I have been led to the study of prophecy; and your volumes afford me a richness, a fullness, in this branch of study, beyond anything I have before seen. Reading them is indeed to me as sitting down to a banquet of 'meat in due season'—predicted truths on becoming due being just this to the household of faith. . . .

"I wish I could be of help to the watchful, consecrated ones; but here in the [Canadian] bush am afraid I cannot do much. I would like to know what the arrangements of the [Society are] with colporteurs and whether they know of any field where there is urgent need of such."

As more and more people learned God's truth and saw the urgent need to declare it to others, the pace of Kingdom activity continued to accelerate. Bible Student classes were developing in one place after another. For instance, 1892 saw the start of Christian meetings held at Victoria, British Columbia.

Matthew Nelson of Carberry, Manitoba, first heard and accepted the Kingdom message in that year. In 1893, Nelson moved to Grandview, Manitoba, and planted seeds of Bible truth there. It was not uncommon for him to drive a wagon 15 miles (24 kilometers) one way on unpaved roads just to reach someone who might be interested! That was not easy on muddy roads. In Nelson's own family, his mother, his sisters and some relatives through marriage all favorably responded to his efforts. On November 22, 1914, the first congregation was established in Grandview, and Brother Nelson was privileged to have oversight. This very active "spark plug" (as Matthew Nelson was affectionately called by local Bible Students) was very encouraging to all his Christian associates until his death in 1945.

GETTING STARTED IN THE MARITIMES

Among those learning the truth around 1892 were Arthur N. Marchant and W. T. Dowden of Halifax, Nova Scotia. They also learned that Christians *do something*. They live the "good news" and they talk about it. Determined Marchant promptly became a colporteur, absolutely convinced that no work was more important than declaring the "good news." As early as 1895, he engaged in systematic witnessing and frequent coverage of all the Maritime Provinces, including Prince Edward Island, thus laying a foundation for excellent future development there.

Arthur Marchant aided interested ones spiritually by establishing study groups and by training some to give a witness to others. He also baptized those desiring to take that important step.

Remember that this work was not carried on with the comfort, convenience and ease of present-day travel. Often Brother Marchant walked many miles. At times he rode a bicycle, and in winter he might use an automobile, if one was available—but that was before the advent of car heaters. Ella Dow recalls an occasion when Marchant was driving an open auto. He arrived at her place in the rurals "chilled to the bone," she says, adding: "I had to rub liniment on his legs and stick them in the open oven to get some warmth back into them!"

Brother Marchant never wavered with the passing of the years. Once, during the first world war, he was arrested in Halifax for distributing the book "The Finished Mystery." His bail was set at $10,000! When the judge asked what his occupation was, he unhesitatingly replied, "A minister of the Most High God!" Arthur N. Marchant completed his course faithfully on May 23, 1940. But what a tremendous work he had done in nearly 50 years of disciple-making! Today in the 51,000-square-mile (132,000-square-kilometer) area that he covered so diligently there are more than 80 congregations and over 4,500 active witnesses of Jehovah.

"LIKE A BURNING FIRE"

Mention of the Maritimes calls to mind a Canadian to whom God's word eventually proved to be "like a burning fire." (Jer. 20:9) He just *had* to talk about it. Born in Canada on July 2, 1877, he was reared by Presbyterian parents in a Catholic community in Nova Scotia. His name? Alexander Hugh Macmillan.

Only about 13 years old when his younger sister died of diphtheria, youthful Macmillan reasoned: "Life is short and uncertain. If what we do here has any bearing on what we will be hereafter, then we would be very foolish if we didn't devote our time to serving the Lord now with the hope of having something better throughout eternity. As for me, I'm going to take my stand and do what I think will be pleasing to the Lord."

At 16, Macmillan decided to become a preacher. Off he went to a school away from home, there to prepare for admittance to a theological seminary. But then, for some reason, he had a nervous breakdown. Nearly brokenhearted, Macmillan returned home. Considerately, his father provided funds and soon the young man was on his way to Boston, Massachusetts. There he obtained a copy of C. T. Russell's book "The Plan of the Ages" (or "The Divine Plan of the Ages"). The truths it contained became "like a burning fire" within Macmillan. Unable to contain himself, he went out on the street and stopped people to tell them what he had learned.

One day, Macmillan approached a total stranger and asked: "Do you know about the great promise God made to Abraham, that through his seed all the families of the earth would be blessed?" Startled, the man replied: "What Abraham are you talking about?—the Abraham that has that pawnshop down on Salem Street?"

Well, at least Macmillan was reaching out for his youthful goal—that of becoming a preacher. In September 1900, this earnest Canadian was baptized in symbol of his dedication to Jehovah God. During succeeding years he traveled far and wide declaring the "good news," visiting congregations and upbuilding fellow believers spiritually. He finished his earthly course in faithfulness as a member of the Brooklyn Bethel family, succumbing at the age of 89 on August 26, 1966.

UPBUILDING "PILGRIM" VISITS

A. H. Macmillan had been a close associate of C. T. Russell, and both of them showed deep concern for fellow worshipers of Jehovah. Russell had been visiting

numerous Canadian groups of Bible Students during
one-day conventions, but new congregations, or classes,
were being established in many places and no longer
was it possible for him to visit all of them. Yet, such
visits, the talks delivered and the good association did
much to strengthen God's people spiritually. Hence,
the September 1, 1894, *Watch Tower* announced that
a number of capable appointed brothers would be
visiting the congregations. Later, this service, rendered
by traveling representatives of the Watch Tower Society, was called the "Pilgrim" work. What was a
typical day like during a pilgrim visit? Some idea can
be gleaned from this letter to Brother Russell:

"Brother [George] Draper has come and gone. . . .
Our meetings were not large, but I feel safe in saying
that there was an intense interest depicted on each
countenance, and that all our little gathering and a few
from outside were deeply impressed with all the meetings, which were held in our new hall [in Toronto].

"On Sunday morning, at 10:30, about forty assembled
at Balmy Beach . . . to witness the symbol of baptism
in water. The morning was bright, cool, and very windy,
causing quite a heavy rolling surf, which rather added
to the interest of the occasion. Four sisters and five
brothers were [baptized] . . . Our little party was indeed a happy, joyous little band as we returned home,
to assemble again at our hall at 3 P. M., and listen to
our dear Brother Draper pour forth more of the
precious things from the Holy Word.

"At 7 P. M. our last meeting commenced, there being
88 or 90 in the hall, quite a number of the friends and
acquaintances of the dear brothers and sisters being
present . . . and about 9:30 our feast of fat things came
to an end for the time, and I think it would have been
difficult to picture a more happy lot of faces than all
wore; all were overjoyed at the precious things they
had heard."

By 1905, William Hersee of Hamilton, Ontario, was
able to arrange his affairs to enter the pilgrim work.
Although he was financially comfortable and could
have remained in Hamilton, Hersee soon became a
familiar figure to many as he traveled across North
America, serving for many years as a pilgrim here and
in the United States.

Brother Hersee, who had been baptized in 1893 at
London, Ontario, was short in physical stature, but
impressive in bearing. Especially in later years did
his white hair enhance a kindly disposition that was
reflected, partly, in his paying special attention to

children and other young persons. One who was a mere boy at that time recalls:

"After he had finished his supper, Brother Hersee took my brother Joe and me out into the fields for an evening walk. We sat down for a while with our backs against a post looking out over the ploughed fields toward the setting prairie sun. Anyone having seen the sun going down on the prairie would appreciate the scene that was before us: the blue of the sky above with the horizon now a crimson red with streaks of orange glow stretching far into the sky as the sun, brilliant in all its color like a big ball of fire, slowly sank out of sight. Around us in the trees were the night sounds of birds settling down to rest, and off in the pasture to our right, horses snorted as they cropped away at the grass. What a beautiful setting in which to discuss God's creations and his kingdom with this quiet, devoted man! It was an occasion that I will never forget."

It is no wonder that till this day, as much as 50 years after Brother Hersee visited their homes, some still recall him with fondness and appreciation for his ministry. Especially in his prayers his depth of spirituality impressed young and old alike. One couple remarks: "He was a great source of encouragement to both of us. His prayers were indeed a stimulus, as he seemed to carry you right into the very courts of heaven itself."

William Hersee served Jehovah—and fellow worshipers of the true God—faithfully for a half century. The end of his Christian course and service on earth came in 1943. It is easy to see how the humble, godly efforts of such pilgrims of the past would spiritually strengthen their brothers and sisters in the faith.

MORE LIGHT IN MANITOBA

The grand message about 'the restoration of all things' first reached Rapid City, Manitoba, in 1898. (Acts 3:19-21) Colporteur Geoffrey Webb then appeared on the scene there and witnessed to businessmen gathered around the potbellied stove at the back of A. W. Leflar's general store. For some time, staunch Anglican Bowen Smith, who ran the local lumberyard, contradicted Webb's remarks. But Smith eventually became convinced, and, with Leflar and several others, organized the first class of Bible Students in that part of Canada.

Leflar put his heart into the work of teaching others. Traveling by horse and buggy, enthusiastically he witnessed in much of the surrounding territory. When

C. T. Russell visited and gave talks in that area, Leflar's horse and buggy came in handy. Why, even now it takes but a little imagination to visualize the driver and his visitor riding in that horse-drawn carriage as they traveled from place to place over those vast prairies!

As the years passed, the Leflar homesite became the center of Christian activities in that part of Canada. It was the stopping place for many colporteurs and pilgrims. Small conventions were held there. When a congregation was formed, A. W. Leflar became the first overseer. However, none of his activities, or those of the area's other Bible Students, took place without sacrifice and the enduring of opposition. People expressed contempt and hatred for "the Russellites," as they called them, and this made the Christian course a hard one. Nevertheless, persecution was endured, and Brother Leflar served faithfully until his death in 1946.

THE TRUTH TAKES HOLD IN ALBERTA

Christian determination and a similar spirit of self-sacrifice also resulted in Jehovah's blessing at Calmar, Alberta. In 1895, Bible Student August Dahlquist arrived there from North Dakota. He was followed by a Scandinavian "flood" in 1899, as families with such names as Anderson, Engberg, Hammer, Melin and Peterson came to Calmar from the vicinity of De Lamere, North Dakota. These families already were active Bible Students when they left the United States.

One of these pioneering families was that of Knud Pederson Hammer. He had been an ordained Baptist minister in North Dakota when A. H. Macmillan placed a book with him back in 1890. According to one of Hammer's descendants, that Baptist preacher "soon came to recognize that it contained the truth. As a result, in 1891 K. P. Hammer stood up in the church and informed the congregation that he, his wife and their babe in arms were walking out of 'Babylon.' They left with their infant daughter, Hannah, never to return to the realm of false religion."

In 1892 Brother Hammer visited his hometown of Skien, Norway. Because of that visit, his mother and sister manifested interest in the Kingdom message.

Providing some later details, a descendant of Brother Hammer reports: "According to plan, in 1899 a group of 50 persons hired a railroad coach. They were planning to go to the Calmar area together. Here, then, was an organized group of Bible Students about to embark on a new life in a new country. At the time that the coach was about to leave, K. P. Hammer received an invitation from Charles Taze Russell to go to Norway as the Society's representative and to form the first congregation there. After discussing the matter with the brothers, it was decided that Hammer should accept the invitation from Russell."

Brother Hammer's family went on to Calmar in the care of other Bible Students, while he traveled to Norway. Although he met certain interested persons while there, no congregation was established. What situation did he find upon returning to his family? The previously cited report continues:

"A pleasant surprise awaited K. P. Hammer upon his return. John Frederickson, a master log worker and builder, had, with the aid of the other brothers, erected a fine cabin on Hammer's homestead. This was but one of the many acts of love and kindness that the brothers showed to each other in the early days." —John 13:35.

Spiritual things came first among those Bible Students at Calmar, among whom was Andrew Melin. His son recalls: "Every time we got our mail . . . we would spend the evening around the table with only a coal oil lamp for light, and we would listen to dad read our copy of the *Watch Tower*. It came in the English language to begin with, but later we got it in Swedish and then mother could understand it as well."

On foot or by horseback, the Melins, John Frederickson and K. P. Hammer witnessed extensively, working with volumes of *Millennial Dawn*. There were not many places where these witnesses of Jehovah were not well known in the Calmar district. It was not that they had a lot of time on their hands. They were in homesteading country and had to work hard to clear the land (at least 20 acres [8 hectares] to obtain title), using horses, oxen and their bare hands. Most of their food had to be grown at the same time. Eventually, some of these Bible Student families included as many as 13 children. So, to earn money for necessary purchases, these brothers accepted any extra work that came along, even at 35 cents a day! Yes, they were self-sacrificing, loving, diligent, faithful—and so Jehovah blessed them richly.

As those Christian families grew, and more newly interested persons associated with them, a log-cabin meeting place was built at Calmar. The good spiritual foundations laid in those days have resulted in many loyal witnesses of Jehovah, and the family names of those early Bible Students now are familiar all over western Canada. Also, there is still an active Christian congregation at Calmar.

A NEW CENTURY DAWNS

It is not possible to mention the early developments in every place or to name all the individuals and families serving Jehovah at that time. Yet, it was evident that God was blessing his people. For instance, the report for observances of the Lord's Evening Meal in 1899 showed that there were quite a few small but growing groups. That year in Ontario, attendances were as follows: Brantford 22, Dorchester 5, Goderich 4, Hamilton 10, London 7, Meaford 5, Niagara Falls 7 and Toronto 21. Memorial attendances in Manitoba were: Brandon 8, Clive 4 and Rapid City 10. Reports from other areas included Wharnock, British Columbia, 5; Regina, Northwest Territories (now Saskatchewan), 7; and Truro, Nova Scotia, 8. Other groups also met that year to commemorate Christ's death.

Truly, then, as a new century dawned, the work of announcing the restoration of all things by God's kingdom was becoming established across Canada. To strengthen the growing groups of Bible Students, pilgrims continued visiting their fellow believers, and spiritually upbuilding conventions were held regularly in various places.

So it was that, here and there, Anglicans, Presbyterians, Baptists and others—sometimes leading figures in those organizations—courageously were abandoning false religion. (Rev. 18:1-4) Spontaneously, such individuals were making known to others the Bible truths they themselves were learning.

GROWTH DESPITE OPPOSITION

Expansion surely was under way. For instance, the growth of Bible Students' classes in various places meant not just gathering for study in private homes, but renting halls for meetings on Sundays. Of course, such expansion brought opposition. Bent on counteracting the growth and influence of Jehovah's people, some religious critics at times went too far. For instance, consider what happened at Nashwaak, New Brunswick, in 1904, as related by Cecil Scott.

Lumberman Hezekiah London, a religious person, had built a church on the corner of the family farm. His seven daughters all sang in the choir. By mail one day, London received some literature from a friend in Connecticut who was a Bible Student. After reading these publications, Hezekiah wrote to the "Bible House"

in Allegheny, Pennsylvania, and received more literature. Shortly after reading it, he was surprised one
Sunday when the local clergyman spoke on "The International Bible Students and Pastor Russell." Not only
was the sermon derogatory; it was the farthest thing
from the truth. About halfway through it, London
stood up, took his wife by the hand, and told his
daughters in the choir: "Come on, girls. We're going
home." All nine walked out. Since Hezekiah London
had donated the building and was the financial main-
stay of the church, that congregation soon "fell apart."
The preacher left and the building was closed.

Shortly thereafter, Hezekiah London made arrangements for pilgrims to visit Nashwaak. For a few weeks
prior to the arrival of a pilgrim (about twice a year),
London would leave home by horse and buggy on a
Monday morning and would not return until Saturday.
During such an excursion, he would place tracts and
booklets with the people for many miles around and
would invite them to the talks to be given by the
visiting pilgrim. And the meeting place? You are right!
It was that former church building on the London
farm at Nashwaak, New Brunswick. Today, as many
as 30 of Hezekiah London's relatives are Jehovah's
Witnesses.

Shortly after the turn of the century, congregations
of God's people were growing in various places. However, in some parts of Canada the situation was still
as it had been in the larger communities a decade or
more earlier. For example, there were areas in Manitoba where solitary individuals had accepted Bible
truth but lacked close association with other Christians
and rarely received pilgrim visits. Nevertheless, these
persons stood firm, and Jehovah sustained them spiritually.

Mrs. John Sample, who lived near Souris, Manitoba,
illustrates this point. She had been in possession of our
literature since 1897 and had taken magazines from
one John Kerslake, but had tried to stay with the
church and teach in local Sunday schools. In 1903 the
day came for a break to be made. She stood up in
church and told all present why she had to separate
from Christendom. Her nearest neighbor tried to get
her back to church, and preachers were brought into
action. But all of this was to no avail. She stood firm.
Later, the neighbor, a Mrs. Nay, also accepted the
truth. But so much had to be done alone. This is how
Sister Sample's son, John, described her situation in
those early days: "No congregation servant [presiding

overseer]. No study servant to lean on. No meetings. A contrite heart. A worn Bible. Long prayerful hours."

THE "GOOD NEWS" CONTINUES
ATTRACTING THE HONEST HEARTED

People with honest hearts, a desire to please God, and a determination to serve him in the face of all odds continued to manifest themselves. Among such persons was a former army captain, William Meneray. In 1906, while cleaning out a telegraph office in Souris, Manitoba, just before returning to his home in Winnipeg, he found some *Watch Tower* magazines dating from 1893 and 1894. Although they were quite old, he took them along. Meneray's wife read some of the journals and recommended them to her husband. The first article he read was a reprint of a Watch Tower Society booklet on hell. Well, that was a start. Meneray immediately wrote to the Society's offices asking if there were any individuals in Winnipeg who shared these beliefs. He was given the names of Mr. and Mrs. Reginald Taylor and Mr. and Mrs. Hamilton. Prior to 1906, there had been some association of those who believed these things. In fact, pilgrim visits to Winnipeg were listed in the *Watch Tower* as early as 1901, and in 1905 it published a letter, likely from Frances Hamilton, telling about observance of the Memorial by her husband and herself. But it appears that the first organized congregation in Winnipeg began functioning in 1905 or 1906.

Not content to witness only in his own district, Meneray established quite a mailing service. By that means, he reached isolated people with tracts and booklets. These had such catchy titles as *Thieves in Paradise* and *What Is the Soul?* Some of this literature was sent clear to the Yukon. George Naish reported that interest also was aroused among the Carments and Rainbows at Kamsack, Saskatchewan.

William Meneray once made a world tour with C. T. Russell and other Bible Students, a journey that made clear the tremendous need for worldwide witnessing. Brother Meneray's faithful course was maintained to the last day of his life on earth, January 21, 1960.

In 1911 Charles Cutforth of Gilbert Plains, Manitoba, became active as a witness of Jehovah. His brother, H. W. Cutforth, also became interested. The H. W. Cutforth home became the local meeting place of the Bible Students. In time, Charles Cutforth became a colporteur and traveling representative of the Watch Tower Society. His son, John, became a pioneer (1941), served as a traveling overseer (1942) and became a member of the Society's branch office staff at Toronto (1943). He attended the Watchtower Bible School of Gilead in 1946 and was sent to Australia. There John Cutforth served as a circuit and district overseer. Later, he was sent to Papua New Guinea, where he is still serving faithfully.

James Gibson of Haliburton, Ontario, was another honest-hearted man who recognized God's truth in the writings of C. T. Russell. That was in 1907, when he received this literature from James and Alexander Brown, his wife's relatives at New Liskeard, Ontario. However, his wife, Margaret, did not see those publications in the right light at the time. After Brother Gibson died in 1908, though, she went to visit the Browns for six weeks. When Margaret Gibson returned, "she had a firm hold on the truth and could think or talk of nothing else," reports her granddaughter, who also says:

"Until her death in 1929, my grandmother would hardly let a day go by without either writing or talking the truth to someone. In the early days in Haliburton, she would travel to her calls by horse and buggy. As she had been an early settler in the vicinity of Haliburton and a zealous worker in the church, she knew everyone in the surrounding area. The way she did her witnessing reminded one of the early Christians, for she would pack a bag with her books and the necessities, hitch up the horse and buggy and go to one of her friends or neighbors, announcing when she arrived that she had come to stay with them until they understood her message. If she could get a hearing ear, she would stay two or three days, and pore over the Scriptures with them, even by lamplight until late at night. By her carrying on the work in this manner, many families were quickly able to see the truth."

By 1911, the Toronto congregation was up to 110 persons present for the Memorial. Other classes, as they were often called, were growing, too. As many as 108 classes across Canada were visited by pilgrims in that year. The Vancouver group was having good success with Sunday evening lectures in Pender Hall. Samuel Withers (who died on March 9, 1971, at 96) was just then beginning to associate with Jehovah's people. His heart certainly was touched by the truth. So impressed was he with the material in "The Divine Plan of the Ages" that he sat up three nights virtually "devouring" it. On the third night, his wife awoke and asked, "What have you got, to keep you saying

'Praise the Lord' so many times at three o'clock in the morning?" Obviously, he was grateful to have his many questions answered.

DETERMINED TO DECLARE THE KINGDOM MESSAGE

Those who gained knowledge of Bible truth were eager to share the good news of the Kingdom with others. As but one example, it was during the year 1912 that Julius W. Lundell made his decision to do something about his contacts with the message proclaimed by the Bible Students. His daughter, Olive Mais, fills in some details, saying:

"Julius W. Lundell first heard of the truth in 1903. He was teaching Sunday school in a 'Free Mission' church in North Dakota when a fellow teacher told him he had heard a lecture proving from the Bible that there is no hell. Then in 1910 my father came to northern Saskatchewan as a pioneer settler to a homestead 20 miles [32 kilometers] north of the village of Maidstone. One day a neighbor loaned him a book on the subject of evolution. Tucked inside was a booklet on the subject *What Say the Scriptures About Hell?* Here was proof of what his friend had told him.

"Two years later an advertisement appeared in the Winnipeg *Free Press*, inserted by Brother Meneray. It asked the question: 'Do you know that the Gentile Times will end in the year 1914?' [Luke 21:24, *Authorized Version*] My father sent for literature, and, when *Studies in the Scriptures* arrived in the mail, he read night and day for a week without letup. By kerosine lamp, he continued reading far into the night. At the end of the week, he knew he had found the truth. With his books and the Bible under his arm, he walked to his neighbors' homes to tell them the good news. Their reaction was: 'Lundell has gone mad!' "

But that was far from true, and it was only the beginning of Brother Lundell's active service to Jehovah. His daughter's account continues: "Completely convinced of the truth, my father ordered and placed cartons of literature in those years . . . Then, in 1917, Brother Andrew Melin from Calmar, Alberta, made a trip to various Swedish settlements to give Bible lectures. Thus he came to our community, Milleton, and was the first to give my father help in organizing his activity. Before long, my father's picture was on advertising material and he was giving talks in all the nearby community schools and halls north and south of the Saskatchewan River."

Yet, the giving of Bible talks was not all there was

to declaring the Kingdom message. When traveling, Brother Lundell always carried a suitcase full of Bible literature. His daughter adds: "Whether at an auction sale or at the Lloydminster Fair, you could always count on finding Dad at the car, a group of men standing or sitting around and a big discussion going on. When it was time to go home, the suitcase was empty of the literature it had carried. Once, when we were stuck in a mudhole and a man with a pair of mules came along, his pay came out of the brown suitcase. At a Greek restaurant in North Battleford, a discussion that began with the owner soon involved everyone in the dining area and, at the end of it, again the suitcase was emptied."

Certainly, this kind of determination to make the Kingdom message known to others was commendable. Because of such an excellent spirit on the part of God's people, fine work was being done in declaring the "good news." Hence, the first decade of the 1900's ended with a marked increase in the number of true worshipers in most parts of Canada. Growth then was evident in all the provinces, and in good numbers in some of them. And similar progress was being made during the second decade of the twentieth century. But it also proved to be a period that tested the faith of these sincere Bible Students.

CLERICS LASH OUT!

One of the earliest congregations of Jehovah's people to be established in Canada was the one at Hamilton, Ontario. That strong, very active congregation naturally had the disapproval of the clergy. Not having any Biblical defense against the forceful thrusts of the truth, the clerics resorted to personal invective. They lashed out in a seemingly desperate attempt to destroy *one man*—C. T. Russell.

A clergyman who used this approach at Hamilton was a bombastic Baptist preacher named J. J. Ross. In 1912, he wrote a scurrilous pamphlet in which he made many false accusations against Russell. Acting on the advice of his legal counselor, J. F. Rutherford, Brother Russell laid a criminal charge of defamatory libel against Ross. As the complainant, Russell attended the trial to give evidence, and he submitted to a long cross-examination of roughly five hours. After the trial, his Baptist opponent falsely charged that Russell had committed perjury when asked about his knowledge of Greek. This "perjury" charge was published in Ross' second pamphlet attacking Russell. In it the cleric *mis-*

quoted what had been said in court, giving the cross-examiner's question and Russell's reply as follows:

Q. "Do you know the Greek?"
A. "Oh, yes."

By omitting the word "alphabet" from this question, Ross sought to establish an exact contradiction with a later question and answer:

Q. "Are you familiar with the Greek language?"
A. "No."

What really happened is clear from the official record (Police Court of the City of Hamilton, Ontario, March 17, 1913). It shows that C. T. Russell did not commit perjury. The cross-examination (by George Lynch-Staunton, K. C.) went as follows, according to the book *Jehovah's Witnesses in Canada*, by M. James Penton:

"*Question:* 'You don't profess, then, to be schooled in the Latin language?'
Answer: 'No, Sir.'
Question: 'Or in Greek?'
Answer: 'No, Sir.' "

After this, Russell was asked if he knew individual Greek letters, and he said that he "might make a mistake of some of them." According to the book just cited, shortly thereafter "Lynch-Staunton asked Russell the question: 'Are you familiar with the Greek language?' Russell's reply was an emphatic 'No.' "

So, there was no question about matters. C. T. Russell had not committed perjury as Ross falsely charged after the trial. The case itself later went before a grand jury, which declined to return a bill of indictment. So, the case never went on for trial before the Supreme Court of Ontario. Under legal practice in Ontario, only the crown attorney is allowed to speak before the grand jury. We do not know how the case was presented to it or what caused that body to reject it. No decision ever was rendered on the merits of the case. In his subsequent writings, Ross treated this inconclusive result as though he had won a great victory. He and others apparently chose to forget that Russell was not the man on trial.

UNDISTURBED BY THE ANTICS OF OPPOSERS

Despite the hatred of Christendom's clergy, Jehovah's people remained undisturbed. In 1913 they held a series of conventions, and these were very successful gatherings. For instance, about 1,000 persons attended the convention in Victoria, British Columbia, and some 4,500 were present for the one in Vancouver. This series of assemblies covered the larger centers of the

West before moving on to the week-long gathering at Toronto. There the audience numbered around 1,200, with about half of the delegates coming from the United States.

Over 200 delegates traveled with C. T. Russell from one convention to another. One press report announced the arrival of the special convention train in Edmonton, Alberta, and then said:

"When asked about the charge that he is a 'no hell' preacher, Pastor Russell replied:

" 'There is no minister in the world that preaches more hell than I do, but the hell that I preach is the hell of the Bible and not the hell of the fire, brimstone, pitchfork and sandpaper-slide variety. The hell of the Bible is a most reasonable interpretation of the original Greek and Hebrew terms—Hades and Sheol—which means the death state, the tomb.' "

Concerning the later 1913 Toronto assembly, *The Watch Tower* said: "Some attended this convention largely because they perceived that an evil spirit of slander and misrepresentation was for some reason endeavoring to do injury to a religious work. Satan and his blinded and misguided servants overdo in their endeavors to injure the Lord's cause. Sometimes the Lord overrules the wrath of man for his own praise and for the forwarding of the truth. As for instance, in the case of a man who, being told that Pastor Russell was Antichrist, went to see what Antichrist might look like. Hearing the joyful message of the Gospel, his heart was captured and now he rejoices."

At the Toronto convention, some opposers went so far as to come on the grounds with a large banner on which there appeared disparaging matter including the prominent wording "Russellism, Millennial Dawnism, Doctrine of Devils." But the police made them move on. According to the Toronto *News* (of July 25, 1913), during that week "the activities of the Toronto anti-Russellites" had not been confined only to that city, for the newspaper said: "Anti-Russell literature has been sent all over the world to different secretaries of that movement, according to Mr. Philip Sidersky of Baltimore, a member of the National Federation of Gospel Missions." But the *News* carried a headline indicating that the Bible Students were "not disturbed" by the antics of opposers.

SPIRITUAL HUNGER SATISFIED

One person who attended the 1913 Toronto convention was Tassey Raycove. In Macedonia, he had been the chanter in the local Orthodox church. He also cleaned the church building, which gave him opportunity to read the Bible kept there, but which the priest never used. Reading the Scriptures created in Raycove a hunger for truth that kept gnawing at him after he moved to Canada. Here he had opportunity to investigate several religions. But, one after another, they failed to satisfy him. He was the head elder of a Bulgarian Baptist group in 1913 when Brother Russell attended the convention in Toronto that religious opposers had tried so hard to disrupt. Tassey Raycove's son, Anthony, reports:

"The news of this visit was greeted with anger and contempt by Toronto's Babylonish religionists, who said, 'That devil Russell is coming to town on Sunday.' My father echoed the words, but under his breath said: 'I am going to hear him just the same.' And this was the turning point in his life because, for the first time, he now heard the soul-satisfying message that the sheep recognize as the voice of the Fine Shepherd."

After listening to Russell's two-hour talk on the soul, Raycove obtained and avidly read a volume of *Studies in the Scriptures.* He then sent away for the other volumes and read them with the same avidity. "The search for truth was now, at last, ended," his son states, adding: "Then came his dramatic break with Babylon the Great. The minister was giving one of his usual hellfire and brimstone sermons when he made the intentional, but 'fatal,' mistake of misquoting a text of Scripture. The head elder leaped to his feet, flatly contradicted the minister's statement and severely censured him for misquoting the scripture." There ensued a brief but hot debate that resulted in many members having their eyes opened.

A HAPPY SLAVE OF JEHOVAH GETS HIS START

It was during the second decade of the twentieth century that Thomas James Sullivan began his faithful service as a joyful slave of Jehovah. While working in Brooklyn, New York, in 1911, Sullivan heard an associate say that Pastor Russell did not believe in hell. That statement made an impression because T. J. Sullivan never had been able to reconcile the doctrine of eternal torment with the God of love. (1 John 4:8) However, the young man heard nothing more about these beliefs until 1913.

In November of that year, Sullivan was in Winnipeg, Manitoba, helping to install an auditing system for a chain of hotels that were being built by the railways. The staff included a young lady who always had a Bible with her, and on display in her office were six volumes of *Studies in the Scriptures* by Pastor Russell. She was so well versed in the Bible that even the management referred many Scriptural questions to her. But why not let T. J. Sullivan continue the story? Some years ago, he wrote:

"Sometimes it was necessary for us to work until midnight or later. Since transportation arteries closed down about midnight and she had a long walk home, I volunteered to escort her. These walks provided opportunity to discuss the Bible further, and the setting for this was indeed inspiring. To appreciate this, one must know the great open prairie lands of the Northwest. The temperature was generally between 20 and 40 degrees below zero at that time of night. Snow was piled up on each side of the walk three to five feet high. A cold, clear, blue sky overhead and the northern lights or aurora borealis sweeping across the heavens emphasized the grandeur and majesty of God's creation. Talking about God's purposes under those conditions was to me very impressive and sacred. It seemed to call on everything within me to reach out for the love and care of such a wonderful Creator."

T. J. Sullivan did reach out for that divine love and care. He began associating with the Bible Students in Winnipeg and was baptized as a dedicated servant of Jehovah prior to the celebration of the Lord's Evening Meal in 1916. It might be added that in September 1918 Brother Sullivan married Sister Evelyn Finch, the first witness of Jehovah he had met on arrival in Canada and the young lady who had done so much to assist him in coming to a knowledge of God's purposes.

In 1924, Brother and Sister Sullivan became members of the Brooklyn Bethel family. Both of them served there faithfully for the rest of their earthly lives. T. J. Sullivan was a happy and faithful slave of Jehovah at Bethel (eventually as a member of the Governing Body of Jehovah's Witnesses) until his death on July 30, 1974, at the age of 86.

"THE APPOINTED TIMES OF THE NATIONS" ARE FULFILLED!

Anticipation ran high with the coming of the eagerly awaited year 1914! Some were expecting more than what C. T. Russell or *The Watch Tower* had forecast. There had been considerable speculation, and failure of some of these personal hopes to materialize could lead to disappointment, especially on the part of those not spiritually mature. But most of those who were mature could see that this very thing might happen. Late in 1913, one Canadian with good insight wrote to the Society:

"Although our heavenly Father sees fit to try the faith of his people along various lines, yet it seems that during the coming year we may meet a more severe testing of our confidence in God and his Word.

"I am aware, however, that the faith of the dear brethren and sisters is very strong, and believe they will continue to fight the good fight of faith successfully to the end.

"Pastor Russell, as I have always understood him, never claimed his interpretation of the time prophecies to be infallible. His writings have always impressed me that way.

"Should the year 1915 come and not witness all that many of the brethren expect, it will matter but little to me. We know still that 'Thy Word is truth,' and that not one jot or tittle will pass till all be fulfilled. We know further that, according to the signs of the times, the Day is not far distant.

"When fiery trials assail us, let us remember the words of inspiration, 'Cast not away, therefore, your confidence, which hath great recompense of reward.'"

Indeed, in the very issue of *The Watch Tower* carrying this letter, the leading article pointed out that not all that was expected to happen in the way of swift and radical changes might occur in one year. But it said, "the Year 1914 is the last one of what the Bible terms 'Gentile Times.'" (Luke 21:24, *Authorized Version*) The article also stated: "It is beyond the power of our imagination to picture an accomplishment in one year of all that the Scriptures seem to imply should be expected before the reign of peace is ushered in."

Some congregations were quite large by 1914. Toronto had an attendance of 204 at the Memorial that year. Vancouver had 195 and Winnipeg, 105. But it would be seen just who were attached to a date, as it were, and who were serving Jehovah out of love.

THE PHOTO-DRAMA OF CREATION

Persons who were busy making disciples and who were not just 'watching the clock' found those to be exciting times. Among the things that aided them to reach many with the "good news" was the audio-visual production that became 'the talk of the town' in its day. Called the "Photo-Drama of Creation," it consisted of photographic slides and motion-picture film accompanied by phonograph recordings of talks and music. All its colored slides and films had to be hand painted. The Photo-Drama was *eight hours long*, and, in four installments, took audiences from creation, through human history, and on to the climax of Jehovah's purpose for the earth and mankind at the end of the millennial reign of Jesus Christ.

An *eight-hour* spectacular with *sound* and *color* in 1914? Who produced it? One of Hollywood's "greats"? No. The Photo-Drama was produced by the International Bible Students Association. All seats were free and never was a collection taken. Moreover, this color and sound production packed with Biblical, scientific and historical facts came on the scene *years before* commercial all-color, feature-length motion pictures and those with recorded dialogue and music were seen by audiences in general.

The quality of the Photo-Drama photography and sound was so good that some viewers thought C. T. Russell was present in person when he appeared on the screen in the opening scene to introduce the presentation. How vivid and touching the portrayal of the resurrection of the widow's son, a miracle performed by God through the prophet Elijah! And what a delight to see the opening of a flower and the hatching of a chick! Yes, the use of time-lapse photography made possible these memorable features of the Photo-Drama.

Local congregations advertised the Photo-Drama and invited the public. Some signs placed on buildings were 11 by 14 feet (3.4 x 4.3 meters) in size. The response was amazing. Theaters were jammed week after week.

In Hamilton, the Photo-Drama was presented for three weeks in the Grand Opera House, and in Toronto at the Grand Theatre. As crowds were leaving one of the sessions, they heard, for the first time, the shocking news that war had been declared in Europe. This must have indelibly impressed on their minds some of the points just covered in the presentation they had seen and heard. At that time in Toronto, the Photo-Drama was also shown at Central Prison (later moved to Kingston).

Among the approaches used to make sure that as many persons as possible saw the Photo-Drama was the inviting of schoolchildren to showings of it. For instance, in 1914 pupils were let out of school for this purpose in Halifax, Nova Scotia. The same thing was done in Victoria, British Columbia, several classes attending there. Charles W. Forbes, 14 years old at the time, saw the Photo-Drama in that way and eventually became a Bible Student. He never forgot what he saw, and tells us: "The theater being crowded, along with others I had to stand up. But the handiwork of the Great Creator, particularly as shown in the immense starry dome of the heavens, was well worth seeing and showed forth what an all-powerful God had produced."

Efforts were made to reach Canada's Poles and Ukrainians with the Photo-Drama. There were showings in the large centers like Toronto and Winnipeg, as well as other places in the West. Translations of the script and of the recordings were made into Polish and Ukrainian.

The beauty and dignity of the Photo-Drama was so tremendous that today, more than 60 years later, there are those who can recall its scenes and message and even the locations of the showings. For some, this educational production holds special significance. For instance, Della Smart, a Christadelphian, was troubled by the course of world events and by some teachings of her religion. She sincerely prayed to God for help in finding his people, in order to get these matters straight in her mind. A few days later, she saw advertising material for the Photo-Drama in Toronto. She attended the first session and realized that her prayers had been answered. That was in 1916. Now in her nineties, Sister Smart continues to serve Jehovah to the best of her ability.

BUT NOT ALL WERE PLEASED

In most places, there was fine cooperation from officials and others, some theaters even being offered free for Photo-Drama presentations. But in other cases, there was opposition. For instance, in Toronto clergymen preached sermons against the Photo-Drama and tried to get theater managers to cancel the engagements. However, this only served to advertise it.

About 1917, the Photo-Drama was due to be shown in Guelph, Ontario. What happened there is typical of the efforts made to stop its presentation and indicates who worked behind the scenes. George Humphries, who died in 1974, was a well-known Bible Student who worked for the local newspaper, the Guelph *Mercury*. In later years, this is how he told the story as he well remembered it:

"The first Sunday showing went off well. There was a good attendance. On the Monday evening at the Town Council meeting, the Council tried to word a resolution as follows: 'Resolved that no moving pictures be allowed to be shown on Sundays.' Of course, this was aimed at the Photo-Drama. Then one alderman remarked: 'Gentlemen, we will have to be careful about this. Suppose such pictures are needed for war purposes.' So the resolution was changed to read: 'Resolved that no moving pictures be allowed to be shown on Sunday, except for war purposes.'

"Of course, it was clear that we would need to have this matter cleared up. The projectionist and I arranged to meet the mayor in his office. In this connection, Jehovah gave us the victory. Two outstanding things were in my favor. The mayor and my employer, the manager of the Guelph *Mercury*, Mr. J. I. McIntosh, were at loggerheads. Mr. McIntosh said to me, 'George, you get all the facts and we will print them.' To say I was thrilled was putting it mildly. The manager of the theater, a Catholic, showed me the book of laws respecting the showing of moving pictures on Sunday. 'When you see the mayor,' said he, 'you show him this page where the law says that since you have a Provincial license to show such pictures on Sunday, then anyone, municipal or otherwise, that would interfere with your showing moving pictures on Sunday will be liable to a fine of 700 dollars.' With these two weapons we approached the mayor in his office. We were ushered in and, when seated, the mayor looked me in the eye and said: 'I am against you and will use any means, lawful or otherwise, to stop you from showing these pictures.' . . .

"First, I showed him the book of laws. 'Where did you get this?' he asked. 'From the theater manager,' I replied. He then rang for the city manager. When this one appeared, the mayor informed him of what had taken place. He then said to the city manager, 'What can we do to him for this?' This worthy scratched his head and remarked, 'We could raise his license fee.' This didn't seem to go over well with the mayor. Then he fastened his gaze on me and asked, 'Do you work at the *Mercury?*' With the most pleased expression on my face, I answered, 'I do.' He looked like a beaten man and remarked, 'I have no authority to stop you and none to say go on.' With that we left.

"I went to the *Mercury* office and gave them all the details. That evening the paper appeared with all the details on the front page . . . It was almost a column long and the heading stated that the Photo-Drama could not be stopped. The next Sunday, there was a lineup waiting for the doors to open. The theater was packed out for the rest of the showing, including the public meeting at the end. The people could be heard to remark, 'Why are the clergy against this?' "

CLERICAL OPPOSITION MOUNTS

Clergymen were also opposing our work in any way possible. For example, consider what happened in the case of Bible Student Charles Matthews in 1914. He became quite active in the Canaan Station and Birch Mountain sections of New Brunswick in talking about war coming in 1914, and some people said he would be sent to an asylum for the insane. But when war came that year, they said: "I guess Charlie's right. It's here. We thought the world too civilized for that."

But clerical reaction was different. Something had to be done to counter the influence that Matthews could now have among the people. Accordingly, clergyman R. M. Bynon arranged for a lecture to be given at the Indian Mountain Reformed Church at Berry Mills in Westmorland County, New Brunswick. Its purpose? To "expose Russellism." The cleric had a missionary with him to support his views. Matthews got an invitation delivered right to his home. At the service, the clergyman and his associate talked against Russell and "his" doctrines. One of them challenged anyone to disprove what they had been saying. But when Matthews tried to talk, they would not allow him to speak. Finally, one of the ministers paused to say "Amen!" Immediately, a deacon responded: "Yes, amen! Now let Matthews talk!" Matthews did speak for about half an hour, using the Bible. Then he thanked the audience for listening. A minister tried to counter by jumping up and shouting: "This man isn't converted. He's a heathen!" With that, however, the crowd got up and walked out.

Sometimes there was downright dishonesty on the part of a clergyman. For instance, in Winnipeg James Kelly had read a volume of *Studies in the Scriptures.* This is what happened shortly thereafter, as reported by his daughter, Mrs. Frank Wainwright:

"Sunday, father, mother and all six of us trooped off to attend Easter Sunday church service at the Fort Rouge Methodist Church. I have never forgotten that sermon, given by [a cleric named] Salton, because it sounded so wonderful. So it was puzzling to me that my father should be scowling and should keep nudging mother's arm and saying: 'Remember that point,' or, 'Don't forget what he is saying,' over and over again. Near the close of this interesting sermon, I wondered why Dr. Salton should spoil his talk by vehemently warning his congregation to have nothing whatever to do with those 'Bible Students,' especially their literature [and falsely charging] that their leader, Pastor Charles

Taze Russell, was an adulterer and an idolater. . . .
"On the long walk home, I overheard father tell
mother that she was to forget about getting dinner
ready and was to sit down and read at least one particular chapter in the book 'The Battle of Armageddon.'
I wondered why mother got so upset as she read.
Finally, she exclaimed: 'Why, Jim! . . . Dr. Salton
quoted word for word from that chapter—and no doubt
from other parts of this book.' Then father made
mother turn to the front page to learn the name of
the author. It was Charles Taze Russell!"

The hypocrisy of clergymen in their attacks upon
Russell only served to open the eyes of righteously
disposed persons. Starting with the very next Sunday,
the Kelly family went to the meetings of the Bible
Students.

WARTIME HYSTERIA

With the coming of war, the clergy found a new
weapon for use against the Bible Students. The enmity
of some envious religious leaders and their urge to
impede the growth of these Christians could be expressed behind a front of patriotism. These opponents
would take advantage of wartime hysteria to brand
Christian neutrals falsely as security risks and a
danger to the State. This would mean that the clerics
themselves would have to become champions of war,
even though this put them in opposition to their
brother-clergymen in other nations. This contradiction
and their denial of the "Prince of Peace" did not seem
to trouble them. (Isa. 9:6, 7) Here is an example of
the clerical viewpoint, as recalled from that era by
Mrs. Frank Wainwright:

"I remember that one of the more outspoken clergymen had it stated in the papers: 'Any man dying in
the front line trenches has a free passport to heaven,
and God himself could not keep him out.' "

The responsibility of the clergy in having promoted
war was evident to some. In 1924, the Toronto *Telegram* reported:

"Two young undergraduates from University College,
R. V. Ferguson and W. S. McKay, came before the
Toronto General Ministerial Association to expound
the views of the 'No More War' group at the University. Mr. Ferguson, who is said to have spent four
and one-half years with the Scots Guards in the war,
declared that he had yet to meet the man who went
into the war for the principle of the thing."

Ferguson was quoted as saying: "We would sing
'Onward, Christian Soldiers,' and then fill ourselves up

with rum so that we could do the dirty work. Thousands of young men enlisted in a state of drunkenness; others enlisted to be seen in uniform; others were lured by propaganda. The pulpit became a recruiting station. The church became a part of the organized sin. The ministers were recruiting sergeants and the cathedrals were hung with banners."

Indeed, the wartime position of the clergy as regards armed conflict did not go unnoticed. But what about their stance with respect to the activities of true Christians?

Does it seem naïve or unfair to say that the aim of some clerics was to silence the Bible Students? Well, consider what Ray H. Abrams wrote after the first world war in his book *Preachers Present Arms*. In discussing the wartime role of the clergy, he stated: "It is significant that so many clergymen took an aggressive part in trying to get rid of the Russellites. Long-lived religious quarrels and hatreds, which did not receive any consideration in the courts in time of peace, now found their way into the courtroom under the spell of war-time hysteria."

But before relating the further actions of our religious opponents, it seems fitting to point out that for Jehovah's people the years 1914 to 1918 brought other notable tests.

CHRISTIAN NEUTRALS DURING WORLD WAR I

Canadian Christians who maintained neutrality and respectfully declined involvement in World War I had to endure various sufferings. (Isa. 2:2-4; John 17:16) Harmless though these individuals were, a number of them endured not only incarceration but inhuman treatment designed to break them down, to ruin them spiritually. For instance, consider what happened to Ralph Naish and Robert Clegg at Winnipeg. George Naish, who served Jehovah faithfully in Saskatoon until his death in 1978, reported:

"One day [Robert Clegg] and my fleshly brother Ralph were taken to the washrooms and, upon refusing again to agree to become soldiers, were held under cold and hot showers alternately until, after fainting several times, they lost consciousness and could not be brought around. They lay on the cold flagstone floor for several hours until the Officer of the Night came across them in his inspection. . . . They were then removed to St. Boniface hospital where, for some weeks, they were very ill indeed. The Winnipeg newspapers gave this quite a little publicity in the following day's papers, but were quickly ordered by the Public Information Board of the government at Ottawa to desist and were told that certain steps would be taken under the War Measures Act if this was publicized further."

Among Canadians receiving harsh treatment as Christian neutrals, besides Robert Clegg and Ralph Naish, were Frank Wainwright, Claude Brown, Lloyd Stewart, David Cook, Edward Ryan and John Gillespie. In time, these men were sent to England, where they eventually found themselves in the infamous Wandsworth Prison.

Life in that prison was strenuous, and the Christian neutrals incarcerated there endured many hardships and tests of faith. For instance, Frank Wainwright recalls: "On one occasion, due to our refusal to undergo military drill, a number of us were taken to a secluded part of the prison yard. Lined up there were a number of men in uniform with canes in their hands. One by one, we were ordered to run the length of the court. If the pace was too slow, we were seized and dragged the distance and subjected to lashes on the back and legs by the men with the canes. We were then taken back to our cells. Our prayers to Jehovah for strength to withstand the pressure of such beatings must have been heard, for such occurrences never again took place."

Claude Brown was the only black man in this group of Christians, and he "came in for particularly rough treatment from guards and soldiers," reports Brother Wainwright, adding: "Once in Wandsworth when he was threatened with the reminder of the prison slogans 'We make you or break you' and 'We tame lions,' Brown replied: 'But you see, sergeant, we're not lions. We're the Lord's little sheep!' . . . After [Brother Brown] was released he continued to serve faithfully. In 1923 he was asked by the Watch Tower Society to serve in West Africa to assist 'Bible' Brown and his wife there."

JEHOVAH'S AID AND BLESSING EVIDENT

Surely, Jehovah upholds his people when they suffer for righteousness' sake, and their faithfulness leads to rich blessings. (Matt. 5:10; Phil. 4:13) Sometimes even cruel persecutors ultimately have 'a change of heart.' And faithful witnessing often produces good results. In this regard, consider the experience of George Naish, who stated:

"The next day [after being arrested] I was taken before the army official in command of the prison and, after a long effort to make me implicate others and especially the family I had been living with, he placed a watch on his desk and informed me that I had three minutes to answer about 20 questions or I would be 'taken down to number six and shot out of hand.' I was assured that this was what was done with 'yellow-bellied so-and-sos who would not fight for their king and country.' The verbal skirmish yielding no results, he bellowed at the top of his lungs, 'Sergeant of the Guards!' On the run came the sergeant with two buck privates. At this, the officer, a major, screamed at the top of his voice: 'Take this yellow-bellied swine down to number six and shoot him!' Never having gone through the process of being shot before, I was, to say the least, disturbed. But I prayed to God for his help. I was pushed and prodded into the basement and, on coming to 'Number 6,' the door was flung open and I was propelled forward with a tremendous kick in the rear. I was not shot, although in the succeeding months sometimes I wished I had been. . . .

"After a period in this prison, I was transferred to the army camp then under canvas on the Exhibition Grounds and I thus had a change both of scenery and of action. While I was standing in between the long rows of tents in front of the quartermaster sergeant's supply quarters, a tall young officer attended by two privates came briskly down the row. I heard enough of their conversation to know that I was the subject of discussion. Standing in front of me, several times the officer ordered me to stand at attention and, when I did not do so, struck me a prize-fighter blow under the chin, throwing me into the guy ropes of the opposite row of tents. Since I was unable to extricate myself, he threw himself upon me and started to throttle me. After some moments of intense pain, I became unconscious. My most vivid recollection of the incident is the rapid change in the expression on the man's face as his burning hatred changed him from human to beast."

Despite these and other hardships, however, Brother Naish said: "It was wonderful to learn from experiences day by day that Jehovah really never does leave us or forsake us. Many times in prayer I told my heavenly Father that I was sure I had reached the end of my own endurance. However, something always happened to revive my spirits and show me over again that it was his power that sustained me."

Moreover, during this trying period George Naish had many opportunities to tell others about Jehovah's purposes, thus building up his own faith and sowing some seed. "Some of this did mature," he said, "as, for instance, in the case of a sergeant who paraded us around the city streets [of Prince Albert] for exercise. Years afterward, when working a rural territory some miles from Saskatoon, I called at a home where I found that former sergeant, now Mr. Roger Barker. He warmly bade me enter. After a few calls, he and his wife began to associate with the Saskatoon Congregation and came into the truth."

Do you recall that major who referred to George Naish as a "yellow-bellied swine"? Well, Brother Naish met him years later at a funeral in Yorkton. "When I stepped to the front to begin the service," reported Brother Naish, "both of us had the look of total surprise. Following the service he asked me to drive to the cemetery with him. He immediately began to apologize for the treatment he had given me years before. It was hard for him to believe that I held no resentment at all. We enjoyed a very warm discussion about the truth. These and other encounters made me realize that, even when we were not able to talk about the things closest to our hearts, our actions made firm impressions on many people during those years of trial."

Consider another experience showing that endurance of suffering may lead to rich blessings. While imprisoned at one location, George Naish had the opportunity to associate with Brother Charles Matthews and to teach the truth to a fellow inmate. Brother Naish wrote:

"We were allowed short periods of conversation before going to the noon and evening meals. Naturally, the three of us quietly talked about spiritual things. Louis Ratz, the fellow inmate I speak of, used to watch Matthews and me with intense interest. Afterwards, he said that this was without understanding the bond of unity we shared. I worked at the table next to him and, as opportunity permitted, he would come over and insist on being told all over again why I was in prison. My constant statement 'because I wouldn't go to kill my fellowman' finally got through to him, causing him to spend much time laughing out loud. I went over to ask him what was amusing him so. He replied: 'Everything very funny. I kill man. I get life. You no kill man. You get life.' . . .

"His interest was tremendous. After my release, I finally secured his release from prison through the parole board at Ottawa. This man, who had served 16 years in the penitentiary, came into the truth and was loyal right up to the time of his death some years ago."

No, it was not easy to maintain Christian neutrality during the World War I period. Nor was it a simple matter to endure harsh, even brutal, treatment for righteousness' sake. Nevertheless, the enduring of these hardships brought fine results. A witness was given, even certain persecutors were impressed, and there were some who embraced true Christianity because they observed the faithfulness of neutral Kingdom proclaimers. (1 Pet. 3:13-15) Despite their sufferings, Jehovah's people surely had his aid and blessing during those difficult war years.

OPPOSITION REACHES A CLIMAX

Of course, not all Canadian Christians of that time suffered in prisons. But they were all put to the test, and they certainly had enemies—religious opposers who were bent on silencing the Bible Students. Yes, for true Christians, the period from 1914 to 1918 proved to be a time of suffering for the sake of conscience. This seemed to reach its climax as the war demanded more and more men, and especially upon the publication of "The Finished Mystery," the seventh and final volume of *Studies in the Scriptures*. Apparently, some clergymen were stung by its expressions on war, perhaps due to their own awkward wartime posture. There was a most vicious, and it appears, *organized* campaign to "get" the Bible Students spreading across North America—and it *started* in Canada.

Have we overstated matters? Not at all. Note what was said in *Preachers Present Arms*. Dr. Abrams wrote: "An analysis of the whole case leads to the conclusion that the churches and the clergy were originally behind the movement to stamp out the Russellites. In Canada, in February, 1918, the ministers began a systematic campaign against them and their publications, particularly *The Finished Mystery*. According to the Winnipeg *Tribune,* the attention of the Attorney General had been called to the Russellites, and the suppression of their book was believed to have been directly brought about by the 'representations of the clergy.'"

In January 1918, leading clergymen of Canada signed a petition asking the civil authorities to suppress the publications of the International Bible Students Association. That no small number of opposers was involved is seen in the fact that the petition had upward of 600 signers. Many of the publications cited had been in use for more than 30 years! Obviously, it was not true patriotism that moved these clergymen to act against the Bible Students.

That clerical pressure moved the government of Canada to ban "The Finished Mystery" is seen in these remarks later printed in the Winnipeg *Tribune:* "The banned publications are alleged to contain seditious and anti-war statements. Excerpts from one of the recent issues of 'The Bible Students Monthly' were denounced from the pulpit a few weeks ago by Rev. Charles G. Patterson, Pastor of St. Stephen's Church. Afterward Attorney General Johnson sent to Rev. Patterson for a copy of the publication. The censor's order is believed to be the direct result."

Official records of the Canadian government that have been opened for public inspection in recent years clearly reveal that the clergy did indeed trigger the 1918 action against true Christians in this country. When it was suggested that the clerics had done this, there was a denial. Yet, *at that very time,* Chief Censor Col. Ernest Chambers had *in his file* a letter from "Reverend" A. E. Cooke, minister of the First Congregational Church in Vancouver, British Columbia, who had written this to the censor:

"I have been instructed by the General Ministerial Association of Vancouver to bring to your attention a matter which seems to us to be of considerable public importance at this time. As you are aware the followers of the late 'Pastor' Russell . . . call themselves 'International Bible Students' . . .

"Would it not also be well to prohibit the propagandist literature of this body which is published in the United States and sent to Canada for distribution by these people?"

The chief censor, Col. Chambers, wrote back. In his letter, which was marked "Confidential," he said to clergyman Cooke:

"Reverend and dear Sir: . . . your communication conveying as it did the views of such an influential body as The General Ministerial Association of Vancouver, proved very useful in securing action in this very important matter. . . .

"I consider that the bitter attacks in these publications upon the Churches of all denominations, without distinction, are noteworthy, even if the statements embodied in these attacks cannot be described as 'militarily objectionable.' "

These confidential documents of the past, now open to public examination, do show that the clergy really did trigger the action of 1918 against Jehovah's people. Yes, these faithful Christians were denied their freedoms because they dared, as did Jesus Christ, to speak God's Word without fear, exposing the hypocrisy of the clergy.—Matt. 23:1-39.

It is most interesting that the Canadian ban came on February 12, 1918, and that in the United States the official act against "The Finished Mystery" came on March 14 of the same year. The U.S. action also came after representations by the clergy.

CARRYING ON IN FAITH

The ban was imposed upon the organization of the Bible Students, as well as upon "The Finished Mystery" and "The Bible Students Monthly." Outstanding during this period were the faith and determination of Jehovah's people, convinced as they were that they had done nothing wrong and that it was only due to clerical interference that they were under ban. Some were up at 6 a.m. or were out late at night distributing tracts.

Faced with an unjust ban, Canadian Christians proved to be "cautious as serpents and yet innocent as doves." (Matt. 10:16) To illustrate: Janet MacDonald noted the press announcement: "The possession of any prohibited books leaves the possessor open to a fine not exceeding $5,000 and five years in prison." But would this intimidate God's people? Not at all! Sister MacDonald wrote: "As soon as we heard this we carried our supply of the book to the chicken coop. We placed newspapers in between the walls to keep the books clean, and packed them in and nailed up the boards. The next day the town constable came and asked my father if there were any copies of this book in the house, to which he replied 'No.'" Of course not! The supply was in the chicken coop.

The fight for pure worship was on in Canada. "We prepared our supplies of 'The Finished Mystery' for a quick and widespread distribution, anticipating opposition," wrote T. J. Sullivan, adding: "When the ban became law, a petition was next circulated by the brothers in the United States and Canada for the government to remove the restrictions placed on the book, so that people might be permitted to obtain this Bible-study aid without interference and molestation." While circulating the petition in Port Arthur, Ontario, Sullivan and another brother were well received by the people in general. But there were repercussions. Brother Sullivan wrote:

"The police obtained a search warrant, searched our [hotel] room, and found our personal copies of 'The Finished Mystery.' We found ourselves in jail that night but were released the next day. In all likelihood the arrest and publicity did more to set the facts before the people than the circulation of the petition would have done. The newspaper blazened our arrest on the front page . . . The police confiscated the five or six hundred copies of 'The Finished Mystery' sent to the territory for distribution. But that night, while the publicity in the newspaper was at its height, the police of Port Arthur carried home copies of 'The Finished Mystery' for themselves and their friends, so that the entire stock was distributed for us!"

Many private homes in various places were raided to locate and destroy Watch Tower literature, including that found in personal libraries. Even Bibles were taken away! For example, as soon as news of the arrest of T. J. Sullivan and his associate reached Winnipeg, this is what happened, as Sullivan reported some years later: "The military sent a truckload of soldiers, who raided the homes where we were now staying in search for banned literature. The military could arrest us and could raid our property and confiscate our goods, but they could not try us. We were still civilians and the civilian court insisted that they were the ones to try us. The civilian authorities, in Winnipeg at any rate, were disgusted with the high-handed manner in which the military were raiding the homes and destroying the property of Christians. When the military raided a home they really upset the house. They would take coal, flour, sugar and other things, mix them all up and leave them practically unusable. This disturbed the civil authorities greatly, and some showed their concern by being as kind as they could in dealing with our cases."

In a surprising number of cases, friendly individuals saw the injustice of the ban and befriended God's people. They knew that the Bible Students were harmless and were good citizens, though having different beliefs. In one place, a police chief once advised one of his men (who was a Bible Student) that it might be best to take the day off since the police were going to be busy that afternoon raiding the I.O.O.F. Hall where the Bible Students met. The objective would be to confiscate any literature found there. That gave the brothers time to relocate their literature. One of the items the raiders found was a list headed "Servants," referring to those in responsible positions. Certain that he had made a great discovery, the policeman finding the list hastened to show it to the officer in charge of the raid. But, not being acquainted with Bible terminology, after uttering some profanity he told the finder: "We don't want their servants. We want the head guys!"

In another instance, Roberta Davies says that during a home raid a police inspector asked a young woman: "Are those your books?" "Yes," she truthfully replied. He ordered: "Put them away, my dear, before I see them." He later quit the force and told a Bible Student he just could not do "that sort of dirty work." He was not the only policeman who felt that way.

In their efforts to locate our literature, government men were known to have intercepted the private mail of humble Christians. Despite this and the raiding of many homes, however, the majority of the publications never were found by the authorities. The literature was stored safely in barns, in basements and elsewhere.

In one classic case in the West, the local police slit mattresses down the middle, tore up the staircase carpet, pulled apart an organ and even sifted the flour in the bin, looking for copies of "The Finished Mystery." But they could not find a single one. Unknown to them, however, there was a copy of this book fastened by straps to the bottom of the very stool on which the officer in charge sat as he directed his men during the search!

When the authorities found our literature, often the possessor was fined heavily or jailed. But consider what happened in the case of 10 Bible Students from the Vancouver area. In the prison library they saw the very books for possession of which they were serving three months as punishment!

PROBLEMS FROM WITHIN

Besides suffering as Christian neutrals and later enduring hardships under a ban, Canadian Bible Students had other pressures and troubles to bear during the World War I period. Problems developed within the organization. But to consider these developments, we must step back somewhat in time.

C. T. Russell had been ailing physically prior to the fall of 1916. But he carried on with his work and kept his speaking engagements. For instance, his great spirit for serving his fellow believers brought Russell to Canada once more in March 1916. His itinerary was as follows: Toronto (March 11), Peterborough and Lindsay (March 12), Midland (March 13), North Bay (March 14), New Liskeard (March 15), Bracebridge and Barrie (March 16), Guelph (March 17), Brantford and Hamilton (March 19) and Niagara Falls (March 20). An exhausting schedule indeed!

Such a heavy routine was taking its toll. At the Toronto gathering, Russell had to sit down while delivering his talks. Thereafter his health declined rapidly. Death came on October 31, 1916.

With this event came sorrow, disappointment and uncertainty about the future. Was the work to go on? Russell certainly had the view that there was a great work ahead for true Christians. During a question session at Vancouver in 1915, he had said: "There is a great work to be done, and it will take thousands of brethren and millions in money to do it. Where these will come from I don't know—the Lord knows his own business."

"A great work to be done"! Thousands to do it! How thrilling—to most. Some, however, started showing a spirit of opposition to direction from Brooklyn in carrying on the very work Russell had mentioned. A few individuals began to have ideas about 'taking over' from Joseph F. Rutherford, who had been duly elected to replace Russell. Not only was that spirit of rebellion seen in certain ones who had enjoyed fine privileges at the Society's headquarters in Brooklyn, but there were those in Canada who got these ideas as well. This, and the arrest of Rutherford and his associates on false charges in 1918, seemed to be about all the sincere ones could bear. It looked as though things were falling apart. Times of testing were upon one and all!

In Toronto about 30 persons withdrew from the congregation and formed their own group. They tried letter writing and other methods to draw away followers. But this activity died out in about two years. Also, at Montreal there were those who went off to themselves. Dissension that continued into the early 1920's greatly affected the Vancouver and Victoria areas. Former pilgrim Charles Heard originated a so-called "Standfast" movement that affected classes all over the Canadian West, many congregations being split 'down the middle' in numbers. Some dissidents formed their own local groups that openly attacked the Watch Tower Society, falsely charging that it had been abandoned by Jehovah.

All this internal pressure caused many to be disturbed. Eventually, however, it became clear that unworthy persons were being separated from faithful ones. (1 John 2:19) It would take men and women of true faith and courage to do the great preaching and teaching work that yet lay ahead.

A BRANCH OFFICE FOR CANADA

But not all was 'bad news' during those years. There was much over which to rejoice. The advancement of the Kingdom-preaching work prompted the establishing of a branch office of the Watch Tower Society at Winnipeg on January 1, 1918. Walter F. Salter was appointed as the first branch manager, and four individuals were invited to be on the staff.

In 1920 the branch office was transferred to Toronto, where it operated first at fairly commodious quarters at 270 Dundas Street West. The building was shared with an auto-top repair shop. (Cars of the day did not have metal tops.) There was good office space at the front and room for shipping at the back. Later, two small printing presses were brought in to print handbills and a booklet on hell. In those days, there were no living quarters at the branch office. So, workers stayed with other Bible Students, or at rooming houses, and looked after their own meals. Those then on the staff were W. F. Salter, Frank Wainwright, Charles Cutforth, Julia Loeb, Winnifred McCombe and Edna VanAlstyne.

THE BAN IS LIFTED!

Adding to the happiness of this period was the lifting of the unjust ban on "The Finished Mystery," "The Bible Students Monthly" and the International Bible Students Association. This came on January 1, 1920, quite some time after the end of the war that supposedly had justified the ban.

Interestingly, the Canadian clergy raised objection to the restoration of freedom of press and religion after the war. They even put themselves on record with a resolution on the matter. Why would they not want wartime restrictions removed? Some idea of their thinking can be gleaned from the fact that they made efforts to have the International Bible Students Association listed in a Department of Labour pamphlet of August 1920 that warned of organizations that were supposed to be subversive. But Brother Rutherford protested to the Department of Labour, and the public was informed about the situation in a printed protest that was distributed.

A REVITALIZING OCCURS

What rejoicing there was when the end of the war made it possible for our conventions to be resumed! And how delighted God's people were that the releasing of Brother Rutherford and his associates from prison enabled *them* to attend some of these assemblies! In 1919 conventions were held at Winnipeg, Calgary and Vancouver. Twelve such Canadian conventions took place during 1920.

The appearance of J. F. Rutherford and some of his associates at Canadian conventions in the years following their release from prison and their exoneration from the false charges against them drew great crowds of interested persons to these gatherings. This was so at the series of assemblies in western Canada in 1921. The first of these conventions was held from August 5 to 7 at Winnipeg. That was the very city in which there lived the clergyman and the politician who had instigated the banning of "The Finished Mystery," which was followed by a wave of persecution, including the imprisonment of Rutherford and his associates. How did the general populace of Winnipeg react to Brother Rutherford's visit? An estimated 6,000 people were present for the public meeting.

The postwar period was marked by a revitalizing of Jehovah's people. Outstanding in that regard was the 1919 convention at Cedar Point, Ohio, U.S.A. It revived the enthusiasm for the evangelizing work among the Bible Students in Canada, as elsewhere. Released there was the new magazine *The Golden Age* (now called *Awake!*), which gave impetus to the work at hand. Then came the year 1922 and another thrilling convention at Cedar Point. Those attending it returned home with a determination to witness even in areas beyond their immediate territory. Jehovah's people surely had been revitalized. They were indeed going to advertise the King and Kingdom!

BRANCHING OUT IN KINGDOM SERVICE

This spirit moved God's servants to branch out in their work of declaring the Kingdom message. Yes, they had been very active before 1922. For instance, in just one year—1920—here in Canada placements of the book "The Finished Mystery" had exceeded 65,000 copies! But now, after that 1922 Cedar Point convention, it was 'back to the field' for Kingdom publicity agents! And they were determined to give a witness, not only in their home territories, but in far-flung areas of the Canadian field.

For example, Charles V. Johnson did colporteur work way up in the Peace River country of northern Alberta, following up the activities of those who had witnessed there earlier. In 1919 a Bible Student named Nielson had been along the railroad as far north as Lesser Slave Lake. That was about 450 miles (720 kilometers) from the U.S. border, quite a distance north in those days! John Hamilton pioneered the Spirit River district from 1923 to 1934.

Concerning a system used by Kingdom proclaimers in Saskatoon, George Naish writes: "Often weekends would see two of the brothers loaded with literature entrain and head for some small town not too far away where house-to-house work would be done until the return of the train, either that day or the next, made it possible to return home. If our return could not be made until the next day, leaving us the evening or part of it after the town had been worked, we would walk in different directions to the farmhouses within walking distance, meaning two to four miles [3 to 6 kilometers] away. We would work in a half-circle back to the village or town, board the train, and arrive home tired but happy about the privileges we had been able to share."

Just how industrious were proclaimers of the "good news" in those days? Well, consider what happened once when a mistake was made in ordering literature, resulting in the arrival of over 2,000 volumes of *Studies in the Scriptures* for a small group to distribute. The one who erred in placing the order recalls: "Great was my mystification one day on returning home . . . I was greeted by the janitor of the building, who asked, 'What on earth have you boys been ordering?' I explained, 'Just some books.' His reply was, 'You must have ordered a public library.' . . . What were we to do with 288 sets of books, a total of 2,016 bound books? My partner refused to go along with my suggestion that I write to the Watch Tower Society's Toronto office about the matter. He insisted that the solution was more and still more field service to place the literature. Interestingly enough, in less than a year we were completely out of *Studies in the Scriptures,* speaking well for the hard work of the brothers in the congregation."

In branching out in Kingdom service, we used all sorts of vehicles—bicycles, buggies and "democrats" (four-wheeled wagons pulled by horses). Also, there were horse-drawn rigs made of old auto bodies. In the wintertime, these were closed in and were called "cabooses." Although they were heated by small wood-burning stoves that kept a passenger warm, there was the danger of being burnt if the caboose turned over. For open buggies there was some warmth provided by fieldstones that had been heated all night and then placed in the buggy at one's feet. Blankets and buffalo robes completed the equipment.

Sometimes Jehovah's people would cover large areas by forming caravans of early-day autos. The outside running boards along the bottoms of the car doors in those days were just the place to prepare meals or sort out literature! Tenting equipment that was taken along served to provide the needed sleeping accommodations.

Loretta Sawyer recalls her colporteur days with horse and buggy in Saskatchewan. She reports:

"The territory allotted me ran, from home, northward about 35 miles [56 kilometers] to the Saskatchewan River, westward 35 miles and was bounded by the same river, southward to the main line of the railroad and then eastward back toward home. It covered about 900 square miles [2,300 square kilometers]. . . .

"Never was I without lodging for the night for myself or my horse. Jehovah always provided. Occasionally there would be a slight charge, but never was anyone nasty or unable to put us up. Along with being bedded down for the night, my horse and I received our breakfast, and my foot-stone was heated for a warm start those chilly fall days on the open prairie."

It was at this time, too, that a small class began to develop well in Wakaw, Saskatchewan. This has had a definite effect on the Kingdom-preaching work in this land. Wakaw became an assembly place for the Bible Students. They made headlines in the community, since as many as 400 sometimes came there from other areas. Emil Zarysky of Wakaw became very active among fellow Ukrainians in the province and did a tremendous work. He served as a colporteur and as a pilgrim for a time. By 1926 there were 104 persons at the Memorial observance in Wakaw and growth was rapid. We can count at least 44 pioneers and missionaries that have come out of that small congregation. As many as 15 are still in full-time service, among them Joseph Lubeck and Olga Campbell (both now serving at Brooklyn Bethel) and Victoria Siemens and Helen Held.

READY FOR EXPANSION

The years 1922 and 1923 found Kingdom-preaching activity on the rise in Canada. By 1922 Memorial attendance had reached 2,335. Surely the early 1920's were years of Christian progress in this land. And Jehovah's people were looking to the future optimistically, for the December 15, 1923, *Watch Tower* stated: "Our new quarters are well lighted, comfortable, roomy.

We have 5,600 feet of floor space—sufficient for our present needs with allowance for further expansion."

"New quarters"? Yes, a better place had been obtained for the Society's branch office. Only later would the staff be housed at the premises. But this roomier location did allow for enlarged printing facilities. Now the advertising of the Kingdom could be carried on in Canada with greater force than ever before.

ADVERTISING THE KINGDOM IN QUEBEC

In 1923, Alexander Deachman and Peter Allan Robertson were sent to Quebec as special colporteurs. A report from the Quebec field during that year states:

"Our average of books [placed] per week has not lessened materially, and at present we can converse with the people intelligently on simple subjects. On Sunday evening, June 10th in the Leboeuf Hall, Valleyfield, we showed the 'Photo-Drama.' The Hall was packed with French and English and as a direct result twenty-five books were [placed]. The gentleman where we roomed requested that we put on the 'Drama' at his home; accordingly on June 13th, it was shown. Seventeen adults were present, all French Catholics. The English parson was going to use our slides to show in the Church on June 18th, but it was impossible to wait over Sunday in Valleyfield. . . . The Protestant pastors greeted us very warmly . . . they never raised a murmur and both of them have some of Bro. Russell's books. At our boarding house one of the youngsters said she didn't think she'd go to Church any more; we were much nicer than the priests. Everything points to an awakening. The King has prepared the way for his message; it only remains that laborers be found to carry forth the glad tidings."

Among those privileged to preach in Quebec in those days was Janet MacDonald (although that was prior to her marriage to Bible Student Howard MacDonald in 1928). Janet began declaring the "good news" in Montreal in 1924. At that time she shared in distributing a resolution that had just been adopted at the Columbus, Ohio, convention. The resolution in tract form was entitled "Ecclesiastics Indicted," and it clearly exposed the death-dealing nature of false religion. Sister MacDonald later reported:

"Following the routing set out by the Society, we went to many towns such as Granby, Magog, Asbestos and others in the Eastern Townships. To avoid opposition, we started distributing the tract from door to door at 3 a.m., and by seven or eight o'clock, when the town was active, our work would be finished. Several times we were arrested by the police, who tried to frighten us out of town. An example was at Magog, where the police took us to court. No charge was made, but we would have to pay $15 to get out. We said we did not have $15, so they reduced it to $10. We said we did not have $10, so it was reduced to $5. We said we did not have $5, so they let us go.

"At Coaticook, we ran into more serious trouble in May 1925. A mob led by the head knight of the Knights of Columbus surrounded us and tried to force us into a truck. We ran to the railway station and took refuge in the waiting room. The stationmaster saw the mob approaching and locked both doors. They milled around, waving their fists and pounding on the window. Soon the leader of the mob came back with the police.

"We were arrested and taken to the town hall, where a court was immediately convened. We were charged with 'publishing a blasphemous libel' because of the criticism of the clergy. The only witness called was the local Catholic priest. We were taken to Sherbrooke and locked up overnight in a filthy, vermin-infested jail, where I was so badly bitten that I required treatment for several weeks.

"The trial came up on September 10 before Magistrate Lemay, who decided to follow the law. He said: 'There is here no blasphemous libel and I dismiss the complaint brought against the accused.'"

Clearly, it was not easy to advertise the King and Kingdom in Quebec in those days. Nevertheless, there, as elsewhere in Canada, faithful proclaimers of the "good news" forged ahead. There was a great work to do and they were eager to do it.

"ON THE AIR" WITH THE KINGDOM MESSAGE!

In the early 1920's there was a new way to advertise the Kingdom, and the Bible Students did not hesitate to take advantage of it. Prior to 1923, they had made some use of the new medium of radio. For instance, Smith Shuttleworth of Brandon had given some Bible lectures on Station CKX. Yet, Canadian Bible Students had no stations of their own.

In the summer of 1923, George Naish of Saskatoon had some contact with a local lawyer who had been a Signal Corps officer during the war. On one occasion, Naish saw some logs about 60 feet (18 meters) long lying on the ground and asked about them. He was told that they were signal-tower material. Later, Brother Naish got to thinking that they would make fine radio towers. Why not have a local radio station that would broadcast Bible truth?

Receiving encouragement from the Society's Toronto office, the local congregation went ahead with the project. By late fall, property was purchased on a height of land in the northwestern part of Saskatoon; the logs just mentioned and other pieces of equipment were obtained as salvage material, and the Saskatoon Bible Students built a radio station. By the spring of 1924, that 250-watt station, CHUC—one of the first religious stations in Canada—went "on the air." At that time, there was just one other station in Saskatoon, with only about seven others in the whole country!

What about program content? During the limited hours of broadcasting, Bible lectures were given, Scriptural questions were answered and musical selections were presented. William Flewwelling, who had a fine radio voice, often gave talks and answered questions. Hilda Essen sang songs, as requested, and choral selections were rendered by talent in the local congregation under the direction of Bible Student Costa Wells who had done that kind of work under the baton of S. Betts at the Crystal Palace in London, England.

Public response was excellent. All mail was carefully looked after and Bible literature was sent to interested persons, or calls were made on them. Station CHUC was the means of reaching many in remote areas. For example, a Mrs. Graham of McKague (about 115 miles [185 kilometers] from Saskatoon) responded well and started the spread of the Kingdom message in the Carrot River Valley territory. When radio reception was especially good, CHUC reached into the foothills of the Rockies in western Alberta and down into the northern part of the United States, some 200 to 300 miles (320 to 480 kilometers) distant. With so many interested persons seeking the truth, expansion was essential, as George Naish pointed out, saying:

"It was not long before expansion became imperative. At this time the Heintzman Piano Company built a very fine store in downtown Saskatoon. I called and spoke to the manager about the possibility of using a part of the main store as a studio three times a week. In return we would, in each program, open and close with the announcement that this was CHUC Studio in the Heintzman Building in downtown Saskatoon. The manager seemed dubious at first, but said he would take it up with his principals. He did, and in a few weeks' time we were broadcasting by what was then an entirely new thing—remote control. Our understanding from the radio station inspector of those days was that our small station CHUC had pioneered this field."

OUR RADIO WORK EXPANDS

In 1925 the Watch Tower Society assumed ownership of Station CHUC, and its studios were moved to the Regent Building, a former theater purchased for this purpose. In Toronto, the Society operated Station CKCX (beginning in 1926). One of its outstanding programs was the lecture "Earth's Greatest Conflict Near," given by Brother Rutherford in 1926 at the Pantages Theatre. CKCX became the center for a nationwide hookup of stations that broadcast the Kingdom message. Incidentally, Margaret Lovell recalls that the station's announcer Neville Maysmith (who had been on stage before becoming a Bible Student) originated the sounding of musical chimes when giving the call letters CKCX. Since then, others have followed that style.

As our radio work expanded, in 1926 the Society started Station CHCY in Edmonton. It also established a fourth station, CFYC, at Vancouver. Besides these radio stations that spread the Kingdom message, either the Society or local congregations of Bible Students sometimes purchased time on commercial stations in various places. For instance, CJCB was used at Sydney, Nova Scotia. Following one broadcast—Rutherford's talk "The Kingdom, the Hope of the World"—a Colonel J. A. MacDonald told Daniel J. Ferguson: "The people of Cape Breton Island heard a message yesterday that was the best that was ever listened to in this part of the world. It was just wonderful."

AN INTERNATIONAL RADIO CHAIN!

The year 1927 was exciting indeed. Toronto, Ontario, had been selected as the site of a convention from July 18 to 26. Delegates came from every state in the U.S., from every province of Canada and even from Europe. When J. F. Rutherford gave the assembly public address, "Freedom for the Peoples," he spoke to more people at one time than any other man had until then. Not only was there a visible audience of about 15,000 at the Coliseum and other locations at the Fairgrounds, but by remote control the facilities of radio station CKCX were put to good use. It was part of an international chain of 53 stations. Yes, millions heard the message by means of the largest radio hookup till that time!

Graham McNamee, the National Broadcasting Company's famous announcer of those days, was sent to Toronto to introduce the speaker. By other special arrangements, the talk was also heard in Australia and England. It is interesting that, although the mayor welcomed the convention delegates to the city, the Toronto newspapers were silent about this historic event. However, to cover the daily story of the convention, the Society published its own paper called "The Messenger."

FIGHT FOR FREEDOM OF THE AIRWAVES

Stung by the growing and effective use of radio to get Bible truth to people, the clergy brought much pressure to bear on government officials. So, on March 8, 1928, the Canadian Broadcasting Corporation abruptly advised that the International Bible Students Association's licenses to broadcast would not be renewed. At first, no reason was given. A strong protest was raised against this attack on freedom of expression, and a petition campaign was launched immediately to keep the stations on the air. Eventually, 466,938 signatures were presented, calling for removal of the ban on broadcasting by the Association-owned stations.

The government's official position was expressed by P. J. A. Cardin, Minister of the Department of Marine and Fisheries and a Roman Catholic. Claiming that there were many complaints against the broadcasts by the Bible Students, but not identifying the complainers, he said: "The matter being broadcast is generally described by complainants as having become intolerable; the propaganda carried on under the name of Bible talks is said to be unpatriotic and abusive of all our churches. Evidence would appear to show that the tone of the preaching seems to be that all organized churches are corrupt and in alliance with unrighteous forces, that the entire system of society is wrong, and that all governments are to be condemned. The Department is persuaded that in the general public interest the licenses of the Bible Students should not be renewed."

From this wording, there is no difficulty in identifying the source of the complaints. Of course, matters were made to sound worse than they were, with some reported points taken out of context. Nevertheless, on these grounds practically any radio station or newspaper that is critical of others should be discontinued. This point was seen in expressions made during the Parliamentary debates resulting from the petition. One Member of Parliament especially summed up the matter very well, saying:

"Now I am not a member of the Bible Students' Association. . . . But I should like to ask, when did we appoint a Minister of this Government as censor of religious opinion? All down through history religious bodies have criticized other religious bodies. I think the great Roman Catholic Church has sometimes spoken very harshly concerning heretics; I think the Anglican Church in its Athanasian Creed utters some very strong things against those who do not believe in that creed; and I have heard evangelists telling the people generally where they would go unless they believed the doctrines then being preached to them. It is stated that the Bible Students condemn other religious bodies. Why should we penalize the Bible Students simply because they follow the footsteps of other religious bodies? If the Bible Students are to be put out of business because they condemn alike Catholics and Protestants, I do not see why the [Orange] *Sentinel* and the *Catholic Register* should not be suppressed."

In reporting on this matter, *The Watch Tower* stated: "We sent one of our attorneys to Ottawa, and in interviewing the Government the only reason that could be found to have been assigned was that some preacher had his sermon cut short by reason of our station going on. Our station, however, was clearly within its time and the preacher had run over by fifteen minutes. But that was no excuse, of course, to refuse to license the other stations in different parts of Canada."

If the Canadian government thought that its arbitrary action could be concealed, it was disillusioned. Protests and demands for explanation mounted. Mr. Cardin obviously was unprepared for the backlash. Members of Parliament demanded an explanation of what the government was doing. A broad generality about "a large number of protests" may have sounded satisfactory to Cardin as he vainly tried to sidestep the issue, but the Members of the House were not satisfied. Two liberal-minded Members of Parliament, J. S. Woodsworth and A. A. Heaps, were unconvinced by the weak explanation given by the Minister of Marine and Fisheries. So they demanded that he table all the correspondence and complaints he said he had received.

Pressure of protests also continued outside the House of Commons. The large petition bearing 466,938 signatures was filed with Parliament. Also, 1,500 telegrams and thousands of letters were sent, complaining about the action of the government. Mass meetings of protest were held in various parts of Canada.

Meanwhile, in Parliament, members who were anxious to see justice done did not let up on their demands that Mr. Cardin table the complaints, which, he alleged, had caused him to refuse to renew the broadcasting permits. There was an unexplained delay. Finally, after repeated requests, the complaints were tabled on May 7, 1928.

Full-scale debate on the question came before the House of Commons on May 31 and June 1, 1928. J. S. Woodsworth set the tone of the debate. He ably pointed out that after all the weeks of delay he had found mainly *newspaper clippings discussing the cancellation!* Mr. Cardin, having been caught with very little in the way of complaints to justify his action in canceling the licenses, had tried to bolster his weak position by inserting material published *after* he had taken his arbitrary action!

Speaker after speaker rose in the House of Commons to attack the action of the government against Jehovah's people. Among them was a Mr. Irvine, who said: "If I have to choose between having my children listening to that sort of thing [jazz] as against some of the elevating and enlightening programs broadcast by the Bible Students, I prefer that some of this other material be taken off the air and that the Bible Students' programs be allowed to remain, even though I may not agree with their religious views. Indeed, I think the question of religion should not enter into this matter in any way; the principle of religious freedom and religious toleration was supposed to have been settled centuries ago."

At 11 p.m. the debate was not finished. It resumed on the following day, June 1, 1928. Cardin struggled to maintain his wholly untenable position while the other members peppered him with questions he could not answer. He had produced a total of three complaints from Vancouver, five from Edmonton, six from Saskatoon and a few from Toronto. (*Jehovah's Witnesses in Canada,* p. 100) Or, as a Member of Parliament put it: "In other words, the Department canceled the licenses, and after they had done so, they looked around for evidence to justify them in taking their action. I do not think that is fair; it is not the kind of action we should care to justify in this house."

The government's arbitrary actions had been brought out into the open. At the same time, a witness was being given. (Matt. 10:18) A relatively small group had occupied the center stage of the nation, and the whole country had to take notice of their righteous demands.

The officials, ignoring the nearly half million signatures on the petition and claiming that they were only giving the public what they wanted, held to their position. The licenses never were granted again. Hence, the work of broadcasting the Kingdom message had to be continued on other stations. By 1931 there were 21 stations carrying Brother Rutherford's recorded lectures as a weekly feature.

INTERNATIONAL BIBLE STUDENTS ASSOCIATION OF CANADA

Increased activity by God's servants and other circumstances brought about the formation of the International Bible Students Association of Canada. This legal body yet serves the interests of Jehovah's Witnesses in this country. For instance, it owns the branch-office property.

When this Association was formed back in 1925 there were 12 members of the Toronto Bethel family. Also, at that time in this country there was an average of 1,000 public proclaimers of the Kingdom busy in the field, along with 71 colporteurs, in 70 companies or congregations.

LEGAL BATTLES BEGIN

All this activity again brought reactions. Clergy-incited officials and police started to interfere more and more with our public evangelizing work. Arrests began in Quebec at Ste-Anne-de-Beaupré, Westmount and Montreal. These and a case at Calgary were won in some of the first of a series of legal battles for freedom of expression.

Regarding the Calgary case, the Calgary *Herald* reported: "NO LICENSE REQUIRED TO SELL RELIGIOUS LITERATURE IN CITY. Selling religious literature, where the element of profit is not a factor, is not peddling within the meaning of the City bylaw to make it necessary for a vendor of such literature to secure a license before making sales. This was the decision handed down by Magistrate Sanders in police court Saturday in the case of H. B. ——————— of the International Bible Society, who had been charged with an infraction of the regulations."

"SCHOOL TEAM" WORK

It might be mentioned that in 1924 Jehovah's people organized a work that had a telling effect in many communities. Called the "School Team" work, it consisted of witnessing in a given area and inviting people to a lecture presented in a local school.

Usually, two Bible Students worked together in this arrangement. Thousands of persons were reached throughout Canada. The workers kept traveling from one community to another, sometimes being in a different place for a lecture each night. Occasionally, two talks would be given on a Sunday. It was not a work for lazy people!

HOUSE-CARS FACILITATE THE WORK

To witness in rural areas, often it was necessary for Kingdom proclaimers to live away from home for weeks at a time. What could be done to provide accommodations under these circumstances? Well, some congregations used a type of house-car. Harry Marshall of Portage la Prairie, Manitoba, probably built the first one. But what were they like?

A homemade body with eating and sleeping equipment was built and attached to a Chevrolet or Ford truck chassis. This was an improvement on the tents that some had used. These house-cars may well have been the forerunners of today's popular "campers" mounted on the backs of trucks.

HOUSE-TO-HOUSE EVANGELISM STRESSED

In the year 1927, emphasis was given to the making of house-to-house calls on Sundays. This type of witnessing work came as quite a shock to some people, for they viewed Sunday as "The Lord's Day" when no one was to work. Of course, they overlooked the fact that their clergymen were 'working' in the pulpit on that day.

There was harassment by police in a few areas, and there were some arrests of Jehovah's servants. But the work of witnessing went ahead. Surprising opposition came from some "elders" in certain congregations of Bible Students. These men felt it undignified to call on people in this way. At least, they claimed this as their reason for opposition. But it is now clear that the ones who thus opposed this work were the remnants of those who showed opposition in 1916 and thereafter. Now, either they had to carry on with the Lord's work or others would see that they were not in line with what the congregation of God's people in general saw to be their privilege and responsibility. So, some of these men fell by the wayside at this time.

With steadily growing groups and successes in public evangelism, and despite a continuing battle with the clergy who were using all methods at their disposal to silence proclaimers of the Kingdom message, another decade ended. There had been many fine accomplishments. For instance, the house-car work did a marvelous job of reaching people where there were no congregations of Bible Students. It is noteworthy that a peak of 125 colporteurs was reached in 1930, a fine increase over the 63 that had been active in 1926.

INCREASED ACTIVITY AMONG
THE FRENCH-SPEAKING POPULACE

Also, it was during the decade of the 1920's that our work began to blossom out among the French-speaking people of Quebec and Ontario. By 1927 a French congregation numbering 18 persons was functioning in Montreal. These and other French-speaking Kingdom proclaimers were energetically declaring the "good news" in the Province of Quebec.

By that time, too, a French class of 30 persons had developed at Chiswick in northern Ontario, the first French congregation of God's people in Ontario.

USING BOATS TO DECLARE THE "GOOD NEWS"

In the late 1920's, J. D. MacLennan was sent to Newfoundland to organize our work there in a better way, and a boat was provided for reaching the people in the otherwise inaccessible outports of Newfoundland. But what about the many inlets and islands along Canada's west coast? Well, in the year 1930, Arne and Christina Barstad and Arthur Melin were declaring the Kingdom message from Vancouver to Alaska aboard the boat *Charmian*. In that year, they were joined by Frank Franske, who had been witnessing on the Newfoundland and Labrador coasts. Theirs was a most unusual assignment—an artist's paradise! Mountains came right down to the sea, dwarfing the hamlets and boats in the narrow channels between their precipitous walls. Tides would rise and fall as much as 25 feet (8 meters) at Prince Rupert to 35 feet (11 meters) in Alaska.

This was a new experience for Arthur Melin. He had witnessed in Alberta and, with his cousin Elmer Melin, had pioneered in the area around Pigeon Lake and Conjuring Lake. But this was a lot more water. Franske had the experience of having spent time in Newfoundland. Yet, the Pacific was different. Barstad was an experienced seaman, however, and so they were in good hands. Enthusiastically, they visited fishing villages, company towns, logging camps and isolated trappers and miners. Also, customs ports in Alaska were called on. Remote Indian villages were visited. Many of the people they contacted responded favorably in time, and congregations have developed as a result of their first calls.

The *Charmian* was equipped with a powerful public address system that could be heard for miles across the water. Hence, it was very useful for reaching people along the coast. After a Bible lecture was broadcast over the boat's sound equipment, witnessing was most pleasurable. Literature was easy to place, sometimes as many as 100 books being distributed in an afternoon or evening.

In 1931 the *Charmian* was rebuilt under the direction of George Young and Frank Franske. The Barstads were able to continue their work along the coast with various crews in the years thereafter. Franske and his wife were back on the *Charmian* with the Barstads in 1940, until a government ban brought an end to the boat service. Authorities later seized the *Charmian*.

After the second world war, Franske took his own boat over much of this same territory with excellent results. Indian families, such as the Schooners at Namu, grasped the truth. Within 12 months, in this part of the Canadian field, Franske and James Quinn obtained over 1,500 subscriptions for our journals. So, for a number of years, boats were used effectively in spreading the Kingdom message.

COLPORTEURS PRESS ON WITH THE WORK

Colporteurs were well organized by the early 1930's. Besides those who worked by themselves, there were about seven "camps" or groups. These colporteur "camps" were in British Columbia, Manitoba, Alberta-Saskatchewan, Quebec, eastern Ontario, southwestern Ontario and the Maritimes. Such groups ground their own wheat, cooked their own meals and traded literature for fresh food. They witnessed in rural areas using house-cars in camping caravans during months when the weather permitted this. In the wintertime, these colporteurs moved into a large house in a city where they could assist a local congregation in covering its territory. At times these groups moved to several cities in one winter.

About that time, colporteurs began to be called *pioneers*. And in some areas they really 'blazed a trail.' For instance, Arthur Melin and David Hadland did fine work in the section around and to the west of Burns Lake, British Columbia. In all that territory, which they worked in the summer of 1932, there was not a single Kingdom proclaimer. With a Model "A" Ford and later with another automobile, they covered a large area. Seed was sown, and Jehovah made it grow. Today there are 10 congregations in that same area.

Naturally, the work was not carried on without problems and opposition. At Hull, Quebec, in 1932, three pioneers were arrested and falsely charged with distributing seditious literature. They handled their own cases before Judge Achim, following directions from Brooklyn as to the procedure to be followed, and were blessed with victory. Convictions could have meant sentences of from five to 20 years!

It was also in the year 1932 that pioneer Frank Lyster was arrested in Sherbrooke, Quebec. Moreover, in that year, a mobbing took place at Lachine, Quebec. Janet MacDonald, one of the special pioneers then serving there, recalls that mobs of 200 and 300 would form in some towns. She adds:

"When we would wend our way through the crowd, some would become more aggressive than others and would kick or punch us. The finale was to come at Lachine. Brother Demorest was hurled down a flight of stairs by an angry son of an alderman. I was working on the opposite side of the street and was informed of the occurrence by a man who was favorable and who advised that I leave the district. Demorest and I both decided to leave at the same time, but had difficulty in getting through the mob and, when we finally got to where the car had been parked, we found that it was not there. Howard (my husband) and the two other brothers had gone to get police protection, which was flatly refused. We had only waited for a few minutes when he returned. When Brother Demorest and I endeavored to get in, an egg-throwing barrage took place. A store owner had pushed a whole crate of eggs out into the street for the mob to use. It was in January and as the eggs broke, they froze, making a very unsightly car."

The Witnesses managed to get away without personal injury, aside from what happened to Brother Demorest. Later, a case was made of this. One of the leaders of the mob was fined and had to pay the costs for damage to the car.

There were also instances of the police trying to interfere with a house-car group working in the Maritimes. The officials tried to make it appear that the pioneers were doing a commercial work and needed a license or permit. This happened at Newcastle, Dalhousie, Bathurst, Campbellton, Grand Falls and Edmundston, New Brunswick. The interference never developed beyond the stage of going to the police station, however, because Daniel Ferguson and Roderick Campbell had obtained from an official in the capital a letter acknowledging that our work was not of a commercial nature. Usually, when that letter was shown to the police, they took no further action against us.

A CLOSER LOOK AT QUEBEC

As already noted, during the 1930's Quebec was becoming a battleground for freedom of worship. And who was behind the persecution of true Christians there? Well, if any doubt remains in your mind, take a closer look at our activities in that province during that eventful decade, and the identity of the principal opposers of Jehovah's people will become evident.

There was much opposition to our work in Quebec during the winter of 1931. Sometimes Alfred Ouellette was picked up by the police daily (at times twice a day) and taken to the station for questioning. This also happened to Ovila Gauthier. Often the police would say: "We received a call from the priest [who said] that you are not authorized to do this work."

In 1932, Quebec authorities began using against us the ancient false charge of sedition—this in cases involving only differences in religious views. (Compare Acts 24:1-8.) The first of such cases in Canada was heard at Hull, Quebec, where Emery St. Amour and Wilfrid Spicer were falsely charged with distributing seditious literature. However, the magistrate dismissed the charge.

In the fall of 1933, a cavalcade of 40 cars bearing 158 Witnesses departed from Montreal after an assembly and made their way some 160 miles (260 kilometers) to Quebec City. At 6:30 the next morning, each one was at his preassigned place and ready to begin a quick distribution of three free booklets in French. Within an hour and a half, 45,000 booklets had been spread throughout the city, causing quite an uproar among the priests. Thirty Witnesses were rounded up and falsely charged with 'seditious conspiracy.' Imagine that!

Only six of these Witnesses were finally committed for trial. The first of these cases to be heard was that of pioneers George Barrett and George Brodie. During their six-day trial before a judge and jury at Quebec City, the prosecution called as witnesses two Catholic priests and two Protestant clergymen, who said that, in their opinion, the literature of Jehovah's Witnesses was seditious. Yes, there was a conviction. The accused were fined $300 each or an additional five months in prison. This case was unsuccessfully appealed to the Quebec Court of Appeal, which decided that criticism of the Catholic Church by Jehovah's Witnesses was sedition. So, appeal was next taken to the Supreme Court of Canada, which reversed the conviction on the purely technical ground that the indictment was improperly drawn. Hence, the decision of the Quebec court that criticizing the Church constituted evidence of sedition was not reversed and remained part of the law of Quebec.

In view of this, Jehovah's Witnesses could be convicted of sedition whenever they distributed a publication disagreeing with Catholicism. The authorities recognized this, and sedition charges became common, with convictions resulting in almost all these cases from 1935 to 1940.

REMOVAL OF ELECTED ELDERS A BLESSING

For some time, a source of trouble in the congregations was the existence of elected elders. Following the understanding of the day, these were democratically voted into office. Of course, many were devoted men who were spiritually minded and a real blessing to their fellow believers. However, others were simply good talkers or were otherwise persuasive. Perhaps they had a good education or position in the community and were the most popular, although they were not always the best suited for congregational responsibility. Frequently, these open elections were a time of tension and hurt feelings.

When the Watch Tower Society appointed service directors, and the public evangelizing work began to be encouraged to a greater extent, the "elective elders" who did not want to witness from door to door began to produce problems. They would not engage in the evangelizing work themselves and they discouraged others from doing so.

Although a few elders and pilgrims became unfaithful, however, there were those who were loyal and true. A splendid example was George Young, who has left a fine record of hard work, Christian deeds, kindness and consideration. Throughout the West he was known as "Evangelist" Young, and theaters were packed out for his excellent talks. He was appointed as a pilgrim and served throughout Canada. Also, he visited congregations of God's people in the West Indies. Later, Brother Young was sent to South America to aid in the development of the Kingdom work there, especially in Brazil. He was even sent to Russia to try to organize the work there, but government opposition resulted in his having to leave that land. After carrying on in other assignments for years, George Young died faithful to Jehovah in 1939.

So, when looking back to the days of the "elective elders," we must realize that many men then shouldering congregational responsibilities served very faithfully. Yet, there were problems, and some solutions were needed.

What a relief and blessing to the faithful when the system of "elective elders" ended in 1932! *The Watchtower* showed that one was an elder Scripturally when he was spiritually qualified and theocratically appointed. Good order, peace and unity now marked the meetings of God's people. Jehovah's spirit was evident. Growth and progress resulted.

BANNING RUTHERFORD'S RADIO LECTURES

In 1933, at the instigation of the Anglican clergy, the Canadian Radio Commission again sought to throttle the Kingdom message over the airwaves. This time the ban was on all recorded lectures of Judge J. F. Rutherford. Please note that *personal opinion* had crept into the official notice of the Commission to radio stations throughout Canada. It said:

"Speeches of one Judge Rutherford, *foreign antisocial agitator*, must not be broadcast by Canadian stations until the continuity or records of same are submitted to the Canadian Broadcasting Commission for approval. Signed, Hector Charlesworth, Chairman." (Italics ours.)

But who was urging Charlesworth on in this course? *The Telegraph Journal* of Saint John, New Brunswick, reported: "Hector Charlesworth, chairman of the Radio Commission, stated a dignified complaint had been received from a *group of Anglican clergymen* in St. John." (Italics ours.) This report named some of these clerics.

A mighty campaign of protest against the radio ban commenced across the land. It got under way with the distribution of 1,350,000 copies of a four-page "Important Notice to the People" to acquaint them with the facts of the matter. Then a petition was circulated from coast to coast. There were 406,270 signers, and it got much publicity in the press. Parliament was flooded with letters of protest and letters of resolution from labor and other organizations. The petition was presented to the Governor-General and this sparked debate in Parliament. The Prime Minister promised to look into the matter, but nothing was done about it.

The determination of Charlesworth to make the ban stick is shown in his response to a station that wanted to take a fair-minded approach to the matter and also preserve itself in difficult times financially. *The Golden Age* (predecessor of *Awake!*) reported:

"One of the Canadian stations sent Mr. Charlesworth a telegram stating, in effect, that 'while we do not agree fully with Judge Rutherford's talks, we have failed to find anything of anti-social or communistic nature. The tenor of his broadcast is directed against other forms of religion and extolling his own creed which we would call fundamentalism. We believe we should accept broadcasts of all nature in the interests of free speech as long as they do not conflict with democratic government. In these times *the loss of revenue is a hardship upon us.*' Supplementing this telegram the station called up Mr. Charlesworth to get permission to continue the broadcast for at least two weeks anyway, and the answer was, 'Not a chance.'"

BUT TRUTH RINGS OUT!

Despite the radio ban, however, recorded Bible lectures continued to be heard throughout Canada. In about 1931, transcription machines had come into use in our witnessing work. They were designed to play phonograph recordings and to amplify the sound over loudspeakers. The transcription machines used in this country were designed and built at the Society's Canadian branch office. These would play the same recordings of J. F. Rutherford's lectures that were used on radio stations. Hence, when religious pressure caused the cancellation of our radio time in 1933, the Society began to make greater use of portable transcription machines. The recorded lectures were played at more and more halls and convention sites.

There was also a model of this machine that could be used with an automobile, thus making it a sound car. These powerful transcription machines could be heard for several miles when the volume was turned on fully. One Canadian innovation was the mounting of the speakers on a telescoping mast that could be raised to about 40 feet (12 meters) to project the sound a greater distance.

Although there was much clerical opposition to our use of transcription machines, the public in general appreciated what Jehovah's Witnesses were trying to do. Many people learned God's truth by this means, and congregations developed as a result of the thought-provoking lectures.

A report from British Columbia states: "One man in Langley was repairing the roof of his barn and he heard a voice discussing the subject 'Where Are the Dead?' He couldn't see anyone, but heard every word

of that talk. What is more, he didn't want to tell anyone what he had heard for fear that they would think
he was crazy. So he kept it all to himself. The next
Sunday morning, when someone knocked on his door
with the very booklet *Where Are the Dead?*, the mystery
was cleared up! In a short time, a congregation was
formed in Langley for all the new disciples."

During the 1930's the portable phonograph also came
into use in our witnessing activities. At first, it was
used for conducting Bible discussions with interested
persons. Later, these phonographs were put to use in
our house-to-house witnessing work, and the Kingdom
message was introduced by means of them. Recordings
of Bible talks by Brother Rutherford (each about four
and a half minutes long) were used in English-speaking
territories, and many subjects were available. These
recordings began to be used in Canada in 1934. In
the one year of 1938, over 900 phonographs were sent
out to Canadian Witnesses, bringing the total then in
use to nearly 2,500.

Yes, this was a period of enthusiastic Kingdom service. Why, by 1935 there were more than 2,200 proclaimers of the "good news" active in 150 congregations
throughout Canada! Also, as 1935 closed, the necessary
adjustments had been made for the 16 members of
the Bethel family in Toronto to be housed at the
branch headquarters.

INTERNAL DIFFICULTIES

Our work was moving ahead. Yet, it seems that
1936 was a year of crisis. There were troubles inside
and outside the organization. On every hand there was
opposition in the field. Around Chéticamp, Nova Scotia,
people threw hot water and even buttermilk on publishers of the Kingdom. In Ste. Anne des Chênes, Manitoba, a mob mistook the automobiles of some American
tourists for those of a group of Witnesses and pelted
the cars with stones, eggs and tomatoes. Residents of
the town were rightly embarrassed. In Quebec fierce
opposition to our work continued.

Internally, however, we also had problems to face.
These centered around the then branch manager, W. F.
Salter. It appears that ever since 1935 he had not been
in full agreement with Scriptural views on the "great
multitude" as presented in the Watch Tower publications. (Rev. 7:9, *Authorized Version*) Imagine his
telling people, "There is no need for house-to-house
witnessing until after Armageddon"! The work of reaching this "great crowd" certainly would be hindered if
individuals adopted that viewpoint.

It became known that Salter felt he was to be a new channel of communication for Jehovah's Witnesses and that *The Watchtower* would in time print his views, such as those on 'universal salvation.' He also wrote to a European branch manager saying that he (Salter) expected to be the next president of the Watch Tower Society. Laura French, a member of the Toronto Bethel family, reports that some of Salter's remarks during the Bethel family *Watchtower* study on Monday nights were disturbing, so that eventually, when a vote was taken as to who would conduct the study, the majority voted against him and for Frank Wainwright.

Matters had to come to a head. Brother Rutherford came to Toronto, had a five-hour meeting with Bethel family members and let some of them read the letters they had written in complaint against Salter. Then Rutherford produced evidence that Salter had been trying to influence brothers away from the organization and to himself, evidence not only from Canada but also from England and Germany. Salter was replaced as branch manager and was given two weeks to move out. (Seven others were asked to leave at that time, most of them being in sympathy with Salter.) Rutherford was very patient with Salter at the meeting and during the time that evidence was accumulating against him.

Percy Chapman, who had served zealously for many years at London Bethel, was made the new branch manager, and peace returned to the Bethel family. But a barrage of letters and literature from Salter, sent to many Witnesses and his followers, made it plain that there was no repentance on his part. Hence, in 1937 he was disfellowshiped by the Toronto Congregation.

REORGANIZATION BRINGS
INCREASED SPIRITUAL STRENGTH

In the following three years, intensive reorganization of the Kingdom-preaching work took place, the entire country being arranged into 14 divisions, each with a divisional servant in charge. Return-visit activity was stressed. Congregational adjustments in 1938 brought about greater peace, unity and working effectiveness.

During this period there were also some adjustments in the Toronto Bethel staff. For instance, Leo K. Greenlees came to Bethel in Toronto on June 13, 1936. He had been a pioneer for five years in Ontario, Montreal and the Maritimes. At Bethel, Brother Greenlees had many fine privileges. Eventually, he became the treasurer for the Canadian branch office and for the International Bible Students Association of Canada. In 1964, Brother Greenlees was invited to Brooklyn Bethel, where he now serves as a member of the Governing Body of Jehovah's Witnesses.

Back on August 24, 1937, Jack Nathan arrived from England, landing first at Montreal and then going on to Bethel in Toronto. In the spring of 1938 he started out in what was then called zone work, which was similar to the activity of a circuit overseer today. Brother Nathan covered all the Niagara peninsula and went as far north as Kitchener and Guelph. At that time, he recalls, there were some 20 congregations in that assignment, with about 700 Kingdom publishers. Since then, however, there has been notable growth in that region.

It has been four decades since Brother Nathan began serving here at the Toronto Bethel, where he still carries on his activities to Jehovah's praise. Yet, in looking back to that early service to his fellow believers in the Canadian field it is evident that he then received good training. It prepared him for the important role he would play a little later, keeping in touch with his brothers and sisters across the country to encourage them and keep them organized for Kingdom-preaching activities under the difficult circumstances soon to be thrust upon them.

THE WORK IN NEWFOUNDLAND

The Watch Tower Society's branch office in Canada had been looking after the work of Kingdom proclamation in Newfoundland. But the summer of 1936 brought a change in the supervision of the work there. Since all the Society's shipping was done from New York and a small depot was maintained in Newfoundland, it was then deemed best to have the United States branch look after the work in Newfoundland.

In 1938 Newfoundland again came under the supervision of the Society's branch office in Canada. That arrangement continued until 1945, when a separate branch was established in Newfoundland. Although in 1949 Newfoundland became part of the confederation that forms Canada, it remains a separate branch of the Society.

THE 1930'S DRAW TO A CLOSE

We were coming to the end of a decade of exciting expansion and congregational advancement. Yes, in

Canada the 1930's gave evidence of steady, healthy increase. The number of Kingdom proclaimers had risen from 798 in 1931 to 4,269 in 1939. Pioneers had increased from 126 to 294 during the same period.

But war clouds loomed on the horizon. The year 1939 brought another international emergency, and with it the aroused feelings of the patriotic elements who so quickly became extreme in their demands upon others. We faced problems with nationalistic ceremonies in schools, problems in connection with secular work, problems because we were determined to remain neutral. Finally, we were confronted with a very formidable problem thrust upon us in mid-1940.

BANNED ONCE AGAIN!

The coming of World War II in 1939 furnished religious enemies another opportunity to try to stop the activities of Jehovah's people. Having failed so far on the open legal front, especially in Quebec, our clerical foes moved behind the scenes to inveigle politicians into doing their bidding.

The summer of 1940 was a dark time for the Western nations supporting the Allied cause in the war. Hitler's armies had overrun most of Europe. France fell in a matter of weeks. In this atmosphere of tension, Canadian Minister of Justice Ernest Lapointe, a Roman Catholic from Quebec City, rose in the House of Commons on July 4, 1940, to announce: "I desire to lay on the table of the house an order-in-council declaring illegal the organization known as Jehovah's Witnesses."

So it was that, suddenly, without warning or any opportunity to defend their position, Jehovah's Witnesses and the International Bible Students Association of Canada were banned on July 4, 1940. The property at 40 Irwin Avenue, Toronto, and the funds in the bank in the name of the I. B. S. A. were confiscated by the authorities. On July 5, 1940, the branch office was locked by the Royal Canadian Mounted Police.

To prevent importation and distribution of our literature, the government also declared illegal the Watch Tower Bible and Tract Society of Pennsylvania and Watchtower Bible and Tract Society of New York, Inc. This took place about one month after the ban on the I. B. S. A. So, happily, we had time to send some of our printing equipment and literature to the United States. However, this time it surely seemed as though Jehovah's Witnesses were finished in Canada.

WE SURVIVED THE CLERGY-INSPIRED BAN!

The ban imposed on July 4, 1940, immediately triggered a wave of persecution against Jehovah's Witnesses in Canada. On the very next day the Mounted Police began raiding the private homes and Kingdom Halls of the Witnesses and seizing stocks of Bibles and other religious publications. The branch office of the Society was occupied by the police.

Following the imposition of the ban, in some areas persecution turned into a veritable witch-hunt. For instance, a meeting for celebrating the Lord's Evening Meal was broken up in Quebec City and another in Montreal. Children were expelled from school and were taken away from their God-fearing parents. Many Witnesses were prosecuted and jailed. In all, there were over 500 prosecutions. Were these Christians charged with any wrongdoing? No. They were penalized merely for *being* Jehovah's Witnesses!

The ban aroused much bitter criticism on the part of the public. It was obvious to many Canadian citizens, including government officials, that the campaign against these humble Christians was totally unjust. Angus MacInnis, Member of Parliament from Vancouver, told the House of Commons: "I wish to say with all the earnestness I possess that the prosecution and persecution of Jehovah's Witnesses under the defence of Canada regulations is a standing disgrace to this country, to the Department of Justice and to the Canadian people."

Finally, Jehovah's Witnesses got an opportunity to challenge the ban. In 1942 a Select Committee of the House of Commons reviewed the ban and allowed Charles Morrell and Robert McNaul, on behalf of Jehovah's Witnesses, to answer the shallow charges made by the government.

On July 23, 1942, the Committee *unanimously* recommended lifting the ban. Here are some comments of the Committee members quoted from the official parliamentary debates:

"No evidence was put before the committee by the Department of Justice which indicated that at any time Jehovah's Witnesses should have been declared an illegal organization."

"It is a *disgrace to the Dominion of Canada* that people should be prosecuted for their *religious* convictions in the way in which these poor people have been prosecuted." (Italics ours.)

In spite of this recommendation, the then Minister of Justice, Louis St. Laurent, still refused to lift the ban.

(St. Laurent had replaced Lapointe, who had died in November 1941.) A year later the ban was still in force. On July 21, 1943, the government was again under attack in the House of Commons for refusing to legalize the Witnesses.

Victor Quelch, a Member of Parliament from Acadia, observed: "It does make one wonder whether the action against Jehovah's Witnesses is largely on account of their attitude toward the Roman Catholics, instead of their attitude of a subversive nature. . . . That question is being asked all over this country. I am asked it from one end of Canada to the other."

Honorable G. C. Crerar, Minister of Defence, hotly denied this suggestion, stating: "He raised the question whether the policy of the government so far as Jehovah's Witnesses was concerned was inspired by their attack on the Roman Catholic church. . . . that inference has *no foundation* whatsoever." (Italics ours.)

But the official archives, since opened to public view, prove Mr. Crerar wrong! It was actually a letter (in French) from the palace of Catholic Cardinal Villeneuve to Minister of Justice Lapointe that caused the ban to be imposed. Here is an English translation of the letter:

Archdiocese of Quebec
The Chancellery

Quebec, 27 June, 1940

Dear Sir:

His Eminence the Cardinal would be happy if you would draw the attention of the Right Honorable Mr. Ernest Lapointe, Minister of Justice, to the enclosed *leading editorial of Quebec,* concerning the publications of the *Watch Tower* or *Jehovah's Witnesses.*

Certain books and pamphlets again recently addressed through the mail, and in particular the periodical *Consolation,* are all that which is the most demoralizing and most destructive of the spiritual strength of the country.

Thanking you in advance, dear Sir, for your kind attention to this letter, I remain

Yours very truly,
Paul Bernier, Chancellor

To: The Private Secretary
       of the Rt. Hon. Ernest Lapointe
       Minister of Justice
       OTTAWA, Ontario

The foregoing letter was, in reality, a demand from the cardinal that Lapointe have Jehovah's Witnesses declared illegal. Lapointe knew his power depended on the cardinal and was quick to respond. The next feature in this drama of secrecy and intrigue is the following letter (translated from French), sent one week later by Lapointe's private secretary to Cardinal Villeneuve's chancellor:

PERSONAL

July 4, 1940

Monsignor Paul Bernier
Chancellor of the Archdiocese
Palace of the Cardinal
QUEBEC

Mr. Chancellor:

Upon receipt of your letter of June 27, I took it upon myself to fulfill His Eminence the Cardinal's desire to direct the attention of the Minister to your representations as well as to the editorial published by *L'Action Catholique* with regard to the Watch Tower, Jehovah's Witnesses and Consolation.

Mr. Lapointe gave me permission to let you know by telephone the confidential information that the said organization of Jehovah's Witnesses would be declared illegal as of today, with the request that His Eminence, the Cardinal, be informed of this.

This letter is to confirm that which I just told you over the telephone.

I understand that His Eminence the Cardinal will be duly informed of the departmental order regarding Jehovah's Witnesses.

Please accept, Mr. Chancellor, my expression of thanks and my warmest regards.

The letter was signed by Lapointe's private secretary. From the time of the cardinal's demand, it had taken just seven days to get the ban imposed. There was great rejoicing in the cardinal's palace. His chancellor wrote to Lapointe's private secretary on July 8, 1940. As translated from French, that letter stated:

I am most obliged by your eagerness to draw the attention of the Right Honorable Mr. Lapointe to the subject of my letter of June 27.

I have no need to add,—since His Eminence will have already written to Mr. Lapointe to state his satisfaction over the departmental order in question, —just how much such a prompt and happy solution deserves our commendation and thanks.

Please accept a renewed expression of my gratitude and of my deepest regards.

Paul Bernier, priest.

So, while the Honorable G. C. Crerar had, in open Parliament, vehemently denied any influence from the Catholic Church, the truth that the ban against Jehovah's Witnesses was engineered directly from the palace of the Roman Catholic cardinal in Quebec City is established from the government's own files.

However, notwithstanding the power of the cardinal and the Minister of Justice from Quebec, pressures on the government from fair-minded members of Parliament and other Canadians resulted in the lifting of the ban on October 14, 1943, when the war was still at its height. Such a reversal of position during that crucial period in history really was an admission that there were no grounds for the ban in the first place.

It took additional months of hard fighting, petitions, letters, briefs and a lawsuit to get the recalcitrant Minister of Justice, St. Laurent, to lift the ban on the International Bible Students Association (June 13, 1944) and the Watch Tower Society (May 22, 1945). But, at last, we were ready for postwar expansion.

WARTIME PROBLEMS AFTER THE BAN

The lifting of the ban reestablished Jehovah's Witnesses as a legal organization free to carry on its religious activities. However, the country was still at war and many legal problems remained for God's people. Among these were: exemption of ministers of Jehovah's Witnesses from military conscription, holding of the Witnesses in government camps as conscientious objectors, and the right of Christian schoolchildren to refrain from saluting the flag. Almost coincidental with the removing of the ban, young pioneer Glen How of Toronto was admitted to practice law in the Province of Ontario. He became very active in the many legal battles that followed.

Conscription for military service had been introduced in Canada in 1940. There was a provision for the exemption of "a minister of a religious denomination." However, none of Jehovah's servants had been able to claim the exemption while the ban was in operation since the religious organization Jehovah's Witnesses was then considered illegal. The lifting of the ban changed the picture. In Toronto an office was opened as *Jehovah's Witnesses of Canada*. There was now a visible organization to speak for Jehovah's people.

FIGHT FOR RECOGNITION

In November 1943 a brief was submitted to the Minister of Labour requesting exemption for full-time Witness ministers in special capacities. The government refused to grant exemption. Although Jehovah's Witnesses in Canada had 15,000 in attendance at the Memorial that year, this was one religion that the officials would not recognize as having even *one* minister.

This issue had to be fought in the courts. The first major case taken was the defense of Earl Kitchener Stewart, tried in 1943 and appealed from the trial court at Vancouver to the British Columbia Court of Appeal. Brother Stewart's fine record as a full-time Kingdom proclaimer since 1938 made no difference. His defense was dismissed and he was convicted.

Undaunted, Jehovah's people got ready to try again. The government wanted to conscript Leo K. Greenlees of the Toronto branch office staff (now of the Governing Body), who had been a full-time minister since 1931. Instead of waiting for the authorities to prosecute, an action for declaratory judgment was instituted entitled *Greenlees* v. *Attorney-General for Canada*. The suit demanded a declaration that Leo Greenlees was a minister not subject to the draft. This was a bold move that left the opposition astonished. The war was still on and anything touching the military was considered almost sacrosanct. Yet, here was an organization that had just come out from under ban. Instead of quietly shrinking away, it was making an unabashed demand for justice and fair treatment. Jehovah's Witnesses were back on the scene and everybody knew it!

The *Greenlees* case was given a full hearing by Mr. Justice Hogg of the Supreme Court of Ontario. Evidence was given by L. K. Greenlees, Percy Chapman and Hayden C. Covington. In spite of the strong evidence, the trial judge dismissed the action on weak and specious reasoning. Appeal was taken to the Ontario Court of Appeal, which also gave an evasive decision, essentially refusing to deal with the true legal issue. Next, application was made for leave to appeal to the Supreme Court of Canada. But it refused to hear the appeal on the technical ground that there was no financial claim involved in the case.

The only remaining remedy was an appeal to the Privy Council in London, England. A motion for appeal was filed in London for hearing during October 1946. Just before the time for argument, however, the government repealed the conscription law. There was no law left to argue about; so the case terminated without a final decision. At least Brother Greenlees had been protected.

RELEASE FROM CAMPS

A number of Jehovah's Witnesses had been classified as conscientious objectors and had been forced to work in camps in the Canadian bush. This practice continued over a period of four years until July 15, 1946. At one point, there were 283 Witnesses in such camps. It was easy to get out of these camps by making a token payment to the Red Cross, a course that most felt was unacceptable. While the labor department said much about putting men in essential services, the real objective often was to prevent full-time preachers of Jehovah's Witnesses from being free to declare the "good news."

By the summer of 1946, all conscientious objectors in Canada had been released except 73 Jehovah's Witnesses. A brief was prepared showing the arbitrary and contradictory position the department had adopted in order to keep these Christians incarcerated after all other conscientious objectors had been released. Copies of the representations were sent to friendly Members of Parliament. Some of them were incensed when they found out what the government was doing. They began to "needle" the labor department with embarrassing questions in the House of Commons.

On July 10, 1946, John Diefenbaker, M.P. (later Prime Minister of Canada), asked: "How many members of Jehovah's Witnesses are still being held in concentration camps?" This kind of pressure became too much for the department. On July 15, 1946, all the labor camps were closed down. Accordingly, these young Kingdom proclaimers were free to participate in the postwar Christian expansion.

FLAG-SALUTE ISSUE

The flag-salute issue involving Christians in Canada roughly paralleled the one in the United States. Publicity from the United States on this question spilled over into Canada and, beginning about 1940, a number of school boards throughout this country began to establish forced flag-salute ceremonies.

A number of lawsuits disputed the power of the school boards to enforce the flag and anthem ceremonies. One of these cases was *Ruman* v. *Lethbridge,* in Alberta. The court ruled that the school board had the power to force the pupil to participate. But the provincial legislature showed fine respect for freedom and changed the School Act so that the children of Jehovah's Witnesses were free to attend school unmolested.

The main legal test, however, took place at Hamilton, Ontario, where a dragged-out case continued from 1940 to 1945. Twenty-seven children were expelled from school in Hamilton for refusing to salute the flag and sing the national anthem. It became necessary to establish a private Kingdom School so that the children would not be prevented from receiving an education.

Legal action was taken, asking the court to order the children readmitted to school without having to participate in the flag and anthem ceremonies. This case was tried at Hamilton on March 30 and 31, 1944. The trial judge, Mr. Justice Hope, a highly patriotic military man, ruled against Jehovah's Witnesses and said that the school board had not only the power to require the exercises but also "an imperative duty to exercise their powers." Essentially, this decision demanded that all other school boards in the province expel the children of Jehovah's Witnesses if they would not participate in the flag salute and anthem exercises.

This case was appealed to the Ontario Court of Appeal, where it was argued in March 1945. The war was still in progress, patriotic fervor was intense, and Jehovah's Witnesses were in the course of reorganization after the ban. When the argument opened, the court was quite hostile. A firm stand was necessary, as the three judges fired rapid questions about Jehovah's Witnesses and their beliefs. The initial antagonism began to wear off, however, and the judges gave a very fair hearing. Subsequently, they rendered a unanimous judgment in favor of Jehovah's people, thus making it possible for our children to attend school and get an education without joining in exercises that offended their conscience.

This decision was a terrible shock to the Hamilton Board of Education and its lawyers who had been loud in their attacks on Jehovah's Witnesses. They tried to appeal the case to the Supreme Court of Canada, but the Court refused leave to appeal. Accordingly, the favorable decision of the Ontario Court of Appeal was the final judgment. For more than 30 years, this fine decision has been very useful in pushing back the "patriots" who, from time to time, have tried to revive this issue.

FIGHTING FOR FREEDOM IN QUEBEC

With the ban over and World War II drawing to a close, in 1944 the time was ripe for renewed Kingdom-preaching activity in Quebec. The premier of the province was Maurice Duplessis, a wily and unprincipled politician who worked hand in glove with the Catholic clergy. Duplessis has been described by a historian as "a demagogue determined to keep the province comfortably safe and backward and corrupt."

At that time there were fewer than 300 Witnesses in all of Quebec. As soon as their evangelizing activity resumed in the Montreal area, "nuisance" charges began to be laid against them under local bylaws. By the end of 1944, there were approximately 40 such cases. The number of prosecutions increased rapidly in 1945, and the eyes of the whole country were drawn to the fight in September 1945, when Catholic mobs attacked the Witnesses at Châteauguay and Lachine. But this small band of intrepid Christians stood firm against such attacks.—Jer. 1:19.

By the end of 1945, the number of legal cases had piled up to over 400. But the end was not in sight. Toward the end of 1946, there were over 800 cases pending in the courts in Montreal, Verdun, Outremont, Lachine, Quebec City, Sherbrooke and other centers! These legal cases and constant arrests were a tiring harassment of Jehovah's people. There is a human side to such proceedings, as you can imagine. It was not easy to bear the arrests, tensions, pressured delays, humiliation, loss of jobs, and continuing frustration.

"QUEBEC'S BURNING HATE"

Something had to be done to relieve the great pressure on the faithful Witnesses in Quebec. So, a special assembly was held in Montreal on November 2 and 3, 1946. On hand were N. H. Knorr, then president of the Watch Tower Society, and the Society's legal counsel from Brooklyn, H. C. Covington. Brother Knorr's concluding talk was entitled "What Shall We Do?"

There was excitement in the air as an expectant and thrilled audience heard Brother Knorr give the answer by reading to the public, for the first time, the now historic document "Quebec's Burning Hate for God and Christ and Freedom Is the Shame of All Canada." It was a sizzling tract! In stern and measured tones, Knorr proclaimed, like a message of doom, Jehovah's indictment of the corrupt administration of the Province of Quebec. The pamphlet was a straightforward, hard-hitting statement of facts that have never been disputed.

Brother Knorr announced that on November 15, 1946 —only 12 days later—a free distribution of this tract would begin across Canada and would continue for 16 days. This was a clarion call for action!

DUPLESSIS ANNOUNCES "WAR WITHOUT MERCY"

Rapidly, the pamphlet "Quebec's Burning Hate" was spread across the country, including Quebec. Now the legal battle really began in earnest. Publicly, Duplessis announced "War Without Mercy on the Witnesses of Jehovah." Instead of 800 legal cases, we soon had 1,700. Duplessis dusted off the old law of sedition and, in a short time, there were over 100 of these charges. The whole country again began watching the struggle in Quebec.

On December 4, 1946, Duplessis, in his rage, threw a legal boomerang that came back and hit him. He unjustly canceled the liquor license of the restaurant owned by Frank Roncarelli, one of Jehovah's Witnesses. This attack on a man's livelihood roused the business community right across Canada. Everyone could see that an unprincipled dictator was in control in Quebec. A large protest meeting was held by prominent citizens of Montreal.

While the country was still sizzling with outrage over the arbitrary action of Duplessis, another boomerang was thrown by Recorder Jean Mercier, a Roman Catholic judge in Quebec City. On trial before Mercier on December 17, 1946, was special pioneer John Maynard How, accused of disturbing the peace, a simple bylaw charge. Recorder Mercier, however, completely lost control of himself. Headlines screamed, "Judge Lashes Jehovah's Sect. Says Deserve Life Terms." One story explained: "Mercier said orders had been issued to Quebec police to arrest every known and suspected witness of Jehovah on sight and pledged his court to continue a relentless purge of all sympathizers."

The man making these statements was a judge thought to be fair and impartial. The behavior of men like Duplessis and Mercier was proving how accurate —in fact, understated—were the accusations appearing in the pamphlet "Quebec's Burning Hate." Typical of the press reaction were the titles of the following editorials:

The Dark Ages Return to Quebec (The Toronto *Star*)

What a Judge! (The Ottawa *Journal*)

Return of the Inquisition (*The Globe and Mail*, Toronto)

The Stench of Fascism (*The Gazette*, Glace Bay)

Instead of retreating from the fray, Jehovah's Witnesses released a second broadside, a pamphlet entitled "Quebec, You Have Failed Your People!" This answer to Duplessis' false charges was distributed in January 1947, and this time the distribution took place at night to avoid the continuing arrests of God's people by the Quebec police.

Parallel with this excitement was a very hot legal battle in the City of Quebec. The small pioneer group there—Laurier Saumur, John Maynard How, Gerald Barry and Russell Herbert Headworth—faced such a rapid-fire series of proceedings in and out of Recorder Mercier's court and in and out of prison that the newspapers dubbed it "The Battle of the Writs." All this activity kept feeding the press, so that Quebec stories became a daily part of the news across the country. Many honest-hearted people admired the intrepid stand of Jehovah's Christian witnesses.

In February 1947, four of the special pioneers from Quebec City—three of whom were out on bail—went to Ithaca, New York, to become students in the ninth class of the Watchtower Bible School of Gilead. While they were at Gilead, the case of Laurier Saumur and Gerald Barry was taken to the Supreme Court of Canada. But the Court refused to hear the case on a technical ground. As a result, Laurier Saumur had to leave Gilead School in June, before graduation, and go back to jail in Quebec City to complete his sentence. This dismissal by the Supreme Court put us back into the courts of Quebec with, by that time, over 1,700 cases pending.

Faithful Gerald Barry, whose case was also in the Supreme Court, died in May 1947. He had been a pioneer since 1908 and had begun serving in Quebec in 1924. Truly, he was like those described by the apostle Paul, in saying, "the world was not worthy of them."—Heb. 11:38.

WHY NOT SHARE IN THE FIGHT FOR FREEDOM?

By now you certainly are aware of the courage and determination displayed by Jehovah's people in the Province of Quebec. But it seems that this is a good place to tell you about two natural and spiritual sisters in their late teens. They had heard of the persecution of their fellow believers in Quebec—how many of them had been mobbed, beaten and imprisoned—and had begun to think: "We have our youth, strength and health; why, an assignment like that would be ideal for us, as we want to have a real share in the fight for freedom along with the brothers already there."

So it was that on May 1, 1946, two young pioneer girls, thrilled at the prospect of being assigned to serve in Quebec, found themselves in Montreal. One of them, Victoria Dougaluk, wrote some years ago:

"It wasn't long before we were experiencing what we had at one time read about. My sister was arrested and taken regularly to the juvenile court and I was a regular attendant at the recorder's court, so much so that the judge one day informed me that I was the biggest nuisance that had ever come into the place. We had many opportunities of witnessing, not only to the court personnel but to other prisoners. A great bond of love grew up between the brothers who shared prison experiences; one occasion I specially recall: Several of us had been brought in together and as the bail would come through, the oldest, or those with families at home, were released first. In the end two of us remained. Six days passed, we not knowing when our turn would come. Finally bail came through, but only for one. The French sister with me said, 'Two or nothing'; so gave up her immediate freedom to stay on with me. This was appreciated more than words could express. Eventually Jehovah's witnesses came to be very much respected for their fight for freedom, as all attempts to discourage us failed. Their efforts to deaden our zeal made us all the more determined to carry on and find the sheep in that area."

BACK TO SEDITION CHARGES!

With the aid of Jehovah's spirit, and with such love, faith, loyalty and determination, God's people in Quebec faced the foe. And the enemy had not given up the fight. The heat of exposure in the pamphlet "Quebec's Burning Hate" sent Duplessis looking for more weapons of threat and oppression. In addition to the swarm of bylaw cases, he resumed the old standby of seditious libel charges. Over 100 such charges were laid against 50 Witnesses. These cases were instituted at Sherbrooke, Amos, Montreal and St-Joseph-de-Beauce. For evidence, the prosecutors relied on the two pamphlets "Quebec's Burning Hate" and "Quebec, You Have Failed Your People!"

The first sedition case tried was that of Aime Boucher, a sincere, mild man of small stature who lived in the hills south of Quebec City, on a farm that he cultivated with oxen. Brother Boucher was poor in this world's goods but rich in love and faith. His trial was heard at St-Joseph-de-Beauce in November 1947 before Justice Alfred Savard, a former law partner of the late Minister of Justice Lapointe, who had instituted the ban of 1940. Justice Savard was extremely hostile and made a very prejudiced address to the jury. Of course, there was a conviction.

The Quebec Court of Appeal supported the conviction and the case was appealed to the Supreme Court of Canada. That Court first ordered the case back to Quebec for a new trial, but Jehovah was with us and an unprecedented rehearing was granted. The Court reversed itself after a second argument and ordered a complete acquittal. Since there was no incitement to violence, the pamphlets of Jehovah's Witnesses could not be seditious. Hence, every single sedition charge laid by Duplessis had to be dismissed. Not one conviction was maintained. Jehovah had vindicated his people!

The *Boucher* decision was probably the most important legal victory Jehovah's people have won in Canada. It broke the back of the Church-State attack on the liberties of Jehovah's Witnesses and all other Canadians. Also, it modernized the law and made obsolete all the standard definitions of sedition in this land. All the lawbooks had to be changed! Dean Bowker, head of the University of Alberta Law School, stated: "A judgment like *Boucher* v. *The King* is worth a dozen declarations of the right of free speech."

POLICE CENSORSHIP DEFEATED

The sedition cases had all been dismissed. That was fine. But there still remained a mountain of over 1,600 bylaw charges. What about these? Basic to these cases was the effort of Quebec authorities to keep all dissemination of information subject to police censorship. Typical was Bylaw 184 of the City of Quebec, which said: "It is forbidden to distribute in the streets of Quebec any book, pamphlet, booklet, circular, tract whatever without having previously obtained for so doing the written permission of the Chief of Police."

To overcome this censorship bylaw, a test case was started in Quebec City in 1947 asking that the bylaw be declared illegal. In court, three clergymen—a Catholic priest, an Anglican cleric and a Jewish rabbi—appeared as witnesses for the City of Quebec. They endeavored to persuade the judge to rule *against* Jehovah's Witnesses. Here was further evidence that politics and the major religions were united against the true servants of God!

This case, styled *Saumur* v. *Quebec*, also was appealed to the Supreme Court of Canada and was argued there for seven days. On October 6, 1953, the nine-judge Court ruled in favor of Jehovah's Witnesses in a split decision of five to four. Victory in this case terminated the hundreds of bylaw cases still pending in the courts of Quebec. The *Saumur* ruling also is acknowledged in Canada as a landmark decision of benefit to all the Canadian people.

One columnist was so moved by this grand decision that the following remarks appeared in the Toronto *Telegram:*

"EQUAL RIGHTS TO ALL
"A large bonfire on Parliament Hill should celebrate the Supreme Court of Canada's decision in the Saumur case; a bonfire worthy of a great occasion. Few decisions in the history of Canadian justice can have been more important. Few courts can have done better service than this to Canada. None has placed Canadians who value their inheritance of freedom more deeply in its debt. . . . The deliverance cannot be celebrated with the bonfires it deserves."

Interestingly, at the time that this case went to trial, the branch office in Canada had sent out word requesting that all the brothers petition Jehovah in prayer as to the outcome of the matter. So much depended on having a favorable decision in this case! (1 Tim. 2:1, 2) The eventual outcome indicates that there was a favorable response from the "Hearer of prayer." (Ps. 65:2) Indeed, "a righteous man's supplication, when it is at work, has much force."—Jas. 5:16.

DUPLESSIS' LAST STAND

By that time all the laws that Duplessis had on the books had been defeated by Jehovah's Witnesses. But still he was not through. In January 1954, he pushed through the Quebec legislature a new law that he claimed would put a stop to the activities of Jehovah's Witnesses. That law, known as Bill 38, went into force on January 28, 1954, at 5 p.m. But at 9 a.m. the very next morning, counsel for Jehovah's Witnesses was at the door of the courthouse to file an action contesting the validity of the new law and demanding an injunction to stop its being used.

The lawsuit over Bill 38 continued over a period of 10 years, and the trial of this action was intensely interesting. Some wonderful evidence upholding Jehovah and his people was given by F. W. Franz (now the fourth president of the Watch Tower Society) when he came to Quebec as an expert witness.

Counsel for Jehovah's Witnesses called one particularly unwilling witness—Maurice Duplessis! He was outraged at having been forced to appear in response to a subpoena from Jehovah's Witnesses. For two and a half hours, Glen How cross-examined this arrogant, snappish little man, much to Duplessis' irritation.

In due course, the Supreme Court of Canada refused to decide on the validity of the law on the technical ground that Jehovah's Witnesses had sued before Bill 38 had ever been used against them. But if the authorities ever did make use of this law, the technical ground used by the Supreme Court would be destroyed. Bill 38 has been ineffective and has remained unused since 1954. Duplessis had made his last stand!

In 1959 Duplessis suffered the ignominy of being the first Premier in the history of the British Empire to be forced personally to pay damages to a citizen for something he had done in an official capacity. The Supreme Court of Canada ordered him to pay damages and costs of about $50,000 to Brother Frank Roncarelli for having canceled his restaurant liquor license. Shortly after this final frustration Duplessis was dead.

Certainly, Duplessis might have saved himself a lot of vexation had he listened to the good advice of Gamaliel. That teacher of the Law stated: "Do not meddle with these men, but let them alone; . . . otherwise, you may perhaps be found fighters actually against God."—Acts 5:38, 39.

EXPRESSIONS OF APPRECIATION

Many Canadian legal commentators have recognized the fine contribution Jehovah's Witnesses have made to law and liberty in this land. Frank Scott, former Dean of the Law School at McGill University, has said regarding Witness cases: "We should be grateful that we have in this country some victims of state oppression who stand up for their rights. Their victory is the victory of us all." He also said: "Five of the victims whose cases reached the Supreme Court of Canada in the last decade, and who have contributed so greatly to the clarification of our law, were Jehovah's witnesses."

Writing in the *Faculty of Law Review* (University of Toronto), another legal commentator described Jehovah's Witnesses as "the group most responsible for buttressing the privileges of citizenship." Also, Ivan

C. Rand, former judge of the Supreme Court of Canada, when describing some of our cases, remarked that "wolves fight in packs but the lion fights alone."

It is clear from these statements of recognized authorities that Jehovah's Witnesses, a minority fighting against great odds, have by their courageous stand made a major contribution to Canadian freedom. Their victory is a victory for the liberty of the people of Canada. Freedom of worship, press, speech and assembly have all been protected through the cases involving Jehovah's Witnesses.

Yes, Jehovah's Witnesses are grateful that their public appearances in court have, indeed, resulted in the giving of a witness and that thereby they have assisted in 'defending and legally establishing the good news' in Canada. (Mark 13:9; Phil. 1:7) But especially are the Witnesses grateful to the Great Lawgiver, Jehovah, who always supports his people. As King Hezekiah once said: "Be courageous and strong. . . . With him [the king of Assyria] there is an arm of flesh, but with us there is Jehovah our God to help us and to fight our battles."—2 Chron. 32:7, 8.

AHEAD, INTO THE 1960'S!

With all these legal battles out of the way, Canadian Christians enthusiastically moved into the decade of the 1960's. In April of 1960, Clayton Morrell, who had served as a pioneer, circuit overseer and member of the Toronto Bethel family for many years, was appointed as the new branch overseer. Manifesting a fine spirit and being a most approachable person, he was also a fine organizer who set about to continue the good work done till then. At that time the Bethel family had 44 members.

Across the land, there were six districts, 61 circuits and 805 congregations. That year, 1960, saw a peak of 38,382 active Kingdom proclaimers, giving a ratio of one Witness to every 465 persons in Canada.

By June 1960 there had been sufficient court decisions in our favor to open up our door-to-door work of witnessing with the Bible and literature offers once again in Quebec. Now that province was the same as the rest of Canada in this respect. The first all-French district assembly, held that summer at Verdun, was a happy milestone in the development of Christian activities in Quebec. More than 3,000 individuals were in attendance, about 1,000 of them being interested persons. What a change in conditions! The legal fight in Quebec was all but over. Priestly influence and opposition were waning. The French-speaking Kingdom publishers outnumbered the English-speaking Witnesses in that province. Growth in the largest city, Montreal, had been such that in 1959 there were seven Kingdom Halls to accommodate 22 congregations, and several other halls were being built throughout the province. Even Quebec City was to have its own Kingdom Hall of Jehovah's Witnesses.

On August 1, 1960, the first Italian congregation in Canada began functioning at Toronto. Though starting with only 40 publishers, it gave promise of rapid growth. Incidentally, today there are 33 Italian congregations across Canada, with more than 2,000 publishers. How pleasing it has been to see the development till now of 14 Spanish and Portuguese congregations, of 12 Greek congregations, and of one Chinese and one Korean congregation!

So, by 1960 all was poised for a decade of intense activity. For the most part, it was a period of peace and spiritual upbuilding.

KINGDOM MINISTRY SCHOOL

January 1, 1961, saw a significant event take place in Canada—the opening of the first Kingdom Ministry School at the branch office in Toronto. By the end of August of that year, 151 overseers and special pioneers had completed the course. Many were the remarks of appreciation for what had been learned. Some even spoke of actually changing their personalities during that four-week course. By 1971 there had been 152 Canadian classes of the Kingdom Ministry School, accommodating 3,370 students. Thus a large number of overseers and special pioneers received this fine training that more fully equipped them for responsible assignments in their local congregations during the 1970's.

Revised Kingdom Ministry School courses in the ensuing years have provided training for all the elders of Canada's congregations, 5,980 going through the latest course in 1977. Truly, since the inception of the Kingdom Ministry School in 1961, it has been a decided help in preparing many for further service in the congregations and in the field.

THE BLOOD TRANSFUSION ISSUE

Over the years in this country, the stand taken by Jehovah's Witnesses relative to the sanctity of blood has resulted in a great deal of unfavorable publicity and animosity. (Acts 15:28, 29) In fact, a climax to the rising tide of public resentment over our refusal to accept blood transfusions came in 1961. Hence, this seems to be an appropriate point in our narrative to discuss this issue in some detail.

Newspapers had used inflammatory headlines and misleading terminology with regard to the supposed efficacy of blood in matters of health and life. Since the 1950's, there had been such an adverse public reaction to our stand on blood that the hostility encountered at the doors when engaging in the Kingdom-preaching work could be compared only to that encountered in the United States during the 1940's, when so many persons challenged Jehovah's Witnesses with respect to our stand on flag saluting and war. Here in Canada, reason and respect gave way to very emotional outbursts and even threatening condemnations.

Going back to a case in 1956 will enable us to provide an example of the irresponsibility of the news media in inciting the public and failing to inform them adequately as to both sides of the matter. In Hamilton, a 17-year-old (and hence one at the legal age in Ontario to make her own decision in a matter of health and treatment) refused a blood transfusion ordered by doctors there. They had been treating her in Hamilton General Hospital for a condition that had been a problem since her birth. She had survived until then, even though it had been thought that she would not live long after her birth. So she made what she felt was a sensible decision for continued treatment without violating Christian principles.

From this simple exercise of a basic human right, what resulted? Well, what did a person see when he looked at the front page of the Toronto *Star* of February 17, 1956? A banner headline in letters that were two and a half inches high—and it read: "NEED GIRL, 17, DIE?" These massive letters—equal to those normally reserved for world war and other global catastrophes—were accompanied by the added heading, *"Jehovah['s] Witness Refuses Blood."* Indicating that this young person would die for refusing blood, the secondary headline in the same article called her a "Doomed Girl." The inclination to incite readers seemed evident in the opening paragraph of the article, in a phrase predicting that the patient's decision "is expected to spark a fresh wave of public indignation in this city."

Why was the *Star* so certain that this young person would die, speaking of "certain death" if she did not receive blood? It was because doctors at the hospital gave that impression. They told the reporter that even with the transfusion "the girl cannot possibly survive for more than two years." Combining remarks of that sort with inaccurate terminology (such as "life-giving" blood) was enough to incite people. The article went on to speak of the girl's life as "ebbing away."

But what happened to this witness of Jehovah? She was not given a transfusion—and she was released from the hospital in good health! But did the doctors then call the newspapers and say: 'We have wonderful news for you! The girl recovered! Everybody should know!'? No! They did not say a word when she was released. Should they have called the press? Well, how did the newspapers find out about the case in the first place?

News of this young person's recovery and release got into the newspapers because a curious reporter started making inquiries about her condition and discovered that she had been sent home. Commendably, the Toronto *Telegram* covered this matter and printed a picture of the smiling young Witness, describing her as "the picture of health." Why, she survives to this day! During the intervening years, she has gotten married and now has a family of her own.

We have taken considerable space to tell you about this one blood transfusion case. But it is so typical of most of them! Press reports customarily start with a big flare-up of front-page headlines and dire predictions. Then there are public outcries and hostility. Next comes a saner view, when unprejudiced medical and legal minds consider the facts. Finally, if at all, there appears a mild story on a back page of a newspaper telling about the patient's recovery and release from the hospital. There have been exceptions, of course, but this sequence of events has been repeated time after time.

TURNING THE TIDE

Among thinking people, however, something began to turn the tide. What? In several places there was publication of facts that gave the other side of the blood transfusion story. For instance, the October 1960 issue of the *Canadian Bar Journal* had carried a penetrating, well-researched article on the legal, medical and religious aspects of the blood transfusion issue. *Canadian Doctor* reprinted the article in a special supplement to its issue of December 1960, giving the material some 24 pages of space. This incisive article reached people in the legal and medical fields, individuals who could affect the situation favorably.

In the August 26, 1961, issue of *Maclean's,* a national magazine in Canada, appeared an article entitled "Three Blood Transfusions Out of Four Are More Likely to Harm Than to Heal." It was written by a medical doctor assisted by Sidney Katz, a journalist who specializes in articles on medicine. The abuses of unnecessary transfusions were exposed in this article, and it was of help to the public, who seemingly had been "brainwashed" to believe that transfusions of blood could *only* be helpful, never harmful, or even a risk.

The May 27, 1961, issue of the *Canadian Medical Association Journal* carried a noteworthy article by Doctors Max Minuck and Ronald S. Lambie. Entitled "Anesthesia and Surgery for Jehovah's Witnesses," it generally brought a halt to the attitude among many doctors that the Witnesses were an emotional religious group difficult to deal with and that problems arising in blood transfusion cases were the fault of 'these naïve people.' In the opening paragraph, the writers put the finger on who really was responsible for the emotional scenes at hospitals when a blood transfusion issue arose. They said that their discussion of cases "pointed up the fact that there exists considerable *confusion, emotional bias, intolerance,* and *ignorance* not only with regard to the tenets of the Witnesses' faith but also to the legal and ethical responsibilities involved in their medical treatment." (Italics ours.) Later in the article, Doctors Minuck and Lambie added that, in other cases where the doctor has to deal with less than ideal circumstances, there is a calm, objective and patient approach to the problem, the physician doing the best he can with these circumstances. Then they said:

"But so often in the case of the Jehovah's Witness[es] the surgical team becomes emotional, confused and irrational, because the patient's liability is religious rather than physical. Jehovah's Witnesses are not the only religious group which must refuse to accept certain aspects of accepted medical practice on religious grounds. Other groups such as Roman Catholics also must refuse some forms of medical treatment, and we accept their point of view. Similarly the Jehovah's Witness[es]' beliefs should be respected and tolerated."

Such reasoning is much more to the credit of the medical profession than the practice of some physicians who tell the patient one thing and then "slip in blood" on the premise that "what the patient doesn't know won't hurt him." Not only is that attitude unethical;

it is dishonest and disrespectful of the rights of others. Really, men who may be wrong in their diagnoses as much as 45 percent of the time, according to some authorities, ought to be more modest. As one balanced physician, Doctor Arthur Kelly (then secretary of the Canadian Medical Association), put it:

"Medical omniscience is a very rare commodity and the dicta of yesterday are being modified and superseded by the new knowledge of today. Let us not, in our pride, become arrogant and demand this subjection of our patient's will. I consider it preferable that certain individuals should die before their time than that we should undermine their ultimate right and duty of being the custodian of their own health."

In more recent years there has been a steadily improving relationship between doctor and patient in these matters involving the blood issue. Many have been the surgeons courageous enough to use their skills while respecting the sincerely held religious views of Witness patients. In the early 1970's, visits were made to the major hospitals in Toronto in order to reach a better understanding with the administrators and directors of these institutions. The visiting Witnesses were most respectfully received, as was the information submitted from medical journals showing what could be done without blood. The Watch Tower Society's booklet *Blood, Medicine and the Law of God* (copyrighted in 1961) was of great aid in reaching these men and many doctors. Interestingly, some physicians now ask for any additional information we can supply from medical journals.

Nowadays, the public seems to get aroused only in the cases of small children who are said by doctors to need a transfusion. But the record shows that Jehovah's Witnesses have not been wrong in their position. Usually, their children have survived despite the dire predictions of some medical men. On the other hand, in a number of cases, children have been seized and given blood transfusions following court orders. Sadly, however, after the forced transfusions 12 of these children have been returned dead to their grieving parents.

However, the material printed in legal, medical and other journals and that produced by the Watch Tower Society has had good results. Happily, too, in 1960 and 1963 it was possible to make successful appeals to the Supreme Court of Ontario to sustain Jehovah's Witnesses in their right to decide on medical treatment for themselves and their children.

SETTING MATTERS STRAIGHT

In 1970 the medical profession sought to get the government of Manitoba to give it added power to force blood transfusions on children of Jehovah's Witnesses. Opportunity was afforded to appear before a legislative committee to show the dangers of this proposed law from the standpoint of families and good medical practice. Two members of this committee had recently suffered the loss of a family member following blood transfusion. Brother Glen How's three-hour presentation before an attentive, very respectful legislative committee was followed by withdrawal of the legislation. A fine witness was given and much favorable publicity resulted.

In connection with a traffic accident in March of 1976, a coroner erroneously reported that one of our sisters died because of lack of a blood transfusion. But it was possible to have some dialogue with the Coroner of Ontario, an impartial man of sound mind. This, in turn, opened the way for Brother Glen How to address a meeting of all the coroners of Ontario. He was well received and a printed submission was provided for all those present. It has taken the pressure off this type of case, where a wrong idea is given to the public and Jehovah's Witnesses would be at the mercy of a prejudiced coroner and any unfavorable recommendations resulting from a coroner's inquest. A more objective view now prevails.

Similarly, due to a newspaper report that the Ontario College of Physicians and Surgeons was planning to adopt some new rulings in cases of Jehovah's Witnesses, a lengthy submission was made to the College in our behalf. This called for continuing respect for the patient's rights, the treating of the 'whole man' and for doctors to look further into the benefits of successful treatments without blood transfusion. A calming effect seems to have been produced by this submission. Nevertheless, continued vigilance appears necessary in this regard in Canada.

FAVORABLE NATIONAL PUBLICITY

In 1977, the Canadian Broadcasting Corporation's program "Access" presented a half-hour television show dealing mainly with the misrepresentation of the blood transfusion issue. During that program millions of viewers across Canada saw three individuals who were supposed to be "dead" according to predictions. But there they were, alive and well! They or their parents were able to explain why they took the steps they did to preserve life and maintain a good Christian conscience.

Then two physicians were interviewed. One of them, Doctor C. B. Baker of Toronto, was asked how many open-heart operations he had performed without blood. Baker responded:

"We've done a total of 37 now . . ."

"With no blood?"

"Right."

"Is it a poorer kind of treatment?"

"It's a better kind of treatment. . . . nurses often say in intensive care, 'Why don't you do all your patients without blood? They do so well.' "

"So, this isn't a Jehovah's Witness[es'] operation, then. It can really be applied to any patient?"

"And we apply it as much as possible to other people now, especially through our Jehovah's Witness experience. Now, that's taught us a great deal, that people that you don't have to use blood on will do better!"

Also interviewed during this program was Doctor Denton Cooley, the famed heart surgeon from the Texas Heart Institute in the United States. He told about some 20 years of open-heart surgery without blood, involving over 600 operations.

The public was impressed, indeed. Many Witnesses had individuals tell them of a definite change of viewpoint after seeing that program. Some persons even wrote to CBC expressing their appreciation for the removal of so much prejudice from the thinking of the public by means of this fair-minded presentation. The executive producer of the program later spoke of "the sheer weight of letters in response to our program on Jehovah's Witnesses," making it impossible to answer them all. He added: "I would say that your program may be counted as one of our most successful efforts of this season."

There has been the more recent countrywide distribution of the booklet *Jehovah's Witnesses and the Question of Blood* (copyrighted in 1977). Copies of it were provided for all doctors, hospital administrators, lawyers, judges and nurses. This reasonable appeal has brought favorable response. Many physicians, administrators and lawyers insisted on taking more time than requested by the visiting Witness in order to discuss at length the material in the booklet. It certainly appears that the distribution of this publication will add another sure foothold in our continuing battle to show respect for the sanctity of blood.

Much more could be said on this subject. However, we cannot close this part of the story of true worship in Canada without expressing appreciation for the many individual Witnesses, including elders, parents and family members who have stood firmly against many odds in order to obey God's law on blood. Often this has meant resisting taunts and pressures for hours while seriously ill and perhaps dying, or enduring insults and threats from nurses, doctors, judges and others. It has called for the spending of many sleepless nights endeavoring to comfort and support those making such a stand, or the making of countless telephone calls to try to find a favorable doctor who would take a serious case. Fellow believers have given of themselves in housing, feeding and otherwise caring for relatives of the sick in these cases. Nor can we overlook the faith of parents who have suffered the terrible experience of having a child taken away from them and given a forced blood transfusion. It would take a book to describe it all.

Neither would it be right to omit mentioning the kindnesses, thoughtfulness and love expressed by many nurses, doctors and judges in a number of blood transfusion cases in Canada. Their compassion will not be overlooked. And come what may, Jehovah's Witnesses in Canada will continue to look to their heavenly Father for aid as they stand fast in their determination to 'keep abstaining from blood.'—Acts 15:28, 29.

A TIME OF STRENGTHENING

We now resume our account of the 1960's. The year 1961 brought the United Worshipers District Assembly program to Canada with all its valuable instruction. The English sessions at Vancouver were attended by 28,952 persons, and 606 were baptized. During that noteworthy assembly the complete *New World Translation of the Holy Scriptures* in English was released, much to the delight of the delegates. At the French-speaking assembly in Ottawa, 2,242 were present, and 37 were baptized.

March 1961 brought another change at Bethel, for it was then that beloved Clayton Morrell died. Eugene Rosam, then teaching in the Kingdom Ministry School, was appointed the next branch overseer. He was to serve in that capacity for about four years.

In an effort to continue the work that had been

initiated in order to strengthen the congregations, Brother Rosam visited all circuit and district overseers in special meetings arranged at seven locations across Canada. A seventh district was formed. Also, efforts were made to try to build activity to a level that would allow for greater experience, advancement and development of abilities as Kingdom proclaimers. The results were good, and with the passing of time it was seen that a stronger organization was developing in Canada.

Due to a situation that had developed over the years, some men who were shouldering responsibility in connection with our assemblies were not being used or had ceased to be used as overseers in their own congregations. But this situation changed. All who served in such capacities at the 11 Courageous Ministers District Assemblies of 1962 (attended by 44,711 persons) and at all subsequent circuit and other assemblies had to be men who qualified as overseers in the local congregations where they lived. Appropriately, then, the desire was to have in positions of oversight only men who were qualified according to the Scriptures.

"FASTEST-GROWING" RELIGION

Jehovah was crowning our efforts with success. He was giving the increase. We knew that, but others observed it, too. For instance, the Windsor *Star* published an article by Maurice Jefferies from Ottawa on the results of the then latest Canadian Census (1961). It agreed with the newspaper headline, which read, "Jehovah's Witnesses Fastest in Growth." The brief note said: "CENSUS NOTE: The latest report on religious denominations shows that Jehovah's Witnesses make up the fastest-growing denomination in Canada. They doubled in numbers from 34,596 to 68,018 in the last decade."

The high figure the census showed had resulted from the way census takers look upon people as "church members." As with other religious groups, they counted children and those studying the Bible with Jehovah's Witnesses. Nevertheless, it was evident that Jehovah was blessing our work in disciple-making.

Of course, we still had our religious foes. The year 1963 saw the prosecution of three Roman Catholic priests as some die-hard remnants refused to accept the force of the Supreme Court decisions that assured freedom of speech and worship in Quebec. One priest was convicted on a charge of assault, while there were appeals in the other two cases.

REACHING REMOTE TERRITORIES

Although there had been increase and fine spiritual development, the mid-1960's still found us with 'plenty to do in the Lord's work.' (1 Cor. 15:58) In 1964, effort was made to reach some people at the extremities of our assigned territories. Many letters were written to Eskimos in the north, and 2,930 pieces of literature were sent to them. There were some encouraging results. Also, it was possible to fly to some isolated Indian villages in northern Manitoba. Then, too, endeavors were made to reach the people in the islands situated off the east coast of Canada, the French possessions of St. Pierre and Miquelon. Christians who went there as tourists were able to witness informally and thus bring cheer to some interested persons. Follow-up letters were sent to these to try to maintain their interest in Bible truth.

This work in remote territories has continued. Many flights and some canoe trips have been made into northern regions in recent years. Certain brothers have provided their own aircraft for the use of pioneers working these territories. Results have been exceptional. Hundreds upon hundreds of pieces of literature have been placed and Bible studies have been conducted by mail. Indians, Eskimos, fur trappers and others have not been missed by the zealous and determined disciple-makers witnessing in these areas.

After many attempts to get our work going on the islands of St. Pierre and Miquelon, in 1975 the Society's branch office in France was able to assign a special pioneer couple there. They have been diligent and faithful in a difficult assignment. But Jehovah has blessed them. Including themselves, there now are five Kingdom publishers there witnessing to the islanders, and meetings are being held regularly.

Speaking of remote regions, during the 1965 service year it was deemed fitting to transfer the Yukon Territory, though a part of Canada, to the Society's branch in Alaska. Access routes and geography indicated that this decision would be wise. Alaska could better look after the needs and the Kingdom-preaching work there.

Early in 1965, due to illness, it had become necessary for Eugene Rosam to leave Toronto Bethel and return to serving congregations in the field. Leo K. Greenlees was recalled from Brooklyn to look after the branch office in this country, taking up these duties in March of that year. But October of 1965 brought Kenneth A. Little back from his special training at Brooklyn to become the next branch overseer for Canada.

FINE PROGRESS IN QUEBEC

An excellent spirit had been displayed by those willing to make sacrifices in order to witness in remote territories. Yet, there also was a need elsewhere—and Canadian Christians did not hold back. Accordingly, for Quebec, 1968 was the year when many individuals and families responded to calls in the *Kingdom Ministry* (Canadian edition) and from district overseers to move from other parts of Canada to assist in getting the "good news" proclaimed in French.

For some years, in Montreal, the Society had operated, from time to time, a class for teaching French to special pioneers assigned to Quebec. During that time a unique textbook system had been devised by our brothers for teaching conversational French in a very short time. It concentrated on expressions Witnesses would need for their evangelizing work and participation in meetings. Successively it took a typical day in a person's life and covered the language he would need to get through that day. The instructors acted out these true-life incidents with assistants and required the student to use the French needed for each situation. Thus more emphasis was given to oral rather than written French so that students got their ideas and thoughts in that tongue. Daily, eight hours were spent studying the language, the length of the course varying from four to seven weeks. More than 1,000 individuals have thus been taught to speak French for their important work in Quebec. Among these are many Witnesses who have specifically moved to that province in order to declare the "good news" there.

This fine spirit of helpfulness was noteworthy. The *1970 Yearbook* mentioned our being 'thrilled by the progress of the preaching work in Quebec' with many more Witnesses to aid our work there. And what about results? Well, people were responding favorably. For example, one person read the book *The Truth That Leads to Eternal Life* in French in just three hours and declared that it was, indeed, the truth.

"PEACE ON EARTH" ASSEMBLY

As the decade of the 1960's drew to a close, we enjoyed a special occasion of spiritual feasting—the "Peace on Earth" International Assembly held at the Pacific National Exhibition Grounds in Vancouver. With an attendance of 65,609, that gathering set a new record for Canadian conventions. The *1970 Yearbook* reported:

"A person who wrote to the Vancouver *Sun* newspaper and whose comment was published in that newspaper said: 'I have been a resident of this city for over forty years and reside close to the P.N.E. Grounds. I would like to express my gratitude to the International Assembly of Jehovah's Witnesses. A more tidy, considerate crowd of people have never gathered in this area before.' . . .

"Delegates were on hand in Vancouver from thirty countries. One television cameraman who was taking pictures of the great crowds and the activity at the stadium said: 'What has impressed me most is the fact that not once have I been pushed or shoved in a crowd of over 50,000.'"

CHRISTIAN PUBLICATIONS APPRECIATED

Through the years, many individuals have expressed deep appreciation for our Bible-based publications. Some of this literature, such as the book *The Truth That Leads to Eternal Life,* has had a profound effect on the Kingdom-preaching work in this country. For example, consider the book *Did Man Get Here by Evolution or by Creation?* (copyrighted in 1967). It had a notable impact on the Canadian field. In the first full year after its release, more than 64,000 copies had been sent out to congregations in this country. The public really took to that book! Some circuit overseers and pioneers found it possible to place two and three copies at one door. A Roman Catholic priest and two young men came to the branch office in Toronto to obtain copies of this book. Seeing one on display, the priest cried out: "There it is! That's the book!" It seems that a visiting bishop from South Africa had strongly recommended that he get a copy of this thought-provoking publication.

Noteworthy, too, were the remarks made in the late 1960's by a newspaper editor in Trenton, Ontario. Commenting on our literature that was reaching his desk, he said:

"Among the interesting plethora of publications, some come regularly from the Watchtower Bible Society, better known as Jehovah's Witnesses. This is an organization which, by any man's standards, must command respect. The magazines are well written, with plenty of research, and quite apart from the special religious theories advanced, with which many may disagree, the society touches on every aspect of human life and the world God gave man. It upholds Biblical principles, and inculcates in its adherents the ideas of honor and purity, good citizenship, and impeccable behavior, which a world rent by the distortions of so-called freedom would do well to read.

"On morals and ethics, the ideas advanced are unimpeachable on any grounds. There are other good publications. We are thankful that the ideas that come in print, new or old, are predominantly sane. But all things considered, Watchtower publications stand head and shoulders above most for sanity of approach and thoroughness of discussion. There may be food for thought for others who are less successful in doing it, that the arguments for standards of conduct advanced in these publications always have a reason why. Arbitrary rules are being rejected nowadays. Here at least are publications which give solid reasons for any course of conduct. They are a refreshing tonic in the midst of a generation which has gone sex mad, and has sullied its publications with the same."

GROWTH IN THE 1970'S

As we entered the 1970's and reflected on the previous 90 years of light-bearing in this land, we were excited and thrilled. What would a full century of Kingdom-preaching produce? Expansion and increase continued into the 1970's.

The 1970 service year saw seven publisher peaks, six of them in succession. In December 1969, Canada went over the 45,000-publisher mark for the first time. The peak for the service year was a very encouraging 46,808 in May 1970.

But what about the years since then? Well, what has happened so far in the 1970's convinces us that Jehovah is pushing the work to a successful conclusion in this generation. Please note the increases indicated by the figures in this chart:

Year	Peak Pubs.	Congs.	Memorial Att.
1970	46,808	788	93,503
1971	49,204	790	97,518
1972	50,166	797	100,755
1973	52,773	863	104,707
1974	58,452	919	110,847
1975	60,759	979	114,744
1976	62,880	1,011	120,533
1977	63,090	1,033	120,958
1978	61,836	1,035	120,060

Increase is evident, is it not? Yes, indeed, and an excellent indication of growth potential is seen in the

Memorial attendance: Almost twice as many persons were present at that celebration in 1978 as there are Kingdom-proclaimers in Canada!

Where are all these people being found? Mainly, among ordinary individuals of humble heart who respond to the things taught in God's Word. Many of these persons have become disenchanted with the false religious systems that downgrade the Bible and its righteous principles. They recognize that Christendom provides only empty religious rituals week after week, with no hope-giving spiritual nourishment. In a report on Canada, the *1971 Yearbook* provides a good example of this, saying:

"One woman heard a radio announcement of a circuit assembly some seventy-five miles away. Although never having been in contact with Jehovah's witnesses before, she traveled by bus in order to attend it. At the assembly she obtained a copy of the *Truth* book and a Bible and met a pioneer who agreed to call on her. Arriving for the first Bible study, the pioneer brother found that the man of the house had distributed twenty-six Bibles to other persons in his vicinity who, like himself, were dissatisfied with the church. After the first Bible study the man stopped smoking; after the second study he destroyed all the images in his household and asked for subscriptions for *The Watchtower* and *Awake!* After the third study he asked how he could attend congregation meetings, even though they were held twenty-five miles away. In less than five months the man, his wife and their oldest son, aged fifteen, had commenced field service. They have already succeeded in interesting a second couple and their twelve children in the truth, with the second family now studying and attending congregation meetings, even though they have to travel forty-seven miles to do so. The first couple have offered to supply lumber for the construction of a Kingdom Hall in that area and are making progress in the way of the truth."

WHEN TELEVISION HONORS GOD

In recent years, television has furnished us with various opportunities to spread the "good news" here in Canada. For instance, consider what happened back in the year 1966. The *1967 Yearbook* reported: "The big event in Canada this year was the marvelous series of conventions. The brothers were truly blessed and thrilled with their 'God's Sons of Liberty' District Assemblies. The publicity given these assemblies from coast to coast was remarkable. Outstanding was the nationwide television network of forty-seven stations affiliated with the Canadian Broadcasting Company that carried an excellent program about Jehovah's witnesses across Canada. There was also another television network with eleven affiliated stations that put on a half-hour program about Jehovah's witnesses. So the Canadian public through the medium of television certainly learned something about the organization of Jehovah's witnesses."

Earlier in this account, we mentioned a fairly recent favorable television program on the blood transfusion issue. However, television has been used to honor Jehovah in yet another way—by the use of cable television programming. Cable TV companies that provide an antenna service to various communities also are required by law to operate a cable station and present programs from the people of the community. About five years ago, after we had used a Toronto cable television station in connection with some publicity for a summer district assembly, the management was so pleased with the quality of the shows that more of them were requested.

In this way, a series began that has continued to this day. However, from being presented on one station, use of these programs has increased until they have been used on as many as 54 stations across Canada. To date, about 200 programs have been produced under such titles as "Finding Joy in Training Children," "Alcoholism—An International Burden," "Women's Role in Religion," "Our Awesome Universe," and "Racial Differences—Do They Matter?" Most of these programs are in English, but some have also been done in Italian and French. The programs are a half hour in length, are in color and incorporate photographic slides and motion-picture film to supplement the discussion carried on in a "talk show" format. Many stations present these programs weekly.

People living in locked apartments are being reached by these presentations. Others, who would not talk to Jehovah's Witnesses in full view of their neighbors, will watch the programs in the privacy of their own homes. As a result, when we witness in those territories, some doors open now because minds have been opened. People acknowledge that the material on the shows has caused them to think. One other benefit of these programs is that a number of unbelieving mates, who formerly would not listen to their Christian marriage partners, will now watch the programs regularly. This has helped them to learn what Jehovah's Witnesses really believe. The result is that some have changed their attitudes and no longer oppose their marriage mates on matters such as attending meetings and assemblies and teaching Bible truths to their children.

OUR EXPANDED BRANCH FACILITIES

As the Kingdom-preaching and disciple-making activities of Canadian Christians increased, so did our need for branch office expansion. So, it was a happy day when approval was received from the Governing Body of Jehovah's Witnesses to build a two-story addition to our factory and a projection on the north side of the Toronto Bethel Home for a new Kingdom Hall. This was tangible evidence of the growth resulting from Jehovah's blessing. The factory space, in particular, was sorely needed. Construction began in November 1974 and was completed by June 1975. More than 2,000 visitors came through on tour on June 28, "open house" day. Brother N. H. Knorr gave the dedication talk on June 29, 1975.

The new Kingdom Hall, with its warm colors and tasteful platform, serves as an excellent meeting place for three congregations—English, Italian and Spanish. And we certainly were pleased to have the 16,000-square-foot (1,486-square-meter) factory addition. It seemed so large at the time! Within a year, however, we were using all the space and were in need of more! For that matter, we were getting crowded in the Bethel Home itself. What could we do?

The crowded situation, the growing noisiness of the 14-lane highway just outside our grounds, and the increasing pollution from the traffic all argued that another location was needed. Besides, we were unable to expand any further at the present location. So, once more there was rejoicing when, in February 1977, we received approval to relocate the Society's Toronto branch office.

With that, a search began. After about six months of searching and more months of negotiating, a suitable country property was found in a new community called Halton Hills, Ontario. Approval for building permits was requested in November of 1977.

Excitement truly was in the air! Many anxious volunteers could hardly wait for work to begin. Major heavy construction was to be done by professional contractors and builders, but much of the inside smaller and finishing work would be the product of the loving hands and energies of Jehovah's people.

While we do not put undue emphasis on material buildings, the new branch structure will indeed be a reminder of Jehovah's goodness. He has given the grand increases in Kingdom proclaimers in this country and this growth has made these enlarged quarters necessary.

SERVING TOGETHER FAITHFULLY

Today, in Canada, 66 brothers are in circuit work. Seven elders are serving as district overseers. Also, during the 1978 service year 1,671 individuals served as regular pioneers and 286 as special pioneers.

At this point it seems appropriate to tell you something about the full-time workers at the Society's branch office here in Canada. There are now 105 men and women making up the Toronto Bethel family. They average 37 years of age, there being many young ones among them. The average number of years spent in full-time service is 14. But, a more complete picture of the age and maturity of this group can be presented in this way: There are two members in their 80's, four in their 70's and 11 in their 60's. Jack Nathan has spent 54 years in various features of full-time work. In such service, Laura French has 51 years, Janet MacRae has 48 and Ralph Brodie has 45. Twenty-seven others have spent 20 years or more in full-time service. Seven members of the Canadian Bethel family profess to be anointed followers of Jesus Christ. Quite apparently, then, there is notable spiritual stability in this family of full-time workers.

Throughout this land a great body of devoted congregation publishers continue zealously proclaiming the "good news." How grand it is for all of us to serve together faithfully to the honor of our heavenly Father!

"VICTORIOUS FAITH" INTERNATIONAL CONVENTIONS

How timely it was that the 1978 assemblies were entitled "Victorious Faith" International Conventions! After nearly 100 years of Christian activity, there was plenty of evidence here in Canada that Jehovah *had* blessed us with a world-conquering faith. And there was no better place to see some of that evidence than at Montreal, in the Province of Quebec. Just imagine: From the days of burning hate in the form of official opposition determined to destroy us, we had now come to commendable cooperation on the part of city and provincial officials! We had come from a period when there were just a few Witnesses in the city to the time when an international convention was held with an attendance of 80,008! Times had changed!

What a delight it was to see the famed Olympic

Stadium filled with English-speaking delegates, to see the Velodrome with a capacity crowd of French-speaking delegates and to see the other buildings of the Olympic complex with their great numbers! There were sessions in seven languages.

Of course, the program was excellent. But, more than likely, the feature that will be longest remembered was the arrangement for visiting the people of Montreal in their homes on the Friday morning of the convention. Wherever a person went that day, he could see Jehovah's Witnesses making house calls or standing at busy corners, offering the literature specially prepared for the people and inviting them to the convention sessions. Newspaper reports were in agreement that Witnesses were everywhere. One radio broadcaster said that the people should listen to the Witnesses and take the literature offered. He added, 'When you do, do not think that you will be doing the Witnesses a favor. They are doing you a favor by bringing that information to you.' And the people of Montreal did respond well. They were friendly and receptive. Many of the older residents must have given thought to the difference now from some years ago: Witnesses who were once mobbed and imprisoned were now in this city as welcomed guests with complete freedom of worship! Christian faith had triumphed in the face of great odds.

Did that mean that the Witnesses would now take undue advantage of the changed circumstances? No, for the Montreal police remarked that the Witnesses were 'the best disciplined' group with which they had ever dealt. That discipline showed up in the good organization of the 110-acre (45-hectare) trailer and tent camp our brothers set up just a short distance from the Olympic Stadium. It housed 15,000 delegates for the five days.

A grand witness to the city was the result. More than 25 hours of TV and radio time and some 500 articles in newspapers gave much publicity to the event.

International conventions were also held in Winnipeg, Manitoba; Vancouver, British Columbia; and Edmonton, Alberta. Total attendance for the four conventions was 140,590. There were 1,226 baptized in symbol of their Christian dedication to God.

JEHOVAH BLESSES ENDURANCE IN RIGHT WORKS

The mere glimmer of spiritual light that came to Canada in the early 1880's has become as bright as midday. From one or two individuals, there are now almost 65,000 very active proclaimers of the "good

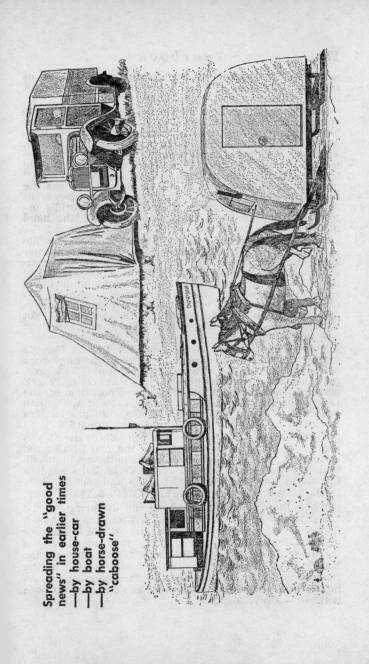

Spreading the "good
news" in earlier times
—by house-car
—by boat
—by horse-drawn
"caboose"

news" in this land. Why, just from the imposition of the ban in 1940 to 1977 the increase in the number of active Witnesses was over 902 percent!

Much more important than statistics, however, is the spiritual state of Canadian Christians. They have faced hardships, survived bans and endured public hostility. Few stood by their side in the matter of free speech. Yet today, informed people admit that Jehovah's Witnesses broke the grip of a clerical dictatorship in Quebec and that their legal battles had the effect of preserving the freedoms of all Canadians. As was the case with the early Christians, Canadian witnesses of Jehovah confidently carry on despite the world's objections. They do so in faith, knowing that "the hand of Jehovah" is with them.—Acts 11:21.

Of course, in this account it has not been possible to mention all the individuals who have given their strength and devoted their lives to the work of declaring the Kingdom message in Canada. Time would fail us to cite all the examples of self-sacrifice and devotion. In addition to all the workers yet here in Canada, 755 Canadians have been sent out as missionaries. Of these, 198 are still in foreign service, with another 130 yet in full-time work in this country. Those sent out have had fine privileges.

Indeed, the acts of Jehovah's Witnesses in Canada during the last 100 years constitute a thrilling story of individual faith. But what of the future? The prospects are excellent! In this country, there were 120,060 persons present for the 1978 commemoration of the Lord's Evening Meal. So, it seems evident that, with Jehovah's blessing, the ranks of Kingdom proclaimers will continue to grow in this land.—1 Cor. 3:6-9.

Therefore, we can happily say that the work of witnessing is being done here before the end of this old system of things. Disciple-making continues in obedience to Jesus' words. (Matt. 24:14; 28:19, 20) Canadian Christians have let their light shine and tens of thousands have responded favorably.—Matt. 5:14-16.

When the final chapter about the declaring of the "good news" in all the earth is written, may Jehovah find that the workers in this part of the field now called Canada have served well, thus meriting the bright smile of his approval and favor. Already, we Kingdom proclaimers in this land can testify to the truthfulness of the statement: "The blessing of Jehovah—that is what makes rich, and he adds no pain with it."—Prov. 10:22.

LEEWARD ISLANDS

In the sun-fleckered Caribbean Sea, sweeping from the American Virgin Islands to Dominica some 350 miles (560 kilometers) south of Puerto Rico, lie the Leeward Islands. For centuries these tiny gemlike dots—Anguilla, St. Martin, Saba, St. Eustatius, St. Kitts, Nevis, Antigua and Barbuda, Montserrat and Dominica—remained unchanged in life-style. Yet, the search for treasure and power had its impact. Even before the arrival of Europeans, roving bands of Carib Indians overran the native Arawaks.

The first foreign salute to a warship of the infant United States boomed from the Dutch island of St. Eustatius in 1776. Sunbathed Antigua, haven for Admiral Nelson's warships, was vital to British naval might in the Caribbean. And some say that it was limes from Montserrat, given to combat scurvy, that gave British seamen the nickname "limeys."

Various cultural backgrounds are evident in these islands. For instance, there are the Norman-Bretons of St. Barthélemy with their frilled white bonnets, hardly changed since the arrival of their early forefathers. Then, too, there are the Dutch, French and Irish dialects—all reminders of early settlers.

FINDING REAL TREASURES

Today little material booty can be found on any of these islands, once famous for their treasures. But found here are certainly a lot of "desirable things"—people with deep appreciation for the Kingdom message.—Hag. 2:7.

Unlike explorers of the past armed with cutlasses and rapiers, early in the twentieth century courageous Christians began serving here with "the sword of the spirit," God's Word, in hand. (Eph. 6:17) They themselves sought real treasures, true understanding of the Scriptures. But they did not hoard these spiritual things. They gladly shared them with others on these scattered islands.—Compare Matthew 12:35.

About the years 1914 to 1920 travel was difficult aboard the schooners and steamships plying these waters. Dangerous reefs and violent storms were numerous. Moreover, after travelers reached one of these islands, they might have had to remain on it for weeks, even months, before a returning ship allowed them to continue their journey.

Despite these difficulties, however, a few persons in the Leeward Islands came in touch with the Kingdom message about 1914. How? Either through personal contact with Bible Students (as Jehovah's Witnesses then were known), by receiving literature sent here, or by hearing such individuals as E. J. Coward give a witness in Barbados and Trinidad. W. R. Roch of Antigua recalls hearing Brother Coward speak (on the 'second advent of Christ') in the courthouse at Roseau, Dominica, back in 1914.

THE TRUTH REACHES MONTSERRAT

In a similar manner, Bible truth penetrated Montserrat, commonly called the Emerald Island because of the strong influence of its Irish settlers. It was on a street corner in Plymouth, capital of Montserrat, that James Lynch, a medical-shop keeper, could be heard in 1916 giving talks on 'Christ's second advent.' Those who knew Lynch say that he was then over 60 years of age. About 1916, he developed a group, mainly of young men, with whom he studied the Bible in his home.

In 1919, the International Bible Students held a convention in Barbados. Among those present was W. H. Rock, then 19 and the only delegate from Montserrat. At that gathering, he met W. R. Brown and invited him to visit the island. Brother Brown did so with his new bride the very next year. Describing that visit, Brown wrote in later years: "In 1920 my wife and I were married, but there was work to be done. Two days after our wedding we left Trinidad for Montserrat with the Photo-Drama of Creation. We witnessed in Dominica, Barbados and Grenada, then returned to Trinidad. It was a joyful honeymoon in Jehovah's service."

The Photo-Drama of Creation (a photographic presentation regarding God's purpose for the earth and man) was shown at a number of locations in Montserrat during the visit of Brother Brown and his wife. Edward Edgecombe, recently deceased, recalled one of these showings and said: "The lantern slides were excellently arranged and very encouraging to everyone. All were impressed with Brother Brown's resource of facts and his ability to present them so clearly." Brother Brown and his wife were quite busy during the visit, moving about and sharing the truth with many.

A START IN DOMINICA

On the way back to Trinidad in 1920, the Browns stopped in Dominica. Brother Brown had been there in 1915 and had placed volumes of *Studies in the Scriptures* with a businessman by the name of De Boin.

He, in turn, passed them on to E. F. Dumas. Mr. Dumas read the books. His interest was aroused and he wrote the Watch Tower Society for a supply of literature to pass on to businessmen, the clergy and others. In the meantime, he wrote Brother Brown, inviting him to visit Dominica. The Browns stopped there in 1920 and the Photo-Drama was shown in a small hall.

Two years later, Brother Brown wrote to J. F. Rutherford, then president of the Society, saying: "By Jehovah's help I have given the witness throughout the majority of the Caribbean islands and made disciples in many. Should I go over them again?" The reply he received said: "Proceed to Sierra Leone, West Africa, with wife and child." So, early in 1923, Brother Brown and family embarked from Trinidad on the *SS Orange Nassau*, heading for their new home in West Africa, where he came to be known as "Bible Brown."

Brother Brown's zeal in declaring the Kingdom message in the islands had helped many. In the smaller islands of the Caribbean, first in Montserrat and then in Dominica, some had made joyful discoveries. They had found real spiritual treasures. But would they put these valuable things to good use and thus realize true blessings from their newfound spiritual wealth?

PUT TO THE TEST

A period of testing began here in about 1922. Some who had embraced Bible truth 'buried their talents,' so to speak, whereas others saw the need to invest. (Compare Matthew 25:14-30.) In Montserrat a division developed and all except Brother James Lynch followed a new group. It took real courage and strong faith to remain with the true Christian congregation, but Brother Lynch did so. He served faithfully until finishing his earthly course in 1926 at the age of 75.

Another 10 years would pass before the Kingdom message would again reach the shores of Montserrat. In the meantime, what was happening elsewhere in the Leeward Islands?

DEVELOPMENTS IN DOMINICA

First of all, let us see what was happening to the seeds of truth that had been planted in Dominica. It might be said that this is an island of "liquid sunshine," for it has quite an unusual rainfall. In sealevel Roseau there is an annual average of 75 to 80 inches (190 to 200 centimeters), but this increases greatly with the rise in elevation. For instance, the yearly average is 360 inches (910 centimeters) at Fresh Water Lake, and the amount is undetermined

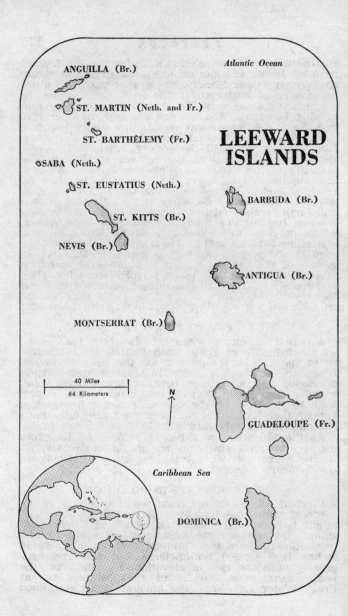

Atlantic Ocean

ANGUILLA (Br.)

ST. MARTIN (Neth. and Fr.)

ST. BARTHÉLEMY (Fr.)

SABA (Neth.)

ST. EUSTATIUS (Neth.)

ST. KITTS (Br.)

NEVIS (Br.)

BARBUDA (Br.)

ANTIGUA (Br.)

MONTSERRAT (Br.)

**LEEWARD
ISLANDS**

40 Miles

64 Kilometers

N

GUADELOUPE (Fr.)

Caribbean Sea

DOMINICA (Br.)

on the highest slopes of Mount Diablotin, which rises to 4,747 feet (1,447 meters). But the precious waters of truth also began flowing in Dominica despite determined efforts to divert them.

Lennard Lee recalls the early 1930's and the struggle to survive the bitter persecution leveled against true Christians in Dominica. Lee himself observed E. F. Dumas preaching on the street in Roseau, but he recalls that many treated Dumas very unkindly, even pinning donkey tails on him and throwing stones at him. A group of lawyers and other influential persons, including the jail keeper, formed what was called the Action Guild. They would come on the scene and warn Dumas that he would "get something" if he even mentioned the bishop's name while preaching on the street. They threateningly waved sticks in Dumas' face. Seeing the injustice of these actions, Lee investigated matters, and this led to his learning the truth.

In those days, Lee was working as a carpenter in the construction of a convent school. At certain times of the day the workmen were expected to make the sign of the cross. Although Lee did not then know all the reasons why this was wrong, he felt that it was improper and refused to do it. This cost him his job but strengthened his determination to stick to true Christianity regardless of the opposition he encountered.

Of course, the priests were bitter toward anyone breaking away from their control. This animosity was displayed in various ways. For instance, Lennard Lee recalls that on one occasion Mr. Dumas was having a house moved from one location to another. Men had been hired for this work, but a priest met them and ordered them to leave the job. Since they were Catholics, they obeyed him—and left the house right in the middle of the street! There it remained for several days until Dumas could get other men to finish the job of moving it.

In time, the town council passed a law requiring that all who desired to preach on the streets of Roseau had to obtain a license. Dumas refused. He was arrested while preaching and, upon conviction, had to spend two days in jail. As opposition to the Kingdom-preaching work continued, local witnesses of Jehovah got in touch with the Watch Tower Society's branch office in Trinidad and were told that someone would be visiting Dominica that year. So it was that in 1934, as promised, a pioneer named Waldo Roberts arrived. In Roseau he found a group of 10 persons endeavoring to serve Jehovah. This visit resulted in the establishment of the first company (congregation) of Jehovah's people in Dominica.

Just how active were these individuals in declaring the "good news"? Well, during what was called the "Kingdom Praise Period" (September 29–October 7, 1934) a report showed that there were 10 workers who gave 463 testimonies during 110 hours of field service. They placed 5 books and 145 booklets with those to whom they gave a witness. This, incidentally, was in addition to Brother Roberts' personal service report. That nine-day period was a happy one, as it was marked by the first organized house-to-house witnessing work ever done in Dominica.

During that period, there was also a small group meeting for Bible study in La Roche, on the east coast of the island. So the waters of truth were becoming more than a mere trickle in Dominica. They were, in effect, welling up in readiness so that they might filter into all parts of the island.

TRUTH SPREADS TO ANTIGUA

At this point, we are going to do a little more island-hopping. So, for orientation, why not glance at the map accompanying our story? From Dominica look about 100 miles (160 kilometers) to the north. Skip over Guadeloupe and you should have little trouble finding Antigua. That is our next stop.

Around the mid-1930's, the "good news" began to reach other islands in the Leewards. This was because zealous Kingdom proclaimers in Barbados and Trinidad were willing to move to new territories, one of these areas being Antigua.

Unlike Dominica, Antigua is affected by prolonged droughts. Why? Because it is almost mountainless, which is a factor contributing to an annual rainfall of only 42 inches (107 centimeters).

Compared with Dominica, where Catholicism is so strong, Antigua has a variety of Christendom's leading religions. Predominant among these was the Anglican religion, although Methodists, Moravians, Roman Catholics and others came on the scene with the passing of time. But how did true Christianity reach this island?

In 1934, William Byam, an Antiguan who had learned the truth in Trinidad, returned to Antigua to spread the "good news" on the island as a pioneer. Apparently, two Christian women from Trinidad also came to Antigua during that year. Their combined annual report indicates that they were quite busy in Jehovah's service. They reported 1,008 hours in field service, 2,720 testimonies, the placement of many publications, as well as the holding of 20 congregation meetings. Reports of Kingdom-preaching activity in Antigua were received for four years thereafter, but then the work ceased as far as the records are concerned.

Nevertheless, some Witnesses today vividly recall that Brother Byam presented fiery truths from God's Word on the street corners of St. John's, the capital. For instance, Brother Donald Meade recalls: "Byam preached about the priests and the clergy and especially about their dress. He called them 'long-gown men.' I remember that he discouraged people from giving support to the clergy." Brother William Tonge, now deceased, once reported that Byam "used to come to Pigotts every Tuesday and give lectures in the pasture."

William Byam was a familiar figure walking from village to village, with a lantern in hand, giving sermons. Byam died in 1939, and it appears that for some time thereafter the only person declaring the "good news" in Antigua was Brother Tonge, although he did not report any activity to the Society's branch office in Trinidad. Nonetheless, seeds of truth had been planted and they awaited further watering.—1 Cor. 3:6.

GETTING STARTED IN ST. KITTS AND NEVIS

Now, please take another look at our map. Some miles to the west of Antigua are the islands of St. Kitts and Nevis. It was during the 1930's and the early 1940's that our work got off to a start in these islands.

During the early 1930's the "good news" spread to St. Kitts, the mother island of the Caribbees, which had its first permanent English settlement in 1624. About 1932 a Dutch couple named Bennett visited the island and witnessed briefly, placing some Christian publications with the inhabitants. It was also in 1932 that Trinidadian E. P. Roberts (brother of Waldo Roberts, mentioned earlier) arrived in St. Kitts.

Some door-to-door witnessing work was carried on in St. Kitts in the 1930's, and good results were forthcoming. Several individuals were baptized before Roberts left for Montserrat in 1936. After his departure, a group met for Bible study in the home of Edwin Saunders in Irish Town.

The Saunders family and Adina Day got our work off to a start in Nevis between 1939 and 1940. At that time there were four or five Kingdom publishers on that island.

TRUTH RINGS OUT!

Indeed, Scriptural truth was spreading in the Leeward Islands during the 1930's. And, certainly, Jehovah

was prospering our efforts to declare the "good news."
But, to round out our review of that decade, we would
like to tell you about a particularly effective feature
of our service to Jehovah.

In 1934 a new means of reaching the public was introduced in the Leeward Islands. At the time, the
Watch Tower Society was producing recorded Bible
lectures to be played on portable transcription machines. These recordings were used with great benefit
here, for the people were not particularly inclined to
read but were very eager to listen. So, much interest
was aroused.

Before long, we were also using portable phonographs in our field service, even as Jehovah's people
were using them elsewhere. The relatively short four-
and-a-half-minute recorded Bible talks that were played
on these machines were received by many with interest and appreciation. We would call at the doors and
people would invite us into their homes, where they
could listen without a feeling of uneasiness, particularly in Catholic Dominica where the priests ruled by
fear and threat over a predominantly illiterate populace.

The transcription machine served a good purpose at
public gatherings. For instance, Sister Beatrice Pond,
who then worked as a domestic servant in Plymouth,
Montserrat, recalls open-air meetings in Salem. "The
people would come out and hear and draw near," she
recalls, adding: "Some would say, 'You had better
listen,' and others would remark, 'Listen to that!'"

ANOTHER KIND OF REACTION

We must admit, however, that some brothers were
not always very tactful in using the transcription machine. For instance, consider what happened back in
June 1936 in Roseau, Dominica, during the Corpus
Christi celebration.

There was a parade in the streets and some brothers
thought that this would afford a good opportunity to
give a witness. Hence, they set up the transcription
machine on the second-floor veranda of a home and
began playing their record that dealt with the "Holy
Year." That recording really infuriated the crowd! A
woman left the procession, ran up the stairs and tore
down the loudspeaker, throwing it to the ground.

At that, a large mass of people charged the iron
gates at the front of the building. A few brothers
managed to shove large wooden shipping crates against
the gates and thus hold off the crowd temporarily. In
the meantime, the Witnesses fled to the backyard.
But they did not succeed in evading the mob. One

brother recalls: "We fought them and, of course, great tumult broke out."

Although the bishop urged the police to arrest the brothers, the officers said that they could not do that because the Witnesses were on their own property. Because of this unfortunate incident, however, there was much opposition to the witness work for some time thereafter. In fact, the brothers even experienced stoning while going to meetings.

RESPONDING TO THE RING OF TRUTH

In general, however, the Bible talks recorded by the then president of the Watch Tower Society, J. F. Rutherford, were well received by the people. In fact, this was the way some of them first heard the "good news."

To illustrate: Charles Payne, a dusky native with a thick Irish brogue, first came in touch with the Kingdom message as it was being broadcast from a sound car in Montserrat back in the year 1936. A hard-working, hard-drinking mountain man who took pride in his carpentry, Payne hewed majestic cedars by hand and used the wood to make fine furniture for the more wealthy inhabitants of the island. Then a man of 31 and the father of two, he was the foreman of a construction group that was building a school in the northern part of Montserrat. He had discovered the Society's book *Deliverance* in the kitchen of a neighbor and had taken it home to read. During a lunch-hour discussion on the job, a woman told Payne: "A man is preachin' at the pierhead and payin' folks two and six pence to join his religion."

Payne had the opportunity to investigate this unusual report when E. P. Roberts called at his home while in the witness work. After obtaining a book, Payne asked Roberts if he was the man paying two and six pence to anyone who would join his religion. The mistaken report was corrected, an explanation of our work followed, and this led to Scriptural discussions with the Payne family.

Charles Payne was a lay reader and Sunday-school superintendent in the Anglican Church. Immediately, he began speaking about his newfound spiritual treasure. This was to cause him some difficulties, but he rode these out with firm determination.

Payne had entered into a contract to build a communion rail for one of the churches in Antigua. He was to be paid according to stages of completion. However, because of Payne's zealous preaching, two Anglican priests sought to take the work away from him. They went to see Payne and, during the discussion, one of them said that he had received the second payment for his work. At this, Payne called the priest a liar and ordered both of them out of his yard.

Because of this, one of the priests brought a court action against Payne. In court, this priest insisted on being called "Reverend," but Payne contended that the man was no reverend to him. The judge threatened to charge Payne with contempt of court if he did not refer to the priest as "Reverend."

Payne answered: "I am in your hands to do with me what you like. But he is no reverend to me. If he wants 'Rector,' he can get it, but not 'Reverend.'"

Finally, the cleric said, "Go ahead, speak." Payne was charged two guineas and costs, but in the end he was paid for building the communion rail as agreed. Sometime later, in the year 1939, Charles Payne and his wife were baptized in symbol of their dedication to Jehovah God.

PERSEVERING DURING THE WAR YEARS

World War II brought special problems to Kingdom proclaimers in the Leewards. During the years of that conflict, there was a ban on the importation of the Watch Tower Society's literature, and it was greatly felt. Nevertheless, Jehovah's people in this part of the world kept busy with the publications they could obtain. They also used the transcription machine and phonographs wherever possible.

In St. Kitts, publications shipped to the brothers were held in the government warehouse. On March 20, 1944, these cartons containing the books *Children* and *The New World,* as well as the Watchtower edition of the American Standard Version Bible, were taken to a sugar factory. For what purpose? Instructions were given to burn the literature in the boiler furnace.

However, Brothers Franklin Nisbett and Arthur Henry were working in the factory at the time. Someone excitedly ran up to them and said: "Some of Jehovah's Witnesses' books are in the boiler room and it looks like they are going to burn them this morning!"

The two brothers left their work and managed to save almost a full carton of the American Standard Bibles and enough books for the congregation. In fact, many workers carried books home so that, despite efforts to destroy the literature, some did get into the hands of the people.

In Montserrat, where the ban also was in effect, two Kingdom publishers were doing what they could and were keeping in touch with the Society despite mailing difficulties. In Dominica, during the 1944 service year three Kingdom publishers spent 74 hours in field service and placed 94 publications, besides making a few return visits. True, the brothers in Dominica, St. Kitts and Antigua were in need of some spiritual assistance. Nevertheless, they persevered in Christian activity and sought to please Jehovah during those difficult war years.

NEEDED—A HARD FIGHT FOR THE FAITH

Why was spiritual assistance so vital? Because internal problems had developed in certain congregations. Indeed, faithful servants of Jehovah had to put up a "hard fight for the faith."—Jude 3.

Some would not associate with the congregation in St. Kitts, for example, because of the conduct of the company servant (presiding overseer). He was replaced, but divisive factions continued and three groups met separately. In time, Franklin Nisbett was appointed as company servant, but help still was needed.

With the passing of time the internal problems in St. Kitts came to an end. In the meantime, however, it was not easy to remain faithful and to continue serving Jehovah. Brother Arthur Henry of St. Kitts says that the words of Psalm 72:4 enabled him to stick with the congregation of God's people during those times of trial. According to the *Authorized Version* he then used, this text reads: "He shall judge the poor of the people . . . and shall break in pieces the oppressor."

DISSENSION IN DOMINICA

In Dominica, the brothers in general were not sharing in the door-to-door witnessing work. At that time, Phillip C. Pemberton was pioneering in Roseau, and he and Lennard Lee were having differences with each other and with E. F. Dumas. All three were holding meetings in their respective homes and were sending the Society critical letters about one another. However, the Society would write back encouraging them to stop quarreling and get on with the Kingdom work.

Many of the brothers would remain at home because of these petty differences, although they witnessed in an unusual way. They wrote scriptures on blackboards posted at the front of their homes. Passersby could read these texts. This practice continued for some years, but was finally discontinued.

Brother Hodge Dominique recalls that there were arguments at times, and on at least one occasion there was no service meeting because of the strife. When

Dumas left for the United States in 1943, Brother Lee
cared for congregational matters. Recalling what happened, he states:

"Well, I saw in *The Watchtower* that others were
going from house to house. So I said to the brothers,
'We have only a gathering like other denominations
unless we go out and do the work.' They refused, so
I left and placed another brother in charge and went
up to La Roche to encourage them also. But they would
not go along with the idea of witnessing from house
to house.

"When Dumas returned, he said that he understood
I had started the house-to-house work, and maintained
that I was threatening his position. We discussed the
matter and decided that I was to do the door-to-door
work and that the others in the group were not to
be bothered."

Like other Witnesses, Brother Lee was stoned and
beaten many times while witnessing in small Catholic
villages around Roseau. About this time, his sister-in-
law died, apparently of grief, just three weeks after
being excommunicated from the Catholic Church for
refusing to put Brother Lee out of her home when she
was told to do so by a priest. Brother Lee's wife,
Lictina, was thrown out of her parents' home because
she refused to stop associating with Jehovah's people.
Nevertheless, Christian activity continued in Dominica.

At that time, the brothers in Roseau were meeting
at a hall in a building owned by E. F. Dumas. He was
opposed to witnessing from house to house. Also, he
resented the fact that the Society had not upheld him
in connection with the use of the transcription machine
in the way that had provoked the riot in 1936.

In June 1947, Joshua W. Steelman came to Roseau
as a servant to the brethren (now called a circuit
overseer). As a result of that visit, the local congregation was reorganized for better Kingdom service. Two
months after Brother Steelman's visit, the Witnesses
were forced to leave the building owned by E. F.
Dumas, and they began meeting in the home of Brother
Lee.

Dumas later wrote tracts justifying himself and
mailed these to the brothers and the Society. In February 1948, Dumas was disfellowshiped from the Christian congregation. He died in 1957.

OUR ACTIVITIES IN ANTIGUA

Now, let us see what had been occurring in Antigua
and its ward island of Barbuda, centers of British slave
trade in the early nineteenth century. When E. P.

Roberts arrived on the island in 1939, he found Brother Byam still preaching on the streets, but with little fruitage resulting from his efforts.

In time, Roberts, who had demonstrated much unselfish zeal in declaring the "good news," started to misuse the precious things entrusted to him. For some years, he kept the brothers in fear, teaching that they were "gatherers of wood and drawers of water" and making them think that they should slave for him because he professed to be an anointed follower of Jesus Christ. (Josh. 9:23) He even referred to himself as a "prophet." Roberts was disfellowshiped in 1948, but by Jehovah's great mercy he was accepted back into fellowship with Jehovah's people in January 1962.

From this brief résumé, it is evident that conditions were not very favorable to the advancement of Kingdom interests when Joshua W. Steelman visited Antigua as a servant to the brethren from July 2 to 5, 1947. However, in St. John's he worked closely with the brothers in the field service, and he gave a spiritually upbuilding service talk before departing. At that time, Brother Steelman also visited congregations elsewhere in the Leewards.

From May 28 to 30, 1948, a fine assembly was held in St. John's, Antigua. Five visiting brothers, along with one or two local speakers, put on the entire assembly program. Four individuals were baptized at that gathering. And a bicycle parade had been put on to advertise the public address "The Coming Gladness of All Mankind." How pleased the brothers were to see 184 persons in attendance for that public talk! Indeed, the hearts of Jehovah's people were stirred by the good things heard at that assembly.

True, the brothers in Antigua had been shaken somewhat by the trials they had endured. But, in the final analysis, their faith had been strengthened. In 1947 there were 26 active publishers in the St. John's congregation. That year, 67 persons attended the Lord's Evening Meal. However, in the year 1948, Memorial attendance was up to 91 at St. John's.

'NEW ERA' DAWNS

With the coming of 1949, a 'new era' dawned in the Leewards. Emphasis began to be placed on spiritual assistance and training of Kingdom proclaimers. For instance, in February 1949 the first circuit assembly was held in Roseau, Dominica. Hodge Dominique (then the presiding overseer there), along with Peter Brown and A. E. Tharp from Trinidad, put on the entire assembly program. All present were elated over the fact that 76 persons attended the public talk despite heavy rains. Two individuals were immersed in symbol of their dedication to Jehovah God. Yes, the entire assembly was a success, and the brothers thanked Jehovah for his loving direction and the spiritual development then in evidence.

Lionel Williams, a beekeeper from Barbados, came to Dominica in 1948. The brothers really appreciated his help in connection with the service meetings and the Theocratic School. When B. H. Berry visited the island as a circuit overseer, Brother Williams accompanied him on an 18-mile (29-kilometer) journey over jungle-like paths and across rivers to organize a group of persons meeting at La Roche.

So, during the late 1940's, there were fine developments in the work of Kingdom proclamation in the Leewards. Truly, a 'new era' had dawned. But before that decade ran out, the preaching work in these islands was bolstered by yet another development.

AID FROM GILEAD

Additional wielders of 'the sword of the spirit, God's word,' began to enter the Leewards in 1949 after graduating from the Watchtower Bible School of Gilead. (Eph. 6:17) In fact, 1949 was a peak year for the entry of Gilead-trained missionaries into these islands. Brother and Sister E. F. Krueger and Brother and Sister L. M. Frazier arrived in St. Kitts, while Brother and Sister Wilfred A. Howlett went to Antigua.

What happy days those were! A typical reception was the one received by Brother and Sister Howlett upon their arrival in Antigua by steamer. Why, the whole congregation was waiting on the pier the morning they arrived, and they were greeted by smiling faces and open arms! In St. Kitts, the Kruegers and Fraziers found a fairly well-organized group of 15 dedicated Kingdom publishers. However, permission to enter the island had not been obtained from the local officials without difficulty. Strong opposition had come from the St. Kitts council members, many of whom were Catholics. Robert Bradshaw, then union representative on the council, argued that if others were allowed into the island, these missionaries should also be granted entry. Until his death in 1978, Mr. Bradshaw, who was premier of the state, was favorable toward the missionaries.

The goals of the new arrivals were to give personal training to the brothers in the Kingdom-preaching work and to help them congregationally. Hence, aid from Gilead was sure to produce some good results.

NEW "SAILORS" IN THESE WATERS

Buccaneers once roamed these waters preying on Spanish ships. It is said that these buccaneers originated on the island of Tortuga but had been former settlers of St. Kitts who had fled from the French. In fact, the name "buccaneer" seems to have originated with the seafarers' custom of roasting meat over a fire or *boucaner* and selling the meat to passing voyagers. Different from the buccaneers of old, however, was a new type of "sailor" that appeared in these waters late in 1949. With these men came an exciting method of spreading the "good news" to the islanders.

On November 18, 1949, the Society's 65-foot (20-meter) schooner *Sibia* set sail from St. Thomas and headed for St. Martin in the Leewards. On board were four preachers of the "good news"—Gust Maki, Ronald Parkin, Arthur Worsley and Stanley Carter. And, of course, the boat was loaded with many cartons of Bibles and Christian literature.

Details gleaned from the diary of Brother Parkin help us to relive the *Sibia's* first voyage. Come aboard!

"We reach St. Martin on the evening of November 19, landing at the French port of Marigot. This is a French and Dutch island. Some young folks, burning with curiosity, meet us upon arrival and we are very happy that they can speak English. They listen to the Kingdom message attentively. Surprisingly, we learn that there already is one of Jehovah's Witnesses on this island. We meet him four days later.

"He is George Manuel, who comes to the dock to greet us and spends the entire day with us in the field service. The people are hospitable and we enjoy some fine discussions. But the Seventh-day Adventist preacher certainly is not pleased with our presence.

"On November 25, we meet a Mr. Duchene, who shows great interest in the Kingdom work. Others, too, are interested and this causes quite a stir in the town. On the evening of November 27, Brother Carter gives an open-air public talk, and around 200 people attend. We answer many questions afterwards.

"On November 29, Brother Parkin gives a public talk out of doors, and around 250 persons come to listen. In an area called Columbier Brother Worsley gives a public talk the next day. A Mr. Flemming has let us use his yard for this purpose and furious priests threaten to excommunicate him. And that Seventh-day Adventist preacher has really become angry. Things are getting 'warmer' as we give more public talks, and the priest begins to warn his 'flock' at morning Mass. But with the people the situation remains the same. They are still listening to the Kingdom message.

"By December 5 we have come to the Dutch side of the island, arriving at Philipsburg. We have to get government permission to give public talks, but our activities go well. After about two weeks we return to Marigot and hold some Bible studies.

"On December 25, we set sail for the British island of Anguilla. There is no transportation on the island at this time; so we must walk from place to place. But our efforts are rewarded as we spread the Kingdom

The "Sibia," a schooner once used to spread the "good news" throughout the Leewards and elsewhere in the Caribbean

message and place Christian publications. At Sandy Ground Village, Brother Carter gives a talk and around 100 persons attend.

"On December 31, we head back to Marigot, where we refuel. Then, it is back to Anguilla for more witnessing. By January 11 we have returned to Marigot, and the next day we leave the island of St. Martin behind, but with pleasant memories of our first witnessing voyage in the Leewards."

GREATER USE OF BOATS

When the Watch Tower Society produced Bible-based motion pictures, the brothers manning the *Sibia* showed the films in various places. At times, the only way to run the projector was to use the boat's portable generator. So the vessel was pressed into service in more than one way.

Those early days of witnessing by boat were filled with satisfying experiences as sheeplike ones were sought in these outlying islands. Yes, those days "were full of missionary work and joys of Jehovah's service," recalls Ronald Parkin. There were "blessings that cannot be described in words," he says, exclaiming: "How good Jehovah is to let us have a share in this great harvest work!"

The Society's boat *Light* eventually replaced the *Sibia*. This later vessel plied the Caribbean waters in a circuit including the Leewards and other southern islands until the year 1957. And, what were some of the developments during those years?

Well, in the early 1950's a nucleus of Jehovah's people had its start at South Hill, Anguilla, at the home of Eugene Bradley. In 1957, two special pioneers were sent elsewhere on the island—to a place called Stoney Ground. The Kingdom work continued to make advancement, and today there are 14 Kingdom proclaimers associated with the congregation in Anguilla.

It was on November 18, 1951, that the first baptism of a dedicated Christian took place in St. Martin. Two brothers were then immersed, George Dormoy and Leonce Boirard, the harbor master. Today there are two congregations with 100 Kingdom proclaimers serving in St. Martin.

So, partly due to the use of boats in spreading the "good news," there has been Christian progress in the Leewards. As we look back to the days when the vessels *Sibia* and *Light* were used extensively in the Caribbean, we have some vivid recollections. For example, in those days the brothers used various methods to attract an audience. E. F. Krueger, deceased, once related how he would stand on the street playing his mouth organ until a good crowd gathered. Then he would take out his Bible and start giving a talk.

Of course, there were some humorous incidents too. Brother Parkin recalls: "I was giving a talk under a tree with a big gas lamp overhead. During the talk a rat chased another animal up the tree and they both dropped at my feet fighting. Then, Whoosh! They were gone, and after them half of the young people in the audience."

At that time, the Society's branch office in Trinidad was supervising the disciple-making work in the Leewards. So we feel justified in telling you what happened in conjunction with a talk to be given by one of the boat's crewmen, Brother Parkin, at a public square in Trinidad. His subject was "Hell Is a Scare." However, the newspapers announced it as "Hell Is a *Square*." Well, 300 persons showed up for the discourse. Perhaps some were curious about the *shape* of hell. Was it really *square?*

OUR WORK GROWS

The Kingdom-preaching and disciple-making work was growing in the Leewards during the early 1950's. For instance, it was progressing in St. Kitts, that fertile island noted for its sugar and molasses production. In fact, the growth was sufficient to warrant the holding of the first circuit assembly in St. Kitts from November 17 to 19, 1950. Samuel McKenzie and Arnold Stoute, two more Gilead graduates who had recently arrived, shared in the program.

Soon Brothers McKenzie and Stoute took up their assignments in Charlestown, Nevis, where they found Brother Walter Joseph, his wife and two other persons proclaiming the "good news." They started to hold regular meetings at the Joseph home, and the small group that had been organized as a congregation back in 1947 began to make notable progress.

In nearby Gingerland, pioneer Benjamin Smith was busy working with nine other publishers. However, the missionaries discovered that six of them were still attending services held by false religious organizations. So they were immediately dropped from the ranks of Kingdom proclaimers.

True, our work was making some advancement in such islands as St. Kitts. Obviously, however, there was need for further spiritual assistance and there was a great work ahead. So, could more be done to advance Kingdom interests in the Leewards?

BRANCH OFFICE ESTABLISHED

The year 1954 was an eventful one for Jehovah's people in these islands. By early spring, the Watch Tower Society arranged for the speeding up of our work by establishing a separate branch office for the Leewards. This arrangement brought our activities under more effective supervision. Brothers Roy F. Bruhn and Kenneth Gannaway were sent here to care for the new branch. Under this arrangement, two new congregations were formed in Antigua, at All Saints and Pigotts.

Initial difficulties in housing the branch office at St. John's, Antigua, were overcome with the aid of a local businessman. Despite pressure from his associates, he insisted that, as long as the Society wanted his building, it was available. So the new branch office had its start at that location. A little later it was moved from that building to a better one on the same block, and there the branch office, a missionary home and a Kingdom Hall remained for the next 14 years.

Milton G. Henschel, from the Society's headquarters in Brooklyn, visited the Leewards from March 30 to April 1, 1954, and a three-day assembly was arranged in conjunction with that visit. The local Witnesses surely appreciated the fine Scriptural counsel provided during Brother Henschel's assembly talks. Imagine, too, the joy of the brothers as a result of the unexpected showing of the Society's film "The New World Society in Action"! Brother Henschel returned to the Leewards as zone overseer in 1961 and again in 1966.

GRADUAL EXPANSION IN EVIDENCE

At this point, perhaps some comparative statistics would help to show the progress of our work after the branch office was established in the Leewards. In 1954, field service reports came in from seven islands—Antigua, Anguilla, Dominica, Montserrat, Nevis, St. Kitts and St. Martin. During that service year there were 193 Kingdom proclaimers and they devoted 34,367 hours to the work of declaring the "good news." Combined Memorial attendance was 303. Ten years later, during the 1964 service year, there were 396 Kingdom publishers reporting 114,047 hours in the disciple-making work. During that year, a total of 575 persons attended the Lord's Evening Meal throughout these islands.

There had been some other notable developments during the intervening years. For instance, brothers aboard the Society's boat *Light* had continued visiting the outlying islands until mid-1957, when the craft was sold and three members of the crew received assignments to missionary homes. For years now, the other crew member, Arthur Worsley, has been serving as a member of the Bethel family in Brooklyn, New York.

In 1957, Alban Joseph became the first native brother to enter the circuit work in the Leewards. Also, during the 1958 Divine Will International Assembly in New York city, Carlton Hull of St. Kitts was the first of three Leeward Islanders to graduate from Gilead School within a year's time. In 1959, Gerald Christopher and Kennedy Phillip, both Kitticians, attended the School.

Jehovah continued blessing our efforts, despite the departure of some for England and the United States in quest of employment. Other 'harvest workers' arrived here to help with the work. For instance, in 1966 Brother and Sister Ernest Jackson, from the United States, took up their missionary assignment on Montserrat. Brother and Sister Paul Ondejko, Canadians, entered St. Kitts a year later. And, of course, the growing number of local Kingdom proclaimers carried on faithfully in their service to Jehovah.

CIRCUIT WORK PLAYS ITS PART

Ever since Joshua W. Steelman visited the Leewards as a traveling overseer back in 1947, this work has played a significant part in the advancement of the Kingdom-preaching work in these islands. So, permit us to tell you a little about this activity through the years.

During the early days of circuit work in the Leewards, the traveling brothers often carried along little folding beds and did their own cooking, since their humble fellow believers simply could not accommodate them. Particularly in Dominica was travel extremely difficult. So, in those days, no circuit overseers were married men. Not until 1956 were Roseau and Portsmouth linked by road. Even then, because of the winding roads, it would take nearly two and a half hours by auto to cover the more than 50 miles (80 kilometers) between these cities, although the actual distance is but 20 miles (32 kilometers). One observer remarked: "The island is such a mass of peaks, ridges and ravines that in proportion to area it is more rugged than

Switzerland." Patois, a broken French dialect spoken by nearly 70,000 inhabitants, presents yet another barrier for Bible truth to overcome.

When visiting Dominica, it was over rugged mountain trails that circuit overseers often had to walk from one town to another. Fred Snow's stamina and zeal moved him to strive to better his previous travel time during each visit as he walked from Grand Bay over Paix Bouche Mountain to La Roche.

Over the years, of course, many brothers have shared in circuit work throughout the Leewards. We cannot possibly recount all their experiences. But one thing is certain: Their efforts have been appreciated.

Looking back to early visits of circuit overseers to Dominica, Hodge Dominique remarks: "When I used to get a letter from the Society stating that a brother was coming to visit us, we would stay by the pier until well past eleven o'clock at night looking out to sea for boats. There was a French boat they used to come on often in those days before the Society opened a branch office in Antigua. I remember how the circuit servant was always so happy to see us, and I would take him right to my house." Indeed, such appreciation, close association and resulting interchange of encouragement have through the years benefited both traveling overseers and those they have visited.—Rom. 1:11, 12.

In the late 1950's, airstrips began appearing at the edge of jungle-like areas on most of the islands, and this resulted in greater tourist trade. However, it also enabled circuit overseers and their wives to travel between islands in minutes. This certainly was much better than waiting for weeks, and sometimes months, for the two boats serving the island chain.

Also, with financial aid coming from Britain, Canada and the United States, improvements began to be made on the islands in connection with the electricity, water and roads. Naturally, these developments benefited the people in general, including the local Witnesses and the traveling overseers.

CHANGES IN LIFE-STYLE

The passing of time has brought many changes to these islands and their inhabitants. Yet, nothing has affected the lives of people more than the Word and spirit of Jehovah God. As the Kingdom message has been spread here, 'desirable ones' have been found and have taken a stand for Jehovah. (Hag. 2:7) By nature, many of these islanders are cautious, though friendly. Some, while being shy like the original Carib inhabitants, are changing their attitude and accepting home Bible studies.

Every part of our territory, each isolated village, has become important to us as we have declared the "good news." For instance, some 400 descendants of the Caribs inhabit a reservation in the Gaulette River area on the Atlantic side of Dominica. These people still hand-shape dugout canoes once used for war but now sold to outsiders for use in fishing. Yes, the Kingdom message has reached these descendants of the Caribs and has affected their lives in a good way. What a delight it was to see the first two of these people get baptized during the 1970 service year!

Encouraging, too, is the fact that younger brothers and sisters have enthusiastically accepted responsibility and have reaped Jehovah's blessing. For example, in recent years several of these younger individuals, like earlier proclaimers of the "good news" in these islands, have organized interested persons into small groups in scattered villages. Such work has had a tremendous strengthening effect on the central congregations, particularly in Antigua, St. Kitts and Dominica.

BUILDING WITH A VIEW TO THE FUTURE

Besides changes in life-style, in recent years the very contour of these islands has changed. Mechanized giants have gouged out huge sections of land for housing developments and swank hotels. But Jehovah's Witnesses also have been building with a view to the future.

Back in 1966, with the continued expansion of our work, a problem developed in connection with housing the branch office and missionary home, then located on the second floor of a rented building in St. John's, Antigua. A sincere effort to locate more suitable living quarters and branch facilities was undertaken that year. This effort, too, had Jehovah's blessing. Accordingly, in November 1966 a piece of land was purchased in St. John's, and there a fine two-story building was erected by the Society. On the ground floor is a spacious Kingdom Hall, as well as literature storage and branch office facilities. Comfortable accommodations for up to eight missionaries were provided on the second floor. The building was dedicated on January 26, 1968, during a zone visit by Robert W. Wallen of the Society's headquarters staff in Brooklyn. Over 200 persons were present on that happy occasion.

Yet, that has not been the extent of our work of building with a view to the future. In various parts of these islands Jehovah's people have constructed fine places of worship. Today Kingdom Halls are owned by all but two congregations in the Leewards. One of the largest halls, which seats 500 inside with provisions for overflow, was constructed during 1976 by the brothers in Antigua.

STRONG BONDS OF CHRISTIAN LOVE

Today, true Christians in the Leewards have no reason to feel that they are isolated islanders far removed from fellow believers in other parts of the earth. Rather, they can sense the bond of love and the closeness characteristic of Jehovah's people earth wide. (John 13:34, 35) Doubtless many factors contribute to this attitude, but it seems especially fitting to mention one of them.

The brothers and sisters on these islands have been greatly stimulated spiritually by visitors from Brooklyn headquarters. For instance, back in November 1968 we were very much encouraged by the first visit of Brother N. H. Knorr, then president of the Society. The 281 persons present to hear his talk were given the opportunity to see themselves in the "mirror" mentioned by the disciple James. They were urged to 'accept with mildness the implanting of God's word,' and were helped to see themselves in the light of the dangerous times in which we live. (Jas. 1:21-24) Thereafter, a group of about 20 to 30 brothers and sisters lingered for an hour at the airport under a canopy of tropical stars while engaging in warm discussion as Brother Knorr waited for the plane that would take him on the next leg of his trip to Caribbean and South American branches.

We have also been upbuilt greatly during recent visits by members of the present Governing Body of Jehovah's Witnesses. Brothers Lloyd Barry, Albert Schroeder and John Booth all visited St. Kitts and Antigua during the month of August 1976. Brothers Barry and Schroeder took an evening out of their busy schedule to fly to St. Kitts. That evening, with less than an hour left before they were to address an audience, the visitors expressed their desire to sample the territory. Doubtless you can imagine the joy of the local Witnesses and their guests as they walked off into the evening dusk and shared in witnessing to the islanders. Just a little later the brothers were delighted when 375 persons gathered to hear the encouraging talks given by the visiting brothers.

John Booth served a district assembly in the Leewards toward the end of August 1976. But other brothers of the Governing Body also have visited us. In October

1976 Lyman Swingle spent two days encouraging the brothers in Dominica. E. C. Chitty paid us a zone visit in 1977, as did Daniel Sydlik in 1978. So, it is not surprising that the brothers and sisters in the Leewards feel close to their fellow servants of Jehovah at the Society's headquarters. And, surely, God's people in these islands treasure the bond of Christian love that unites them with worshipers of Jehovah earth wide.

"VICTORIOUS FAITH" INTERNATIONAL CONVENTION

How thrilling it was for the brothers and sisters in the Leeward Islands to host the "Victorious Faith" International Convention held from August 23 to 27, 1978, at St. John's, Antigua! They were delighted that the delegates included brothers and sisters from Sweden, England, the United States, Canada and the Caribbean. The peak assembly attendance was 1,717, and 35 persons were baptized.

Most encouraging to the missionaries, and attesting to the spiritual stature of the local brothers, was the fact that the entire operation of the assembly was handled by Leeward Islanders. Brother Karl Klein of the Governing Body served the assembly, and a number of members of the Brooklyn and London Bethel families shared in the program.

EVER REJOICING IN JEHOVAH'S SERVICE

"Should I go over them again?" wrote W. R. Brown to Brother J. F. Rutherford in 1922 after having made disciples in these lovely islands. Brother W. R. Brown was then sent elsewhere, but in the years since then many others like Brother Brown have 'gone over these islands again and again,' and many precious ones have rallied to Jehovah's house, serving him in faithfulness. (Isa. 2:2-4; Hag. 2:7) But what of the future? The prospects are excellent! Today there are 716 Kingdom proclaimers in the Leewards. At the Lord's Evening Meal on March 23, 1978, there were 1,594 present in the 18 congregations and two isolated groups.

In reviewing the years of Kingdom witnessing in the Leewards, it is apparent that an inerasable record of faithfulness is in evidence. We have enjoyed Jehovah's great love and patient direction through the "faithful and discreet slave." (Matt. 24:45-47) And, we are joyful in God's service. Until he says the work is finished, true Christians in the Leeward Islands will continue rejoicing as they spread the grand news: "Jehovah himself has become king! Let the earth be joyful. Let the many islands rejoice."—Ps. 97:1.

PERU

Land of the Incas. That is Peru, once the domain of the Inca empire. Today it is the home of some 17,000,000 people, among them the Quechua Indians, whose forebears founded the highly developed Inca civilization of over seven centuries ago.

Out of every 100 Peruvians of today, approximately 46 are either Quechua or Aymara Indians. For the most part, the balance of the populace are of mixed Indian and white descent. Actually, the towering Andes mountains, which split the country into an arid coastal region on the west and a luxuriant and steaming jungle on the east, have had much to do with the ethnic groupings of Peru's inhabitants. In the jungle areas there are dozens of Indian tribes with customs and languages quite different from those of the "altiplano" Indians living in the lofty heights of the Andes. In the 1,400-mile (2,300-kilometer) Pacific coastal region are found the majority of Peru's Spanish residents, not a few of whom have mixed in with the original inhabitants of the land.

To the north of Peru lie Ecuador and Colombia. Eastward are the countries of Brazil and Bolivia, and to the south is Chile.

It was to this country, the ancient Land of the Incas, that the Spanish conqueror, Francisco Pizarro, came in the sixteenth century C.E. Accompanying him, in 1535, were priests and friars from Spain. For that newly introduced Catholic religion to "stick," the priests found it convenient to adopt many Indian traditions, customs and ideas. Never has the Catholic Church in Peru totally rooted out the age-old practices of the descendants of the sun-worshiping Incas. Hence, spiritism, animism and the worship of the dead all have been smeared over lightly with a veneer of Catholicism, and modern-day Peru is a land of fusion religion. But through the hills, mountains and valleys of this ancient Land of the Incas, spiritual light has been shining. (Ps. 43:3) How did this grand development have its start?

SPIRITUAL LIGHT BEGINS SHINING

During the 1930's, traveling witnesses of Jehovah passed through Peru, leaving Bible literature here and there. Also, friends in other lands lovingly sent Christian publications to relatives in this country and urged them to look into the pages of God's Word. In time, some of this literature found its way into a number of secondhand bookstores in Lima, the capital.

It was in one of these stores, during 1938, that Victor Lura came across a book entitled "The Harp of God." That title enthralled him! "Was it possible that God had a harp? Indeed, what manner of harp would it be?" mused Mr. Lura. Buying the book for an insignificant price, he lost no time "devouring" its contents. Like a beautiful melody played on a ten-stringed harp, the newly acquired book brought its reader joy as it clarified ten fundamental teachings of the Holy Scriptures. How these truths differed from Catholic doctrine and his own Pentecostal belief!

Soon, Mr. Lura was back in the bookstore, combing it thoroughly for more publications of the Watch Tower Society. He found several. At that time, he was the janitor at the local meeting place of the Pentecostals. As the months progressed, Mr. Lura felt compelled to copy from these valued books excerpts that exposed evolution and spiritism. Moved with zeal, he had these portions printed, at his own expense, as handbills. Out these went to many residents of Lima and nearby Callao. During that period, Mr. Lura met a young lady, Lastenia Casana, who also attended Pentecostal meetings. In 1939 they were married, and together they pored over Bible prophecies so clearly outlined in the Christian publications they both prized so highly.

One day in 1943, Victor rushed home with electrifying news. "One of Jehovah's Witnesses is in town," he excitedly told his wife. Freida Johnson, a full-time Kingdom proclaimer traveling along South America's west coast, had stopped in Lima. She had been witnessing to an evangelical woman, and the lady kindly had offered Sister Johnson accommodations in her home near the top of a large hill at the edge of the city. The house lacked sewerage facilities and running water, and had only straw mats for walls. But it sufficed. Our intrepid pioneer, though in her sixties, bathed in the river Rimac along with the local residents.

Without delay, Victor Lura went to meet Sister Johnson. At long last he had come in contact with Jehovah's own people! A meeting was arranged for that very evening, and friends and neighbors were invited. That first meeting was not too successful. Mostly Pentecostals were present, and they did not let Sister Johnson say very much, always interrupting her with their own pet religious phrases. So, invitations to the meeting to be held the next night were extended only to those who had manifested real interest in Bible truth. At that gathering, Sister Johnson gave a concise, pointed witness touching repeatedly on the establishment of God's kingdom in the heavens in 1914. A number of listeners were convinced. Among them were Pedro Garay and Victor Romero.

Sister Johnson remained in Lima for four days, witnessing and encouraging newly interested ones. Following through with her Christian commission, she sent their names and addresses to the Watch Tower Society's headquarters in Brooklyn, New York. Then she left for Huancayo, in central Peru, and thereafter headed southward. Later, Peruvian Witnesses learned that Sister Johnson had died around 1945 during a bout with malaria at Medellín, Colombia.

Victor Lura, Pedro Garay and Victor Romero got together $20 and sent that sum to the Watch Tower Society in Brooklyn. They keenly desired information about what they could do to spread the "good news." Just a month later, literature arrived, along with a phonograph and recorded Bible talks in Spanish. At times, letters and instructions arrived. Although these were in English, Victor Romero knew that language and translated them. So it was that, in 1943 and 1944, spiritual light was beginning to spread out in the ancient Land of the Incas.

CONTACT UPBUILDS US SPIRITUALLY

One of Victor Lura's letters to the Society asked if help could be sent to Lima. The thrilling reply was that missionaries were indeed being prepared to go forth as witnesses "to the most distant part of the earth." (Acts 1:8) Thus hope was kindled for the eventual arrival in Peru of missionaries trained at the Watchtower Bible School of Gilead. In fact, on June 10, 1944, the Watchtower Society's president, N. H. Knorr, had called into his office seven missionaries and had told them that their assignment would be Peru.

But something very significant was to take place before those missionaries arrived. The small group in Lima learned that Brothers N. H. Knorr and F. W. Franz would pay them a visit, arriving on February 26, 1945. What joy of heart there was at the thought of having contact with Jehovah's organization through association with these brothers!

The long-awaited day finally arrived. Five joyful brothers and interested persons were at Lima's airport, vigorously waving *La Atalaya* (the Spanish edition of *The Watchtower*) as the incoming plane roared to a halt. Soon enthusiastic greetings were exchanged, and visitors and Peruvians alike were looking forward to a gathering at the home of Victor Lura.

That evening, eight expectant faces were turned toward the speaker, Brother Knorr, as he outlined the

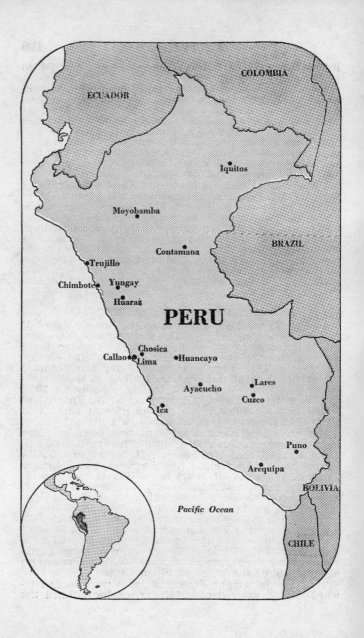

great responsibilities resting upon those desiring to serve Jehovah God. For one thing, Christian meetings should be held regularly. The problem of getting missionaries into Peru was mentioned. This would not be easy since the country had concordat relations with the Vatican. Moreover, the president of Peru had ruled that, with the exception of Roman Catholicism, no organization would be permitted to hold religious exercises in public. The penalty for doing so? Two to 30 days in prison and a fine of from two to 50 soles, or either one of these penalties. But how did Brother Knorr's listeners feel about all of this? They were fearless and determined to spread the Kingdom message from house to house. It was with that spirit that the meeting was adjourned.

After a trip southward, the visitors were back in Lima on March 26. Eighteen people were crowded into the meeting place that night, four of them being the two travelers from Brooklyn and Brothers Albert Mann and Jack Powers, Gilead School graduates who were stopping over in Lima briefly before heading for their assignments to the south. Using Brother Franz as his interpreter from English into Spanish, Brother Knorr highlighted the importance of making return visits. He also discussed the possibility of organizing a local congregation of Jehovah's Witnesses. Did the new ones desire that? Indeed they did! Also, a number of those present expressed their wish to be baptized in symbol of their "consecration," or dedication, to Jehovah. It was arranged that Brothers Mann and Powers should return the next evening for another meeting and that they should also come back the following night to celebrate the Memorial of Christ's death. That occasion provided the opportunity for the first Christian baptism in Peru. Three persons then symbolized their dedication to God, one of them being Pedro Garay.

MISSIONARIES LEND A HAND

The government had refused entry to Witness missionaries. However, in October 1945 the Society arranged for two Gilead graduates from Bolivia to get in touch with the Department of Foreign Affairs in order to find out what was holding up the visas for our missionaries. Through inquiry, it was learned that by coming into the country as tourists, and then paying $25 per person, missionaries could in time get their visas to remain here. So it was that after much correspondence and many efforts eight Gilead missionaries finally arrived in Peru on October 20, 1946. That original group included Walter and Christine Akin and Nellena and Verda Pool, who would spend decades here aiding sheeplike ones.

So, late in 1946, they were here—eight enthusiastic missionaries. Now what? Before them was a newly opened territory. 'A large door leading to activity had swung open to them.' (1 Cor. 16:9) They had a new language to master. But, first things first. Although not knowing Spanish, they sought and found hotel accommodations, limited though these were. The four single girls piled into one room, a room that had neither lock nor bars on the door. Being wary of foreign surroundings, they took the precaution of stacking all the furniture against the door before retiring that night.

House-hunting while lacking knowledge of the language and of currency values proved to be quite a job. During their second week in Peru, the missionaries found a house for rent, but it proved to be too expensive; and a month later another house was rented. The sisters carried their baggage and few possessions, while Brother Akin took the heavier things in a taxi. But, at least, they were getting settled.

The first meeting of the missionaries with the interested persons living in Rimac showed that the new ones needed much help. Therefore, the Lura family and the Garays were invited to attend meetings in the new missionary home. At the first congregation meeting held there, just four Peruvians were present with the missionaries.

During those early weeks, when much incidental witnessing was done by the missionaries, it became evident that they should quickly learn the language of Peru. So, it was decided that the group would take a two-month course in Spanish at the Peruvian-North American Cultural Institute. Each paid for his own course. Now they had to prepare for their studies and they had to do more talking in Spanish. A concerted effort was put forth to increase their vocabulary. While walking to and from classes, street names and words appearing on various signs were laboriously pronounced and one missionary would correct another. But they were making progress, much to their delight.

Learning Spanish has been an "adventure" for many Gilead-trained missionaries assigned to Peru, and teaching methods have been varied. For instance, during one period these newcomers were given intensive instruction for two months after their arrival. During the first month, for eleven hours a day, they virtually "soaked" themselves in Spanish. For the second month, half of their time was spent studying the language at home and the other half was devoted to using that knowledge in field service. Of course, the newer missionaries just learning Spanish could always benefit from listening to their "older" brothers speaking in that tongue as they sat together sipping cups of coffee around the kitchen table in a missionary home.

Unquestionably, though, the best language training was received in the field service. On the "testimony card," used some years ago in the Kingdom-preaching work, there was a fine witness printed in Spanish, and the householder could be asked to read this card. However, the new missionaries also learned short presentations that they were able to recite, parrotlike. So, how might matters go at the door? Edna Waterfall, one of the later missionaries to come into Peru, admits:

"I'll never forget the first house at which I had to give a witness all by myself. Jehovah gave me the strength to get through it. . . . I broke out in a cold sweat. The maid asked me what I wanted, and I asked for the lady of the house. . . . I quietly prayed to Jehovah for help, the maid reappeared, and I was ushered into the living room. An elderly lady came, smiled kindly, and sat down to listen to what I had to say. I stumbled through my memorized sermon, showed her the testimony card, and offered her the book *'The Kingdom Is at Hand'* in Spanish. She took the book and I arranged for a Bible study, but that was the end of my Spanish. As I was sitting there wondering how to make a graceful exit, I think she realized my situation. She smiled and then said, in perfect English: 'All right, that is all very fine. I will study with you and we will do it all in Spanish to help you learn Spanish.' Shocked, I said: 'You know English? And you let me do all of that in my wobbly Spanish?' 'It was good for you,' she replied. It was, too, and we had a wonderful study."

OFF TO A GOOD START IN LIMA

On December 5, 1946, a prayer of thanksgiving went up to Jehovah as the missionaries received official notice that they could stay in Peru as nonimmigrant residents. Ah, that was fine! It was then that the normal door-to-door witnessing work began. The missionaries were delighted because they could now use their time and energies fully in declaring the "good news."

The original group of eight missionaries divided Lima into eight territories. It fell to Brother and Sister Akin to work the section called Lince, which proved to be a very fruitful field. How could Sister Akin ever forget witnessing at her first door there? She presented her testimony card to the lady of the house, read a verse or two from the Spanish Bible, and mentioned the contribution for the literature. The lady seemed interested, rattled off something in Spanish, and started to push Sister Akin down the street. They came to a halt in front of a tailor shop. The lady pointed to her wedding ring, and it dawned on Sister Akin that she wanted her to talk to her husband, the tailor. Imagine our sister's surprise at seeing, not just one, but five tailors in that shop! With a prayer in her heart to Jehovah, she courageously gave a witness and offered the book *"The Truth Shall Make You Free."* All five men tried to converse with Sister Akin, and finally the owner pointed to her wedding ring. That meant, Come back with your husband. Well, this led to a home Bible study and to some "letters of recommendation," eventual associates in Jehovah's service. (2 Cor. 3:1-3) Years later the Akins could point to their "letters" resulting from that first Bible study in Lima. Luis and Adriana Sanchez later became regular pioneers. Another of those five tailors, Flavio Ramos, eventually became a special pioneer in Lima. One young man who accepted the book from Sister Akin in that tailor shop later became a special pioneer serving high in the Andes.

As our work spread out in the capital city, it found its way into Barrios Altos, the oldest section of colonial Lima. There, many of our books were placed in one of the large passageways or "interiors." When the Witnesses returned to continue their work, a man came out of one of the houses looking for Nellena Pool. He had accepted the book *"The Truth Shall Make You Free"* from her companion, Lastenia Lura, a week earlier and had read all of it. The man had a long list of questions, and in time he got his answers. Before long, this man—Leopoldo Sanchez—was attending Christian meetings and engaging in field service. He was baptized in January 1948, and four years later he became the first special pioneer to be enrolled from among the local brothers in Peru.

INTO THE INTERIOR

By mid-1947 some 20 persons were attending Christian meetings in Lima. But what about other parts of the country? Well, the missionaries' first venture outside the capital into Peru's interior was undertaken in June 1947. The Garay family, associated with God's people since 1943, had property in Huancayo. That city, high in the Andes and about 12 hours by train from the capital, was in typical Indian territory. And what was the predominant language? Quechua —the age-old language of the Incas.

Sister María Garay was witnessing diligently at Huancayo and was finding interested ones there. She was using a testimony card, and, in place of a briefcase, she had one of our magazine bags over her shoulder. No, Sister Garay was not doing magazine street work. That was not permitted in Peru. The law of the land prohibited any religions, other than the Roman Catholic State religion, from going into the streets for any type of religious activity. That would be defined as proselyting. Also, whereas in most parts of the world Jehovah's Witnesses speak of themselves as "placing" literature with people for a nominal contribution, in Peru we are considered officially as "book salesmen." So, we are viewed as "selling" Bibles from house to house, something that is permitted by law.

At any rate, Sister Garay was busy in God's service, although she was not having an easy time of it. Priests followed her from door to door and confiscated the literature she left with the people. These clerics also urged the young boys of the neighborhood to throw stones at her and to cry out "Heretic," or "Protestant." Nevertheless, sufficient interest in Bible truth had been sparked at Huancayo to warrant a visit from Lima's Witness missionaries.

Going 'over the hump' to Huancayo is a unique experience indeed. The train grinds its way upward to almost 16,000 feet (4,800 meters) before beginning the long descent toward the valley and the city of Huancayo, situated at an altitude of about 10,950 feet (3,340 meters). Lack of sufficient oxygen affects many travelers by causing splitting headaches, giddiness or even attacks of fainting and vomiting.

Upon arrival, the missionaries had a joyful reunion with Sister Garay. Help and counsel were given, a congregation of God's people was established, and, at the end of the 1948 service year, five Kingdom publishers were reporting field service at Huancayo.

SPREADING TRUTH WITH MAGAZINES

By the late 1940's, increased use of *The Watchtower* and *Awake!* was opening the way for many new ones to come into association with Jehovah's people in Peru. At that time, about 1948, each full-time Kingdom proclaimer was being sent seven free copies of each issue. Distribution was increasing, but not all the brothers were placing their magazines. So, these began to accumulate. Then some of the missionaries got an idea—'Why don't we make a special day and go out and place those magazines?' Soon several missionaries in the Rimac area of Lima were using magazines in their witnessing work every Saturday. Noticing their success in this activity, others joined them. Before long, therefore, every Saturday the local Witnesses were busily engaged in presenting just our magazines to people at their doors. And, in a short time, more and more magazines were being requested for this productive activity.

Later, when Brother Knorr came to Peru, he was very interested in learning why so many more magazines were being distributed in Lima than in various other places. The reason? Why, the brothers and sisters were using them every Saturday for group magazine work! Was it then that the idea of having a regular "Magazine Day" took hold? We in Peru are not sure, but that seems quite possible. At any rate, many magazine routes were developed and numerous Bible studies were started as a result of magazine placements.

BRANCH OFFICE ESTABLISHED

Excitement ran high in early 1949 when we learned that N. H. Knorr and his secretary, M. G. Henschel, were to pay us a visit. Accordingly, on March 5, some 50 brothers and interested ones greeted the travelers upon their arrival at Lima's airport. Coinciding with the visit was an assembly held in the Kingdom Hall of the missionary home at 256 Ramón Dagnino. We were delighted to see 224 persons present for Brother Knorr's public talk "It Is Later than You Think!" During this visit, a large group of Witnesses went out to one of the beaches where 20 persons were baptized.

But Peruvian Christians were in for a surprise. A little later Brother Knorr delighted the missionaries by explaining one of the principal reasons for his visit. What was that? The Watch Tower Society was establishing a branch office in Peru. One of the missionaries was appointed as the first branch overseer.

Starting in October 1950 the new branch suffered an upset of sorts. The original branch overseer was replaced and his responsibilities were assumed by Robert Hoyt, a graduate of Gilead's fifteenth class. Our work in Lima was expanding rapidly, and so at the year's end, a new missionary home was established in the San Isidro area of the capital. Also, the branch office-missionary home was moved to a new location, on Pasaje Velarde, nearer the center of Lima. Immediately, Brother Hoyt started getting the branch well organized and ready for the hard work ahead.

INTO THE PROVINCES

Now that the new branch office had been organized, our activities were expanding. For instance, public talks were being prepared and presented in various places. Even so, the great amount of work to be done in this country, then having a population of some 7,000,000, staggered the imagination. How earnestly the brothers prayed that the "Master of the harvest" might send out more workers! (Matt. 9:37, 38) Soon the answer was forthcoming. Twenty-one new missionaries of Gilead's thirteenth class were on their way to Peru. They arrived in the months of December 1949 and January 1950. Six were sent north to Trujillo. The large southern city of Arequipa was the destination of seven others. And a missionary home for eight workers was set up at Callao, Peru's major seaport situated eight miles (13 kilometers) west of Lima.

Being a port city, Callao had a high degree of crime and immorality. Nevertheless, Kingdom-preaching activities proved fruitful there. In fact, some individuals were found who had been contacted years earlier by Victor Lura when he had distributed tracts in that seaport city. Before long, a number of Callao's residents were attending Christian meetings. Among them were Arturo Guzman and his wife, as well as Manuel Calderon, Victor Cespedes and the Carlos Vega family. Today six lively congregations with a total of 367 Kingdom proclaimers are declaring the "good news" in Callao.

Arequipa proved to be 'a tough nut to crack.' For years this town has been known as the "Little Vatican," for its populace is steeped in Catholic tradition and custom. The new missionary home there became the center for congregational meetings and activities. Progress was slow, although interest was found after diligent house-to-house searching. On one occasion, however, things worked out the other way around—an interested person earnestly looked for the truth. A young man, Eliseo Balboa, spied a "gringo" sitting alone in a park reading a book. Why had he come to Peru? Mr. Balboa wanted to know. The brother, Horace Criss, explained that he was a Christian, a minister. That struck Mr. Balboa as rather strange because all the ministers he knew wore long, black robes. So it was that a witness began, and it led to a Bible study.

After just a few studies, Mr. Balboa left Arequipa in search of secular work. In time, he went to Callao, where he kept inquiring about Jehovah's Witnesses and their meeting place. Finally, he met Sister Charlotte Barron, who was distributing magazines from stand to stand in the marketplace. Obtaining the branch address from her, Mr. Balboa attended a few Christian meetings. Then his search for secular work took him away once more, this time to a vanadium mining camp at Jumasha, high in the Andes. However, contact was maintained through correspondence with the branch office. Also, despite a long and arduous trip, Robert Hoyt visited Mr. Balboa. This strengthened the young man spiritually and also afforded opportunity to help him with the witness work, which he carried on alone thereafter. Later, returning to Arequipa, Brother Balboa was helped spiritually by the missionaries to the point of entering the full-time preaching work.

Up north, in Trujillo, missionary Harvey Conrow found sheeplike Encarnacion Leiva. She virtually soaked up Bible truth, but only by ear, since she could neither read nor write. However, being a determined 51-year-old woman at the time, she obtained a book that could help her to understand letters and how to group them into words. With the aid of her daughters, she soon was able to read and write, becoming an able Kingdom proclaimer in Trujillo. As she later admitted, without the truth behind her as an incentive, she never would have made the attempt to become literate. Sister Leiva died in 1967, an able and faithful witness of Jehovah.

The Theocracy's Increase Assembly on July 30 through August 6, 1950, at New York city's famed Yankee Stadium aroused excitement here in Peru. Twelve missionaries made the trip, accompanied by three local publishers. The humble and loving Peruvian Witnesses who were left behind thought they never would see the missionaries again. Not so, however! All of them returned to their assignments.

HOODLUMS IN CHOSICA

In 1950 Emil and Clara Müller moved from Switzerland to Chosica, an inland city about an hour's ride east of Lima. Later, pioneer Leopoldo Sanchez contacted them while witnessing in this town, where Brother Müller was working at the hydroelectric plant. Still later, in July 1955, special pioneer Betty Myers began to serve in Chosica.

One day Sister Myers knocked at the door of a lady who proved to be a fanatical Catholic and a close friend of the local priest. The woman was furious that one of Jehovah's Witnesses should be knocking at her door. Sister Myers and her young pioneer associate had gone just a short way down the street when the enraged lady, together with a gang of young boys, hoodlums, accosted them.

Just what did the two Witnesses think they were doing in that Catholic neighborhood? The mob wanted to know. Why, they were doing a good Christian work and had every right to do it, replied Sister Myers! Soon the priest was on the scene. He demanded that the two Witnesses leave at once. But the young pioneer sister, who once had been the Catholic girl friend of that very priest, asked him to show her where the Bible said she should not be out preaching the "good news." It was his turn to be furious. After all, she had put her onetime boyfriend on the spot in front of those young hoodlums.

The situation was almost comical, but what followed was not. As the two sisters turned away and started down the road, the boys began to pelt them with mud balls packed with small stones. These were thrown until the two Christians were completely covered with mud. One stone cut the young pioneer sister on the ear, and it bled profusely. Finally, an elderly black gentleman—himself an ardent Catholic—called them into his patio-garden and shamed the boys away.

Sister Myers went directly to the police station, reported the incident, and requested protection. As a result, a plainclothes policeman was assigned to accompany the sisters in their work. Not long thereafter, several of the boys tried to repeat their stone-throwing harassment. But the plainclothesman caught them, got their names, and 'laid down the law' to their families. That stopped the mob action in Chosica.

A NEW ARRANGEMENT FOR MISSIONARIES

Gilead-trained missionaries continued to come into Peru in considerable numbers during the early 1950's. For instance, by the end of 1952, 46 missionaries had come to this country. Of that number, 20 had left, some of them due to dissatisfaction with missionary life. But, 26 remained active in the Peruvian field.

In the year 1952 a different arrangement was made for missionaries coming into Peru. No longer could they be brought in as instructors, as had formerly been the case. They had to come into the country as tourists. Once having entered Peru, they were enrolled in San Marcos University, the oldest in the western hemisphere. They studied the language and, on that basis, could apply for a permanent residency permit as students. Only when they received their permanent carnets, or official papers, were they able to carry on their missionary activities as did the other Gilead graduates. This arrangement was quite effective and lasted for about four years.

'AND THEN, TO CHINA'?

During early 1953 our attention was focused on the New World Society Assembly to be held in New York city, from July 19 to 26. Charter flights carried 20 missionaries and a couple of Peruvian Witnesses, along with about 18 brothers from Bolivia, to the assembly city. Soon after that spiritually rewarding convention, more missionaries arrived in Peru. But it was toward the very end of 1953 that Kingdom proclaimers in this land enjoyed an especially upbuilding event.

In December 1953, Brothers N. H. Knorr and M. G. Henschel visited Peru. After days of searching, we had found a highly suitable meeting place for that occasion, the Salón Majestic in Pueblo Libre, a residential section of Lima.

Particularly memorable was a comment made by Brother Knorr during his final assembly talk. Why were the missionaries in Peru? To help the Peruvian brothers attain the necessary maturity to be able to reach out and shoulder various responsibilities in the congregation of God's people, Brother Knorr indicated. Once that was accomplished, he said, the missionaries would be freed for work in other fields. "And then," he remarked, looking around the hall, "we will send the missionaries to China!" Of course, that did not happen. Nevertheless, Brother Knorr certainly had made clear the privileges and responsibilities of Peru's missionaries.

As it was, we had plenty to do among the Peruvian people themselves. Accordingly, a feature of our work that opened up in 1953 and was being pushed ahead with more vigor during 1954 was that of caring for unassigned territory. The congregations from Lima and Callao spread out into all the surrounding districts, intent on declaring the "good news." Callao's Witnesses went down as far as Cañete and Chincha Alta, while those from Lima headed out to Puente Piedra, Ancón and Huaral.

A TIME OF SPIRITUAL STRENGTHENING

Aside from the 26 missionaries serving in Peru during 1952, there were 260 Kingdom publishers associated with the seven congregations then functioning. There were two congregations in Lima, as well as one each in Callao, Arequipa, Trujillo, Chosica and Huancayo. Three years later, in 1955, the average number of publishers in Peru was 460, with a peak of 563.

With the continuing increase during this general period, it became necessary to give attention to the spiritual strengthening of Peruvian Christians. For one thing, consideration had to be given to the upbringing of children, not allowing them to be contaminated with false religious teachings. The law requires that the national Catholic religion be taught in all the schools. Nevertheless, non-Catholics may apply for and receive exemption from this religious instruction. Hence, it was necessary to prepare letters to the effect that a certain person was one of Jehovah's Witnesses and was receiving adequate religious training from other sources. These letters were submitted to the school authorities and applications were considered by the Ministry of Education before exemption was granted. Particularly from that time onward have Peruvian Witnesses used this method to prevent the exposure of their school-age children to the false teachings and practices of Babylon the Great.

It also became necessary to place great emphasis on the need for moral cleanness. Some men in Peru have lived with one, two or three women at the same time, and might have had children by each woman. In other cases, a man and woman might be living together in a respectable home with several children but had never legalized their union. So, some serious decisions had to be made in an effort to ensure that marriage received the honor it Scripturally should. (Heb. 13:4) While individual circumstances have varied, it seems sufficient to say that a number of today's Peruvian Christians have the deep satisfaction of knowing that they have resolved their moral problems in a godly way.

CIRCUIT WORK A CHALLENGE

Back in 1953, the entire country of Peru comprised just one circuit. When Sidney Fraser became the branch overseer in that year, Robert Hoyt began serving in the field as the circuit overseer. It was quite a challenge to travel throughout the land visiting the seven congregations and the various isolated groups manifesting interest in Bible truth.

During one unforgettable trip, Brother Hoyt had to sit for nearly 20 hours in the back of a truck on a load of dried fish that was being carried to the sierra. Hotel accommodations in the sierra always left something to be desired. Communal rooms were favored there. In one room there were many beds, available for any man or woman who happened to come along and needed a place to sleep. Making good use of the chain and padlock he customarily carried with him, Brother

Hoyt chained his suitcase to the head of one bed and went off to find a bathroom or its equivalent. Upon returning, he found a woman in his bed! She had decided that she was going to sleep there. Since there was no other bed available, this posed a problem. But there was evidence of priority padlocked to the head of that bed! Happily, the hotel administrator managed to straighten things out so that our circuit overseer got that bed for himself and enjoyed a much-needed night's rest.

Naturally, as Jehovah prospered our Christian activities, circuits grew in number, and more circuit assemblies were scheduled. At one of these, held in the Surquillo section of Lima, among persons in attendance was a dentist, whose wife opposed him bitterly. When he arrived, it was quite noticeable that he was wearing his bedroom slippers. What had happened? "Well," he said, "my wife hid my shoes to stop me from coming. But here I am!" Yes, there may be large or small obstacles to overcome, but how important it is that we remain firm in the truth!

FILM SHOWINGS AID MANY

A new feature of our work had its start in Peru during 1954—the use of motion pictures to aid persons spiritually. The first of these films produced by the Watch Tower Society was entitled "The New World Society in Action." What an impression it made on viewers! Hundreds flocked to see this movie that provided fine insight on the activities of Jehovah's Witnesses.

One place where this film was shown was a workers' hall in the Andean mining town of Casapalca, situated at an elevation of 15,000 feet (4,600 meters). The hall was next to a hydroelectric plant, and consequently the voltage was very high. Although the projector was set at its slowest position, the film raced along at a speed faster than the script-reader could maintain. Add to that the rarefied atmosphere at that elevation, which made breathing difficult. As you might imagine, a few gaps were evident here and there. Nevertheless, all those present enjoyed the presentation.

At a circuit assembly film showing in Callao during September 1954, everything went well when running the first reel. But the projector's take-up spool ceased to function during the second reel. Oh, the film was going through the machine all right! When we finally became aware of the malfunction, there was a pile of film all over the floor. Yes, a few minutes passed while the brothers wound it up by hand. For the rest of that showing, the take-up reel had to be turned manually, but the show went on.

In later years, the Society's film "Proclaiming 'Everlasting Good News' Around the World" was shown throughout Peru, and it certainly struck a mighty blow against Babylon the Great, the world empire of false religion. At Toquepala it was shown to an audience of 3,251. True to type, a certain priest had done his best to hinder the exhibition of the film. Not being able to do so, he sneaked into the dark hall after the film showing had started, obviously curious about it. Well, the film ended, the lights went on, and there he was in plain sight. Becoming very self-conscious, the priest got up and sort of danced out of the hall, childishly and loudly singing: "Babylon the Great has fallen. Babylon the Great has fallen." Present were many Catholics who watched their priest make this 'Babylonish' spectacle of himself.

MISSIONARY ENTRY EASED

As of the year 1955, all missionaries coming into Peru were still entering as tourists and going to San Marcos University while endeavoring to obtain residency papers. However, while witnessing from door to door in Lince shortly after her arrival in this country, missionary Lucille Rapraeger called at the home of an official of the Ministry of Foreign Affairs. He recognized that she was working as a missionary and, of course, obtained her name.

Several days later, Nellena and Verda Pool, as well as Sister Rapraeger, met up with a lawyer with whom Nellena had placed literature. Calling her aside, he said: "Nellena, one of your missionaries is in trouble." What did he mean? Well, while in the Office of Foreign Affairs, this lawyer had noticed that Sister Rapraeger's application for permanency papers was lying on a desk, ready for refusal. Evidently, this was a result of her earlier call at the home of that official of the Ministry. Immediately, the matter was reported to the branch office of the Society.

This lawyer, who already had shown interest in Jehovah's Witnesses, was able to use his influence in working out this problem. The missionary stayed in Peru. Through the services of this lawyer, other missionaries were helped into the country—but now as *missionaries*, not as university students. From that time onward, the Society was able to get visa clearance for missionaries assigned to this country.

COURAGEOUS CHRISTIAN NEUTRALS

Peruvian Christians, young and old, have faced tests involving God and the State. For instance, according to the law, all males reaching 19 years of age must register and perform two years of military service. This posed problems for certain special pioneers sent to witness at Cuzco, Arequipa and elsewhere in the interior back in 1956, for many of them were young men around 19 or 20 years of age.

In fact, many brothers in Peru attempted to file as conscientious objectors and/or ministers, but the authorities recognized only Catholic clerics as religious ministers. Hence, in not a few cases, young Witnesses who sought recognition as ministers were beaten, thrown into filthy jails, and subjected to all kinds of abuse because of their stand as Christian neutrals. (Mic. 4:2, 3; Jas. 1:27) In this country, there never has been an arrangement for exempting from military service individuals who have objections to 'learning the art of war.'

Maintaining Christian neutrality is also of concern to godly parents and their children. In Peru, schoolchildren must take a course in premilitary training. There is no arrangement for exemption, and at the end of the term anyone not taking the course does not receive recognition for the school year. Such a pupil cannot advance toward getting a diploma. Although several things can be done to help the children get their education in another way, some have compromised and have permitted their youngsters to 'learn the art of war.'

However, to overcome the problem, one congregation in Chimbote asked if it could organize a class in the Kingdom Hall using volunteers among the brothers to teach the children different subjects. This has worked out well, especially since some Christian activity also is encouraged and participated in after the regular school studies.

Yet, this does not mean that parents and children encounter only minor problems in maintaining Christian neutrality, avoiding idolatry and ascribing salvation to Jehovah. (Ex. 20:4-6; Ps. 3:8) During 1970, for example, in the mining town of Toquepala, 10 Witness children were expelled from school for not saluting the flag and singing the national anthem. In other isolated cases, Christian children have been called before the authorities to explain why they do not take part in such ceremonies.—Mark 13:9; 1 Pet. 3:15.

Because of our stand as Christian neutrals, we have faced problems through the years. For instance, in 1975 we had to change an assembly site from the university city of Trujillo to another town because of a wave of patriotism that had arisen due to the fact that a Witness schoolboy would not participate in singing the national anthem or saluting the flag. Local authorities refused to acknowledge our neutral position, and newspapers in northern Peru carried such banner headlines as, "Jehovah's witnesses refuse to honor national emblems." Some articles falsely accused us of "brainwashing" the people by means of a "six month study course" during which we supposedly taught doctrines not in line with the interests of the country.

In Lima, the capital city, a Catholic priest preached the same type of message over the radio twice a day for a week. Actually, however, what he said resulted in a good testimony for the truth. He stated clearly and concisely what we believe, but then floundered around trying to refute our Biblical viewpoint of 1914 and the Trinity doctrine.

Paralleling the adverse publicity, the government decreed that in January 1976 all young men and women 18 years of age were to register for obligatory military service. Of course, Jehovah's people complied with the law by registering. Since so many young Witnesses were regular pioneers, they were supplied with a certified letter attesting to the fact that their chosen vocation was that of being preachers of God's Word. As far as is known, all these pioneers chose to prepare a file on their dedicated life of service to Jehovah and to present that material along with an appeal for exemption from military service because they were preachers. In previous years, the Military Manual of Law provided for exemption for members of the clergy or laymen without any specification as to religion. However, something new had now been added, and any application for exemption had to be signed and approved by the archbishopric of the Catholic Church, the State-recognized religion. Nevertheless, our brothers presented their documentary file and application when registering. Although some of these files were not accepted because they lacked a stamp of approval, there was acceptance of others. And, when the first lists were issued in January 1976, it was noted that at least some brothers had received exemption on the basis of their religious activities.

ASSEMBLY "FIRSTS"

Now that we have rounded out our story of Christian neutrals in this country, let us return to the late 1950's.

The year 1957 opened with a well-planned visit by Milton G. Henschel of the Society's headquarters in Brooklyn. Witnesses from all over Peru gathered for the assembly scheduled to coincide with this helpful visit. Only 389 persons were in attendance on the first day. But for the main talk on Sunday the audience numbered 1,044. What a joy it was to see over 1,000 present for the first time at an assembly in this country!

Another assembly "first" was enjoyed in 1958. During that year, for the first time, a district assembly was held in Iquitos—on the banks of the Amazon in the very heart of the jungle. In that equatorial region, rain was unpredictable and plentiful. It was quite paradoxical to hear a brother speaking on The Song of Solomon and saying, 'Come, my dear one, for the rainy season has passed and the downpour is over,' while the assembly hall's tin roof amplified the sound of the torrential downpour of the moment.—Song of Sol. 2:10, 11.

Care had to be taken in choosing a place for the baptism during that assembly. Although the flesh-eating piranha fish are not often found in the Amazon, we could not be sure about the inland rivers and streams. Happily, though, the baptism was held with no casualties.

ASSEMBLING DESPITE DIFFICULTIES

The Divine Will International Assembly of Jehovah's Witnesses held in New York city during the summer of 1958 caused excitement throughout Peru. Many Witnesses had been saving for that trip, and, when the time came to leave, we had 82 delegates. At the time of departure, it was very touching to see about 350 brothers on the veranda at the airport and to hear them sing Kingdom songs.

Toward the end of 1958, arrangements were being made for a district assembly to be held the following January in the stadium of a Lima soccer club. But the then Director of Government, an ardent Catholic, had decided to close down our assembly, although he did not act until the very day it was to start. All the equipment had been transported to the stadium, the cafeteria groups were preparing the noon meal, and preparations were under way for the afternoon meetings when a truckload of policemen pulled up at the stadium and began to move us out. Efforts to contact the Director of Government were to no avail.

The assembly had to be moved to Lima's two largest Kingdom Halls, and it was necessary for the speakers to give their talks in both places. Nevertheless, we had a good assembly and the difficulties only served to strengthen the brothers for further trials.

We would like to mention the 1958 assembly talk "Serving Where the Need Is Great Overseas." It showed that there was a need for more Kingdom proclaimers in many lands. In time, quite a number of individuals and families interested in expanding their service moved to this country. Actually, however, among the first arrivals in Peru was Eileen Sobie, who came from Canada as early as September 1957. But brothers and sisters kept coming. For various reasons, many have had to leave, but we can say that all have contributed something toward building up the faith of their Peruvian brothers and sisters.

LEGAL REGISTRATION

While attending the 1958 New York assembly, the branch overseer was told to register the Watch Tower Bible and Tract Society of Pennsylvania upon returning to Peru. Among other things, such registration would be necessary in order to hold property.

Accordingly, the Society was duly registered on April 29, 1959. From that time forward, all property bought by congregations or donated by brothers for building Kingdom Halls has been registered in the name of the Society.

NIGHT OF THE "GREAT DISASTER"

Naturally, not all developments are of major proportions. Sometimes, however, relatively minor incidents can create big problems. So, let us tell you something about what we have humorously called the night of the "great disaster."

Missionaries Edna Waterfall and Lucille Rapraeger had been sent to Puno, situated on the shores of Lake Titicaca at an elevation of some 12,500 feet (3,800 meters). These sisters had kerosine heaters that did not work just right at that altitude. After a fine meeting in the Kingdom Hall one Sunday evening, Sister Rapraeger went upstairs to the bedroom. But, when she turned on the light, she could not see it or anything else. The heater had been smoking for two hours. Naturally, she turned it off and opened the window before coming downstairs.

Edna Waterfall took one look at Sister Rapraeger and groaned. Why, her face had been blackened by the soot! Everyone trudged upstairs to have a look at the black "snowfall." Well, a big clean-up job had to be done that evening and the next day. What a task to clean that sticky soot from walls, clothes, blankets and books! But spirits were lifted when 60 persons showed up that week for our first assembly in Puno.

CLERICS FOMENT OPPOSITION

Of course, we have also had serious problems and tests of faith. At times we have encountered outright opposition, even mob violence. For example, consider what happened to missionaries Frances and Elizabeth Good in the remote jungle town of Moyobamba. The only way to get there was by plane, and because it was so isolated the town was very, very religious. The Spanish priests ruled the people with a tight grip and had instilled the feeling that 'woe would befall anyone daring to speak against the images of the Church.'

Almost as soon as they arrived in Moyobamba, our missionary sisters began witnessing from house to house and started inviting people to come to the newly established Christian meetings in the town. They had invited only a few honest-hearted persons when leaflets began to appear on the streets. The message? "There are two dangerous elements that are in Moyobamba —two women who don't believe in Hell nor in our images. Do not listen to them; do not accept their literature. Bring any that you have to us and we will take care of it."

Almost immediately, the two missionaries were the objects of a clergy-inspired campaign of hate. During one Christian meeting a mob of about 50 men and boys led by three priests stormed up to the one-room adobe Kingdom Hall. The sisters had bolted the door shut and it held against the blows of the opposers. But, among other things, the mob threw cow manure all over the outside walls. Also, the two missionaries were threatened with bodily harm if they did not get out of town.

The next day our sisters went to the mayor of the town and explained what had happened. He was appalled, and they formulated a letter of protest to the Prefect of the Department. The sisters received a promise of protection, but the threats and general harassment continued.

The priests promised to give a comic book to every boy that brought one of our publications to the parochial school. Quite some time later, the prefect sent a policeman from Lima to stand outside the Kingdom Hall door while Christian meetings were in progress. The opposers had lost the battle, for up to 26 persons were present at meetings during visits of the circuit overseer, and two sheeplike individuals were baptized despite the clergy-fomented opposition in Moyobamba.

Now, please consider another example of foiled clerical opposition. In November 1959, Reginald and Irene Wallwork opened up the Kingdom-preaching work in Ayacucho. Later, they were joined by Merle Laurens and Phyllis Wepener. As the people began to know these Christians as Jehovah's Witnesses, it did not take long for the priests to work up opposition. This they did in a subtle way. They went to the political authorities and pressed them to do something about expelling the missionaries from that town. Consequently, one day Brother Wallwork was called into the office of the Investigation Department. There he was plied with many questions, but was also shown a petition signed by nine priests and by the prefect. This paper had been sent to Lima, and so an investigation had been ordered. This could be serious.

Brother Wallwork promptly refuted all the lies spoken by the priests. It was also explained that only recently he had talked to the prefect and found him to be a reasonable man, quite interested in the Bible. What, then, had happened? Well, someone in the prefect's office was working in cahoots with the priests. That individual had slipped the petition in among other papers so that the prefect had signed the document without really knowing its true nature. All of this was reported to the Society's branch office and, since our work was well known in Lima, the whole scheme "fell through" without further difficulty.

Of course, the priests were not happy about that. Whenever they passed by the missionary home carrying religious idols during processions, they never failed to stop, look up at the balcony of the home and mutter a few incantations against all those living there.

A TIME FOR EXPANSION

The work of declaring the "good news" was making fine advancement in Peru when Brother N. H. Knorr visited us in December 1959. An assembly was to be held in connection with that visit. However, just the previous year we had been ousted from our chosen assembly site. So, to prevent a recurrence of this, we instituted a writ of habeas corpus against the Director of Government. When confronted with it, he disclaimed any responsibility for what had happened to us the year before and even proclaimed himself a friend of Jehovah's Witnesses. So, we had a fine assembly in the "U" Stadium, where the main talk was attended by well over 2,000 persons. That was almost twice the number of Kingdom publishers in the country. Incidentally, we shelved the writ of habeas corpus, although it is still on file in the Palace of Justice at Lima.

At the time of Brother Knorr's visit, Bent Pedersen was appointed branch overseer. But expansion was the big item on our visitor's agenda. Consideration was given to the building of a new branch-missionary home in Lima.

Construction got under way in Miraflores the following June. The Society had acquired two lots covering an area of 7,948 square feet (738 square meters). There a beautiful two-story branch-missionary home was erected. The first floor housed the office and stock rooms, a large entryway and a Kingdom Hall capable of seating 200 persons. On the second floor were living accommodations for 12 missionaries or members of the Bethel family. The new building truly was a "home" in every sense of the word. Construction was completed in October 1961, and the new building was dedicated on the 21st of that month.

It might be mentioned that because of personal responsibilities Brother Pedersen had to leave the missionary field and return to the United States with his wife. So, in April 1961, Brother Don Burt was appointed as branch overseer in Peru.

DISASTER STRIKES ICA

Disciples of Jesus Christ have the identifying mark of love. (John 13:34, 35) How well this was demonstrated in March 1963, when disaster struck the town of Ica, 170 miles (270 kilometers) southeast of Lima! Because mistakes were made by those controlling the floodgates on the river, the town and many vineyards were inundated. The waters swept away the local Kingdom Hall, as well as many homes, including those of some Witnesses.

However, Christian love went into action. All over Peru Jehovah's people acted as one. Quickly, a relief fund was set up and two tons of clothing and food also were sent to stricken fellow believers in Ica. Yes, God's servants really care about each other.

OVERCOMING KINGDOM HALL
CONSTRUCTION PROBLEMS

Besides the love they have among themselves, Jehovah's people manifest other godly traits that often contribute to the success of their endeavors. This can be illustrated by what happened in Trujillo in the mid-1960's. Because of rapid growth in the congregation the Kingdom Hall was unable to accommodate everyone and a new hall was needed. Happily, Jehovah opened the way for the brothers to obtain a plot of land and a loan for Kingdom Hall construction.

Before long the local Witnesses were busy carrying bricks, hauling loads of iron and working hard at the construction site. Why, even the sisters became very adept at mixing cement "by hand," as they did not have a cement mixer!

There were many obstacles. For example, the brother assigned to complete the "paper work" needed an engineer's signature on the plans. Well, to sign them one engineer wanted $110, another, $150—prices the brothers could not pay. But the problem was overcome in an unusual way.

One day the brother doing the "paper work" was standing in line at a bank when a man came along and pushed in front of him. The brother was annoyed, but exercised the Christian fruit of self-control and said nothing. That very day someone suggested that the brother contact a certain engineer to obtain the signature needed on the plans. Well, that engineer turned out to be the same individual who had pushed in front of our brother at the bank. The man was very friendly, said he liked to help good work, and readily signed the papers, asking only $11 as his fee. Truly, displaying Christian qualities can be rewarding. Today the Kingdom Hall in Trujillo stands as a silent testimony to the fine traits and hard work of Christians in that vicinity.

ANOTHER ASSEMBLY "FIRST"

Our first large international assembly was held in Lima from January 4 to 8, 1967. The Peruvian brothers were thrilled that the delegates included many fellow believers from other lands, as well as certain directors of the Society. Almost 500 Witnesses from various countries were on hand and their presence certainly upbuilt their Peruvian brothers and sisters.

Brother F. W. Franz gave the principal talk to 5,940 conventioners on Saturday night. But the largest crowd that had ever attended an assembly in Peru up to that time gathered to hear Brother Knorr speak the next day. That audience numbered 6,925. That was a fine attendance, for in 1967 the peak number of Kingdom publishers in Peru reached only 2,810.

In 1969, 51 missionaries, circuit overseers and others in Peru came under provisions made by the Society to assist them financially so that they could travel to assemblies abroad. This certainly was appreciated and these conventioners returned with a wealth of spiritual things to share with their fellow believers in this land. However, we had our "Peace on Earth" District Assembly in Lima during January 1970. What a delight it was to have a peak attendance of 7,414 at that gathering! Increased activity truly had borne fruit by the late 1960's, for our 1969 Memorial attendance reached 13,751.

We had entered the 1970's, and the work of declaring the "good news" was going well in this ancient Land of the Incas. But what awaited us in the months and years ahead?

THE EARTH QUAKES!

One of the worst disasters in Peru's history struck at 3:30 p.m. on Sunday, May 31, 1970. A gigantic earthquake then literally shook down villages and towns in the Andes and coastal areas. Many of Jehovah's people were affected, and Kingdom Halls were damaged or completely destroyed at Chimbote, Casma, Huaraz, Trujillo and other places.

News of the earthquake flashed around the world. Almost as quickly, Jehovah's people went into action. It was heartwarming indeed to see their response. Christians in Peru and other lands quickly came to the aid of their stricken brothers. From the Watch Tower Society's headquarters in Brooklyn came $25,000 for relief and reconstruction, as well as 15 tons of clothing. Peruvian brothers themselves contributed $3,091, and $2,084 came from others all over the world. Seven tons of clothing were gathered from the congregations in Lima. Later, over a period of time, funds were provided to rebuild three Kingdom Halls in Chimbote, one in Huaraz and the halls in Máncora and Sullana that were damaged by subsequent earthquakes.

Although the major earthquake struck on Sunday afternoon, roads were not open until late Tuesday evening, and there was much speculation over the radio as to whether private cars would be permitted to use them. Undaunted, the brothers loaded supplies into four cars or panel trucks and one 10-ton truck and headed for the disaster area at 1 a.m. on Wednesday.

The first town reached was Casma, which then had a congregation of 20 publishers. Most of Casma's structures were adobe buildings that had been shaken down into a pile of suffocating dust and rubble. Even the town's hospital, although built with reinforced steel, had collapsed. Unfortunately, one brother, confined to a wheelchair, was unable to escape, and he died in the disaster. Supplies intended for distribution among the brothers were left with a special pioneer.

Then it was on to Chimbote, with an estimated population of about 200,000. Some 300 Witnesses were associated with the three congregations in that city. All the homes had been destroyed and the Kingdom Halls had been ruined. Nevertheless, the brothers had cleared the rubble from the cement floor of one hall, had put up straw mat walls and held their weekly congregation book study there on Tuesday night. The first of the relief supplies of food, drinking water, blankets, clothes and so forth arrived the next morning.

But how were the Witnesses faring in Huaraz and Caraz, high in the Andes mountains? According to radio reports, these towns had practically been wiped out, either by the quake or by a mammoth mud slide caused when a portion of Huascarán mountain fell into a nearby lake. Although planes and helicopters had been dropping supplies into the stricken areas, eight days passed before it was announced by radio that the road was passable. Immediately, two vehicles were packed with supplies, and some brothers headed for Huaraz, where there was a congregation of 20 publishers and two special pioneers.

There were delays and dangers on the road. Finally, however, early on Wednesday morning the brothers reached Huaraz at an elevation of about 10,000 feet (3,000 meters). Little camps had cropped up all around the city and it was quite a job locating the brothers and sisters. However, finally at 5 p.m. they were found in huts made from branches of eucalyptus trees. What a delight it was to see them! And how glad they were to get the supplies, which included food, medicine and kerosine stoves that would help them to keep warm during the extremely cold nights!

Only two persons associated with the Huaraz Congregation had been injured; no Witnesses there had died in the disaster. By helicopter an injured sister had been taken to Lima for medical attention. And a young brother, who had been buried under adobe debris but had been dug out with no more than a broken jaw, accompanied the brothers to Lima on their return trip.

ON TO CARAZ

Only some time later were we able to reach the town of Caraz, where there was an isolated group of seven brothers. A mud slide had completely covered two towns between Huaraz and Caraz, blocking all traffic by land.

Around July 1, 1970, we applied for a permit to travel into the mountains through Huaraz and on to Caraz. It turned out, however, that our schedule called for a trip up the mountain when traffic was actually supposed to be coming down the mountain. Nevertheless, the brother assigned to obtain the permit found that he had held Bible studies with the man handling the permits. As matters turned out, the official gave the brother a permit for a five-car caravan and wrote on the document the words "First Priority—Jehovah's Witnesses' Caravan." Although our brothers were stopped three times, in each case the permit got them through.

After a stop at Huaraz, four of the five cars headed for Caraz. Without difficulty, they got through the first mud slide—the one that had hit the town of Ranrahirca. The engineers had made a makeshift road across the mud. While the brothers were thinking about what to do next, a captain of the Civil Guard approached the car and asked if they would take him on to Yungay, the next town that had been covered over by the mud. That was fine with everybody.

Huge boulders and rocks were strewn everywhere. At one point, the cars had to go down into a newly formed swiftly flowing river. Three of them made it, but one car had to turn back.

At Yungay, the other covered town, the smell was not too pleasant, for many dead bodies were in evidence close to the edges of the mud slide. Leaving Yungay, the brothers and the captain continued on to Caraz. They went as far as they could across the ground prepared by the road workers. Then they started out across the trackless waste. Everything went fine until they hit a soft spot and both rear wheels sank in up to the axle. Everyone got out. The captain called about 20 workers of the road gang and, though the ground had a shaky movement to it, they pushed until the car was free. From there on to Caraz the going was not too difficult.

Caraz was in the path of the mud slide that had followed the course of the river, but the slide had swerved just before reaching the town. Although most of the adobe houses had been damaged by the quake, generally the people had been able to salvage their personal possessions. Our brothers were all right but sorely in need of food and medicine. We left them tents, food, blankets and lanterns.

The brothers from Caraz accompanied us to Yungay. As they started loading additional supplies on their backs to carry them back to Caraz, the captain who had accompanied us stopped a truck and told the driver: "Here, take these things and these people over as far as you go." So our brothers, as well as those heavy supplies, were taken at least three quarters of the way across the mud slide of Yungay. From there, the journey was comparatively easy for them. Incidentally, all of this took place while no traffic was permitted in the area. So, Jehovah's Witnesses were the first to get through to Caraz by car.

In succeeding weeks our fellow believers in the devastated areas were further fortified through visits of their spiritual brothers from other parts of Peru. In fact, during that period a circuit assembly was held in Chimbote, much to the surprise of the city's residents. That gathering showed them that Jehovah's people care for one another.

Outstanding throughout the crisis was the guiding hand of Jehovah, so evident in directing his people. Certainly, the brothers and sisters in the stricken areas deeply appreciated the assistance and generosity of their fellow worshipers of God. Of course, especially do we credit Jehovah with the outworking of matters during that time of disaster and we are deeply grateful for his unfailing direction and aid.

REACHING UNTOUCHED TERRITORY

Throughout Peru on April 9, 1971, a total of 18,397 persons attended the Lord's Evening Meal. That year we had a peak of 5,384 Kingdom publishers, or one publisher to every 2,600 inhabitants. So, we still had plenty to do in God's service. In fact, although there was a need for much witnessing in urban areas, we had long been wondering how we were going to cover our vast rural territory. Situated here and there throughout the rugged Andes mountains was one populated valley after another—a great untouched territory.

True, some inroads had been made by special pioneers and a few brothers who served where the need was great. For example, special pioneer Alfredo Diaz and 16 others had taken a 20-day witnessing journey into northern Peru. They had placed hundreds of publications and had found many honest-hearted individuals. But there was so much more to do throughout the country!

Happily, Jehovah's hand never is short. Accordingly, in May 1971 something happened that led to better coverage of our untouched territory. While visiting their son in Peru, one married couple also wondered how all the isolated inhabitants of this country could be reached with the Kingdom message. On returning home to the United States, they made arrangements to send a fully equipped, self-contained motor home to their son for use in the Andes. Two motorbikes also were sent for this purpose.

With this development, a whole new field of activity was opening up. Missionary Joe Leydig and three special pioneers (one of whom spoke the native dialect, Quechua) were assigned to use the house-car. It was dubbed the *Casa Luz*, or "Light House." The four brothers also used a Land Rover that had been obtained locally.

On May 21, 1972, the four full-time Kingdom proclaimers started out. Their assignment? The Urubamba Valley, once sacred to the Incas. It is located high in the mountains between the cities of Cuzco and Macchu-Picchu, the last Inca stronghold.

EARNEST EFFORTS BRING GOOD RESULTS

In three and a half months of preaching throughout the valley, the four brothers placed 5,042 books and 9,146 magazines. For efficient coverage of rural sections, our brothers rose at five o'clock in the morning and witnessed to farmers on the way to their fields. Villages along the roadside were covered quickly. But what about those perched high up on the side of a mountain and surrounded by terraces and ancient ruins? Reaching those villages required hiking up steep paths while loaded down with bulging book bags.

Interestingly, each village seemed to have its own personality. In one, books were placed only with the children—10- to 14-year-olds. The parents wanted nothing. In another village, everyone—men and women alike—literally had "passed out," apparently under the influence of a local beverage that must have flowed liberally during the fiesta of the previous night.

Only three people were found in the next town; all the others were in the fields. Reaching the following village required some climbing. But it was worth the effort. Much interest was found. Few had money for the literature, but all were willing to trade something for it. At the end of the morning, our brothers were loaded down with foodstuffs as they hiked back to the *Casa Luz*. One had a sackful of corn; another a book bag full of sweet potatoes. Joe Leydig had pocketed two eggs in exchange for several magazines, but unfortunately forgot them until he leaned against the Land Rover.

Later in the day, a book and a Bible were traded for a live sheep—fresh meat for the table! Another book and two magazines were exchanged for 15 avocados. A combination of five books was given for some 200 bananas. And one interested man gladly gathered up about four pounds (1.8 kilograms) of coffee beans to offer for a book. At the nearest town of any size, such items could be sold and the money used to buy needed gasoline.

How quickly will some abandon Babylonish practices? Well, when two brothers made a return visit on one man, a discussion of doctrine ensued and it was shown that the Bible condemns idolatry. At that, the man shook his head and looked up at the images adorning his adobe wall. One by one, he took them down, walked outside, poured kerosine over the images and burned them in front of the brothers.

Working outlying sections that are isolated because of numerous mountain ridges and almost inaccessible valleys required patience and determination. At times the trail bikes came in handy. For instance, with difficulty, two of the pioneers used the bikes to reach the town of Lares. They arrived there with briefcases full of publications and several boxes of literature tied to the bikes. A wonderful day was spent witnessing in the town. That evening, several interested persons gathered for a Bible talk. So, that trip, too, was rewarding.

"THE ARK" AND "THE SCORPION"

Up to this point, the *Casa Luz* had been used mainly in the southern part of Peru. But what about the central and northern sections? Well, it was possible to obtain a truck chassis and construct a new house-car, one strong enough to meet the rigors of rural roads and trails. Because this vehicle was oblong and boxlike, it was named "The Ark." That name may also be fitting because the five special pioneers using the vehicle often brought in live sheep, chickens, guinea pigs, turkeys and ducks received for literature placed with the people.

Besides "The Ark," which was put in service during 1973, a third vehicle became available for use in what we might term our witnessing expeditions. It was called "The Scorpion," a name chosen with the figurative language of Revelation 9:3-5 in mind.

So, then, all sections of Peru—north, central and south—have been reached through the hard work of full-time Kingdom proclaimers covering the unassigned territories in this country. Thousands of books, booklets, tracts and magazines have been placed with the Quechua-, Aymara- and Spanish-speaking Indians. Wherever our three mobile units have gone—whether into the jungle or up to mining towns at altitudes of 16,000 feet (4,900 meters)—something fine has been accomplished. In 1978, the *Casa Luz* was still working in unassigned territory and carrying the Kingdom message to some remote areas of Peru.

SPREADING TRUTH IN THE AMAZON JUNGLE

But wait! There was a section of the country that the house-cars could not reach—the vast jungle in northeastern Peru. For the most part, it, too, was unassigned territory. What about that area?

The Amazon region is composed of thousands upon thousands of square miles of tangled jungle criss-crossed with rivers large and small. Along their shores are hundreds of little "chacras," or farms, with villages dotted here and there. It is said that about 37 different Indian tribes live in the Amazon territory. Some of these have been influenced little by so-called civilization, whereas others have been attracted to modern ways. How were we to spread the truth to these isolated jungle peoples?

In 1973, Cesar Chavez, Manuel Molina and Americo Matsuda got together to talk about building a boat for use in witnessing along the shores of the jungle rivers. Soon such a craft was being built at the port town of Callao, with missionary Walter Akin in charge of construction. When completed, the boat was separated into two parts. These sections were hauled to the town of Pucallpa, where they were rejoined. Dubbed *El Refugio*, the 15-ton boat was launched in the Ucayali River.

The special pioneer list had been combed and much care had been taken in selecting a proper crew. For one thing, all six brothers had to know how to swim. Also, these men would have to be able to stand the rigors of life in the jungle. Theirs would not be an easy assignment by any means.

One of the first settlements covered was New San Juan, where about 500 people lived in thatched-roofed, open-air homes. When the brothers arrived, the villagers (most of whom were Protestants) were sure they would be able to convert the newcomers to their religion. But, in a short time, just the opposite happened. The pioneers began many home Bible studies, and soon, on an average, 23 persons were attending the talks and meetings that had been organized in that small village.

Among the Shipibo and Conibo tribes the pioneers effected what might be called a 'strange exchange' with the natives. They traded languages! Yes, the tribesmen would teach their dialect to the pioneers who, in turn, taught them Spanish, along with Bible truth.

The town of Contamana, between Pucallpa and Iquitos, was full of people interested in the Bible. Day and night, individuals sought out the pioneers to ask Bible questions and obtain literature. Copies of the book *Your Youth—Getting the Best out of It* went like "hot cakes." Among many of Contamana's 10,000 inhabitants, it was possible to establish Bible studies, a number of which later developed into congregation meetings.

RIVER PERILS

Besides the general hardships of jungle life, the crew members of *El Refugio* faced other perils. Even as the apostle Paul experienced "dangers from rivers," these pioneers found the Ucayali to be a swift-flowing, treacherous river.—2 Cor. 11:26.

At 3 a.m. on Wednesday, August 10, 1977, hurricane winds suddenly exploded over the area, causing a flash flood. Rapidly, the volume of water increased and the river rose in choppy waves. Because of the rising waters, the mooring ropes of *El Refugio* broke away from their stakes, requiring that the crew member serving as watchman go ashore and try to secure them. But the buffeting wind soon tore away all the ropes and the boat was adrift. The other crew members, who had slept through all of this, awakened and tried to start the motor in order to fight against the raging current. However, their efforts were to no avail and they had to watch helplessly as the waters slammed the craft against the steep riverbank.

At that very moment, a large section of the bank, undermined by the rushing waters, fell into the river. This caused the boat to tilt to starboard with the brothers trapped inside. Fortunately, though, one of the sliding doors was open. Though this permitted the boat to sink more rapidly, it did provide an opening for the pioneers to fight their way out of the craft. They all got out! In the pitch black of the night, the brothers swam safely to shore. Yes, all their literature, clothing, cooking utensils, book bags and personal effects had been lost to the hungry river. But they were there —alive! A fervent prayer of thanks went up to Jehovah for his protection.

At early dawn, the brothers could see their boat, one end apparently being held up by a large air bubble in the prow. The craft was floating gently in the then-calm waters, but there was no time to lose. At seven o'clock, with cables and two tractors kindly loaned by the townspeople, the boat was pulled to the shore. Later that day, an enormous floating boat-crane belonging to a petroleum company was able to right the 15-ton boat and put it afloat once more. Thanks again to Jehovah, this time for opening the way to recover their floating home so quickly!

As news of this mishap reached the brothers throughout Peru, contributions and supplies came pouring in. Consequently, it was possible to equip the pioneers for further service along the rivers of the Amazon basin.

EXPANSION CONTINUES

Meanwhile, increased activity on the part of Jehovah's people throughout Peru impressed upon us the need for larger branch facilities. Memorial attendance in 1972 reached 19,772. It was not surprising, then, that during a brief visit by Brothers N. H. Knorr and M. H. Larson arrangements were made to buy an empty lot next to the branch building.

Work on the branch addition began in March 1973. The project was well supported by the brothers and, in spite of an increased shortage of building materials, the new structure rapidly took shape. On the first floor was a spacious Kingdom Hall that could comfortably seat 300 persons. Living accommodations for missionaries assigned to work in nearby congregations were provided on the second floor. The branch addition was dedicated on January 19, 1974, by Brother N. H. Knorr, who then spoke to a happy audience of 456 witnesses of Jehovah.

During that same month the "Divine Victory" International Assembly was held in Lima. That gathering certainly was significant in the eyes of those who had watched our work grow in this country over the years. Among the 19,738 persons present (our greatest assembly audience till that time) were delegates from Canada, the United States and Europe. Interesting English-language programs and tours had been arranged for these visitors. Colorful folkloric dances rounded out the informative historical presentations. Indeed, that assembly was a delight to foreign delegates and Peruvian Christians alike.

With continued growth, most sites were too small for our assemblies. Also, we could not use most sports stadiums because religious gatherings were prohibited in them. So, the Lima circuits appointed a committee and before long an ideal spot for an assembly site was obtained in an undeveloped area called Campoy, just a 20-minute ride from the center of the capital city. In that quiet, peaceful setting enthusiastic volunteer workers labored until an excellent assembly field with essential facilities had been prepared. It was ready in time for the two 1976 district assemblies attended by a total of 18,914 persons. About a year later, the assembly grounds and various structures were dedicated during a visit of A. D. Schroeder, a member of the Governing Body of Jehovah's Witnesses. On that occasion, 14,353 persons were present, representing 96 congregations of greater Lima and nearby cities.

In 1977, the love and care of the Governing Body certainly was impressed on us here in Peru because during that year we enjoyed, not just one, but two visits by members of the Governing Body. Brother Grant Suiter, along with his wife, Edith, spent six fast-moving days at the branch office. Brother Suiter also spoke to a crowd of 15,056 at the assembly site in Campoy.

WE CONTINUE "SHINING AS ILLUMINATORS"

The year 1978 has proved to be a very busy one for Jehovah's people in Peru. Our four "Joyful Workers" District Assemblies drew a total of 28,063, with 636 being baptized at these gatherings in symbol of their dedication to Jehovah God. We now have 12,925 Kingdom proclaimers spreading spiritual light and truth in this ancient Land of the Incas.

How grateful we are for Jehovah's many spiritual provisions through the years! For example, not only have we benefited from the missionary work of brothers and sisters sent here after being trained at Gilead School, but certain Peruvian Witnesses have received such training. Also, since its inception here in 1962, the Kingdom Ministry School has been very beneficial. And, how grateful we are for the present Pioneer School! All this beneficial schooling, along with the many other rich spiritual provisions made by our loving heavenly Father, enables us to continue serving as effective light-bearers.

So, with confidence in Jehovah, Peruvian Christians look to the future. We are determined to press on in Kingdom service, whether in the towering Andes, along tangled jungle paths, or elsewhere in our vast territory. Delighted we are indeed to serve faithfully with our fellow believers earth wide while "shining as illuminators in the world"!—Phil. 2:15.

SENEGAL AND NEIGHBORING LANDS

Senegal is a land of contrasts. Situated on the westerly tip of Africa's big bulge, it is constantly swept by the parching desert winds of the Sahara to the north or by the cool ocean breezes of the Atlantic to the west and south. The northern stretches of open desert sand merge gradually into the humid jungle-like regions of the southern district. But the contrasts do not end there. They carry right over into the people and their origin, customs and religion.

Apparently attracted by the life-sustaining waters of the huge Senegal River, wandering nomadic tribes of northern Mauritania gradually pushed southward in about the eleventh century of the Common Era, bringing along their Arabic language and customs, as well as the Moslem religion. They were the Berbers, or Zenaga, the latter term probably providing the basis for the name "Senegal." But the descendants of Ham, who had also migrated to the African continent, were attracted to this land of contrasts as well. Drawn by its more moderate climate and refreshing ocean breezes, African tribes from the south slowly moved northward settling in the fertile valleys of the Casamance and Gambia Rivers. With them came their customs, languages and animistic religion. By the gradual fusing of these two diversified ethnic groups, meeting, as they did, in a land that links the scorching desert of the north with the steaming jungle of the interior, the foundation for a new nation and a new people was being laid. Eventually, it would become the Republic of Senegal.

But other eyes were turned to this strange, yet inviting, land. Thus it was that in 1455 the first Europeans arrived. It was then that the Venetian explorer Ca Da Mosto (commissioned by Prince Henry of Portugal) set foot on the rocky cape that juts out into the Atlantic. Now known as Cape Vert, it is the present-day site of the modern capital city of Dakar, the gateway to West Africa. The Europeans brought with them new customs, new languages and, yes, a different religion, thus adding to the already existing contrasts.

The sixteenth century saw the beginning of the slave trade to provide cheap labor for plantations in the Americas. The Dutch settled on nearby Gorée Island, and soon Spanish, Portuguese, English, Dutch and French traders regularly visited the west coast of Africa. In 1635, Catholic missionaries came and opened up parts of the country for the colonial powers. Selfish greed soon resulted in conflicts and war, with the

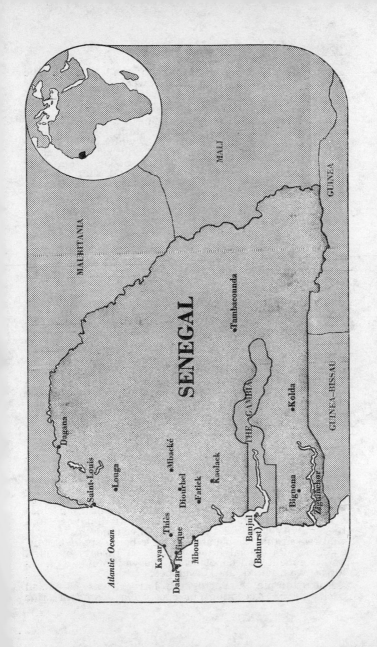

French finally winning the upper hand in 1817. The real colonization of Senegal followed.

SEEDS OF TRUTH ARE PLANTED

As worldly authorities were vying for the domination of Africa, in 1914 the loving Creator, Jehovah God, set up his heavenly government, which will in due time relieve the oppressed and bring refreshment to all races. But when would this good news of the set-up kingdom reach Senegal? It was in 1951 that the first rays of spiritual light penetrated this land. One of Jehovah's Witnesses, then working for a commercial firm, was able to spend six months in this country. Did he let his light shine? He certainly did! In the short time he spent in Senegal, he very actively sowed the first seeds of truth.

But to grow, planted seeds need water and care. (1 Cor. 3:5-9) Who else would come to this land of hot sun and refreshing rain to help the seed take root and develop? Who would be willing to leave the comforts of his home to come to a new land, strange in so many ways, to bring comfort to depressed souls? How lovers of truth rejoiced when in 1953 the call was answered by a full-time Kingdom proclaimer sent here by the Watch Tower Society!

Would the colonial authorities welcome these sincere efforts to bring a message of peace and hope to people hungering for truth? On the contrary. This first special pioneer had to enter Senegal as a representative of a textile firm. He comments: "The isolation was a little difficult at first, living without Christian fellowship and no meetings. But the preaching work kept me busy, and I soon found persons willing to listen."

The people of Senegal are warm and hospitable. Living in a land of contrasting religions, they generally welcome religious discussions. Since about 80 to 90 percent of the population are Moslem, many questions come up about the differences between the Bible and the Koran, and these queries often lead into serious discussions. But there was opposition, too, in those days of small beginnings. A large quantity of our magazines was distributed in a section of Senegal that year, and this activity aroused the ire of Christendom's clergy, who feared that their pastures were being spoiled. However, despite official interference and threats of fines, imprisonment and deportation, the work took root. Interest was found and developed.

For example, a Portuguese barber was contacted back in 1953. Accepting our book *"The Kingdom Is at*

Hand," he made steady progress and soon was attending the small meetings that had been organized in the home of an interested person. What would be the result? Well, he became the first congregation publisher in Senegal. But since 1953 this seed has produced abundant fruitage and 17 members of his family now are actively glorifying Jehovah's name.

In 1954, a special pioneer couple arrived to provide further help. Aside from the problem of adjusting to the climate, customs and food, these early pioneers faced other difficulties. Many of the people contacted could not read French (the national language) and hours upon hours were spent first teaching them how to read and then helping them to understand the Bible. But with much patience and the blessing of Jehovah, the work started to gain momentum. The message of God's kingdom was beginning to be felt in Senegal.

For instance, by 1954, three Bible study groups were functioning in Senegal, with an average attendance of 20 persons. During house-to-house witnessing here, people from Gorée were contacted, and it was learned that the majority of that island's residents had read our literature. In fact, they had been telling others that it contained the absolute truth. Hence, although we had not yet worked from door to door on Gorée, "that island has already been witnessed to," wrote one Kingdom proclaimer.

MISSIONARY ACTIVITY BEGINS

The year 1955 saw further increase. On May 15 the small group was thrilled to see six new ones take their stand for Jehovah. Toward the end of the year, there was another response to the 'Macedonian call.' (Acts 16:9) Jean Queyroi, a graduate of the Watchtower Bible School of Gilead, arrived in Senegal and our work became established on a more solid footing.

But what kind of territory awaited this missionary? What were the people like? How would they respond to the Kingdom message?

Senegal had come a long way from the time that the Arabian nomads of Mauritania discovered the refreshing waters of the Senegal River, or the migrating African tribes first settled along the Casamance and Gambia Rivers, back in the early eleventh century. Throughout the following centuries, several distinct tribes had developed in this land of contrasts.

The most populous are the Ouolofs (Wolof), a tall, stately race noted for very colorful dress. The men wear baggy trousers and a *boubou,* a large outer garment flowing to the ground in a dazzling array of colors. Often Ouolof (Wolof) homes are square and made of straw or clay. Polygamy is widely practiced. Then there are the Sérère (Serer), whose prime occupation is farming, the growing of millet and peanuts. The Peuls (Fulani) are thought to be the descendants of intermarriage between the Berbers and the local African tribes and are generally cattle breeders. The Toucouleur (Tukulor) tribe was the first to accept the Moslem religion. And then there are the Sarakolé (Soninke), the Mandingue (Mandingo) and the Diolas (Dyola), the rice farmers and tradesmen.

Although nearly all residents of Senegal claim to be either Moslem or Catholic, the practice of ancient animist religions is obvious everywhere. *Gri-gris,* or good-luck charms, are seen attached to individuals' arms, waists, legs and ankles, or interwoven in their hair. Often these articles are suspended from the necks of sheep, goats and even horses. Large sums of money are paid to have these charms blessed to protect the bearer from evil spirits or to guard the affection of a husband or wife. Senegal was certainly a land of contrasts awaiting the zealous servants of Jehovah— a land of bush and forest; of wild birds and ferocious beasts; of clear refreshing water and malaria-infested regions; of peanuts and rice; of oil and textiles; of cattle raisers and people casting their nets for fish; of quaint African villages and a large modern capital city, Dakar, with over 798,700 inhabitants.

Missionary Jean Queyroi had much to do when he appeared on the scene in 1955. He comments: "There was only a small isolated group in Senegal when I arrived. But I found a territory ripe for harvesting. And what variety! Dakar is a large cosmopolitan city with Senegalese, Guineans, Malians, Togolese, Dahomians, Mauritanians, Lebanese and Syrians, as well as Portuguese and other Europeans, especially the French. There was a great work ahead of us. The Moslem population did not show much interest in the truth but always gave a hearing ear. Bible studies soon were started, and people began developing an interest in the truth."

One difficulty encountered by early Witnesses was getting sufficient Bible literature into the country for use in field service. All books and publications had to be sent through the mail in small packages, and every time they went through customs it was a delicate situation. Occasionally a zealous customs official would open a package and, upon seeing all the literature, would ask many questions. Several packages were confiscated in this way.

GROWTH BEGINS

Although true Christianity here still was in its day of small beginnings, Jehovah's loving organization did not overlook the little nucleus developing in this land. With great joy and excitement, these hardworking Kingdom proclaimers prepared for a visit by a director of the Watch Tower Bible and Tract Society of Pennsylvania, M. G. Henschel, who was accompanied by Harry Arnott. And it was an added privilege to taste some joys of the 1955 assemblies! Six of the main convention discourses were delivered by the visiting brothers at a three-day assembly from December 5 to 7, 1955, a gathering held for just a small group of publishers. As a result of this visit, a congregation was formed in Dakar, the first in Senegal. It reported a peak of 18 publishers during the 1956 service year.

How thrilled we were to see 42 persons present at the Memorial in 1957! That year there was a peak of 22 publishers, a 50-percent increase over the previous year. Of course, during this period Senegal was still a colony of France, and many French people were working here. These were contacted, and a number started out in the witnessing work. But since they did not stay in Senegal, they would bring only temporary increase to the local congregation, returning to France after a short while.

It was in 1956 that a family was contacted that would later play a prominent part in the development of Kingdom interests in this land of contrasts. A study was started with a young Catholic lady, and shortly thereafter she was joined in the study by her husband —a man prominent in the tax administration of the local government. These people were from very well-known families in Dakar and Saint-Louis. Many doctrinal points had to be cleared up, but the truth steadily produced good results. The husband was a very heavy smoker, and in his office there was a large display of pipes on his desk, not to mention cigarette lighters, tobacco pouches, and so forth. Then one day there was nothing! "Yes," he said with confidence, "I've thrown them all out. That's finished with me— I don't smoke anymore!" Certainly, a step in the right direction.

The entire family courageously took their stand. And what an uproar this created in Dakar! "What! The Fourcaults are going to become Jehovah's Witnesses? What a shame!" Since they were from well-known families with certain members in high positions, their new stand for Bible truth hardly pleased anyone. Resisting all the opposition, however, they progressed rapidly to the point of symbolizing their dedication to Jehovah by water baptism. The result was that, in time, all the members of the family became active witnesses of Jehovah.

OPPOSITION ENCOUNTERED

The work was progressing well, but not without official opposition. Endeavoring to reach other large population centers in the interior, one day our brothers were working in Kaolack, a city of over 106,800 situated about 110 miles (177 kilometers) from Dakar. There they encountered the commissioner of police, and a missionary recalls: "He asked me to step inside, saying: 'I know what you are doing here. Follow me!' He took me into his office and asked me to sit down. 'I am well acquainted with you people and I have a file on you,' he said. It seemed that one brother already had been expelled. 'He was of this city and was asked to leave because he did what you are doing!' the commissioner exclaimed, adding: 'Your work is banned here in Senegal. You cannot preach here.' And there I was sitting before him with a bag full of books and booklets, which he well saw! He asked us to return to Dakar and said he would be obliged to make a report on us. What were we to do? We were in this untouched area and did not want to leave without doing something. So we went to another part of town and worked all morning in the service, placing 55 books and hundreds of booklets." Happily, the brothers heard no more from the authorities. But our work was to go on for several more years without legal recognition.

INCREASING OUR EFFORTS

The pioneer couple attended the Divine Will International Assembly at New York city in 1958 and returned with greater enthusiasm to build up the new ones. Brother Wilfred Gooch visited us as zone overseer in January 1959, and his fine counsel was greatly appreciated by the 31 attending his main talk. However, one joy followed another, and so it was that in February Brother N. H. Knorr, then president of the Watch Tower Society, came to Senegal for the first time. Certainly, this was the most outstanding event till then in the development of our work in this land of variety. We enjoyed four thrilling days, with a peak of 42 attentive listeners present for Brother Knorr's special discourse.

With the desire to open up the field in other French-speaking West African countries, Jean Queyroi was sent to Guinea in April of 1959. There were two active brothers in Conakry at the time, and he was able to strengthen them for the work ahead despite their isolation. The visit was not without excitement, though. On the very night that Brother Queyroi stepped off the plane in Conakry there was serious trouble among the different tribes, resulting in intervention by the army. "Some persons were killed," recalls Brother Queyroi. "Others were injured, and there was some burning. But this did not stop us from visiting interested persons the next day. Some of the streets were barricaded, and the inhabitants were frightened. However, things calmed down to the extent that I was able to help the two faithful brothers to continue their peaceful work of making disciples despite turbulent conditions."

In May 1959, the Society asked Brother Queyroi to visit the Cape Verde Islands, a group of islands under Portuguese control situated in the Atlantic off the west coast of Africa. This visit was of great benefit, as many of the persons coming into the truth in Senegal had emigrated from these islands in search of employment. Brother Queyroi took along a Portuguese brother from Dakar and, although they were able to visit only one of these islands, they contacted many interested persons and placed much literature, most of it being distributed free because of the extreme poverty. In the islands it was unlike Dakar with its many different religions. Here, the Catholic Church was still very powerful and evoked much fear among the populace. Everyone passing a church had to salute it; the women were required to kneel with one knee touching the ground, whereas the men were supposed to take off their hats. All made the sign of the cross. Despite this strong religious domination, though, the brothers, to the best of their ability, sowed seeds of truth.

Up to that time, most of those heartily embracing Bible truth in Senegal were of Portuguese and French origin, with many of the latter returning to France after spending a limited period in Africa. Hence, 1960 saw a small decrease, but the places of those leaving were being taken by other interested ones. So the number in the congregation remained about the same.

In 1960, loving concern prompted the Society to arrange for African pioneers to serve here in order to contact the local population better. Many people were pleased to have a European, or *toubab,* come to their homes, but, in general, our message was not taken very seriously. In March of that year, an African pioneer arrived from Cameroon. How he was touched by the warm welcome he received! He carried all his worldly possessions with him in one suitcase as he anxiously stepped off the plane at the airport. Tears of joy streamed down his cheeks when he learned that, to show their appreciation for his coming, the brothers had rented a small apartment and had furnished it with a bed, a stove and the necessary cooking utensils. He was a great help in taking care of the interested Senegalese, who now saw that the truth was not just for the *toubab,* but for the African as well. That year the brothers rejoiced that 10 Africans were among the 45 present for the Memorial.

But this intriguing land of contrasts, with its ever-changing climate, can also pose health problems, as Brother and Sister Queyroi learned. How sad they were that they had to leave behind their spiritual brothers and sisters!

In the early 1960's, surely 'the harvest was great but the workers few' in Senegal. (Matt. 9:37, 38) More workers were needed. Who would answer the call? In the very month of June 1960, when one couple who were full-time servants left, another pioneer couple stepped off the boat in Dakar's famous international port. Brother and Sister Casimir Krawczyk vividly recall these first impressions:

"We were filled with enthusiasm despite the rather rough voyage we had just had. But we noted quite a contrast—the heat! Would we be able to adapt to the change? With Jehovah's help we were eager to try."

By working along with the couple about to leave, Brother and Sister Krawczyk were helped to adjust to their new environment. But they comment: "We remember remarking one day how difficult it was to work the territory and especially to make return visits because, in some quarters, all the houses seemed exactly alike. They were just wooden huts leaning together in the hot sand. But someone replied that we could at least be grateful that the houses did not move —they would always be there in the same place. In time one learns how to distinguish between all the similar dwellings."

QUEST FOR LEGAL RECOGNITION

An important development that affected the lives of all the people, and which eventually was also to have favorable effects on the witness work, was the granting to Senegal of independence from the French colonial power in 1960. Already in 1958 we had made the first attempts to legalize our work, but without success due to the hostility of the colonial powers toward Jehovah's Witnesses. Now that independence had been declared, a second attempt was made, in 1961, but again without success, as the same French officials were still directing National Security. When Brother M. G. Henschel stopped at Dakar in 1963, he encouraged us to continue working toward legalizing our work in Senegal. That third attempt, in 1963, brought no reply.

Then, beginning in 1964, we pleaded our cause before the director of political affairs, who was involved in the false accusations made against us—that we are a secret society inciting insubordination, religious hostility, and so forth. The director was invited to attend our meetings and to come unexpectedly. Information on our subjection to the "superior authorities" finally convinced him that Jehovah's Witnesses respect law and order. (Rom. 13:1-7) Furthermore, the brother handling our case signed a declaration to the effect that all the accusations made against us were false. A final step was a visit to the Minister of the Interior. Thus the Senegalese authorities were convinced. Their decision to grant us legal recognition certainly was to the government's credit, for the authorities had refused to base their judgment on the accusations of our enemies, but had examined the case with impartiality.

Now that the "Association les Témoins de Jéhovah" was registered, much more could be done in bringing in literature and additional workers for the field in the way of specially trained Gilead School graduates. How evident it is that we must not only pray for things to happen, but also take the initiative in order for God to bless our efforts! And Jehovah's arm has not been short.—Isa. 59:1.

GETTING BETTER ESTABLISHED

For several years our work here had continued without the help of Gilead graduates, the first ones having found it necessary to leave. How beneficial it was, then, to have Brother George Amado arrive in Senegal on September 24, 1963, to be followed shortly thereafter by other specially trained missionaries! Now, for the first time, a missionary home was opened and several special pioneers were invited to come under the missionary arrangement, even though they had not attended Gilead School. This enabled more full-time servants to remain in their assignments.

Up to this point the Kingdom-preaching work in Senegal had been under the direction of the Watch Tower Society's branch office in Paris, France. But in order to improve the supervision of our activity here, a branch was established in Senegal itself. Thus on August 22, 1965, Emmanuel Paterakis, accompanied by his wife, arrived in this land of contrasts to enjoy the happy privilege of organizing the local branch office. It was to start functioning on September 1, 1965, and also was to care for the Kingdom-proclamation work in The Gambia, Mali and Mauritania. First, a suitable location for the branch-missionary home had to be found—not an easy task by any means. But with Jehovah's blessing and through perseverance the local office was set up in Dakar.

EXPANDING OUR FIELD OF ACTIVITY

In view of the urgency of the times, arrangements were made to expand the field of activity further in Senegal. Earlier, when the African tribes settled along the Casamance River, they found the area to be very fertile, a land of forests and water, of rice and millet. Ziguinchor became the capital of the Casamance region. Today it is a thriving city of over 72,700 inhabitants. And just as an abundant supply of literal water had been available to the early settlers, so in 1965 refreshing 'waters of truth' were made available by other "pioneers" for the benefit of the people of the Casamance region. Two special pioneers were assigned to Ziguinchor, and they found this predominantly Catholic region to be a productive field for cultivation.

But what about other areas in this land of differing customs and languages? These, too, had to be reached. When a missionary couple were expelled from the land of Mali in September of 1965, they were assigned to open up a missionary home in Saint-Louis. This city of some 88,400 residents is located at the mouth of the Senegal River, the important waterway that attracted early desert tribes to this land of contrasts. Saint-Louis, situated mainly on an island, was founded in 1659, when Louis XIV ruled France, and it once was the capital of the French colony in Senegal. Now mainly Moslem, this city has proved to be one of the more difficult territories to develop. Nevertheless, the first full-time servants to work in Saint-Louis started a number of Bible studies, some of which later bore fruit.

Thiès is a city of some 117,300 inhabitants located about 40 miles (64 kilometers) inland from Dakar. Toward the end of 1965, arrangements were made to cultivate this "field." Initially, the first two special pioneers had a hard time, as nearly all the streets were of loose, dusty, red sand and even walking was difficult, not to speak of trying to use a bicycle. How refreshing was a cool shower after many hours spent there searching for sheeplike ones among the quaint little shacks and straw huts!

Public talks were arranged, films produced by the Society were shown and Bible studies were started. Two missionaries assigned to Thiès increased the ranks of workers in the "harvest." But there were difficulties, too—opposition from the outside and, due to the unwise conduct of some, problems from the inside. Corrective measures were taken and good results were forthcoming. Today, there are 13 Kingdom publishers in Thiès, assisted by the missionaries now assigned there.

UNDETERRED BY OPPOSITION

One Catholic woman had chosen to join the Protestants because they were more inclined to read the Bible. Soon she realized that, although they did more Bible reading, they did nothing to help the people understand the Scriptures. Years later, her Moslem husband came home with three booklets he had obtained from one of Jehovah's Witnesses. He mocked the statement that God had a Son. However, the man's wife, on reading the booklets, recognized the clear ring of truth and wrote the Society for help. Despite much opposition from her husband, this sincere truth-seeker, along with her young daughter, made efforts to study the Bible. The husband indignantly sent his 17-year-old daughter to Lebanon to learn and practice the Moslem religion. The result? She returned, fully convinced that Jehovah's Witnesses have the truth!

Both this girl and her mother were put out of the house by the angry father. But this did not prevent either of them from being baptized in symbol of their dedication to the "God of peace." (Phil. 4:9) Despite many trials, they did not waver in faith but became the first Kingdom publishers in Rufisque, a small city several miles down the coast from Dakar.

GETTING STARTED IN THE GAMBIA

In 1965, the newly established branch office at Dakar began to care for the Kingdom work in The Gambia, that small country that bites like an alligator snout right into the middle of Senegal. Seemingly, it is only due to its occupation by the colonial powers that The Gambia exists as a country separate from Senegal, as its origin and people are the same. Inasmuch as this land hugging the mighty Gambia River was first penetrated by the English, it was the English language, rather than French, that came to be spoken by many of the local people. In 1816, Captain Alexander Grant founded the city of Bathurst, which has since become the capital, with 50,000 inhabitants. The Gambia itself is the home of about 493,000 people.

It is very difficult to determine when the "good news" was first declared in The Gambia. Brothers working in Bathurst (now Banjul) have met persons who have *Studies in the Scriptures*, books written by Brother C. T. Russell. These publications may have been left by "Bible" Brown, a witness of Jehovah who served in The Gambia for a while years ago. Or perhaps this literature was brought in from Sierra Leone.

In 1949, two full-time Kingdom proclaimers entered The Gambia. That year there was considerable activity, with the two missionaries and one congregation publisher reporting the placement of over 1,000 pieces of literature and the conducting of eight home Bible studies. These early missionaries stayed for nearly four years; after they left, the handful of local publishers served for several years without any pioneer help. However, on December 21, 1958, Gilead School graduate Samuel Akinyemi and his wife were assigned to The Gambia. They left family and friends in Nigeria, anxious to tackle the work before them. During this period, The Gambia was cared for by the Society's branch in Ghana.

Diligent work by a small nucleus of two special pioneers and two congregation publishers soon produced fine fruit, for a peak of nine publishers reported field service in 1959. Regular visits by zone and circuit overseers did much to build up faith and strengthen the organization. Although 41 persons attended the Memorial of Christ's death that first year, ties to Babylon the Great, the world empire of false religion, were strong, and ancient superstitions and practices were deep-rooted. Few embraced the truth, and The Gambia has proved to be a rather difficult assignment for Kingdom proclaimers.

CLERICS CRY OUT

The distressed cries of Christendom's false religious shepherds soon were heard ringing throughout the land. They were trying hard to put out the light of truth that was now beginning to shine. (Ps. 43:3) Only 10 months after their arrival, or on October 16, 1959, Brother and Sister Akinyemi were notified by the local police that they were prohibited immigrants and had 14 days in which to leave The Gambia. And the reason for this action? They were "Jehovah's Witnesses." That was all! But the case was taken to court in order to 'defend and legally establish the good news,' and the brothers were blessed with victory, enabling the special pioneers to stay in The Gambia.—Phil. 1:7.

The Anglican clergy threatened the proprietor of a local theater where our meetings were being held. Refusing to be intimidated, the man stated: "These people are talking about God, not the Devil. So why should I drive them out, if I am a man of God myself? No! I will refuse to do as the priests say!"

As of December 1960, the Kingdom work in The Gambia came under the direction of the Society's branch office in Sierra Leone. The regular visits of traveling overseers proved very upbuilding spiritually and resulted in a peak of 15 publishers in 1961.

The years 1961 and 1962 brought action on the legal scene, for the authorities were bent on labeling Jehovah's Witnesses as prohibited immigrants. Two cases, involving two special pioneers from Sierra Leone and a visiting circuit overseer, were taken to the Supreme Court and were decided in our favor—an evident proof that Jehovah was backing his servants! Thus a door for increasing activity remained open.

Another milestone was the formation, in 1962, of the first Gambian congregation of Jehovah's people. Also, the law declaring Jehovah's Witnesses prohibited immigrants was rescinded, giving the brothers greater freedom and peace of mind. Then in September 1965, the newly organized branch in Senegal began caring for the needs of the Gambian brothers. That same year, regular visits of the circuit overseer from Senegal contributed toward the steady advancement of theocratic activities in The Gambia. It was much nearer for Gambian Witnesses to attend circuit and district assemblies in Dakar, where a special program in English was arranged for them.

Now that the law branding Jehovah's Witnesses as prohibited immigrants had been rescinded, would it be possible to have our missionaries come in to give a helping hand? An effort to that end was made in 1967, but without success. The authorities have put out an order limiting to three the number of foreign representatives that Jehovah's Witnesses can have in The Gambia. Despite consistent efforts by the Society and local brothers to have this order removed, no missionaries or other full-time servants have been able to enter The Gambia to bolster up the small congregation in Banjul.

THE "GOOD NEWS" REACHES MALI

A third West African country that came under the care of the Society's Senegal branch was Mali. A huge inland area reaching well into the Sahara Desert and bordered by Algeria on the north, Mali is a land of sand—hot, dusty sand under a burning sun—mainly in the northern Sahelian and Saharan regions. However, the southern regions, especially the part watered by the majestic Niger River, are green, with some forests and luxurious vegetation. The beautiful capital city of Bamako lies on both banks of the Niger River.

Mali's 5,000,000 inhabitants, ranging from white Arabian desert nomads to dark-skinned African tribesmen, are a friendly, hospitable people, contrasting sharply with the uninviting desert that surrounds them. The first "waters" of truth began to flow in Mali during 1962 when the Society invited four Ghanian brothers to open up the field there. After a 'crash course' in French at Abidjan, Ivory Coast, Brother Ewuley Sarpey and his three companions were eagerly anticipating their new assignment. Would it be very different from Ghana?

It certainly proved to be! At first the scorching sun seemed almost unbearable, but the four Kingdom proclaimers soon learned to take advantage of the cooler hours of the day. Meetings for field service were at seven o'clock in the morning. After about three hours of service, trudging along in the hot, loose sand, it was time to head for the cooler protection of home to rest, eat and take a much-needed siesta before preparing to leave for the field again at four o'clock in the afternoon. Often, the work would continue into the cooler hours of the late evening.

Two of these pioneers returned to Ghana in 1964. To replace them, special pioneers Rene Peyronnet and his wife were invited to leave their assignment in Algeria to give a helping hand in Mali. But the climate can be harsh and, after only a few months, health problems came up that necessitated their return to France. They were replaced on May 10, 1964, by Brother and Sister Lucien Frizon, who were assigned to the city of Bamako.

The people of Bamako lived within small, crowded courtyards with several families very close together, often sharing the small dwellings. Animals mingled freely with the chattering women who might be preparing a meal. And in the middle of all this commotion, as if in another world, an elderly Moslem might be sitting on a straw mat under a mango tree with a kettle of water at his side. The water would serve for his ablutions before praying. It was not easy to penetrate the thinking of such people.

In this primitive setting, the "good news" was to be declared. Praying for the aid of Jehovah's spirit, the pioneers tackled the work at hand. Tirelessly, day after day, they served, faithfully declaring a message of peace and comfort. They were joined by another special pioneer couple in the summer of 1965. But the message of God's kingdom was not welcomed by all, and soon official interference was experienced. In September of 1965, just as the Kingdom-preaching work came under the care of the newly established branch office in Senegal, the four special pioneers were deported from Mali. All were reassigned to Senegal.

But the Adversary has not been able to burn up the seeds of truth that were planted and then sprouted in Mali. Brother Sarpey remained in Mali and carried on faithfully there as a special pioneer, also caring for his wife and two children. Brother John Ansah, then a very zealous regular pioneer, was of great help at this critical time due to his friendly contacts with men in authority. What a blessing it is for our work that Brother Ansah continues in full-time service, now as a special pioneer! Indeed, he provides a fine example of endurance and perseverance!

EARLY EFFORTS IN MAURITANIA

The work of declaring the "good news" in the sparsely settled Islamic Republic of Mauritania also is supervised by the Society's branch office in Dakar. In 1966 the first reports of witnessing activity were received from that territory. This indicated the existence of a small spiritual oasis for the desert dwellers of that land. The populace, composed mainly of wandering Arabian tribes, enjoy few modern conveniences, and the camel remains one of the chief means of transportation. The official language is French, although Arabic is the national tongue and is spoken by most of the inhabitants. But the official attitude toward our work is very unfavorable, and it is not easy to make disciples under the present conditions. The two publishers in 1966 were sisters, the wives of men sent to Mauritania on work contracts. They left the country at the end of May 1967.

Nevertheless, the light of truth was kept burning in Mauritania by a brother who moved to the capital, Nouakchott, at the end of 1968. Although newly baptized, he accomplished much in distributing our literature and in starting some home Bible studies. Later, when he moved to France, an isolated publisher at Rosso, on the Senegalese border, began to witness each month. This interested woman was able to travel to Dakar quite frequently and thus could receive spiritual encouragement. Additionally, a sister in Dakar conducted a Bible study with her by mail.

FURTHER PROGRESS IN SENEGAL

Our work in Senegal continued to move ahead, and, after the branch office was set up in Dakar, the closer supervision resulted in a real strengthening of the local organization. There was an increase of 33 percent, with 98 publishers reporting in 1966, including 16 special pioneers and missionaries. Regular circuit and district assemblies contributed to greater spirituality.

In 1967, about 15 years after the first rays of truth shone in this land of contrasts, the number of 100 publishers was surpassed, with a peak of 120 engaging in the service. Enthusiastic reports were coming in regularly from Saint-Louis, Thiès and Ziguinchor. The two congregations in Dakar were expanding steadily, despite the large number of brothers leaving Senegal each year because of the government's program of "Senegalization" of jobs. Twenty full-time Kingdom proclaimers were spearheading the activity, constantly combing the diversified territory. What a thrill to see 268 gathered for the Memorial celebration that year! Senegal is a fisherman's paradise and also, in keeping with Jesus' words, more and more men were being 'caught alive' and were being trained to let down their spiritual nets for a catch.—Luke 5:9-11.

The publications of the Society certainly have served well here in getting people acquainted with their Creator, Jehovah God. Particularly is the *Awake!* magazine well known. Its value is recognized by people in all positions, and almost everyone contacted has either read or seen *Awake!* Many listen with respect when they learn that the publishers of this magazine are Jehovah's Witnesses. Frequently, we are stopped on the street and asked for the latest copy, and many Bible studies have been started, thanks to *Awake!*

During the late 1960's, the ranks of full-time servants in Senegal were growing steadily. The year 1968 saw more missionaries enter this land of contrasts, with a new peak of 139 publishers being reached and 339 gathering together in commemoration of Jesus' death. For the first time, total hours spent in the witnessing work surpassed 50,000, with 266 Bible studies being conducted each month. The stage was being set for future growth.

"PEACE ON EARTH" ASSEMBLIES

And what blessings 1969 had in store! With the help of the generous contributions of the brothers through-out the world, many of the missionaries were privileged to attend one of the "Peace on Earth" International Assemblies in Europe or America. What a joy! In addition to the missionaries, more than 50 of the local Witnesses attended assemblies in Paris, Nuremberg and New York. The three special pioneers then serving in The Gambia went to an assembly in London, England. All conventioners returned refreshed and strengthened for the work ahead.

Of course, many could not leave Senegal to attend one of the larger assemblies in 1969. So, the "Peace on Earth" District Assembly held in Dakar from December 25 to 28 had special import for them. Thirteen newly dedicated persons stood up to answer *"Oui!"* to the two questions posed during the baptismal talk.

Hence, 1969 proved to have many blessings for the work of making disciples in this land of contrasts: a new peak of 158 publishers, a 15-percent increase in Kingdom proclaimers, and 30 pioneers active in field service, 19 of whom were specially trained Gilead graduates. Also, the Memorial attendance was 383.

WE ENTER THE 1970'S

But what would the 1970's bring? Unfair action against Jehovah's Witnesses was taken in certain lands of Africa. How would this affect God's people in other African countries?

Often at the instigation of the clergy, unfavorable publicity began to appear in certain religious papers. The brothers were encouraged to progress spiritually and to instill the truth in the hearts of new ones so that they could withstand the test of persecution. The result? More increase, in that 22 were baptized during the 1970 service year.

AN EXCEPTIONAL GATHERING

The year 1970 concluded with something special to the praise of Jehovah—an exceptional assembly from December 1 to 4. For Senegalese Christians, this "Men of Goodwill" District Assembly proved to be the most important event up to that point. How thankful we were that Jehovah and his visible organization had so lovingly arranged the visit of 140 brothers and sisters from the United States and Canada! Their presence transformed the small oasis of the Dakar Congregation into a larger garden and gave the assembly a truly international flavor.

A special effort was made to give the visiting brothers a taste of the real Africa. They were accommodated in African-style "huts" with thatched roofs. Also, a special program was prepared, mainly by the local missionaries, to make the life and scenes of Africa unfold before our visitors' eyes right at the assembly hall. A market scene in Senegal, the witnessing work here, many customs, local songs and dances—all of these were part of the special program.

This was a never-to-be-forgotten assembly, exceptional in so many ways. Twenty-five candidates presented themselves for baptism, which was more than had ever been immersed in Senegal during a whole year up to that time!

A LOOK AT OUR PROGRESS

Interestingly, although it had taken 17 years' work to reach the first 100 Kingdom witnesses in Senegal, in just four more years the 200 mark was passed, for 207 shared in declaring the "good news" during April 1971. And an indication of the potential for future growth in Senegal was the number observing the Memorial that year—459 persons!

In The Gambia the brothers were carrying on steadfastly despite their rather difficult assignment. They rejoiced in seeing 24 persons gathered together for the Memorial in 1971, a real source of encouragement to the seven local publishers. The small isolated group then in Mali was receiving help from a special pioneer and a regular pioneer. During 1971, Mauritania had three isolated publishers reporting field service activity. That year, for the first time, the Memorial was celebrated in Mauritania, with 22 persons in attendance.

How encouraging it was to see 45 persons baptized in Senegal during 1972, the most ever in one year! A Memorial attendance of 577 and a peak of 241 publishers brought us joy. Whereas it had taken 21 years to reach 200 publishers, in just three years (1971 to 1974) the 300-publisher mark was passed. We were overjoyed at seeing 302 in field service in 1974, and a Memorial attendance of 705, a leap of more than 100 over the previous year. An event that certainly contributed to this increase was the "Divine Victory" International Assembly, the most refreshing event of 1973. About 100 visiting brothers from distant lands stimulated us by their presence. The peak attendance was 510, the highest ever up till then, and 23 individuals were baptized. Those in attendance made the firm resolution to share in Jehovah's victory by staying faithful.

The increase continued to be encouraging, with 327 Kingdom proclaimers in 1975 and a fine Memorial attendance of 826. But most of these new ones live in the big cities, especially Dakar. What about the small villages, many of which never had received a witness?

"FROM VILLAGE TO VILLAGE"

During the 1976 service year, concerted efforts were made to visit large portions of unassigned territory. Problems were encountered because of the lack of good roads, but with Jehovah's help much good was accomplished, as the following comments reveal:

"We prepared well, with a supply of food and cooking equipment, a tent and much literature. The main problems, apart from the poor roads, were illiteracy and our own ignorance of local dialects. With the help of volunteer interpreters and tape recordings in the main dialects, however, we made out well. In one village the chief eagerly accepted a set of books, and, seeing their value, led us to the village meeting place where we waited while he went from hut to hut, inviting everyone to come there. In less than half an hour 50 books were placed.

"Due to the condition of the tracks between villages, we sometimes used the 'beach highway,' skirting rocks and trying not to get bogged down in the sand. Once we were brought to a rapid halt when a jagged piece of wood, hidden by the sand, punctured two tires! Hastily, we rented a cart to carry the wheels to a nearby village for repair before the incoming tide could wash away the car and its contents. We made it! In four days, during which we visited 20 villages, we distributed 347 Bibles and books, 320 booklets and 663

Effective witnessing is done from hut to hut. The people of Senegal rarely are too busy to listen carefully to the good news of God's kingdom

magazines, and more than 20 subscriptions were obtained."

We pray for Jehovah's continued blessing on those who find joy in declaring the "good news" in such territories. Like Jesus, Senegalese Christians are spreading the Kingdom message, not only in the cities, but also "from village to village."—Luke 8:1.

FAITH THAT SUSTAINS

The number of publishers continued to grow. Senegal's Memorial attendance for 1976 was 835, showing fine potential, and 1977 saw a peak of 334 participants in field service. Sometimes the increase is quite slow. But what of those already in the truth? Are they firmly anchored in the faith? Some do fall away, but the majority have become strong in faith, and the increase is in quality as well as quantity.

An example of this can be seen in connection with the Fourcault family. We have already mentioned how they found the truth. Yet, how strong would their faith be in the face of terrible calamities? First, an automobile accident severely injured all members of the family, except the two oldest boys. Most were confined to hospital beds. Nevertheless, family faith was maintained by regular Bible study together, and this time of distress showed the vital importance of developing spirituality. To this end the pioneer spirit was cultivated. Henri, the eldest boy, took up regular full-time service and then special pioneering. His brother Jean-Marc did the same thing a little later. Their mother became a regular pioneer. Soon, though, this zealous and united family faced an even greater time of crisis. Sister Fourcault entered the hospital for a serious operation. She made wise use of her time, witnessing and starting a Bible study in the ward. Then tragedy struck again! Just before Sister Fourcault was to leave the hospital, she died suddenly, due to a blood clot.

Sister Fourcault would have been happy to see the mature reaction of the family, including the little ones. Their faith in the resurrection was wonderful to observe. (John 5:28, 29; 11:21-25) The only daughter, Sylvie, 11 years old at the time, courageously gave her first presentation in the Theocratic School a few short hours after the funeral. Her hospitalized mother had been promised that this part of the program would be tape-recorded for her benefit, and this was done in spite of her death. When presented with the tape, little

Sylvie held it to her heart and said earnestly: "I shall keep this very carefully, so that after the resurrection my mother will be able to hear my first sermon."

The three oldest Fourcault boys now are in full-time service. Two of them have studied at Gilead School, Henri attending the fifty-fifth class, and Jean-Marc the fifty-ninth. They have returned to serve in Senegal.

ACTIVE FAITH AMONG THE GAMBIANS

The Gambia, too, has its examples of faithfulness. Ralph Phillott, a loyal elder in the Banjul Congregation, died after a long period of bad health. A fine witness was given to the hundreds of people attending the funeral talk.

A very important event for our brothers in The Gambia was the outstanding circuit assembly held in May 1976. For the first time, three were baptized at a Banjul assembly. Two were local Gambians. One had first been contacted in 1959. For years he had frequented the congregation, at the same time trying to reform his church. Finally, he saw the need to get out of Babylon the Great, and thereafter he got baptized. A woman immersed at the same time is a well-known retired schoolteacher, and their baptism in the Gambia River was a fine witness to the community.

What a pleasure it was to see a 67-percent increase in publishers in The Gambia during 1977, with a peak of 11 Kingdom proclaimers! The recent campaign of sending letters to members of the medical profession, along with the booklet *Jehovah's Witnesses and the Question of Blood*, has helped to make our work and Scriptural position better known in that country.

The little group of publishers in the city of Banjul are grateful that, each time a zone visit is planned for West Africa, they are not forgotten. In February 1978, they seem to have received C. W. Barber of the Governing Body, his wife, and his traveling associate David Mercante, with as much joy as the early Christians had when they were visited by the apostle Paul. A total of 38 persons attended the special meeting held during this zone visit to The Gambia.

MALI'S CHRISTIANS ENJOY RICH BLESSINGS

An important milestone in the history of our work in Mali was reached during January 1973, when three special pioneers moved from Dakar to Bamako. Their earnest efforts amid difficult conditions have produced fine results. Monthly, they spend up to 200 hours in field service, place an average of 300 magazines and conduct up to 23 Bible studies each! One pioneer obtained 100 subscriptions in a month. A fine increase followed. During 1973 there were only 7 Witnesses in Mali, including the pioneers. But in 1975, 23 were declaring the "good news," and 1977 saw 32 Kingdom announcers in the field.

The "Joyful Workers" District Assembly in December 1977 proved to be of great encouragement to the Malian brothers who were able to travel to Dakar, Senegal. They were deeply impressed by the Christian hospitality and friendship they experienced, and several were planning to be present at the 1978 "Victorious Faith" International Convention in Paris. Of course, the same rich spiritual banquet was planned for the Dakar assembly in December 1978.

WE CONTINUE CALLING OUT TO "THIRSTY ONES"

In Senegal's eight congregations, 56 pioneers and missionaries are working shoulder to shoulder with some 300 fellow believers. True, the more than 380 Kingdom proclaimers in Senegal, Mali, The Gambia and Mauritania are seemingly an insignificant handful when compared with a total population of around 11,000,000. Yet, confident in Jehovah, they continue to combat spiritual drought.

Although some have lost their spiritual vision in recent years, "the solid foundation of God stays standing," and "Jehovah knows those who belong to him." (2 Tim. 2:19) Thus, with ever-renewed zeal, happy declarers of the "good news" continue inviting the honesthearted to 'come and take life's water free.' (Rev. 22:17) In Senegal, this land of contrasts that is severely affected by persisting drought, we keep on serving Jehovah and preparing for the day when, like the spiritual paradise of the present time, "the wilderness and the waterless region will exult, and the desert plain will be joyful and blossom as the saffron."—Isa. 35:1.

In the meantime, like small oases in parched country, Jehovah's faithful servants in Senegal, Mali, Mauritania and The Gambia will keep on sounding out the heartwarming invitation to come to the Fountain of all waters, Jehovah God. In unison with our fellow believers earth wide, we continue crying out: "Hey there, all you thirsty ones! Come to the water. . . . Listen, and your soul will keep alive."—Isa. 55:1-3.

Giving Evidence of Victorious Faith

After reading this "Yearbook" report on the activity of Jehovah's Witnesses and the history of their work in several countries, one thing is clearly evident. Faith is not something for a person merely to profess. Millions of religious individuals are doing that. As witnesses of Jehovah, however, we are giving proof that our faith is alive and active, accompanied by works. (Jas. 2:18, 26) This has resulted in our giving a tremendous witness in all parts of the earth even though having to undergo various trials. Despite persistent efforts of opposers in many lands to stop the Kingdom proclamation, Jehovah God has kept open the door to such activity. (1 Cor. 16:9) All who have shared in works of faith in the worldwide field are truly thankful to the Most High God for his rich blessings upon all that has been done during the past year. As long as Jehovah God indicates that there is more Kingdom witnessing to be done, we are determined to press forward with this work, thus demonstrating our faith in imitation of our Leader, Jesus Christ.—John 16:33; 17:4.

All those who attended the "Victorious Faith" International Convention this year were able to appreciate more fully what is involved in this matter of faith. This was forcefully brought home to us on the second day of the convention when the "Declaration of Our Faith" was presented. Let each one of Jehovah's Witnesses who said "Yes" in response to what it expresses earnestly continue to display an active and meaningful faith. In order to make this important declaration available for the benefit of Jehovah's Witnesses, it is set out below as part of a permanent record in this "1979 Yearbook." Our reading through the Declaration and referring to it from time to time will bring to our minds the spirit of heartfelt appreciation and enthusiasm that was manifest at the time that this information was presented at each convention.

DECLARATION OF OUR FAITH

As witnesses for Jehovah God and followers of his Son Jesus Christ, we thank God for his precious Word of truth and for "the faith that was once for all time delivered to the holy ones." (Jude 3) But we also feel the need to apply the apostle's exhortation: "Keep testing whether you are in the faith, keep proving what you yourselves are." (2 Cor. 13:5) Are we—heart and soul—"in the faith"?

"Faith is the assured expectation of things hoped for, the evident demonstration of realities though not beheld." (Heb. 11:1) Real faith is based on knowledge of the truth, on facts. What, then, are the facts that cause us to believe, live, work and worship as we do? Why are we Jehovah's Witnesses?

With our own eyes we have seen the results where faith is lacking, for "faith is not a possession of all people." (2 Thess.

3:2) The world has gone its own way, independent of God, and continues getting deeper and deeper into difficulty, with no prospect of genuine relief. We have seen the arrival of the "space age" and spectacular advances of science in many fields. Yet science has done little if anything to solve the major problems facing humanity—poverty, sickness, hunger, crime, hatred and violence. These problems are still all around us, and are becoming more complex. On the other hand, all that modern science has revealed about the marvels of the universe confirms for us the truth simply stated at Hebrews 3:4: "Every house is constructed by someone, but he that constructed all things is God." The evidence of an all-wise universal Designer and Architect is there for us to see on every side. In the words of Hebrews 11:6, we "believe that [Jehovah] is and that he becomes the rewarder of those earnestly seeking him." We believe firmly that his kingdom by Christ Jesus is the only hope for ourselves and for all mankind and we are determined to keep it ever first in our lives.—Matt. 6:33.

We have seen what ignorance of the Bible, or a failure to put faith in it and live by it, produces. We see marriages breaking up, families falling apart, young lives scarred or even ruined by immorality, a steady deterioration in the quality of life and of people's enjoyment of life; less and less friendliness and unselfish concern and more and more mistrust, fear and insecurity. By contrast, we have seen and personally experienced what the faithful application of God's Word can do, the remarkable changes it has accomplished in our own lives and homes, the benefits in contentment and peaceful relations and the warmth of unselfish love. We have seen the power the "good news" has in appealing to honest-hearted persons of every conceivable background, in the Western world and in the Orient, in all continents and islands of the sea. We have seen what faith can produce on a global scale; how God's spirit has produced something that remains unique: an earth-wide "association of brothers." (1 Pet. 2:17) "By this all will know that you are my disciples," Christ Jesus said, "if you have love among yourselves." (John 13:35) We rejoice to be part of the *only real international brotherhood* on the face of the earth, a brotherhood bound together in unbreakable love—for God and his Son, for truth, for what is right, and for one another.

We have also seen what God can accomplish while using fragile 'earthen vessels,' imperfect humans, and how, even though we are but a small minority, he has used us to make his own name, Jehovah, known throughout all the earth. (Ps. 83:18; Rom. 9:17) We have seen how, in this twentieth century, nations have fought to prevent this and have tried to smash a people that is tiny by comparison. But we take heart in knowing that faith has conquered even when our brothers have been subjected to the most brutal of treatments! With the apostle we say: "Who will separate us from the love of the Christ? Will tribulation or distress or persecution or hunger or nakedness or danger or sword? . . . To the contrary, in all these things we are coming off completely victorious through him that loved us." Like the apostle, we are convinced that there is absolutely nothing that will be able to separate us from God's love that is in Christ Jesus our Lord.—Rom. 8:35-39.

Our brothers in Nazi Germany had that confidence, and our

brothers in Malawi, Mozambique and many other countries today have that same confidence.

While enjoying rich blessings in many ways, we are all faced with the grim realities of our imperfect state—aging, sickness, accidents and death. We cannot believe and we do not believe that this brief life is all there is. We have faith in God's provision of the ransom, that by Jehovah's undeserved kindness he arranged that Jesus Christ "might taste death for every man." (Heb. 2:9) While finding it true in our daily lives right now that "godly devotion is beneficial for all things," we are grateful indeed that it holds promise not only of the "life now" but also "that which is to come." (1 Tim. 4:8) We believe wholeheartedly in Jehovah's promise of life without end in his righteous new order.

Because of all that we have seen, heard and experienced in our own lives, we here at this "Victorious Faith" International Convention of Jehovah's Witnesses express anew our firm determination to *move forward* in the service of the Most High God, Jehovah, following the lead of his Son Jesus Christ. We have full faith in their direction of us as a united body. We are convinced that there is no need for uncertainty today nor for any feeling of lack of positive direction as we move straight onward in the course that God's Word lays before us. Nothing about God's purposes has changed; these remain solid and unchangeable. We know that the time for his day of judgment has not shifted, has not moved backward in the slightest. We do not know the time of its arrival, but we do know that it will come as God's Son said—with shocking suddenness. (Luke 21:34, 35) Not reliance on some specific time period, but our wholehearted trust in God and our conviction that his purposes are absolutely certain of fulfillment—this is what gives us a sense of clear direction in our lives. (Heb. 3:14; 4:12) We believe that, by continuing through faith to conquer the pressures and temptations of this world, we will see the day when we can look back and say, as did God's servants of old: "Not a promise failed out of all the good promise that Jehovah had made . . . it all came true." "Not one word of them has failed."—Josh. 21:45; 23:14.

We will not, we cannot, stop speaking about the things we have seen and heard and experienced. (Acts 4:20) We are impelled to give expression with our lips to our strong faith in Jehovah's victorious kingdom and we sincerely want to share the blessings of this "good news" with all. Like the faithful apostle, our plea is: "Become reconciled to God." (2 Cor. 5:20) That is *our determination,* to make public declaration of this good news of Jehovah God's kingdom from here on until the end of this system of things.—Matt. 24:14; 28:19, 20.

We know we must give proof of our faith in Jesus Christ as our Ransomer and Head and King, and we have his words that "everyone, then, that confesses union with me before men, I will also confess union with him before my Father who is in the heavens; but whoever disowns me before men, I will also disown him before my Father who is in the heavens."—Matt. 10:32, 33.

We will never turn our backs on the One who has done so much for us, who has given meaning and purpose to our lives. We will never turn our eyes from the light he has given us that has enabled us to see through all the confusion of our times and understand why the world of mankind is in its present distress, and what today's conditions signify as to the nearness of his new order of righteousness. Instead, we will keep our faces and our hearts turned ever toward him and his Son, seeking their guidance, their favor, proving obedient to their direction in all our lives. We will let neither materialism erode our faith nor opposition crush it.

Jesus' apostle John said: "This is the conquest that has conquered the world, our faith." (1 John 5:4) Ours is not faith in human organizations, their leaders and plans, but in Jehovah God and in his grand purpose in connection with Jesus Christ. We have complete confidence that our faith will be victorious. We are sure that this faith is solidly based, and it will therefore lead to success and not to failure, to the realization of our hopes and not to disappointment. "For the Scripture says: 'None that rests his faith on him will be disappointed.' "—Rom. 10:11.

We are confident that by displaying such a living faith, one that is actively at work each day of our lives, we will be privileged to be used even more wonderfully in the remaining days between now and the sudden arrival of God's expression of judgment. We confidently expect that such remaining time will be filled with grand evidences of God's backing of his name people. By our daily lives and by our faithful witnessing, moved by love of neighbor, we are determined to extend the word of life to all who will hear. As we meet people at their homes, in the streets and in all our daily contacts, we will make known to them the "good news" that God's kingdom is at hand to bring grand blessings to mankind. Our hope is that the remaining time may see grand expansion of the spread of the Kingdom good news, indeed, the finest ever. We pray to the One who, as Ephesians 3:20 says, "can, according to his power which is operating in us, do more than superabundantly beyond all the things we ask or conceive," and we ask that he use us in just that way so that "to him be the glory by means of the congregation and by means of Christ Jesus to all generations forever and ever. Amen."—Eph. 3:21.

If, after having heard this entire declaration of faith, it expresses the way that all of you feel, and you say "Amen" to this declaration, then let us hear your "Yes!" in response.

The reading of the Declaration was repeatedly interrupted by spontaneous applause, and, having heard this entire declaration of faith, the conventioners responded with their own loud "Yes" of agreement. You, dear reader, may have been one of these. And certainly it is the aim of Jehovah's Witnesses everywhere to live in accord with this declaration, for unequivocally it sets forth our determination to move forward in the service of the Most High God, making known the good news of his kingdom. May we stand firm in one spirit with Jehovah's people world wide, "with one soul striving side by side for the faith of the good news."—Phil. 1:27, 28.

Your brothers,
GOVERNING BODY OF JEHOVAH'S WITNESSES

YEARTEXT FOR 1979

"My Father is glorified in this, that you keep bearing much fruit and prove yourselves my disciples."
—John 15:8.

In its 1,950th year of life, and yet it is still bearing much good fruit! That is the case record of the "vine" that Jehovah God planted back in the year 29 C.E., and what a credit this is to him! How the abundance of fruit of this "vine" glorifies him! We who have tasted of its good fruit know that very well.

"I am the true vine," said the Son of God, Jesus Christ, "and my Father is the cultivator." Just as this great Cultivator made the literal grapevine to be fruitful for the enjoyment of others, so he purposed for this spiritual "vine" to be a fruitful thing. From its first planting he has cultivated it that it may never fail to produce, but, rather, that it may increase its fruitage. Jesus Christ, the Son of this Cultivator, would not want his heavenly Father to suffer any loss of glory by being an unproductive "vine." Exemplarily he himself was most fruitful, and he worked to produce "branches" in union with him. These were disciples who would imbibe the sap, the spirit, of the "vine" and then produce much fruit.—John 15:1-5.

This is just what the first "branches" did. On the day of Pentecost, by means of the glorified Jesus Christ, "the true vine," God's holy spirit was poured out on about 120 "branches." These proved themselves to be his disciples, his "branches," by giving a live witness to the thousands of Jews and Jewish proselytes who were attracted to the scene. About 3,000 of these partook of the spiritual fruit held out to them. They accepted the witness as setting out the truthful facts about Jesus Christ and then testified to their belief by getting baptized in water in the name of the Messiah Jesus. By thus becoming united to the "true vine" they too received the holy spirit and became "branches" in the Christ "vine."

Did this work out for the glory of the Cultivator of the "true vine"? Yes, for concerning the growing numbers of the disciples the sacred record says that they were "praising God and finding favor with all the people. At the same time Jehovah continued to join to them daily those being saved."—Acts 2:47.

Today those who are spirit-anointed "branches" of the Christ "vine" make up only the final remnant of the foreordained 144,000. What Jesus said 19 centuries ago to his apostolic "branches" applies to this remnant also: They are under obligation to bear much fruit. By doing this they prove their discipleship, their union with the "true vine," Jesus Christ. This calls for them, of course, to produce the "fruitage of the spirit." (Gal. 5:22, 23) They have offered the benefit of this spiritual fruitage to the people of all the nations of the earth in this time of spiritual famine. How? By their activities in giving a worldwide witness.

A grapevine is a plant organization. True to form, the "branches" in the Christ "vine" must act in an organized way in union with Jesus Christ. As a united organization they must offer to all mankind the benefits of their spiritual fruitage, displaying true Christian qualities in giving the final worldwide witness to the now-established kingdom of God.—Matt. 24:14; Mark 13:10.

Those who are already an international "great crowd" have benefited. For this they are glorifying Jehovah God. They have associated themselves intimately with the vinelike organization. Rather than enjoying the goodness of the "vine" by themselves, they seek to develop Christlike qualities and to express these in activity. They cannot keep their joy to themselves. It is something to be shared.—Rev. 7:9, 10, 15.

The end of the world's joyless system of things is becoming more threatening every day. The opportune time for preaching "this good news of the kingdom" is nearing its limit. So the urgency for getting "this good news of the kingdom" to the people of this imperiled world increases all the time. Those who respond to the increasing urgency will display genuine Christlike qualities. Who, then, will share in causing God to be glorified by the bearing of much fruit? May it be each one of us!

DAILY TEXTS AND COMMENTS

There is a text for each day and a comment on that text. The comments are taken from *The Watchtower* (*W*) of the year 1978. Figures following the date of the *Watchtower* issue refer to paragraphs in the first study article, where further comment on the text may be found. When "a" follows the paragraph number, comment is found in the second study article; when "b" is shown, it refers to the third study article.

Monday, January 1

They will be certain to fight against you, but they will not prevail against you, for "I am with you," is the utterance of Jehovah, "to deliver you."
—Jer. 1:19.

As the tempest of destruction sweeps over the earth, the national "shepherds" and "majestic ones" of their flock will howl and wallow about, and "fall like a desirable vessel." They will be "rendered lifeless because of the burning anger of Jehovah" God. (Jer. 25:31-37) Happily, honest-hearted persons out of all nations who learn of Jehovah's goodness are joining themselves to the Jeremiah class. They will find deliverance when God's burning anger breaks forth, to "make *all the nations*" drink the bitter potion of destruction. (Jer. 25:17) The execution of that judgment hastens on! For a short time longer Jehovah's enemies may fight against the Jeremiah class and their companions. But as a "fortified copper wall" we will continue to resist enemy pressure against our speaking "all the words" commanded by Jehovah. (Jer. 15:20; 26:2) Always, we draw strength from his promise noted above. *W 1/1 17, 18*

Tuesday, January 2

Both if we live, we live to Jehovah, and if we die, we die to Jehovah.—Rom. 14:8.

Whatever Christians do, they are to do wholeheartedly as to Jehovah God. One Christian may not fully understand why another sees or does things in a certain way. But he realizes that God is the Judge of his servants. And, just as we try to do all things to the best of our understanding and ability in order to please Jehovah, so we attribute the same conscientious motives to our brothers. Even the most sincere, conscientious Christian has imperfections and faults and therefore does not always stay free from selfish acts. But it is *not his great object in life* to become rich or to indulge in a life of pleasure and ease. He is not living with regard to himself or for himself only. His main pursuit in life is to please Jehovah God by doing His will. He is willing to die at any time if his death can serve God's purpose. And just as he lived his life as belonging to God, so in death Jehovah counts him as His, because of the resurrection.—Matt. 22:31, 32. *W 3/15 3, 4*

Wednesday, January 3

In themselves the days of our years are seventy years; and if because of special mightiness they are eighty years, yet their insistence is on trouble and hurtful things; for it must quickly pass by, and away we fly.—Ps. 90:10.

Many normal persons make the complaint that the system in which we live offers little to encourage real purpose. These individuals point to the fact that a person may start out with a goal, spend years getting an education in his chosen field and then find that he cannot get employment. Then, again, death of a loved one can doom a person to a life of loneliness. Looking at things in this way, some conclude that God has no concern for human affairs. But, having designed and brought forth the universe, God *does* have intense interest in dealing with it. In fact, in the mind of God there is a future for man. But it must be admitted that mankind is powerless to change matters. The inspired psalmist Moses described our helpless condition. *W 2/1 1-5*

Thursday, January 4

Your people will be my people, and your God my God. Where you die I shall die, and there is where I shall be buried. —Ruth 1:16, 17.

What a moving expression of loyal love! It is, in fact, much more than that. Ruth has chosen a life of service to Jehovah, and Naomi's people —those in a covenant relationship with the true God —will be her people. The Moabitess is determined to serve Jehovah faithfully. Hence, Naomi ends all efforts to send the young woman away and the elderly Judean and the younger Moabitess resume their arduous journey side by side. Had Ruth, like Orpah, allowed herself to be entreated to return to her native land, she, too, could have returned to it. But Ruth displayed loyal love, not just for aged Naomi, but especially for Jehovah. She manifested a self-sacrificing spirit and a determination to serve the true God in faith. Observing these contrasting decisions, we also are encouraged not to "shrink back" but to "have faith to the preserving alive of the soul."—Heb. 10:38, 39. *W 2/15* 14, 15

Friday, January 5

Now have come to pass the salvation and the power and the kingdom of our God and the authority of his Christ. —Rev. 12:10.

The kingship of Jehovah God is what is exalted even in what is said in connection with the birth of an offspring by God's heavenly "woman." The offspring is pictured as a male child, "who is to shepherd all the nations with an iron rod." That doubtless means that this symbolic male child is to break all the political nations of the earth to pieces as one does when

smashing clay pottery. So it has a governmental role to fulfill. But who, basically, wields the kingly power? This is spelled out for us in the words: "And her child was caught away to God and to his throne." (Rev. 12:1-5) God is the One who enthrones this symbolic male child. God is the Source of all rightful rulership. The symbolic child is given a position subsidiary to God's kingship. Yes, the kingdom is said to be that of our God. He is the One who really does the reigning, and his Christ, Jesus, gets "authority" to rule in a secondary way under the Lord God. *W 3/1* 11, 12a

Saturday, January 6

As a cage is full of flying creatures, so their houses are full of deception. That is why they have become great and they gain riches.—Jer. 5:27.

Let the clergy continue to preach Babylonian falsehoods. Let them make themselves prominent in support of corrupt politicians. Let them wink at, or even come out in support of, permissive sex, homosexuality, gambling and other practices condemned in God's Word. This may be popular, appealing to the masses. Many people love to have it that way. (Jer. 5:29-31) But God declares that he will execute judgment on all such religious hypocrisy in the very near future. In the days of Judge Samuel, Israel suffered a crushing defeat at Shiloh by the Philistines. According to Jehovah's words, Jerusalem of Jeremiah's time was doomed to suffer as Shiloh suffered. (Jer. 7:13, 14) The religions of Christendom, which claim a relationship to God through Jesus Christ, would do well to heed these words. It is our obligation to sound the warning to all such wicked ones. *W 1/1* 7, 8

Sunday, January 7

Whenever people of the nations that do not have law do by nature the things of the law, these people, although not having law, are a law to themselves.—Rom. 2:14.

Yes, God made man with a desire for order and with a conscience to distinguish right from wrong. He has also made known his own righteous principles through the Bible, and, as a result of this, most of the nations of earth have embodied some of these principles in their constitutions. That is why most governments have generally set out with good intent. They have tried to serve for the benefit of the people. They have written constitutions containing fine ideals and principles. And yet, whatever their measure of success, governments everywhere today recognize that the human race is far from enjoying a world of peace and security. Why? God's Word gives the answer and, far better, it gives the promise that the joyful living conditions of a united world are certain to come, by means of Jehovah's kingdom. It is our blessed privilege to make that kingdom known. W 1/15 2, 3

Monday, January 8

He is the image of the invisible God, the firstborn of all creation . . . All other things have been created through him and for him. Also, he is before all other things and by means of him all other things were made to exist.—Col. 1:15-17.

Are you a disciple of the Lord Jesus Christ? Do you recognize his vital place in God's arrangement? If so, does your daily life reflect appreciation for the Son of God and what he has done on your behalf? The apostle Paul helps us to see just how important the position of Jesus Christ is. As noted above, the firstborn Son, the start of God's creation, is the preeminent One among all intelligent creatures. He is the image of his heavenly Father in that he is a spirit person who perfectly reflects such admirable qualities as love, wisdom, justice, mercy, graciousness and long-suffering. Through him, Jehovah God brought into existence millions of angelic sons, the vast universe with its billions of galaxies and the earth with its abundant variety of plant and creature life. W 4/1 1-3

Tuesday, January 9

What God has yoked together let no man put apart.—Matt. 19:6.

We can be assured by what Jesus said at Matthew 19:4-9 that he and his followers accepted the Bible as inspired. Such acceptance is an important distinguishing mark of true religion. And what Jesus said there also illustrates the consistency of true religion with regard to right conduct. Jesus Christ agreed that marriage is sacred and that the marriage covenant is binding; divorce and remarriage are to be permitted by God's Word only if one's mate is guilty of gross immorality. By holding to this godly standard, true religion motivates married persons to work at making a success of their union. They should not view marriage as a temporary social contract easily terminated by the State. Accordingly, in practicing true religion the early Christians avoided promiscuity, holding to Jehovah God's view of marriage as a sacred, binding union. W 4/15 4-6a

Wednesday, January 10

Jehovah, Jehovah, a God merciful and gracious, slow to anger and abundant in loving-kindness and truth, preserving loving-kindness for thousands, pardoning error.—Ex. 34:6, 7.

Of all the names in the universe, the name of *Jehovah* excels in brilliance, dignity and reputation. Not only is he the Creator, almighty and with limitless knowledge, executing perfect justice, but even more than that, his loving-kindness and mercy make his name deserving of the greatest honor and praise, yes, reverence. When Moses asked to see God's glory, he was directed to go up into Mount Sinai, and "Jehovah proceeded to come down in the cloud and station himself with him there and declare the *name* of Jehovah. And Jehovah went passing by before his face and declaring" the above. The love and mercy of Jehovah are here shown to be among his dominant qualities. But the Most High will not let the wrongdoer pervert his mercy as an excuse for continued wantonness. Otherwise, he could not govern the universe for the good of those who want to do what is right. *W 5/1 2, 3*

Thursday, January 11

*Where is the wise man? . . . Did not God make the wisdom of the world foolish?
—1 Cor. 1:20.*

It was to the Christian congregation at Corinth that Paul wrote the above words. The Corinth of Paul's day was a cosmopolitan city, with Romans, Greeks, Orientals and Jews. In the Christian congregation there, some divisions existed because certain groups aligned themselves with prominent individuals. (1 Cor. 1: 10-13) There may also have been a tendency for some to cling to certain features of the Law, or for some of those of other races to be impressed with the eloquent ways of the Greek philosophers. (1 Cor. 1: 17-25) But the Gospel was not to be preached with lofty words, nor was it to be adulterated with the wisdom of religious traditions or philosophical speculations. Whatever the case was there in Corinth, Paul saw fit to bear down hard to limit preaching to "Christ impaled." Today, too, we want to avoid lofty words, speculations and the wisdom of this world in presenting the truth to the people in our territory. *W 5/15 1*

Friday, January 12

*Trust in Jehovah with all your heart and do not lean upon your own understanding.
—Prov. 3:5.*

Why has it turned out that "man has dominated man to his injury"? (Eccl. 8:9) Because, in the beginning, God did not purpose for humans to rule over other humans. (Gen. 1:28) Only over the animal creation was man to exercise dominion. But men went beyond this and assumed domination over other men. Violence and wars have resulted, with contending sides struggling for domination. The ancient nation of Israel serves as a pattern to teach mankind the lesson that human rule can never bring the kind of life that people everywhere seek. In that nation the rulers often did well for a while. But as time went on, these rulers began to look to sources other than Jehovah God for wisdom. Ignoring the law that he had given them, they had more and more problems. They began to rely on their own wisdom and to listen to men, who had only human wisdom. May we never make the mistake that they made! *W 1/15 6, 7*

Saturday, January 13

A king will certainly reign and act with discretion and execute justice and righteousness in the land. . . . And this is his name with which he will be called, Jehovah Is Our Righteousness.—Jer. 23:5, 6.

This prospect reminds us of how Jehovah strengthened faithful Abraham by holding before him the hope of "the city having real foundations," whose builder is God. (Heb. 11:10) And now we are living in the day when Christ's "bride" is nearing its completion, in the heavens, whence figuratively it will 'come down' to bestow everlasting blessings on mankind. (Rev. 21:2-5, 9) This city is the heavenly kingdom toward which God, through Christ, shepherds the remnant of his "sheep." At present the elders among these serve as faithful undershepherds to his congregated people on earth. (Isa. 32:1, 2) How eager we should be to make known to others Jehovah's words concerning that righteous kingdom! But Jehovah *also* commissions the modern-day Jeremiah class to proclaim a message of doom, in all of which work the "great crowd" of "other sheep" gladly share. *W 1/1 4, 5*

Sunday, January 14

This good news of the kingdom will be preached in all the inhabited earth for a witness to all the nations. —Matt. 24:14.

Our maintaining faithfulness to God gives, first of all, a better life *now*, with a *purpose*, and great freedom from the problems and worries that this world experiences. Then there is the prospect of being a part of the foundation of the "new earth." Yes, there is an exciting future before us —a fine purpose in the life ahead! But we do not want to belittle the marvelous opportunity we have to serve God *now*. For this is the last time that people will have an opportunity to take their stand for God's side of the issue of universal rulership *amid a world of people that do not know God.* It is the last opportunity to proclaim the "good news" to these people under conditions of opposition. What a fine way to *prove* our loyalty to God! Doing this brings the greatest reward. Now is the opportunity to work as a member of God's household in sharing and proclaiming the Kingdom good news to others. *W 2/1 22, 23a*

Monday, January 15

I shall put enmity between you and the woman and between your seed and her seed. He will bruise you in the head and you will bruise him in the heel.—Gen. 3:15.

God said for the encouragement of *all* peoples: "My own house will be called even a house of prayer for all the peoples." (Isa. 56:7) However, away back in the garden of Eden, God made a prophecy that has meaning for all peoples. There he said the above to the great Seducer of all mankind. Those prophetic words indicated that, just as all the descendants of the first human couple were hurt by the deceptive action of the great Seducer, so *all* of them would be able to benefit from the bruising of his head by the triumphant "seed" of God's "woman." That bodes good for us today, does it not? Happily, Yes! And when Jehovah God spoke of the Bruiser of the head of the Adversary, he was speaking of the government agency that he would set up over all mankind. That government was to be *of* and *by* Jehovah God. *W 3/1 3, 4*

Tuesday, January 16

If possible, as far as it depends upon you, be peaceable with all men.—Rom. 12:18.

Yes, true Christians are interested in living at peace with others. Members of the Christian congregation do this by giving attention to the more important things and minimizing the things that are not essential for promoting faith. (1 Tim. 1:4) Among the important things, they seek to have unity of faith and action. As an illustration of this unity, Paul points to the human body. Just as the members of a healthy body operate in a unified way in the interests of the whole body, which enables it to get worthwhile work done, so it is in the Christian congregation. There should be no division in this "body," but "its members should have the same care for one another." (1 Cor. 12:25) However, this unity is not uniformity. No, each Christian differs from the others, more or less, in his way of arranging affairs and of doing things, even in daily routines of work, and relaxation. But this difference is no reason for their not endeavoring to be peaceable with each other. *W 3/15 1, 2*

Wednesday, January 17

By means of him all other things were created in the heavens and upon the earth, the things visible and the things invisible, no matter whether they are thrones or lordships or governments or authorities.—Col. 1:16.

What are these "thrones," "lordships," "governments" or "authorities" that came into existence through the Son? They could not be worldly governmental positions or offices, for such are referred to in Scripture as human and not divine creations. (1 Pet. 2:13, 14) Hence, these must include those forms of rulership for which Jehovah God is responsible through his Son, including the kingdom of Melchizedek and that of David at Jerusalem. As to the place of Jesus Christ in relation to the congregation, Paul states: "He is the head of the body, the congregation." (Col. 1:18) Hence, the congregation rightly looks to him and not to any human as the preeminent one, the head. A failure to recognize this fact results in disunity. This was well illustrated by what happened in ancient Corinth.—1 Cor. 1: 11-13. *W 4/1 3-6*

Thursday, January 18

What! Do you not know that unrighteous persons will not inherit God's kingdom? Do not be misled.—1 Cor. 6:9.

Many might say that while the Bible's high morality is admirable, basically it is not possible to hold to it in our time. But it definitely is possible as can be seen by what is taking place among Jehovah's people. Yes, even from the beginning, we find in true worship insistence on sexual morality and respect for marriage. This is even involved in the Bible's concern for property rights and condemnation of stealing. That would include stealing another's mate or the moral purity of another person. (Gen. 2:24; Eph. 4:28) Furthermore, the Bible plainly states that persons professing true religion but who unrepentantly continue to be 'fornicators, adulterers, thieves or greedy persons,' must be expelled from the Christian congregation. (1 Cor. 5:11-13; 6:9, 10) Firm adherence to such divine morality has consistently identified true religion. But each one should ask himself, 'How does my worship measure up?' *W 4/15 8, 9a*

Friday, January 19

Wives, be in subjection to your own husbands, in order that, if any are not obedient to the word, they may be won without a word through the conduct of their wives.
—*1 Pet. 3:1.*

A wide door that is open to most of us for sanctifying Jehovah's name is in connection with our relatives who are not Witnesses. We may be sincere in presenting the truth, but may not have the advisable consideration for our relatives, who do not know or perceive and accept matters concerning the Bible in the same way that we do. For example, a wife may come to a knowledge of the truth, and may discern that some of the former practices of herself and of her family are wrong. However, her husband and other relatives are likely to view her as a fanatic if she tries to impose her ideas on them. She could come right out and tell them that all these practices, such as observing certain holidays, are wrong, and possibly turn them away from listening. What might be a better way? Exercise patience, consideration and empathy in line with the advice of the apostle Peter. *W 5/1* 12-14

Saturday, January 20

Certain ones of both the Epicurean and the Stoic philosophers took to conversing with him controversially, and some would say: "What is it this chatterer would like to tell?"
—*Acts 17:18.*

Paul cautioned against any efforts to copy the ways of the Greek philosophers. In Athens, those philosophers referred derogatorily to Paul as a chatterer, a translation of a Greek word meaning "seed picker." It signified a bird that picked up seeds. Figuratively, the expression referred to a man who picked up scraps of information and used them to impress others, but was actually an ignorant plagiarist. However, Paul was no idle babbler. He preached to them about "the God that made the world and all the things in it," that "he himself gives to all persons life and breath" and that "he made out of one man every nation of men." (Acts 17:24-26) But when Paul spoke of God resurrecting Jesus from the dead, some of them mocked; however, others believed. When we today speak of the resurrection some likewise mock, while others believe. *W 5/15* 3, 4a

Sunday, January 21

The prophets themselves actually prophesy in falsehood; and as for the priests, they go subduing according to their powers. And my own people have loved it that way.
—*Jer. 5:31.*

The clergy of Christendom claim to be Christian. But do their teachings and their actions support this claim? Or, rather, do they fall into the same class as the religious leaders of Jeremiah's day? (Jer. 5:26, 27) They too have coveted men, either by attracting them with an outward display of piety or converting them at swordpoint, as in the days of imperial colonization. Among their false teachings are the Trinity, immortality of the soul, hellfire, purgatory and the sacredness of the cross. They deck the images and icons of their saints with halos and rosaries. In Jeremiah's time, the majority of the people chose to remain with the doomed system. They loved its dishonesty, its corruption, its immorality. Is it not the same with many persons in Christendom today? It is our privilege to make known to all how God views this. *W 1/1* 6, 7

Monday, January 22

Let every soul be in subjection to the superior authorities, for there is no authority except by God.—Rom. 13:1.

Over the centuries mankind has lived under hundreds of governments. None have truly satisfied the needs of all the people. Whatever the complaints made, however, the fact remains that some sort of government is clearly better than no government at all. Without government there would be no order; it would be no less than mob rule. And if you have ever seen a mob in action you know what that would mean—for in a mob people take the opportunity to vent hatred, greed and viciousness, feeling that no one will identify them for punishment. The God of heaven knows all of this. And because government by man is far better than anarchy, God has permitted earthly governments to operate for thousands of years. For the most part, this has benefited people with a measure of security, protection and order and an opportunity to earn a livelihood. For such reasons Christians should heed the words of Paul as given above. *W 1/15 1, 2*

Tuesday, January 23

Help us, O God of our salvation, for the sake of the glory of your name; and deliver us and cover over our sins on account of your name.—Ps. 79:9.

Man's helplessness in getting free from enslavement to death is expressed in the forty-ninth psalm, verses six to nine. The writer of the psalm knew that the price was too precious, too high, beyond the reach of all mankind. As far as imperfect man's ability was concerned, relief was so far away that it was "to time indefinite," actually beyond

hope. This sad, helpless situation is upon us all because our forefather Adam sold his future offspring into slavery to sin and death. The price he received for the "sale" was the selfish doing of what he wanted to do, stepping out in independence, in rebellion against God. So, if man was ever to be delivered, God had to act and make provision. Sincere ones cry out as above. Does Jehovah God hear this prayer? And, if he does, can he answer it? Yes, indeed, for man's powerlessness is no problem to Jehovah God. *W 2/1 6-9*

Wednesday, January 24

You are a priest forever according to the manner of Melchizedek.—Heb. 7:17.

In showing the difference between the glorified Jesus Christ and the imperial Caesars and other political rulers, Paul spoke of the immortal Ruler, Jesus Christ, as "the King of those who rule as kings and Lord of those who rule as lords." (1 Tim. 6:15, 16) Besides that, the apostle Paul compares this immortal Son of God, Jesus Christ, with King Melchizedek of the twentieth century before our Common Era. When was Jehovah God's Son made King-Priest like Melchizedek? This was 40 days after his resurrection from the dead, when he ascended to heaven. Then he appeared in the presence of Jehovah God with the value of his perfect human sacrifice in behalf of the redeemed humans who were to become his subjects in the future. Since Christ has been reigning in the heavens only since the end of the Gentile Times in 1914, how could it be said that he has been reigning in heaven since 33 C.E.? In that he has been reigning over a spiritual kingdom. *W 3/1 14-16*

Thursday, January 25

Give orders to those who are rich in the present system of things not to be high-minded, and to rest their hope, not on uncertain riches, but on God, who furnishes us all things richly for our enjoyment; to work at good, to be rich in fine works, to be liberal.
—1 Tim. 6:17, 18.

The most important work a person can do is to help others to gain and maintain a good standing with God and Christ. Every one of us has his own view as to what material things he needs, while continuing to put Kingdom interests first, sharing zealously in the urgent work of preaching the "good news" to others. (Matt. 6:33; Mark 13:10) A man may be of the nature that he cannot control riches and is tempted to let them take him away from spiritual things. He needs to 'pummel his body' and learn to exercise self-control, having in mind his foremost obligation to proclaim "the good news." (1 Cor. 9:16, 27) Another Christian, while not presuming to judge him, may offer kindly help and counsel to one who is succumbing to a love of money, even as noted above. *W 3/15 5, 7*

Friday, January 26

When they heard of a resurrection of the dead, some began to mock, . . . but some men joined themselves to him and became believers.
—Acts 17:32, 33.

Why did Paul's mention of resurrection cause some to mock? Because it clashed with some of their philosophical wisdom. Scripturally, resurrection makes sense. Since a person dies in the same manner as a beast perishes, is unconscious, returns to the dust, is a dead soul, resurrection is his only hope to live again.

(Ps. 146:4; Eccl. 3:18-21; 9:5, 10; Ezek. 18:4) But resurrection made no sense to those Greek philosophers! Many of them taught that man had an immortal soul, and therefore needed no resurrection. The Stoics believed that the soul lived on after the body died. Pythagoras said that after death the soul went to Hades to be purged, then returned to enter a new body. "The soul plainly appears to be immortal," Plato quotes Socrates as saying. Clearly, Christendom obtained its teaching regarding the soul not from the Scriptures but from pagan philosophers! *W 5/15 4, 5a*

Saturday, January 27

Keep bearing much fruit and prove yourselves my disciples.
—John 15:8.

Are you striving to share fully in bearing witness and in making disciples? (Matt. 28:19, 20) Are you keeping awake spiritually, not allowing yourself to become weighed down by the daily cares of life or by overindulgence in food and drink? (Luke 21:34-36) Do your dealings with others show that you really want to display the self-sacrificing love that identifies true disciples of Jesus Christ? (John 13:34, 35) When you obediently assemble with fellow believers to commemorate the Lord's Evening Meal, do you think seriously about the benefits that have come to you through Jesus' sacrifice? Are you moved to take careful note of your conduct so that you might maintain the clean standing that resulted from your accepting, in faith, the atoning benefits of Jesus' shed blood? We should never forget that as long as our sins were not atoned for, we were alienated from God.—1 Pet. 1:14-19; Col. 1:20. *W 4/1 22, 23*

Sunday, January 28

O magnify Jehovah with me, you people, and let us exalt his name together.—Ps. 34:3.

Jehovah God's name and that of his Son must be sanctified in all that we do. This means that our object must be to make known and to exalt God's sovereignty, his mercy and his other fine qualities, even as the psalmist asks us to do. If we do not do this, either we or someone else will be credited for what is done, with no good result. An instance highlighting this fact is found in a situation that developed after Israel's settlement in the Promised Land, namely, their demanding that Samuel appoint a king to rule over them. Thereafter, Israel suffered much under their kings. This was the result of not recognizing that Jehovah was their real king. From this example we can see that, in every problem confronting us and in all our undertakings, Jehovah God is involved. Like the psalmist, we must have God's will and name in mind. Then we can lay matters before him and know that the firm establishing of our plans is in his hands. If it works out, Jehovah gets the praise. *W 5/1* 8, 10, 12, 13a

Monday, January 29

I will give them a heart to know me, that I am Jehovah; and they must become my people, and I myself shall become their God, for they will return to me with all their heart.—Jer. 24:7.

According to Jeremiah chapter 24, Jehovah made the prophet see two baskets of figs. The one basket contained bad figs, representing those who do not act in faith on Jehovah's promises, so that they suffer loss. The good figs were very good and pictured, in the first instance, those Jews who would act in faith in returning from Babylonian exile after 70 years to restore Jehovah's worship in Jerusalem. In modern-day fulfillment, they represent the faithful remnant who have returned from captivity in Babylon the Great, particularly from 1919 onward. Concerning these restored ones, and others, the "other sheep" who would join them later, Jehovah said the above. These "good figs" develop a very intimate relationship with their God, Jehovah. Having a right heart condition, they trust implicitly in Jehovah to direct their steps. *W 1/1* 14

Tuesday, January 30

These were bought from among mankind as firstfruits to God and to the Lamb, and no falsehood was found in their mouths; they are without blemish.—Rev. 14:4, 5.

Jehovah God has not wasted time. Jesus' earthly life proved that he was from God. After his resurrection he was raised to power in the heavens, to take over Kingdom authority in due time. But God purposed to have more than one person as ruler in the Kingdom. Christ would possess complete power, but God purposed to have 144,000 others with Christ as associate kings. Just as any ruler, before going into office, is concerned about those whom he will associate with in his rule, Jesus was selective in choosing his apostles, those who would become secondary foundations of the new government. Using these men, he caused the kingdom of God to be preached throughout all Israel, and later, to all nations. In the long period of time until now God has been selecting the 144,000 persons who will be associate kings. *W 1/15* 23, 24

Wednesday, January 31

All these men act in opposition to the decrees of Caesar, saying there is another king, Jesus.—Acts 17:7.

Jehovah God had intervened to make the first-century believers suitable for a share in the brighter life. (Acts 26:18) In this way they were brought into the realm of light. But with what was their enlightened condition connected? It was connected with a kingdom. Yes, when God "delivered [them] from the authority of the darkness," he at the same time "transferred [them] into the kingdom of the Son of his love." (Col. 1:13) At the time that the apostle Paul wrote his letter to the congregation in Colossae, Jesus Christ was spoken of as being a king and as already having a kingdom. That is the way that the enlightened Christian congregation in Colossae understood the matter. Even their enemies came to understand the matter that way. For instance, what was the charge that the mobsters brought against the Christians in the city of Thessalonica? In order to incite the city rulers against the Christians, these mobsters said the above. *W 3/1 11-13*

Thursday, February 1

My Father has kept working until now, and I keep working. —John 5:17.

Do we know how long Jehovah has been working? Amazingly, there is a scripture that helps us to answer that question and that evidently refers to Jesus in his prehuman existence as "the Word." This one, speaking under the personification of wisdom, says, as recorded at Proverbs 8:22, 23: "Jehovah himself *produced me* as the beginning of his way, the earliest of his achievements of long ago . . . from times earlier than the earth." Ah! yes, Jehovah is a *productive* worker and that is the key to being a *happy* worker. Jehovah is a happy worker because he produces good things that reflect his fine qualities. (Deut. 32:4) From Proverbs we can see that the one who became Jesus Christ was a worker, sharing joyfully with his Father, "being glad before him all the time." (Prov. 8:29-31) This close cooperation was evident right through to the act that crowned earthly creation. —Gen. 1:26-28. *W 6/1 4-7*

Friday, February 2

He himself gives to all persons life and breath and all things. For by him we have life and move and exist. —Acts 17:25, 28.

What is more precious than our life? Without it, we could not enjoy anything. Yet, there is evidence all around us that many have little real appreciation for the value of life—either their own or that of others. Can we not see such evidence in the reckless driving habits of many? Then there are those who seek thrills in dangerous sports that admittedly take many lives each year. And how about the millions of persons who know that they may be shortening their lives by using tobacco or by gluttonous eating? In the face of such attitudes, we each can ask, 'Do *I* really have an appreciative outlook on life?' A key to having real appreciation for life that even affects one's thinking and actions is to recognize that life is a gift from Jehovah, even as the apostle Paul notes above. Logically, our view of life should conform to God's. Does it? —Jer. 10:10. *W 6/15 1-3*

Saturday, February 3

Let the word of the Christ reside in you richly in all wisdom. Keep on teaching and admonishing one another. —Col. 3:16.

Thus Paul writes after encouraging us to be thankful. What does he mean by "the word of the Christ"? It is the message from Christ, the whole deposit of Christian teaching, which should become a part of us. (*The Bible in Living English; Good News Bible*) It should be as if the entire body of teaching as given by Christ has taken up residence within us. For that to be the case, we must be fully absorbed with the message of Christian truth, meditating upon it. When the "word of the Christ" is actually a part of us in all its richness, it will serve as a guide to us, helping us to make our way successful. That word will move us to act wisely. When we are filled with the "word of the Christ," we will be encouraging and upbuilding to our brothers. Then, as persons loved and approved by Jehovah God and Jesus Christ, we can be confident of gaining the reward of everlasting life.—1 John 2:25. *W 4/1 30, 33*

Sunday, February 4

See, I have commissioned you this day to be over the nations and over the kingdoms, in order to uproot and to pull down and to destroy and to tear down, to build and to plant. —Jer. 1:10.

Christendom's clergy have been like apostate Jerusalem, which Jehovah condemned. (Jer. 19:3-5) As he severely punished Judah's inhabitants, Christendom's people are in line for a like punishment. The Jeremiah class, together with those of the "great crowd" of "other sheep," have been proclaiming God's judgment for many years. The time draws near for the execution of those judgments. So this foretells a work of uprooting, pulling down the error of false religion. It also foretells a building and planting work by making known to honest persons the "good news" of God's kingdom that will replace the corrupt rule on earth today. It involves building in their hearts an appreciation of Jehovah, of his goodness and the opportunity for everlasting life under paradisaic conditions, made possible through the sacrifice of Jesus Christ. Are you having a full share in this work? *W 1/1 11, 13*

Monday, February 5

Your kingdom is founded on righteousness and justice; love and faithfulness are shown in all you do.—Ps. 89:14, Today's English Version.

Adam brought the human race into the position of enemies of God. (Rom. 5:10) Nevertheless, Jehovah loved his creation, knowing that they could not help themselves. But in his love for humankind, could he condone the wickedness that Satan, along with Adam, had brought into the universe? No, for in harmony with his justice and righteousness he could not ignore sin and let it go unaccounted for. If he should do that, he would be undermining the foundation of his government. We have an example in some nations of earth today of the results of condoning lawlessness. Criminals have been let run loose. The result has been that people lose faith in the governments. Disorder results. We can be thankful, however, that the Universal Ruler, Jehovah God, will not let that take place with the laws he has made. *W 2/1 9-11*

Tuesday, February 6

Let us not be judging one another any longer, but rather make this your decision, not to put before a brother a stumbling block or a cause for tripping.—Rom. 14:13.

What a man is spiritually, not what he appears to be from a fleshly, material standpoint, is what counts with God. We should hold to this evaluation of matters. In the congregation at Rome some had been judging the actions and motives of others who had different opinions and different conscientious scruples. This was wrong and dangerous to all involved. It was displeasing to the great Judge, before whom none had a preferred standing. Paul shows a far better way. To those who were prone to judge, he said the above. They could turn their propensity for judging others to a good advantage by judging themselves instead and by determining to supervise their own conduct more closely. To cause another to stumble would be to incite him to sin, for sin is represented in the Bible as a *fall:* "Let him that thinks he is standing beware that he does not fall." —1 Cor. 10:12. *W 3/15* 9, 12-14

Wednesday, February 7

"This is the covenant that I shall covenant toward them after those days," says Jehovah. "I will put my laws in their hearts, and in their minds I shall write them."—Heb. 10:16.

The Jewish nation had been under the Mosaic Law covenant for more than 15 centuries by the time their Messiah, Jesus, came. He denounced the oral traditions of their wise men and scribes, said he would end the Mosaic law by fulfilling it, and finally was impaled as a blasphemer. Thereafter his followers preached his resurrection and spread his teachings throughout Palestine and the Roman world. Not only Jews but also Gentiles flocked into their ranks by the thousands, and Christian congregations sprang up everywhere. The Law covenant was ended. It had served its purpose as a tutor to lead persons to Christ and had been nailed to the torture stake of Christ. Now Jehovah's worshipers were under a new covenant. Law was no longer written on stone tablets but on human hearts. How thankful we can be for this improved provision! *W 5/15* 1a

Thursday, February 8

The holy spirit and we ourselves have favored adding no further burden to you, except these necessary things, to keep . . . from blood and from things strangled and from fornication.—Acts 15:28, 29.

Thus, with the assured guidance of God's holy spirit, ruled the conference of the apostles and other Christian elders at Jerusalem. Though many clergymen say that this requirement was just a temporary step to avoid offending Jews, the facts show that more than a century later the prohibition on the partaking of blood was being observed generally by Christians. Also, numerous writings from the second and third centuries prove that Christians in that period realized that this prohibition was not a thing of the past. Why, then, are not Christendom's churches holding to this "rule" today? They, as Martin Luther admitted, realize that, because obeying this decision is difficult and ignoring it is so common, it would be impossible to require all churchgoers to follow it. So as Luther himself would not do so, neither do they. But we are happy to obey that decision. *W 6/15* 9-12a

Friday, February 9

His name will be called Wonderful Counselor, Mighty God, Eternal Father, Prince of Peace. To the abundance of the princely rule and to peace there will be no end.
—*Isa. 9:6, 7.*

Today, instant communication and fast transportation have "shrunk" the world, so that what happens in one place affects people everywhere else. Governments can make some minor adjustments and make conditions a little better for the people. But such help proves to be only superficial and temporary. What is required? First of all, a ruler that possesses *absolute authority*. He would also need a *perfect law* to follow, one that is just and fair in every respect. *Wisdom* and *love* would also be needed. He would also need *complete knowledge of human nature* and *of the whole creation*. Furthermore, for his administration to be one of happiness, accomplishment and productivity, the ruler would need to *know what is in the hearts and minds of people*, so as to be able to get their full cooperation. Of such a ruler Isaiah prophesied, and it is our privilege to tell others about him. *W 1/15* 9-12

Saturday, February 10

The one that without fail goes forth, even weeping, carrying along a bagful of seed, will without fail come in with a joyful cry, carrying along his sheaves.—Ps. 126:6.

Psalm 126 quite likely was one of the psalms that the Israelites sang on their way up to Jerusalem when they joyfully attended the three annual festivals held there. It tells of those who have come into Zion, God's organization. The above is the last verse, indicating an encouraging change in occupation.

Though at first this one had a hard time of it, with seemingly nothing to show for his labor, his diligence in patiently continuing to sow is at last rewarded with a harvest more bountiful than his fondest expectations. Yes, this is harvesttime. We are now in the conclusion of the system of things, even as Jesus said in one of his parables. (Matt. 13: 39) Jesus had some interesting things to say about the harvest and the work in connection with it, and especially about himself as a worker, namely, "My Father has kept working until now, and I keep working."—John 5:17. *W 6/1* 3, 4

Sunday, February 11

They will certainly fight against you, but they will not prevail over you. For I am with you, to save you and to deliver you.—Jer. 15:20.

Jeremiah was a faithful prophet. Because he was zealous in proclaiming Jehovah's "words," the entire nation called down evil upon him. But when he cried to Jehovah for relief, his God reassured him. Jeremiah minced no words in exposing the wickedness of the Jewish nation, its rulers and its people. (Jer. 26: 2) This called for courage on Jeremiah's part, and for explicit faith in Jehovah's power to sustain His prophet. Correspondingly, in modern times, Jehovah has raised up the small remnant of his anointed witnesses to serve as a Jeremiah class, particularly in the realm of hypocritical Christendom. They, too, must speak all the words that Jehovah commands. These words contain a message, not only of doom for Christendom and all other nations, but also of encouragement and hope for all those sharing in the witness work today. *W 1/1* 1-3

Monday, February 12

Faithful and deserving of full acceptance is the saying that Christ Jesus came into the world to save sinners.
—1 Tim. 1:15.

From the human viewpoint, there was no solution to the problem resulting from Adam's sin. But Jehovah God works out seemingly impossible problems in a marvelous way, still maintaining the dignity of his universal sovereignty and, at the same time, extending mercy. After seeing the outcome, we are moved to say, 'It just couldn't have been done in any other way and have been so thorough, righteous and altogether good.' So at the very time that God pronounced judgment upon Adam for his sin, God revealed that he would come to the rescue of the human race. (Gen. 3: 15) Who, particularly, would be designated by God to rescue the human race and to crush Satan's head? Jehovah's only-begotten Son! He was chosen as the primary one to serve for the settlement of the issue regarding the worthiness and righteousness of Jehovah's rulership or sovereignty, which had been challenged. *W 2/1 12, 13*

Tuesday, February 13

May Jehovah reward the way you act, and may there come to be a perfect wage for you from Jehovah the God of Israel, under whose wings you have come to seek refuge.
—Ruth 2:12.

Boaz was moved to say this because of Ruth's loyal love and humility. When evening came, Ruth was still threshing what she had gathered. Why, Ruth's gleanings for the day amounted to over a half bushel of barley! Unselfishly, Ruth also took out the food that she had left over at mealtime earlier that day and gave it to her needy mother-in-law. Again Ruth displayed loyal love toward Naomi. Add to this the young woman's love for Jehovah, her industriousness and humility, and it is no wonder that people viewed her as "an excellent woman." (Ruth 3:11) Surely, Ruth did not eat "the bread of laziness," and because of her hard work she had something to share with someone in need. (Prov. 31:27) By thus caring for her mother-in-law, Ruth knew the happiness that results from giving. Ruth is, indeed, a fine example for any godly woman. *W 2/15 21, 23, 24*

Wednesday, February 14

He delivered us from the authority of the darkness and transferred us into the kingdom of the Son of his love, by means of whom we have our release by ransom, the forgiveness of our sins.
—Col. 1:13, 14.

We do not depend upon the United Nations to set up the sorely needed world government. In the first century C.E. Jehovah God made a gracious move that was related to world government. He set up a spiritual kingdom. Over whom was that kingdom, inasmuch as the privileges of the kingdom of God were taken away from the nation of fleshly Israel? Who on earth are the subjects of that spiritual kingdom? The apostle Paul specifically called attention to that kingdom in his letter to the Christian congregation in Colossae when he said the above. Yes, away back there in the first century Jehovah God began making the believers suitable for his purpose even though they were from the Gentile nations. He forgave their sins. Thus they were made suitable for a share in the inheritance with God's holy ones, who were in the light. *W 3/1 9-11*

Thursday, February 15

If because of food your brother is being grieved, you are no longer walking in accord with love. Do not by your food ruin that one for whom Christ died.—Rom. 14:15.

While the example used here is food, the principle covers anything that we might have a right to do, and yet is an optional matter. However, there are things that God commands must be done, involving integrity, righteousness and obedience. These are the "important things." (Phil. 1:10) No Christian may properly compromise or fail on these points. But to go ahead stubbornly on matters of personal preference or opinion, not caring for the feelings of other Christians, is not acting in accord with love. That which is not done out of love is of no value to the doer. Furthermore, headstrong action would be very unwise. It could pain another brother, even though that brother's opinion that the action is wrong might not be well founded. He could become downhearted, angry, or even disgusted. The injury could go so far as to bring his faith to ruin. *W 3/15 20, 21*

Friday, February 16

Become imitators of me, even as I am of Christ. —1 Cor. 11:1.

From 1 Corinthians 1:11-13, we can see that because of giving undue attention to men, the members of the Corinthian congregation split up into factions. They failed to appreciate that men taking the lead among them were but slaves of God and Christ. Happily, Paul, Apollos and Peter were not responsible for the situation that developed in the Corinthian congregation. They personally set the example in looking to Jesus Christ as head. That is why the apostle Paul could say the above. And certainly elders today should want to be like Paul. This requires that they speak in agreement. (1 Cor. 1:10) Once elders publicly express widely divergent personal views, members of the congregation will be inclined to look to those whose opinions are more in line with their own thinking. The situation becomes especially serious when an elder downgrades his fellow elders, perhaps implying that he is more zealous and more faithful than they are, or perhaps more discerning. *W 4/1 6, 7*

Saturday, February 17

Blessed is the able-bodied man who puts his trust in Jehovah, and whose confidence Jehovah has become.—Jer. 17:7.

As the Jeremiah class and their companions proclaim the tidings about the time of distress foretold at Daniel 12:1, 4, they endure in faithfulness. To their faith they supply endurance. (2 Pet. 1:5, 6) The Jeremiah class, along with all those newly flocking to the ranks of Kingdom publishers, need continued encouragement to press on to victory. Jehovah provides just such encouragement. In contrast to the one "who puts his trust in earthling man and actually makes flesh his arm," the Jeremiah class put their trust in Jehovah and make him their confidence. They "become like a tree planted by the waters," so that they can send forth roots to drink in all of Jehovah's life-giving provision. Neither the "heat" of persecution nor the "drought" resulting from bans and restrictions can make them "leave off from producing fruit." Like a productive tree, they are "luxuriant" in bringing forth praise to Jehovah. In this, they are blessed. *W 1/1 3, 4a*

Sunday, February 18

They will sanctify my name, and they will certainly sanctify the Holy One of Jacob, and the God of Israel they will regard with awe.—Isa. 29:23.

For what was Jesus Christ living and dying? To take away all the reproaches heaped upon Jehovah God so that people would have the right view of his Father, and so that they might come to know and praise God. How can the Christian today, upon whom Jehovah's name has been called, be sure that he is always sanctifying God's name? Of course, he does this even in private by holding God's name as sacred in his heart and mind. He does it in his family by speaking of right things and by showing a loving concern. Toward his brothers in the congregation he sanctifies God's name by helping them at every opportunity, bearing the weaknesses of those not as spiritually strong as he is. (Gal. 6:10) Because Jehovah's name is called on him, he knows that what he says and does will reflect on the divine name. In such ways he will be doing what the prophet Isaiah foretold that the restored remnant would do. *W 5/1 6, 7*

Monday, February 19

The kingdom of the world did become the kingdom of our Lord and of his Christ, and he will rule as king forever and ever.—Rev. 11:15.

That announcement heralds a world government! How, then, is Jesus Christ to gain a share in that world government? The Lord God recognizes his Son as having a right to share in such a world government. Why so? Because God gave his Son to die for all the human race, and this Son died as a perfect human sacrifice. By this he re-deemed the whole human family. (Heb. 2:9; 1 Tim. 2:5, 6) However, the Lord God set a time for giving his self-sacrificing Son a share in the world government. When? At the end of the Gentile Times. All the intervening centuries have allowed God to go ahead with transferring additional approved disciples of Jesus Christ into his spiritual kingdom. He has done this by begetting them with his spirit. (Jas. 1:18) These 144,000 must be such as will steadfastly remain in that kingdom in spite of all the trials, hardships and persecution experienced in this world.—Rev. 2:10. *W 3/1 23-25*

Tuesday, February 20

The word of God went on growing, and the number of the disciples kept multiplying in Jerusalem very much; and a great crowd of priests began to be obedient to the faith. —Acts 6:7.

Immediately after telling the disciples to beg the Master to send out workers into his harvest, Jesus sent out the twelve. (Matt. 10:1-10) His instructions stressed the urgency of their harvest work. Jesus did not want them to get involved with a lot of other things. He does not want us today to get sidetracked by materialism or any other diversion. It is harvesttime! We might ask, Was there a harvest in the first century? There certainly was! Consider what happened in Jerusalem on that Pentecost day. After listening to Peter's "thorough witness" and exhortation, "about three thousand souls" were baptized and were added to the original congregation of about 120. (Acts 1: 15; 2:37-42) And the congregation itself was really only *one day* old! Though ordered by the rulers not to teach, the apostles kept talking and the harvest kept coming in. *W 6/1 12-14*

Wednesday, February 21

You must not pollute the land in which you are; because it is blood that pollutes the land. —Num. 35:33.

How does Jehovah God view life? He considers it sacred, not something to be squandered. We can tell that from his repeated condemnations of murder and the emotions that often lead to it. (Ex. 20:13; 1 John 3:11-15; Rev. 21:8) Moreover, in ancient Israel, Jehovah God arranged for cities of refuge to which a person could flee for sanctuary if he unintentionally caused another's death. Why did an accidental manslayer have to take the major step of leaving his home and remaining, for perhaps years, in the city of refuge? Because he had caused the loss of life, sacred life. You can see that the divine provision of these cities would promote further respect for the sanctity of life. (Num. 35: 9-29) After outlining that provision, Jehovah God told the Israelites the above. Why was that? The "blood" here mentioned stood for the life of the victim. Jehovah God thus called to the fore the vital link between our life and our blood. *W 6/15 3-5*

Thursday, February 22

I know that in me, that is, in my flesh, there dwells nothing good.—Rom. 7:18.

When witnessing to people we should keep in mind that those to whom we are speaking do not view matters in the same light that we do. They more readily observe our kind, helpful and sincere manner than they do our words. If they do not see these things, they will not listen to what we say. Also, in calling from house to house, we do well to have a positive approach. To condemn what the householder believes or the things that he is practicing will not help him. We have to help him to see that what we present to him in Jehovah's name is *good*. It has to appeal to him as something better, or something that will help him, not condemn him. Also, our attitude toward him, and toward all persons in the world, should be that displayed by the apostle Paul. Just because he was favored by having the truth, he did not consider himself any better personally as an imperfect human creature than those to whom he preached, as can be seen by his words above.—1 Tim. 1:12-16. *W 5/1 9-11*

Friday, February 23

The Jews ask for signs and the Greeks look for wisdom; but we preach Christ impaled, to the Jews a cause for stumbling but to the nations foolishness. —1 Cor. 1:22, 23.

The apostle Paul would not water down the word of God with Jewish or Greek impurities to make it more acceptable to a world whose wisdom was foolishness to God. Neither should we. Both Paul and Peter foresaw the time coming when false teachings from both Jewish and Gentile sources would contaminate the truth of Christ impaled, and they sounded warnings. (Acts 20:29, 30; 2 Tim. 4:3, 4; 2 Pet. 2:1) Subsequent history confirms that the warnings of the apostles were well founded. Little has changed down to our day. The vast majority of the churches of Christendom still teach such doctrines as immortal soul, Trinity and others, which filtered into apostate Christianity. It is our privilege to bring the truth about these matters to all honest-hearted persons by our preaching from house to house and making return visits. *W 5/15 9-11a*

Saturday, February 24

This good news of the kingdom will be preached in all the inhabited earth for a witness to all the nations; and then the end will come. —Matt. 24:14.

Since 1914, the "kingdom of our Lord and of his Christ" has had a right to interfere with Gentile nations. Does this mean that we now have a right to meddle in worldly politics? May we take sides, as Catholics and Protestants do, with this or that political party, even conspiring against established political government or stirring up revolution? Not at all! Uncompromisingly we copy the example of the Lamb, Jesus Christ, in being "no part of the world." (John 17:16) We hold strictly to the kingdom that was brought to birth in heaven in 1914. In spite of the fierce persecution leveled against us because of our Christian neutrality toward worldly conflicts, we carry out the prophetic word of our heavenly Leader, Jesus Christ, when he said the words above. This Kingdom witness has to be done before this system of things ends and Christ's 1,000-year reign begins. *W 3/1 12, 13b*

Sunday, February 25

King Zedekiah . . . went on to say: "Does there exist a word from Jehovah?" To this Jeremiah said: "There does exist!" And he said further: "Into the hand of the king of Babylon you will be given!" —Jer. 37:17.

It was the last king of Judah, Zedekiah (617-607 B.C.E.), that called on Jeremiah to pray to Jehovah on Judah's behalf. (Jer. 37:3) But Jeremiah continued to proclaim the impending destruction of Jerusalem. Later, after being harshly treated and imprisoned many days, he was brought before the king, who asked him privately about Jehovah's "word." Jeremiah gave back to him a forthright answer. In like manner, Jehovah's Witnesses today are forthright in pointing to the divine judgment. We are not interested in interfaith movements or in softening the message proclaimed against Christendom. It is a joy to note that there are still on earth today persons of the same caliber as Jeremiah and his friends, Baruch, the Rechabites and Ebed-melech. Our annual worldwide field service report proves this to be so. *W 1/1 19, 21a*

Monday, February 26

I shall put enmity between you and the woman and between your seed and her seed. He will bruise you in the head and you will bruise him in the heel.—Gen. 3:15.

Jehovah God has regard for the feelings and rights of those he governs, and so he first educates them in his way, building up their faith in his righteous rulership. That is why the bringing in of God's kingdom has taken time. Rather than being idle or merely waiting, as some suppose, Jehovah God has been making progressive moves toward the complete establishment of this kingdom ever since mankind rebelled at the first, even as implied in the first Kingdom promise. He is now nearing the complete end of these preparations. His purpose is to have people enlightened and educated to know him and willingly submit to his rule. To this end he graciously provides a knowledge of the standards and principles of his righteous administration and how it operates. God's people gladly follow these principles. *W 1/15 16-18*

Tuesday, February 27

If errors were what you watch, O Jah, O Jehovah, who could stand?—Ps. 130:3.

As Jehovah views the earth and sees the many distresses that men undergo, he has deep feeling for humankind. His desire is to help each one of them. Though he does not 'turn a blind eye' to wrongdoing, he is looking for people's good points, rather than their faults, even as the psalmist noted. When on earth, God's Son was *anxious* to use his power to help people. (Mark 1:40, 41) Jesus' healing of people who came to him for help was accompanied by deep feeling. In the same way Jehovah God and his Son are at this time showing concern and love for anyone who has paused in the affairs of everyday life to give consideration to the "good news" about God's purpose. Are you right now looking into God's Word in a genuinely searching way and getting some knowledge about Him? If so, this in itself is evidence that God is interested in you. How can this be said with assurance? Because God sees some goodness of heart in anyone sincerely inquiring into his Word. —John 6:44. *W 2/1 6-9a*

Wednesday, February 28

Do not, therefore, let the good you people do be spoken of with injury to you. —Rom. 14:16.

Differences of opinion, taste and inward feelings exist also among sincere Christians. These can upset the peace and unity of the congregation if its members view their own opinion as superior or as being the one to which all should conform. In Romans, chapter 14, Paul points out that mature Christians have a wide latitude of freedom in these things. But he also cautioned against the unbridled exercise of this liberty or a Christian's attempting to restrict another's freedom. One Christian might feel conscientiously free to exercise a certain right. However, Paul encouraged such a one to temper his actions if he knew that they offended the conscience of a brother. Conversely, the one having a conscience overly tender in some respects was counseled not to condemn his brother for doing what the Scriptures allow, even though he himself could not conscientiously do it. Failure to respect the consciences of others would be going contrary to Paul's advice above. *W 3/15 1-3a*

Thursday, March 1

They must rebuild the long-standing devastated places; they will raise up even the desolated places of former times, and they will certainly make anew the devastated cities.—Isa. 61:4.

Ministers of State participated in the great reconstruction work that was made necessary by World War I. After World War II, reconstruction work became necessary once more, but on a far grander scale. However, a more impor-tant work of another kind began in the postwar year of 1919. In spite of the destructiveness of World War II, it has continued on determinedly, yes, irrepressibly. It was restoration work of a spiritual kind, backed by a power such as the ministerial departments of human governments did not have. Those who have pioneered the restoration work of the spiritual kind have been God's servants of a far higher order than those mentioned at Romans 13:4. *W 7/1 1, 2*

Friday, March 2

Sovereign Lord, you are the One who made the heaven and the earth and the sea and all the things in them.—Acts 4:24.

What does the term "sovereignty" mean to you? You doubtless think of supreme power, the power of a ruler —the power of government. Rulership can be one that strictly metes out full justice; or it can be one that deals with partiality toward some. Few man-made rulerships act out of real love for their subjects. God's Word speaks of Him as the "Sovereign Lord." By what right does he have sovereignty? By reason of his having "created all things." (Rev. 4:11) What kind of sovereignty does Jehovah exercise? Is it different from other forms of rule? King David, who exercised rulership over ancient Israel under Jehovah's sovereignty, said: "Yours, O Jehovah, are the greatness and the mightiness and the beauty and the excellency and the dignity; for everything in the heavens and in the earth is yours." (1 Chron. 29:11) To gain everlasting life we must submit to Jehovah's sovereignty. *W 7/15 1-3*

Saturday, March 3

My food is for me to do the will of him that sent me and to finish his work. . . . Look! I say to you: Lift up your eyes and view the fields, that they are white for harvesting. —John 4:34, 35.

When Jesus commenced his earthly ministry he worked and showed others how to work. He expressed himself about this in connection with harvesting, even as noted above. From Matthew 9:35-38 we can know what kind of harvesting Jesus had in mind. So in both these accounts it is evident that the harvest about which Jesus spoke was one of *people,* whom Jesus wanted very much to see gathered in. There is a close parallel between that day and our day, and Jesus wants us who are his followers to enter into the *spirit* of harvesting. And that spirit is one of rejoicing, a spirit of keen appreciation of how worth while the work is, prompting a desire in one to see it fully accomplished. That is why we beg the Master to send out more workers. Jehovah does not provide these 'more workers' miraculously. It is up to us to make disciples. *W 6/1 8-10*

Sunday, March 4

I have made myself the slave to all, that I may gain the most persons. . . . I have become all things to people of all sorts, that I might by all means save some. But I do all things for the sake of the good news, that I may become a sharer of it with others. —1 Cor. 9:19, 22, 23.

God, by favoring us with a knowledge of the truth, has actually put us under obligation to people on the outside, as well as to our brothers, even as the apostle Paul shows at Romans 1:14, 15. And in this regard Paul also said the above. Consequently, when we pray, "Father, let your name be sanctified," we are asking God to help us to set all other things aside so that what we do will always glorify his name and cause it to be held sacred. We will then follow up our prayer by seeking not to put anything in front of others to stumble them in their search for the truth. We will watch to be more loving and less critical. We will ever keep in mind that by being all things to all people we can 'become a sharer of the good news and its blessings' with others. *W 5/1 17, 18*

Monday, March 5

Get out of her, my people, if you do not want to share with her in her sins, and if you do not want to receive part of her plagues.—Rev. 18:4.

A high regard for life and blood should move us to be careful when driving a vehicle, to obey safety regulations and to keep our vehicle in a safe driving condition. Similarly, reasonable care ought to be exercised to eliminate hazards in the home or in one's business so as to minimize the likelihood of a fatal accident occurring either to oneself or to others. Another feature of avoiding bloodguilt relates to organizations or institutions that are bloodguilty in God's eyes. For instance, God specifically charges Babylon the Great with bloodguilt for shedding the blood of true worshipers. (Rev. 17:6) She has also endorsed various institutions that have shed seas of blood over the centuries. A sincere desire to be free from bloodguilt requires our separating ourselves from and our being careful not to support present-day organizations that God thus judges adversely. *W 6/15 20, 21a*

Tuesday, March 6

Solid food belongs to mature people, to those who through use have their perceptive powers trained to distinguish both right and wrong.—Heb. 5:14.

What of Christians who accept the personal philosophies and opinions of others as a guide for determining the rightness of a particular course? They may well injure their conscience and hinder their spiritual growth. Why? Because the Bible shows that 'perceptive powers must be trained by use.' So, when others are unduly influencing or even controlling an individual's decisions, this person is not going to grow spiritually but will remain a babe, unable to distinguish right from wrong. Those who allow themselves to be unduly influenced by the personal opinions of someone else may later experience problems that could have been avoided. Whenever God's Word is displaced by the views of imperfect men as a source of guidance, serious problems can result. But we are always safe when we make decisions based on the example and teachings of the perfect Son of God. *W 4/1 20, 21*

Wednesday, March 7

Let the lowly brother exult over his exaltation, and the rich one over his humiliation, because like a flower of the vegetation he will pass away. —Jas. 1:9, 10.

The lowly one, not having possessions or prominence in this system of things, can exult because in the world he was disregarded, but now he is considered as being on the same level as the rich man in the judgment of Jehovah God and of his fellow Christians. He is a 'fellow citizen of the holy ones and a member of the household of God.' (Eph. 2:19) He has the surpassing riches of serving Jehovah God, and ahead of him lies the reward of life. The rich man can exult over the fact that he has been brought to see that it is useless to spend his energies in the amassing of wealth. From his new Christlike, humble position he can appreciate the "deceptive power of riches" and the folly of trusting in them. (Mark 4:19) He knows that "the things seen are temporary, but the things unseen are everlasting." He now looks to the same reward as does the lowly one. —2 Cor. 4:18. *W 3/15 8*

Thursday, March 8

Instead of your shame there will be a double portion, and instead of humiliation they will cry out joyfully over their share.—Isa. 61:7.

Let us not fail to note this: Those upon whom this encouraging prophecy is fulfilled must first suffer shame and humiliation, the denial of their "portion" and "share." During World War I such disagreeable, unjustified things did befall Jehovah's anointed remnant, even at the hand of war-mad Christendom. However, those spiritual Israelites are no longer in the land of Babylon the Great, suffering captivity and religious slavery there. In the spring of 1919, when the Babylonish clergy of Christendom no longer had marshaled nations to use as henchmen, Jehovah liberated his faithful anointed remnant. He restored them to "their land." In that God-given estate was where they were no more to suffer shame, humiliation and lack of spiritual provisions. Theirs was now a spiritual paradise, in which they enjoy a "double portion." How faith-strengthening it is to see the fulfillment of this prophecy! *W 7/1 8, 9a*

Friday, March 9

I am Jehovah, the One exercising loving-kindness, justice and righteousness in the earth; for in these things I do take delight.—Jer. 9:24.

When Moses asked to see God's glory, he was told that he would not be able to see God's face, because no man can look on God and live. (Ex. 33:18, 20) Nevertheless, God did come down in a cloud on Mount Sinai and the first things he brought to Moses' attention were mercy, graciousness, slowness to anger, loving-kindness, truth and forgiveness. (Ex. 34:6, 7) And he expressed like sentiments through his prophet Jeremiah. However, when anyone sins against God, even though forgiven for his sin, he cannot escape the consequences of the chain of events that he has set in motion. For example, one committing adultery affects others close to him. His whole family is bound to feel the effects. And while God punishes those who reject his sovereignty, he does not take delight in punishing them. (Ezek. 18:32) These truths should inspire in us both love for Jehovah and fear of displeasing him. *W 7/15 4, 5*

Saturday, March 10

Jehovah strong and mighty, Jehovah mighty in battle. —Ps. 24:8.

Thus the Levite priests promptly and without shame reply to the question: "Who, then, is this glorious King?" Ah, yes, it is no lowly person who asks entrance into the royal city. It is the loftiest Personage in all the universe, Jehovah "the glorious King." For that reason the gates and the long-lasting or ancient entrances seemed to be too low. Hence, they should heighten themselves for the passing through of so lofty a king. (Ps. 24:7) He was far loftier than King David, who sat on "Jehovah's throne" at Jerusalem. (1 Chron. 29:23) In earlier times other kings may have passed through the ancient entrances of the city, but none as glorious or as mighty as Jehovah, the Most High God. He was the One that did battle and gave the victory to King David over the former pagan occupants of the city, the Jebusites. He, too, will be the One to give the victory to his Son, Jesus Christ, at Armageddon. Today both the "remnant" and the "other sheep" welcome this glorious King. *W 3/1 21b*

Sunday, March 11

Yours is the kingdom, O Jehovah, the One also lifting yourself up as head over all. —1 Chron. 29:11.

Jehovah God has taken time to reveal his principles and qualities by having *dealings with people*. It has been instructive, convincing and moving to see in the Bible's historical record the proof that what he *says* he also *carries out* in righteousness and justice. Thus, in laying the foundation for his government over the earth, Jehovah has first given us the benefit of: (1) a firm basis for faith in the administration that he would provide, (2) a knowledge of the principles of his government, (3) a demonstration of his qualities as universal Ruler and (4) a sure and unmistakable identification of the Messiah. At the same time a comparison with man's rule and its results over the years has clearly demonstrated the superiority, deservedness and rightness of God's rulership, to which King David testified in the above words. It is in our interest to show our allegiance to that kingdom by sharing in making it known. *W 1/15* 19, 20

Monday, March 12

The things I was fond of were with the sons of men. —Prov. 8:31.

Why did Jehovah choose his only-begotten Son, who was so close to his heart, for the settlement of the issue? Well, when Satan made his challenge it called into question the loyalty of all creatures in the universe, right up to this Son of God. More than that, the question of loyalty would focus more on him than on any other one of God's creatures, because he was the chief Son of Jehovah, next to Him in the universe. Furthermore, speaking of God's creative work, this Son, symbolized by wisdom, says the above. Yes, he deeply *loved* mankind. He gladly took this assignment to vindicate his Father, first out of loyalty to Him, and, additionally, out of the love he had for mankind. Because of the universal issue involved, Jehovah the Universal Sovereign permitted sin to exist for a time in order to settle the question of his sovereignty and of the loyalty of his great family of intelligent creatures. He also laid a foundation for the removal of sin. *W 2/1* 13-15

Tuesday, March 13

Look! My own servants will rejoice, but you yourselves will suffer shame. Look! My own servants will cry out joyfully because of the good condition of the heart, but you yourselves will make outcries because of the pain of heart. —Isa. 65:13, 14.

Our *Yearbook* shows that even in countries where our work is banned, thousands are baptized each year. Certainly that is cause for rejoicing. To work, and to work hard, under conditions of fierce opposition is not a new experience for Jehovah's servants. It is now as it was in the days of Nehemiah, when they were building Jerusalem's wall and the neighboring peoples intensified their opposition to such building. (See Nehemiah 4:17, 18.) In that same chapter, at verse 6, it says that "the people continued to have a heart for working." Do we know the secret of that fine heart condition? It is mentioned at Nehemiah 8:10: "For the *joy of Jehovah* is your stronghold." The same is true of us today, is it not? Are we not reminded of the above words of Jehovah through his prophet Isaiah? *W 6/1* 1-3a

Wednesday, March 14

Christ entered, not into a holy place made with hands, which is a copy of the reality, but into heaven itself, now to appear before the person of God for us.—Heb. 9:24.

There is no denying the emphasis that the Bible places on the death of Jesus. (Rom. 5:8; 1 Cor. 15:3) His dying, willingly giving his perfect human life, paid back or balanced what Adam had lost for us and which led to our sinful state. However, the Bible's references to the *"blood* of the Christ" should convey to us important things that might not be appreciated in speaking of just his death. (Eph. 2:13) Christ did not, and could not, simply die and remain dead. Jesus had to enter heaven, into the very presence of God. There Christ could present the value or merit of his lifeblood, just as on Atonement Day the high priest took the sacrificial blood into the Most Holy, a parallel that Paul sets out above. Furthermore, in heaven Jesus Christ *is alive* and able to plead for all who exercise faith in his ransom and assist them toward salvation.—Rom. 5:10. *W 6/15* 18-20

Thursday, March 15

They led him to the brow of the mountain upon which their city had been built, in order to throw him down headlong. But he went through the midst of them and continued on his way. —Luke 4:29, 30.

Till Jesus became 30 years old he had been a carpenter in Nazareth. There the synagogue was in which Jesus read the significant words of Isaiah 61: 1, 2. This change of profession he announced to his Nazarene audience when he finished reading Isaiah 61:1, 2 and said: "Today this scripture that you just heard is ful-filled." Then he demonstrated this fact by giving a Bible talk that his fellow countrymen thought the former carpenter incapable of giving. They had heard that Jesus had become a physician. So they wanted him to 'cure himself' by performing cures in his "home territory" on his own townspeople. By means of Bible illustrations Jesus explained why he would not do so. At this they became highly displeased and tried to kill him. Today there are likewise many opposers who are not "meek" enough to accept "good news." *W 7/1* 9

Friday, March 16

Happy is the man that keeps on enduring trial, because on becoming approved he will receive the crown of life, which Jehovah promised to those who continue loving him. —Jas. 1:12.

The "crown of life" is the gift of life that God gives to "those who continue loving him" through the many trials that God causes to work together to perfect his servants, if they endure them steadfastly, uncomplainingly and, by his help, triumphantly. This does not mean that we earn the right to life by our works or endurance, for life is the free *gift* through faith in Jesus Christ. But the enduring Christian has proved that he has that faith. Its quality is tested and found strong and complete. Consequently, we as Christians CAN endure whatever trials come upon us, even the most severe ones. We should not enter into these trials trusting in our own strength. God's wisdom and strength must be sought through prayer in the name of Jesus Christ, who, when on earth, set the perfect example of endurance.—1 Pet. 5:10. *W 7/15* 18, 19a

Saturday, March 17

Your words were found, and I proceeded to eat them; and your word becomes to me the exultation and the rejoicing of my heart . . . I have not sat down in the intimate group of those playing jokes.
—Jer. 15:16, 17.

As a sign that his message was sure, Jehovah commanded Jeremiah not to marry. Thus he would not bring forth children for destruction. He did not complain about his single status, but became absorbed in the work at hand. In time, Pashhur, an official in the house of Jehovah, took offense at Jeremiah's words, struck him and put him in stocks overnight. But on his release Jeremiah once again fearlessly declared that all Judah would be given into the hand of Babylon's king. (Jer. 16:1-4; 20:1-6) Jehovah also gave Jeremiah a powerful prophecy to pronounce when wicked King Jehoiakim came to the throne in 628 B.C.E. (Jer. 26:1-9) At all times Jeremiah found joy in Jehovah's words and in bearing His name. He found no pleasure in the empty joking of godless men and wisely avoided their company. Should we do any less? *W 1/1* 7, 8, 6a

Sunday, March 18

Our Father in the heavens, let your name be sanctified.
—Matt. 6:9.

It is our privilege not only to pray for God's name to be sanctified but also to have a share in its being done. How so? By imitating God and letting people know why we do so. So we must love them even as God does. God could have looked at all mankind as worthless, self-seeking, disgusting sinners. But instead, "God loved the world so much that he gave his only-begotten Son, in order that everyone exercising faith in him might not be destroyed but have everlasting life." Yes, Christ died for us "when we were *enemies.*" (John 3:16; Rom. 5:6-10) One of the most direct ways of sanctifying God's name is by telling others about God's provision for mankind through Christ. In speaking to these persons, whether they appear to be interested or not, we must always keep in mind the sanctifying of Jehovah's name. This means that our conduct and speech should be that which will, if possible, encourage the person to have a more friendly viewpoint toward God. *W 5/1* 8, 9

Monday, March 19

Deaden, therefore, your body members that are upon the earth as respects fornication, uncleanness, sexual appetite, hurtful desire, and covetousness, which is idolatry.
—Col. 3:5.

We must deaden wrong fleshly desires, not allowing them to cause our body members to sin. One thing that can help us to gain the mastery over wrong fleshly desires is a recognition of the seriousness of covetousness—an inordinate desire for something to which a person is not entitled. Covetousness is idolatry because the object of a person's wrong craving begins to take on too much importance in his life. It becomes an idol to him and so interferes with his giving Jehovah God exclusive devotion. It also prevents him from being wholehearted in his love for Jehovah God, as his selfish craving prods him to disregard divine law. When a Christian becomes aware that wrong desire is building up within him, he does well to call to mind how precious his relationship with God is and how senseless it would be to forfeit this by making himself an idolater. *W 4/1* 24, 25

Tuesday, March 20

Make melody to God, make melody. Make melody to our King, make melody. For God is King of all the earth. —Ps. 47:6, 7.

It is for *us on earth!* It is perfectly suited to our pressing needs—this world government of which we speak. It is about to take over the care of all our affairs. That is why we speak of it as "our incoming world government." It comes from a source far higher than from us puny human creatures, who have failed so miserably in managing our affairs on earth. It comes from the One who knows how to run, not only our tiny earth, but also the whole universe. It comes from the Creator of all things. The world government is His kingdom that he promised six thousand years ago. For all of this ought we not to be glad and make melody to Him? Yes, indeed! In being a world government, God's kingdom will not deal with just one nation as God did with Israel from 1513 B.C.E. until 33 C.E., at which time he was their heavenly King. He gives his own word for it that he will be King over *all* the earth. *W 3/1 1-3*

Wednesday, March 21

He who in this regard slaves for Christ is acceptable to God and has approval with men. —Rom. 14:18.

It is the teaching about the kingdom of God that will produce the far superior fruitage of righteousness in its proclaimers and in those who hear our message. If a Christian really allows the holy spirit to work in him and direct him, he will have joy because of his confidence that he is pleasing to Jehovah God. The design of the kingdom of God is to promote these vital things of the spirit. In view of his having these majestic goals, a mature Christian focuses his attention on the matters that really have to do with the characteristics and principles of the kingdom of Jehovah God. If he slaves for Christ in promoting these important things, he will certainly have God's approval, and other Christians will love him for his reasonableness. His life course will commend him to people on the outside. Even though some may not want to take up Christianity, his conduct will recommend itself to their consciences. *W 3/15 9, 10a*

Thursday, March 22

They must be called big trees of righteousness, the planting of Jehovah, for him to be beautified.—Isa. 61:3.

From Pentecost onward Jehovah planted "big trees" in the spiritual estate of his dedicated people that their enemies had devastated and desolated. Such figurative "big trees" were the stalwart, steadfast, immovable Christians that reared themselves up loftily for the righteousness of Jehovah God. He, as their Planter, was "beautified" by their presence in the newly established Christian congregation. On the day of Pentecost, thousands became anointed ones after their repentance, their acceptance of the Messiah and their baptism in water at the hands of the 12 apostles. These also came under the obligations of the anointing with Jehovah's spirit through Christ. Their Leader, Jesus, had pioneered the way for them to get the perfected faith and life and salvation. They became "ministers of our God." (Isa. 61:6) As such, they must now pioneer the way for yet others to gain reconciliation with God through Christ. *W 7/1 24, 25*

Friday, March 23

Thanks to God that you were the slaves of sin but you became obedient from the heart to that form of teaching to which you were handed over.
—Rom. 6:17.

Among the dominant features of Jehovah God's rulership are loving-kindness, mercy, righteousness and impartiality in administering justice. (See Exodus 34:6, 7; Jeremiah 9:24.) The good news of the Kingdom is directly connected with God's sovereignty. Paul wrote to Christians in Rome as above. Those who hear with a good heart and obey are not there told that the "good news" was handed over to them, but that *they* were 'handed over to that form of teaching,' the gospel or good news of the Kingdom. They are now willing subjects and supporters of God's sovereignty. When they, in turn, proclaim the "good news," the receivers are handed over to such teaching. What does this promote in the earth? Righteousness, loving-kindness and mercy. For instead of our former uncleanness and lawlessness, we 'now present our body members as slaves to righteousness.'—Rom. 6:17-19. *W 7/15 6, 7*

Saturday, March 24

I am clean from the blood of all men, for I have not held back from telling you all the counsel of God.
—Acts 20:26, 27.

One way to be free from bloodguilt is by enthusiastically preaching the Kingdom message. Consider in this connection God's counsel to Ezekiel before Jerusalem's fall in 607 B.C.E. God told him that if he, as a watchman, failed to sound the warning message, he would be held accountable for the blood of the Israelites who perished. (Ezek. 3:17-21; 33:2-16) Yet, what satisfaction we can find in discharging our Christian responsibility to spread the truth about the coming end of this wicked system and about the paradise to follow! Doing that allows one to feel as did the apostle Paul, who told Christian elders the above. What a privilege! While personally avoiding bloodguilt, we can aid others to gain life everlasting by their exercising faith in Christ's blood. Based on God's Word we appreciate Jehovah's view on life and blood. Let us be resolved to uphold that view and to live in accord with it. *W 6/15 22, 23a*

Sunday, March 25

After these things I saw, and, look! a great crowd, which no man was able to number, out of all nations and tribes and peoples and tongues, standing before the throne and before the Lamb, dressed in white robes; and there were palm branches in their hands.
—Rev. 7:9.

Today, we observe the good news of the Kingdom proclaimed in virtually every corner of the earth, and we see over two million persons gathering together in peace and unity in true worship of Jehovah God. These are proclaiming the "good news" to still others. Where do these fit into God's purpose? The Bible tells us that they are a "great crowd" who will survive the crushing of the governments of the earth by the Kingdom "stone" mentioned by Daniel, to become the foundation for the "new earth." They will be the first to enjoy the rulership of the Kingdom over the earth, and they will be on hand during Christ's 1,000-year reign to welcome back millions of dead persons by a resurrection and to help them to learn and practice true worship. *W 1/15 25*

Monday, March 26

Let us, therefore, approach with freeness of speech to the throne of undeserved kindness, that we may obtain mercy and find . . . help at the right time.—Heb. 4:16.

We know that God has communicated his purpose to us. Can we, in turn, communicate our inmost thoughts and heartfelt desires to God? Yes, and that is by means of prayer. You need not fear that God will not listen to you. His only requirements are a sincere heart and the acknowledgment that one is a sinner, needing help. One who cries out to him will be shown what to do. Such a person will come to know that prayers addressed to God must be through Jesus Christ as God's appointed High Priest. (Heb. 4:15) What are proper subjects for prayer? Anything that will affect our relationship to Jehovah God, anything that will affect us spiritually. The apostle John said we are to "ask according to his will." (1 John 5:14) Asking "according to his will" would mean that we would not pray for things that promote strictly selfish interests, such as riches. *W 2/1 13-15a*

Tuesday, March 27

If anyone ministers, let him minister as dependent on the strength that God supplies; so that in all things God may be glorified through Jesus Christ.—1 Pet. 4:11.

As Christians we have to be alert at all times not to lapse into the natural tendency of the imperfect flesh, forgetting that we are simply God's servants, planting and watering the seed, but that it is Jehovah God who makes it grow. (1 Cor. 3:6, 7) The part that God performs as we serve him can be compared with the way our bodies function. The organs God designed for us function without our being conscious of their operation. We can only partly explain how they work. Also, the food we get grows with only minor effort on our part, and in some cases none at all, yet it is filled with all the vital nourishing factors. Sun, rain, soil and seed do the major tasks. So, in reality, our life is wholly dependent on the things Jehovah God supplies. He does practically all the work. Our service to God rests on the same principle, even as the apostle Peter shows. *W 5/1 14, 15a*

Wednesday, March 28

It was in the name of Jehovah our God that he spoke to us. —Jer. 26:16.

The priests and prophets called for Jeremiah's death. But in a stirring speech he made it plain that Jehovah God had sent him to prophesy and that they would shed innocent blood if they put him to death. (Jer. 26:10-15) Then it was that the princes and all the people spoke up on his behalf. Certain elders also supported him. Jeremiah continued, therefore, fearlessly prophesying. This temporary letup in the Judeans' hounding of Jeremiah reminds us of some relief that came in the experience of our brothers in Malawi. Some recent reports have indicated that many of the brothers have been released from prisons, and have been permitted to return to their homes and cultivate their fields. Some youths who were formerly their persecutors are said even to be studying the Bible with them. However, in other parts of the country, local officials and relatives make it hard for Jehovah's people to live a normal life. But Jeremiah-like, they continue to endure. *W 1/1 8, 9a*

Thursday, March 29

Deliver me from bloodguiltiness, O God the God of my salvation.—Ps. 51:14.

The faith that we as Christians have, and in harmony with which we are firmly resolved to live, involves faith in the saving power of Christ's blood for gaining everlasting life. So our everlasting destiny is tied up in our faithfulness to Jehovah. This includes our being obedient to what he says about blood. It is altogether right for us to strive earnestly to avoid overstepping God's law on blood, whether medically or otherwise. Violation of that law would make us guilty before Jehovah God. King David manifested the attitude that we need to cherish when he prayed the above. Many persons think of bloodguilt solely in terms of deliberate murder. God certainly is on record as hating such bloodshed. But the Scriptures show that because life is sacred a measure of bloodguilt could even result from causing someone's death unintentionally. Do we personally evidence high regard for life and blood in our daily affairs? We should. *W 6/15 18-20a*

Friday, March 30

This tested quality of your faith works out endurance.—Jas. 1:3.

Some have said, "I wonder if I could have endured," when they read about the trials suffered by Christians of the first century, as well as those in Nazi countries during World War II and, in more recent times, in lands all around the earth. Even in the day-to-day life of all Christians, problems occur that are not only hard to bear but often very difficult to handle. Can one who expresses faith in Christ and who is a servant of God endure? It was to persons undergoing trials and facing such questions that James wrote. His words are of great comfort, for he wrote when Christians, not only were undergoing strong persecution, but were approaching a time when affairs of the Roman nation would be more turbulent, as far as Christians were concerned. So James' letter was timely. We have need of endurance, for we live in a world that flouts Christian principles and, in addition, we have to deal with sickness and many other problems. *W 7/15 1, 2, 4a*

Saturday, March 31

He has sent me to bind up the brokenhearted, to proclaim liberty to those taken captive and the wide opening of the eyes even to the prisoners.—Isa. 61:1.

The anointing of Jesus with holy spirit in 29 C.E. occurred 565 years after Jesus' people had been released from Babylonian captivity in 537 B.C.E. and had returned to their devastated homeland, the province of Judah. They had 'made anew the devastated cities' of the land, including Jerusalem, the temple of which they had rebuilt. They had 'raised up the desolated places' of the former 70 years of their lying waste and had converted the land into somewhat of a paradise. At the three annual feasts of the Jews, Zion, or Jerusalem, would teem with millions of worshipers. Why, then, when Jesus was anointed, should there be any brokenhearted Jews or Israelites? Why any "taken captive"? Why any "prisoners"? It was because of the spiritual state into which the nation of Israel had come. Today we find the people of Christendom in a like sorry spiritual state. *W 7/1 12, 13*

Sunday, April 1

We, for our part, shall walk in the name of Jehovah our God. —Mic. 4:5.

The true God has given himself a name (Ps. 83:18) and we are grateful that he has revealed to us his own personal name. But walking in the name of Jehovah involves much more than being able to speak his name. It means more than recognizing the divine name in Bible manuscripts. Walking in the name of Jehovah does not mean merely saying that he is our God. It involves more than attending Christian meetings at the local Kingdom Hall. And, naturally, preaching activity is not all that is connected with walking in Jehovah's name. While all these things are important, they alone do not prove that we truly are walking in the "name" of Jehovah. The determining factor is not merely what we say and claim about ourselves, but what we actually do with our whole heart, soul, mind and strength. Those walking in God's name are dedicated to him, and they really "slave for Jehovah." (Rom. 12:11; 6:16) Have you taken a firm stand for Jehovah? Are you walking in God's name? *W 8/15 7-9*

Monday, April 2

If anyone wants to come after me, let him disown himself and pick up his torture stake day after day and follow me continually. For whoever wants to save his soul will lose it; but whoever loses his soul for my sake is the one that will save it. —Luke 9:23, 24.

Just the opposite of the attitude of the world in these last days, as described at 2 Timothy 3:1-4, is the spirit of self-sacrifice. It is a course recommended by no less an authority than Jehovah God himself. But such a course of self-sacrifice—is it not outdated in these modern times? Why should anyone want to be interested in that when more and more people are not? It is very important that we have the right view of this matter of self-sacrifice as opposed to self-indulgence. Regarding this, Jesus said the above. Jesus was here describing a course of self-sacrifice. And he took the lead in demonstrating what this meant. The reason he undertook such a course of self-sacrifice was so that he could fully accomplish the will of his heavenly Father. *W 8/1 3-5*

Tuesday, April 3

He has sent me to bind up the brokenhearted, to proclaim liberty to those taken captive and the wide opening of the eyes even to the prisoners. —Isa. 61:1.

The leaders in Judaism, the scribes and Pharisees, maneuvered Jerusalem into rejecting the real Messiah, Jesus, and having him put to death on a stake as if he were a false Christ. Those religious leaders kept Jerusalem on the path of being a killer of prophets and a stoner of those whom God sent to her. (Matt. 23:1-37) So, did the "meek" ones of such a nation need to have "good news" told to them? Were those "taken captive" needing to have liberty proclaimed to them? Were there "prisoners" that needed to have a "wide opening of the eyes" by being brought out of the dungeon of religious darkness? Was Jerusalem as the center of Jehovah's worship in such a religiously devastated state that there was real cause for mourning over her? Yes, indeed! And the anointed Jesus saw that there was then a remnant of such "mourning ones." *W 7/1 14*

Wednesday, April 4

To earthling man his way does not belong. It does not belong to man who is walking even to direct his step.—Jer. 10:23.

After thousands of years of human existence, why do we not see the peaceful, prosperous and happy world that people everywhere long for? Not just *humility*, but *reality* and *honesty* oblige us to admit that it is because all men are imperfect. The fault lies, not just with those who rule, but also with those who are ruled. That is why human efforts to make this earth a joyful home for all mankind fall so far short of what God promises by means of his own rulership. Right in the Bible we find proof of Jeremiah's above statement in the history of ancient Israel. That nation had a perfect law, given by God himself. At first it had God alone for its invisible King, with prophets and judges representing him to the people. Later, the choice of a human king led Israel to problems and loss of freedom, even as God forewarned. Truly the wise course is for us to be guided by what Jeremiah 10:23 says. *W 1/15 4, 5*

Thursday, April 5

The dragon . . . went off to wage war with the remaining ones of her seed, who observe the commandments of God and have the work of bearing witness to Jesus.—Rev. 12:17.

Satan the Devil will be responsible for the everlasting "woe" that strikes the Gentile nations at the battlefield of Har-Magedon. How can we escape that woeful destruction with those nations? We must refuse to march as allies with the Gentile nations in their march to fight against Jehovah God. Such refusal has brought great hardship on Jehovah's people. Especially since the ouster of Satan and his demon angels from heaven, the remnant of prospective joint heirs of Christ have been the main target of the wrathful Satan. His aim is to break their integrity toward God. In this way he would make them unfit to rule as kings with Christ during the 10 centuries when all the demons are imprisoned in the abyss. Satan is bent on preventing Christ from having the full number of 144,000 associate kings in the heavenly world government. Will Satan succeed? Never! *W 3/1 14, 15b*

Friday, April 6

When those of the nations heard this, they began to rejoice and to glorify the word of Jehovah, and all those who were rightly disposed for everlasting life became believers. —Acts 13:48.

When a woman came into the house where Jesus was eating a meal and poured perfumed oil on his head, Jesus said the words recorded at Mark 14:3-9. And his words have proved true, because the woman's good deed, though small, is recorded in the Bible and has been called to the attention of millions. We, in turn, should show appreciation for God's kindness in helping us to know about his purpose and in giving us the opportunity to get everlasting life. We should be thankful that God has seen fit to allow us to be like the people to whom Paul preached in Asia Minor. There certain Jews who claimed to serve God opposed the truth. But the Gentiles rejoiced when they heard of the opportunity to be accepted by God. Those people appreciated God's kindness. Such appreciation will help us to be the kind of people that God is pleased to accept. *W 2/1 11, 12a*

Saturday, April 7

Make disciples . . . teaching them to observe all the things I have commanded you. —Matt. 28:19, 20.

A good Christian will represent God's sovereignty properly when he studies with others, by making effort to teach these people *all that he can,* as Jesus directed. If he is an overseer, he will not be jealous about his knowledge or be afraid that someone else might eclipse him by knowing more or by developing greater ability. The overseer should teach *all he knows* to others around him so that they will be able to do the job. Not only does he help them thereby, but also they become capable of handling matters if he is absent. In this way the overseer shows himself to be really concerned about the welfare and progress of the congregation, not just thinking about himself. For what if he should be sick, or die, or move away? Paul had met the men who became the elders of Ephesus first while he was doing public witnessing. He did not teach them merely to the point of baptism. He told them "all the counsel of God." (Acts 20:27) We should do so today. *W 7/15 13, 14*

Sunday, April 8

They must rebuild the long-standing devastated places; they will raise up even the desolated places of former times.—Isa. 61:4.

After first telling how the Sovereign Lord Jehovah would be "beautified" by his producing "big trees of righteousness" (Isa. 61:3) in a spiritual paradise, Isaiah's prophecy goes on to say the above. The rebuilders here spoken of are those referred to in the preceding three verses who receive comfort and who are given religious liberty and re-stored to the favor and "goodwill" of Jehovah. These are set to the restoration work. The facts show that the fulfillment of this prophecy extends down to our 20th century, to our day. World War I had a devastating effect on the anointed remnant of Jehovah's servants. But in 1919 came release, not only from literal imprisonment, but, more importantly, from Babylon the Great. Restoration work of a spiritual kind got under way without delay. It has continued down to this day, and great is our privilege to have a share in it. Are you doing your part? *W 7/1 3-5a*

Monday, April 9

I seek, not my own will, but the will of him that sent me. —John 5:30.

This is the course that Jesus recommended to his followers. He said that they should be willing to "disown" themselves, meaning that they should subdue their own personal desires and make the doing of God's will the main thing in their lives. (Luke 9:23-25) True, such a life of self-sacrifice is not easy. It involves a cost, which includes time and effort. In some cases it may even mean the loss of one's life at the hands of those who persecute God's servants. However, as Jesus showed, the one doing God's will would 'save his soul,' or life. In what way? In that he would gain Jehovah's approval and the eventual reward that God promises all those who serve him. (Heb. 11:6) For most of God's loyal human servants, that reward is eternal life in a righteous new order here on earth. Even death itself will not be able to stand in the way of this reward, because Jehovah guarantees that there is going to be "a resurrection of life." —John 5:29. *W 8/1 5, 6*

Tuesday, April 10

The fruitage of the spirit is love, joy.—Gal. 5:22.

Love is the first fruit mentioned by Paul. "God is love," wrote John. (1 John 4:8) Hence, a godly person who manifests love is imitating God in that respect. Furthermore, "by this all will know that you are my disciples," said Jesus, "if you have love among yourselves." (John 13: 35) The love among Christians attracts attention now, even as it did in former days. It is "a perfect bond of union" within the Christian congregation. (Col. 3:14) And no wonder! 'Love is long-suffering and kind. It does not brag, get puffed up, behave indecently, look for its own interests, become provoked, keep account of injury or rejoice over unrighteousness. Rather, it rejoices with the truth and bears, believes, hopes and endures all things.' Truly, "love never fails." (1 Cor. 13:4-8) *Joy,* another fruit of God's spirit, is said to be "deeper-rooted than *delight,* more radiant or demonstrative than *gladness.*" The pleasant, joyful countenance of a Kingdom proclaimer has brightened the face of many a listener. *W 8/15* 10, 11a

Wednesday, April 11
Memorial Date
After Sundown

See, the Lamb of God that takes away the sin of the world!—John 1:29.

Today the political governments consider their citizens to be the property of the State. In this way such governments push God the Creator and his sacrificed Son out of the realm of property rights. But shortly in the heavenly Court of Divine Justice it will be established that the Lamb of God was slaughtered here on earth for those who make up the citizenry of all nations. So by right of purchase they all belong to him, and not to any man or men. They are Christ's property, yes, also the property of his heavenly Father, Jehovah God. So this purchase does not limit itself to just the 144,000 who will be kings with Christ in the heavenly government. (Rev. 5:9, 10) We must have the broad view of the Son of God that John the Baptizer had, when he pointed to the baptized Jesus and said the above. In full harmony with that fact, the incoming royal government will be global, earth wide. *W 3/1* 4, 5a

Thursday, April 12

Keep from becoming causes for stumbling to Jews as well as Greeks and to the congregation of God.—1 Cor. 10:32.

A Christian could make a brother stumble in this way: He might do something that he has the Christian freedom to do, without first ascertaining whether this might hurt the conscience of the brother. For example, this brother may have qualms of conscience with regard to alcoholic beverages. Yet the Christian may drink before the brother, or offer him a drink. The brother may think, 'Well, he is a mature Christian, so maybe I can follow his pattern.' So he is emboldened, and goes ahead. But at the same time his conscience is telling him that it is not right. It is condemning him. He is not acting out of faith, or as unto God. Therefore, he has been made to stumble. His conscience is wounded and he is dejected because he feels that he has sinned. It may be hard for him to recover. (Rom. 14:23) Or, the action of a Christian could cause the weaker one to start entertaining false suspicions. *W 3/15* 14, 15

Friday, April 13

Look out: perhaps there may be someone who will carry you off as his prey . . . according to the elementary things of the world and not according to Christ.—Col. 2:8.

Christ's perfect example and teachings do not have to be supplemented by human philosophies and traditions. Back in the first century, Christians were in danger of being led astray by the "elementary things," which included the unscriptural concepts of the Greeks and other non-Jewish peoples as well as the non-Biblical traditions of the Jews. On the surface, some of the philosophies and teachings may have seemed very plausible. They may have been accompanied by reasoning and argument that had a certain appeal to human thinking. But they lacked a solid foundation. These baseless teachings—whether on doctrine, on human conduct, or as to how things should be done in the congregation—were really "empty deception." So, there was good reason for Christians to be on guard against becoming the prey of some false teacher and being turned aside from the way of the truth. *W 4/1 11, 12*

Saturday, April 14

Do you despise the riches of his kindness and forbearance and long-suffering, because you do not know that the kindly quality of God is trying to lead you to repentance?—Rom. 2:4.

When dealing with your own relatives, think of the time that you spend calling on strangers at the doors, the time you take studying with them, carefully helping them to get a good foundation before trying to get them to change their ways, their associations, and so forth. So, why be overhasty and make attempts to push your views on your relatives? Before you either cut off your association with them or cause them to withdraw from you, why not look at the matter as actually one way of serving Jehovah God while you are still being as friendly, kind and helpful as ever? In this way you will be displaying the godly quality of long-suffering and sanctifying his name so that when you do have an occasion to bring to their attention the *good* things of God's provisions, they may be ready to give you a hearing, because they see God's qualities in you. *W 5/1 14*

Sunday, April 15

Be wise, my son, and make my heart rejoice, that I may make a reply to him that is taunting me.—Prov. 27:11.

Are there still people to be gathered in during this harvesttime? Worldwide reports indicate that there are. What are we going to do about it? Will we keep on working together with Jesus Christ, under his yoke? (Matt. 11:28-30) We are assured that he would be with us right down to the conclusion of this system of things. (Matt. 28:20) So, let us all keep working with Christ until the harvest is completely gathered, all working joyfully together. This is Jehovah's work for his people today. Paul rejoiced because he was entrusted with the "glorious good news of the happy God." (1 Tim. 1:11) Surely we have even more reason to rejoice as we are entrusted with the good news of the established Kingdom. Our taking a firm stand on its side and loyally working for its interests will cause even Jehovah's heart to rejoice. What a privilege is ours! What an incentive to share in God's work! *W 6/1 23-25a*

Monday, April 16

When Christ came as a high priest of the good things that have come to pass, . . . he entered, no, not with the blood of goats and of young bulls, but with his own blood, once for all time into the holy place [heaven itself] and obtained an everlasting deliverance for us.—Heb. 9:11, 12.

In Leviticus chapter 17, Jehovah God himself explained the underlying principles of the sacrificial requirements and there he plainly stated his decision: Blood (representing life from him) was to be put to one use only—in sacrifice. God thus put a value on blood, setting it aside as sacred. Under the Law, it was not to be eaten or drunk, or put to any other use that men might devise. The animal sacrifices of the Law covenant could not completely cover sin, or else they would not have had to be offered year after year. Those sacrifices, especially the ones on the Day of Atonement, were but a "shadow of the good things to come." (Heb. 10:1-4) The reality that was foreshadowed was the ransom sacrifice of Christ that could fully atone for all our sins. *W 6/15* 12, 14

Tuesday, April 17

A God of faithfulness, with whom there is no injustice; righteous and upright is he. —Deut. 32:4.

Those walking with Jehovah have come to appreciate his qualities, his personality. Such have also learned that love, joy, peace, long-suffering, kindness, goodness, faith, mildness and self-control are fruits of God's spirit. (Gal. 5:22, 23) These are therefore qualities that originate with Jehovah. Now we associate them with his holy name, and they move us to love and trust the God in whose name we are walking. Moreover, we have come to know of Jehovah's purpose to uphold his universal sovereignty and vindicate his name by means of the heavenly kingdom in the hands of Jesus Christ. Moreover, godly persons realize that Jehovah is able to accomplish his purpose and to vindicate his name. Why? Because Jehovah has a record of mighty deeds. He is not like the worthless gods of the nations. (Ps. 115:1-8) At Exodus 15:11, 12, 19 Jehovah is described in song after his miraculously delivering his people Israel at the Red Sea. *W 8/15* 11, 13, 14

Wednesday, April 18

Pay attention to yourselves that your hearts never become weighed down with overeating and heavy drinking and anxieties of life, and suddenly that day be instantly upon you as a snare.—Luke 21:34, 35.

When Jesus spoke of Jehovah's day of destruction coming, he said it would come "as a snare." A snare closes in on an unsuspecting animal when the animal walks heedlessly in the pathway of danger. So, too, this system's end will come suddenly, when most people do not expect it. Such people could include some who have started on the "road leading off into life," but who have allowed themselves to become absorbed in worldly pursuits, and have strayed too far in the wrong direction. (Matt. 7:14) Yet, would not a less-threatening world situation give some justification for feeling that the end is not close? Actually, it could mean just the opposite, as can be seen from Jesus' words at Matthew 24:37-39, 44. The apostle Paul, too, noted the suddenness with which this system would come to its end, unexpected by most people. —1 Thess. 5:2, 3. *W 8/1* 14-16

Thursday, April 19

Strangers will actually stand and shepherd the flocks of you people, and the foreigners will be your farmers and your vinedressers.—Isa. 61:5.

In 1919 the first convention of the International Bible Students Association at Cedar Point, Ohio, proved meaningful. It notified the world that the true Christian remnant anointed with the spirit of the Sovereign Lord Jehovah was again alive, as if from the dead. They had been restored to his favor and were once more openly active in 'preaching this good news of the Kingdom for a witness to all the nations,' as foretold in Matthew 24:14. The effect of that pioneering effort at spiritual rehabilitation shows up on a worldwide scale even at this late date. To his own praise, Jehovah God has established a spiritual paradise for his spirit-anointed remnant. Strange as it may sound, the spiritual rehabilitation of this remnant was due to excite international attention. After first telling of the rebuilding of the long-standing desolated places, Isaiah's prophecy foretold this.—Isa. 61:4. *W 7/1* 6, 7a

Friday, April 20

There will not be cut off from Jonadab the son of Rechab a man to stand before me always.—Jer. 35:19.

Among Jeremiah's friends were the Rechabites, the descendants of Jonadab. He had given them the command that they must drink no wine "to time indefinite." Jeremiah placed wine before them. But they refused it, in loyal obedience to their forefather, Jonadab. Jehovah then contrasted the disobedience of the Jews with the enduring loyalty of the Rechabites and declared the above. Thus these received a grand reward, deliverance during the tribulation on Jerusalem. These Rechabites have their counterpart today—persons of honest heart and right principles, who may even have tried to find escape from these critical times in the religious confines of modern Christendom. But their real refuge lies in Jehovah's provision through Christ. He sends to them the modern-day Jeremiah class, with the message that means their salvation. Yes, their safety is to be found squarely on the side of Jehovah's modern-day "prophet." *W 1/1* 17, 18a

Saturday, April 21

Take this cup of the wine of rage out of my hand, and you must make all the nations to whom I am sending you drink it. And they must drink and shake back and forth and act like crazed men because of the sword that I am sending among them.—Jer. 25:15, 16.

Jeremiah was a true prophet. He spoke in the name of Jehovah, directed the people to Jehovah's worship, and every word that he uttered concerning Jerusalem, Judah and other nations came true. Likewise, the major fulfillment of his prophecy is certain today. And note, in its modern-day fulfillment, this utterance of doom embraces, not only the nations of Christendom, but all the nations of the entire earth. After the destruction of all the nations that oppose God's righteous will, the ruler of this world, Satan the Devil, will be abyssed. This will prepare the way for lasting peace and happiness here on earth. Should we be fearful that we now stand face-to-face with this final execution of judgment? Jeremiah was not afraid. Neither should we be. *W 1/1* 15, 16

Sunday, April 22

Dignity and splendor are before him, strength and joy are at his place.—1 Chron. 16:27.

If each of us keeps in mind the fine qualities of God's sovereignty, we will promote joy. Without joy, which is a fruit of God's spirit, there is discouragement. Paul asked the Christians in Galatia who had become spiritually weak, "Where, then, is that happiness you had [when first you believed the good news]?" (Gal. 4:15) An atmosphere of joy is the atmosphere that God's sovereignty prompts among all those who love God and serve him wholeheartedly. (Ps. 89:15-17) From the starry heavens, which "are declaring the glory of God," to the earth itself, it is evident that God's creatorship is grand and beautiful. (Ps. 19:1) Imagine what a fine place the earth will be when 'the knowledge of Jehovah fills the earth as the waters cover the sea.' (Isa. 11:9) In anticipation of that most joyful time, let us joyfully expend ourselves now, in making known to all who will hear the "glorious good news of the happy God."—1 Tim. 1:11. *W 7/15 15-17*

Monday, April 23

Love does not work evil to one's neighbor; therefore love is the law's fulfillment. —Rom. 13:10.

Already, today, Jehovah's people are making diligent efforts to apply the law of love as best they can in their imperfection. This does not mean that they fail to obey the laws of the nations in which they live. Not at all! In fact, in many places they have been described as the most law-abiding citizens. And why is this? It is because the law of the Kingdom, the law of love, is written on their hearts. For conscience' sake they respect and obey the "superior authorities" of the nations and their laws, but their highest allegiance they give to the supreme authority of Jehovah God and his kingdom by Christ Jesus. No, God's kingdom does not load them down with oppressive rules and restrictions, for Micah writes appreciatively concerning Jehovah: "He has told you, O earthling man, what is good. And what is Jehovah asking back from you but to exercise justice and to love kindness and to be modest in walking with your God?" —Mic. 6:8. *W 1/15 30*

Tuesday, April 24

God saw good for all fullness to dwell in him.—Col. 1:19.

When an elder downgrades his fellow elders this can result in his undermining the efforts of the body of elders to care for the spiritual interests of the flock. (Compare 2 Samuel 15:2-6.) On the other hand, when elders strive to speak and act unitedly, allowing themselves to be guided fully by the Scriptures in their decisions, there will be unity in the Christian congregation. The whole congregation will then be encouraged to look, not to humans, but to Jesus Christ as the head of the congregation. Recognition of Christ's headship also includes recognizing that, according to Jehovah God's good pleasure, Jesus Christ occupies the foremost place in the congregation, not only as regards pre-eminence and authority, but also in having the "fullness" of everything that Christians need. He is the embodiment of divine qualities, including wisdom. Hence, he is *the one* to whom true Christians look as their exemplar and the appointed source of guidance and instruction. *W 4/1 7, 8, 10*

Wednesday, April 25

Demas has forsaken me because he loved the present system of things.—2 Tim. 4:10.

From God's viewpoint, can any way of life in this system of things be "normal"? This world is under the influence of Satan and his demons, dominated by harsh political systems, greedy commercial interests and selfish false religions. It is filled with fear, hatred, violence, immorality, corruption, economic difficulties, sickness and death. All of this is far from the normal life that Jehovah has purposed for mankind, which includes perfect health, complete security and happiness, as well as eternal life, and all of this on a paradise earth. Hence, life now is far from normal. It is very abnormal, and it will stay that way until Jehovah crushes out of existence this entire wicked system. So it is a self-delusion to search for normality in an abnormal world. What a calamity it could be, at this late date, for a Christian to ignore Jesus' warning, relax his guard and endanger his relationship with Jehovah, as did Demas!—Luke 21:34-36. *W 8/1 12, 13*

Thursday, April 26

I, Jehovah, am loving justice, hating robbery along with unrighteousness. And I will give their wages in trueness . . . And their offspring will actually be known even among the nations.—Isa. 61:8, 9.

"Ministers of our God" should carry out their responsibilities and conduct themselves in a way that honors their standing before God. (Isa. 61:6) People may misunderstand them. They may be robbed of their good reputation or be denied proper recognition and a deserved consideration. (2 Cor. 6:8-10) But the Supreme Judge of all will correct matters just when it suits his purpose. He believes in justice, even as he assures us. To become "known" the remnant of spiritual Israel had to get out among the nations and peoples. During World War I and World War II they had been subjected to "robbery." Because of being falsely accused and misrepresented by religious foes and their patrons, they underwent great persecution. But Jehovah, by making them his witnesses and preachers of the Kingdom good news showed whom he himself approved. *W 7/1 24, 26a*

Friday, April 27

It does not belong to man who is walking even to direct his step.—Jer. 10:23.

What is the motivation for submission to God's sovereignty? It is love for God because of his divine qualities, and also love for what is right and good for all creation. The one who understands what Jehovah's sovereignty means prefers it above all other sovereignties. In fact, those supporting Jehovah God's rulership prefer it to having absolute independence, if that were possible. Why? Because they know that they will be much happier under God's sovereignty than they would be if they could do altogether as they pleased. They realize that the wisdom, love, knowledge and power of God are so far superior to theirs that there is no comparison. Humans cannot keep themselves living everlastingly, neither can they bring about peace, righteousness and justice throughout the earth, even as noted by Jeremiah, a faithful supporter of Jehovah's sovereignty. It is, therefore, also the course of practical wisdom for us to submit to Jehovah's sovereignty. *W 7/15 8*

Saturday, April 28

Symeon has related thoroughly how God for the first time turned his attention to the nations to take out of them a people for his name. —Acts 15:14.

A great responsibility rests on those walking in Jehovah's name. To walk in his name necessitates our being unreservedly dedicated to him. It requires living in harmony with God's name, being representatives of everything for which Jehovah's name stands. Yes, it means representing the divine name before all the world in a correct manner. Walking in the name of our God means honoring the name Jehovah, fighting for it spiritually, giving that divine name its proper place in the Holy Scriptures and declaring that holy name boldly. (Ps. 9:1, 2) Jehovah God had a people for his name in the first century of the Common Era. Comparably, Jehovah has his name-people today, the remnant of Jesus' anointed followers. Associated with this remnant is a "great crowd" who have the hope of life eternal on earth. Are you making use of every opportunity to represent Jehovah's name? *W 8/15 20, 21*

Sunday, April 29

Praise Jah, you people, because Jehovah our God, the Almighty, has begun to rule as king.—Rev. 19:6.

At the end of the "seven times" of Gentile domination Jehovah's universal sovereignty was to express itself again toward the earth. At that marked time in God's schedule of events the occasion would call for 'the kingdom of the world to become the kingdom of our Lord and of his Christ.' (Rev. 11:15) Valid reason that would be for tremendous joy on the part of all those in heaven and on earth who had prayed for God to assert once again his full sovereignty toward our earth, where the Gentile powers had held world domination for so long. The foregoing proclamations put in bold relief the fact that it is the Sovereign Lord Jehovah who takes up reigning again toward our earth at the close of the "seven times" of Gentile domination. It is He who takes his great power to himself and takes over "the kingdom of the world." Then he gives to his Son, Jesus Christ, a share in that kingdom. *W 3/1 15, 16, 18a*

Monday, April 30

May Jehovah fulfill all your requests. Now I do know that Jehovah certainly saves his anointed one. He answers him from his holy heavens with the saving mighty acts. —Ps. 20:5, 6.

Some months have passed since Boaz said to Ruth: "May Jehovah reward the way you act, and may there come to be a perfect wage for you from Jehovah." (Ruth 2:12) Now, by fathering Obed, Boaz has become an instrument in the blessing he had wished for the young Moabitess. One day, Obed will have a son named Jesse, who will become the father of David, Israel's second king. (Ruth 4:18-22) Surely, the "perfect wage" granted by God to loyal Ruth should move thoughtful persons to approach him in implicit faith, confident that Jehovah exists and that "he becomes the rewarder of those earnestly seeking him." (Heb. 11:6) Yes, the book of Ruth portrays Jehovah as a God of love who acts in behalf of those devoted to him. Moreover, it proves that God's purposes never fail. Hence, we can and should have confidence in his promises. *W 2/15 23, 25a*

Tuesday, May 1

Unless you eat the flesh of the Son of man and drink his blood, you have no life in yourselves.—John 6:53.

Jesus' flesh, which served as symbolic manna for the spiritual Israelites, also serves "in behalf of the life of the world." (John 6:51) The disciple that "feeds" on the antitypical manna (Christ's "flesh") before the coming of "the last day" will, as Jesus said, "live because of me," for the living Jesus will resurrect him "at the last day." (John 6:54, 57, 58) In heaven, when having 'life in themselves,' the resurrected spiritual Israelites will no longer need to feed on Jesus' flesh and drink his blood. They will be privileged to serve as "priests of God and of the Christ" and will thus be able to pass on to mankind the lasting benefits of Christ's atoning sacrifice. (Rev. 20:6; Heb. 7:23, 24) Like the High Priest, Jesus Christ, they will be able to serve as underpriests continuously throughout the whole millennium. In this way they will share with Jesus Christ in uplifting mankind to human perfection on earth. *W 9/1 24, 25b*

Wednesday, May 2

If I speak in the tongues of men and of angels but do not have love, I have become a sounding piece of brass or a clashing cymbal.—1 Cor. 13:1.

What is the surpassing way? (1 Cor. 12:31) It is the way of love. Yes, the Christians at Corinth needed to make changes in their evaluation of "gifts" and to put love in action. Pointing out how love is of greater value than abilities and gifts, Paul wrote the above. A Christian's being able to speak languages other than his native tongue would certainly be a valuable gift. Even greater would be the ability to speak in the language of angels who are a creation higher than man. But if the individual were to use the gift to enhance his prominence or would in some other way be wrongly motivated, he would not be upbuilding to his fellowmen, including his Christian brothers. He would be just like a big noise made by a brass instrument or a cymbal. Moreover, without love, the gift of prophesying, miraculous knowledge and miraculous faith would not serve for the encouragement of others. *W 9/15 5, 6a*

Thursday, May 3

Present your bodies a sacrifice living, holy, acceptable to God, a sacred service with your power of reason.—Rom. 12:1.

Jehovah God is certainly worthy of any sacrifices that we make for him. He is the Creator of the awesome universe and the source of all living things. He is also the Maker of a new order of righteousness that will remedy all mankind's problems. Because Jehovah is so worthy, we are urged to 'present our bodies as a living sacrifice' to him. Just what does being a living sacrifice to Jehovah involve? One definition of the word "sacrifice" is "to surrender something prized or desirable for the sake of something considered to have a higher claim." An additional meaning of "sacrifice" is "the offering of life to a deity." Since God does not ask us to be killed literally on some altar, the offering of our lives would be in *service* to him. Acceptable sacrifice to God involves positive acts, as well as abandoning practices that he disapproves or that could interfere with our service to him.—2 Pet. 3:11. *W 8/1 1, 2a*

Friday, May 4

Then he started to say to them: "Today this scripture that you just heard is fulfilled."—Luke 4:21.

The first-century restoration worker Jesus Christ showed just when the words of Isaiah's prophecy recorded at Isaiah 61:4-6 would begin to come true. The time for this would be when a centuries-old nation was breaking down and a new and better nation was to be brought into being. The new nation would be made up of the disciples of Jesus Christ, who were begotten by the spirit of Jehovah God. It would be a spiritual Israel. But how did Jesus Christ indicate the time for the fulfillment of Isaiah's prophecy? He did this when he quoted from the words that lead up to this prophecy and applied those words to himself. Jesus was then visiting the synagogue of his home-town, Nazareth, sometime after the Passover of 30 C.E. He stood up to read. He unrolled the scroll of Isaiah's prophecy to what is now sectioned off as chapter 61 and read at least part of verses one and two. Then he said the above to his audience. *W 7/1 4*

Saturday, May 5

"You are my witnesses," is the utterance of Jehovah, "even my servant whom I have chosen . . . Before me there was no God formed, and after me there continued to be none." —Isa. 43:10.

Ours is indeed a unique privilege and position before all mankind. In the eighth century B.C.E., through the prophet Isaiah, Jehovah God challenged all the gods of the nations to produce their witnesses, so that these might testify regarding the deity of those gods. All those false gods failed to produce witnesses. But Jehovah God did produce people to testify to his Godship, even as shown by the above quotation from Isaiah 43:10. Today we gladly bear the divine name. We consider it a grand privilege to represent the Universal Sovereign and to acquaint mankind with him, witnessing about this true God and his purposes. Compared with this marvelous privilege, everything else becomes of relatively little importance. Often great courage is required for one to walk in Jehovah's name as his witness. But doing so results in rich blessings, even as can be seen from the examples of Enoch and Noah.—Gen. 5:24; 6:9. *W 8/15 22, 23*

Sunday, May 6

With your blood you bought persons for God out of every tribe and tongue and people and nation, and you made them to be a kingdom and priests to our God, and they are to rule as kings over the earth.—Rev. 5:9, 10.

Notice, please! That inspired statement does not say that the sacrificial Lamb of God bought persons for God out of only the 12 tribes of the one nation of Israel. The governing factors of that world rulership will not have their roots in just the fleshly nation of Israel, even though the Lamb of God, Jesus Christ, was himself a Hebrew-speaking Jew or Israelite, when a perfect man on earth. As he is now in heaven, he is to be known no more according to the flesh that he sacrificed. (2 Cor. 5: 16) In harmony with this he will have associated with him in the world government persons whom he bought "out of every tribe and tongue and people and nation." It is our privilege and obligation to make this grand incoming government known by sharing in both formal and informal witnessing. *W 3/1 2a*

Monday, May 7

Let the lowly brother exult over his exaltation, and the rich one over his humiliation. —Jas. 1:9, 10.

Most Christians today are of humble birth. (1 Cor. 1:26) Being of low estate, their economic condition may make it harder for them when persecution comes. Nonetheless, they can rejoice because, in the Christian congregation, their lowly estate is no disadvantage. They are children of God. The poor man can forget his earthly poverty because of the surpassing riches of his relationship with God and Christ, and the love of his Christian brothers. And he can be happy that he is able to help others by imparting the "good news" to them. Over these things he can boast. As for the rich man who has become a Christian, he can exult "over his humiliation." Now it is not his wealth that really counts. Rather than high-mindedness, which riches often produce, the spirit of Christ is one of lowliness of mind. He can rejoice over the understanding that he can now discern that riches are not the thing in which to put trust.—Matt. 13:22. *W 7/15* 15, 16a

Tuesday, May 8

This is the will of my Father, that everyone that beholds the Son and exercises faith in him should have everlasting life, and I will resurrect him at the last day.—John 6:40.

Those particular ones exercising faith in Jesus as the Messiah during this present system of things have the prospect of everlasting life. Why so? Because Christ will raise them up from the dead at the last day. This guarantees to them a resurrection. Jesus' listeners had begun murmuring among themselves in a contention about the origin of Jesus. From the comment that Jesus made about this we should identify the particular ones to whom he directs his speech. Jesus quoted from the prophecy of Isaiah 54:13, which is addressed to the heavenly Zion, and which refers to the spiritual sons of God. These are the ones whom he draws to Jesus by their present belief in him. These are the ones of whom Jesus speaks as entering into everlasting life by his resurrecting them at the last day. Their life would be everlasting in God's heavenly organization. *W 9/1* 6-8b

Wednesday, May 9

Love is long-suffering and kind.—1 Cor. 13:4.

The person who gave generously, simply so that he could brag, would receive no reward. Since love is so important, we do well to consider how we are individually measuring up in our display of this fine quality. What do the above words require of us? When provoked, oppressed, irritated or misrepresented, how should we react? The long-suffering person avoids hasty action or emotional outbursts. He will patiently bear up under trying circumstances, doing so in the hope that those responsible for the unpleasantness will be helped thereby to change their ways. For the same reason, we should be kind, not rough, harsh or hateful, but tender, mild, friendly and helpful. Because of genuine concern for fellow believers, we should gladly put up with their idiosyncrasies and any weaknesses of conscience that they might have. We should not insist on our rights but refrain from using our Christian freedom to the full. Thus we will not stumble others, giving them an excuse to forsake true worship. *W 9/15* 6, 7a

Thursday, May 10

Become imitators of God, as beloved children.—Eph. 5:1.

A person's friends can have either a good or a bad effect on him, because one may be inclined to imitate the ways of one's associates. Well, those walking worthily in Jehovah's name as his friends can be certain that intimacy with God will always have a good effect on them. Trying to imitate Jehovah is highly beneficial, for which reason the apostle Paul urges us to do this. A person, though imperfect, can imitate God by accepting the guidance provided in Jehovah's Word and by yielding to the influence of God's holy spirit, or active force. Surely, we desire to cultivate and demonstrate the fruitage of God's holy spirit—love, joy, peace, long-suffering, kindness, goodness, faith, mildness and self-control. (Gal. 5:22, 23) As we manifest these fruits, other people will be moved to think of these qualities when Jehovah God is brought to mind. Of course, this requires that we display the fruits of God's spirit everywhere, before all persons, whether at home, at work, at school, or elsewhere. *W 8/15* 7, 8a

Friday, May 11

If anyone does commit a sin, we have a helper with the Father, Jesus Christ, a righteous one. And he is a propitiatory sacrifice for our sins, yet not for ours only but also for the whole world's. —1 John 2:1, 2.

By his faithful course Jesus qualified to become the Helper of all who desire to serve God, even as the apostle John shows. Now, the Devil has tried to find fault with God's servants from the time of Abel. In fact, Satan is called "the accuser of our brothers ... who accuses them day and night before our God." (Rev. 12:10) So, in due time in the contest with respect to integrity, Jesus Christ has appeared before God as a helper. He has access to the throne of God in our behalf. When faithful servants of God have made a mistake, have committed a sin, and have sincerely repented and confessed, Jesus has presented the merit of his sacrifice so that they should not be destroyed—for his propitiatory sacrifice can cover their mistakes and sins. For in spite of their best efforts, they do make mistakes. —Rom. 7:19, 20. *W 2/1* 21-23

Saturday, May 12

Strangers will actually stand and shepherd the flocks of you people, and the foreigners will be your farmers and your vinedressers.—Isa. 61:5.

Fully counting the cost of their decision and course of action, these forsook Satan's organization and have lined up with Jehovah's visible organization. Of course, they could not serve him as spiritual Israelites, but they really desired to help the anointed remnant in heralding the good news of Jehovah's kingdom. So they got baptized as dedicated followers of Jesus Christ. They took up active service with the spiritual Israelites. Consequently, with delight the anointed remnant see fulfilled to them the above words. Humbly the "great crowd" consider it an honor and a privilege to serve in the spiritual paradise with those "priests of Jehovah" and "ministers of our God." (Isa. 61:6) They appreciate that the anointed Christians thus designated by Jehovah God must specialize on spiritual matters in his spiritual temple. All of this aids in beautifying the spiritual paradise. *W 7/1* 28, 29a

Sunday, May 13

To Jehovah belong the earth and that which fills it, the productive land and those dwelling in it. For upon the seas he himself has solidly fixed it.—Ps. 24:1, 2.

Behold now, with eyes of faith, the victorious march of the Sovereign Lord of all creation! He brings with him world government by Christ for the blessing of all the families of the earth, living and dead. Let us acknowledge his rightful sovereignty and say as did the psalmist David. Ah, yes, no subterranean waters will ever rise to overflow the earth like a flood, while at the same time the seven seas have their bars set for them by the Creator. We now have reason to be like the citizens of ancient Jerusalem in the year 1070 B.C.E. King David was then having the sacred ark of the covenant carried by the Levite priests toward the city gates. As the joyful city watched the approaching procession conducting the symbol of God's presence, they heard the cry ring out: "Raise your heads, O you gates, . . . that the glorious King may come in!"—Ps. 24: 7, 8. *W 3/1 18-20b*

Monday, May 14

If, now, you practice carrying out the kingly law according to the scripture: "You must love your neighbor as yourself," you are doing quite well. —Jas. 2:8.

The rulership of God's kingdom is a unifying one. It really works among those who give allegiance to that heavenly kingdom. It is beneficial. We can see this in the loving harmony so apparent at our assemblies. On the other hand, man-rule is based on restrictive laws, which in themselves may have some good, but which are obeyed, very often not out of love, but grudgingly or out of fear of punishment. If they can 'get away with it,' many persons will flout the law, and in recent years these lawbreakers have at times included high government officials. Our remarkable unity throughout the earth is one of the rewarding benefits that we enjoy due to giving prior allegiance to God's kingdom and following its law of love. It is a foretaste of the harmony and the love that will flourish among the entire world of mankind under the rule of the heavenly kingdom. *W 1/15 32, 34*

Tuesday, May 15

I always do the things pleasing to [God].—John 8:29.

To us humans Jehovah God, at Jeremiah 9:23, 24, describes what we should make our real treasure, our boast, namely, knowing Jehovah. Therefore, the name of Jehovah and all that it stands for should be uppermost in our hearts. When Jesus was on earth, the things that hurt him most were the reproaches that were brought upon God's name, particularly by God's own people. In his ordeal in the Garden of Gethsemane, the greatest concern to him was not that he was going to die. He came to earth, being born as a human for the very purpose of a sacrificial death, and he walked undeviatingly toward that end. But what put such a weight on him that last night before his death was the reproach that his death under the charge of blasphemy against God would bring upon Jehovah's name—he, the Son of God and God's representative, dying in this reproachful manner before the whole world. About him it was written, "The reproaches of those who were reproaching you have fallen upon me."—Rom. 15:3. *W 5/1 4, 5*

Wednesday, May 16

He who has died has been acquitted from his sin.—Rom. 6:7.

Jesus, at John 5:28, 29, spoke (1) of "those who did good things" and (2) of "those who practiced vile things." This does not refer to what the resurrected ones are at the moment that they come out of the memorial tombs. Why not? The determining factor as to how these resurrected humans will turn out is not what they were before they died, because at death they paid the penalty for their sins. (Rom. 6:23) Also, Jesus Christ died as "the Lamb of God" in order that he might 'take away the sin of the world.' (John 1:29) So what he "takes away" cannot be charged to the world of mankind after they are resurrected from the dead. Hence, by being resurrected no redeemed human comes into "double jeopardy," to be punished again for what he did before his death. Consequently, the determining factor for resurrected mankind will be, What will they henceforth make of their lives, now that they are given a new start under Christ's 1,000-year kingdom? *W 9/1* 7, 8a

Thursday, May 17

Love . . . does not become provoked. It does not keep account of the injury. —1 Cor. 13:4, 5.

Love has nothing in common with the "me first" philosophy. It is wholly unselfish. And since love "does not become provoked," it would certainly be wrong for us to flare up in anger. We should be "slow about wrath," avoiding fits of rage. (Jas. 1:19) In the family, this requires that all strive to be patient with one another's shortcomings. And in the congregation, elders espe-cially must set an example in being patient when brothers and sisters seem to be forgetful and negligent or fail to take Christian responsibilities seriously. Moreover, in harmony with the Bible's description of love, we should "not keep account of the injury" done to us. It would be unloving to harbor grudges and to review just how certain ones wronged us, as if we were keeping a scorecard. The past should be pushed aside, and kindness should not be withheld from those who may have done us injury.—Prov. 20:22; 24:29; 25:21, 22. *W 9/15* 10-12a

Friday, May 18

Jehovah is our Judge, Jehovah is our Statute-giver, Jehovah is our King; he himself will save us.—Isa. 33:22.

Persons walking in Jehovah's name recognize him as their Judge, Statute-giver and King. Since he is the Universal Sovereign, Jehovah God certainly has the right to make and enforce laws, establish moral standards and make provisions for the everlasting benefit of all his intelligent creatures. And consider this: Our showing respect for Jehovah's laws, our having regard for the moral standards of God, our expressing appreciation for his provisions for our well-being and everlasting salvation—all of these give evidence that we are walking in Jehovah's name. Certainly, those who truly walk in Jehovah's name eagerly await the time when God will act in the best interests of all lovers of righteousness and will take action against those who profane his name. (Ezek. 20:9; 39:7) Indeed, lovers of Jehovah are looking ahead to the fulfillment of the Model Prayer taught by Jesus Christ. *W 8/15* 18, 19

Saturday, May 19

I said: "I am not going to make mention of him, and I shall speak no more in his name." And in my heart it proved to be like a burning fire shut up in my bones; and I got tired of holding in, and I was unable to endure it.
—*Jer. 20:9.*

Jeremiah was bitterly opposed by his own townsfolk in Anathoth, and his own brothers and the household of his father dealt treacherously with him. It seems that he had enemies everywhere that were calling down evil upon him. But Jeremiah found strength for enduring. Where? In prayer to Jehovah, and in realizing the privilege that he had of bearing Jehovah's name and word. (Jer. 15:16, 17) Have some today set their eyes on material goals, rather than on the priceless treasure of Kingdom service? Have some found it hard to endure? Well, remember that, at times, Jeremiah found it hard to endure. He even thought of quitting. But then it was that he found the word of Jehovah to be in his heart 'like a burning fire shut up in his bones.' That word impelled him to fight on and to triumph over his enemies. *W 1/1* 6, 5a

Sunday, May 20

The one working with a slack hand will be of little means, but the hand of the diligent one is what will make one rich. The son acting with insight is gathering during the summertime; the son acting shamefully is fast asleep during the harvest.—*Prov. 10:4, 5.*

Part of the harvest work is not only bringing the truth to people, but, as Jesus said, 'making disciples' of them. (Matt. 28:19, 20) That is the spirit we need to show. We want more workers in the field. That means keeping busy and wide awake ourselves. What a contrast the above depicts! And still another thing about harvesttime is that it is a special time for farmers. They cannot and do not consider that the ordinary routine is good enough, that what is not done today can be done tomorrow. When the crop is ready it must be harvested. All the farm workers know that too—there is no time to be lost. They are ready to work in the fields from sunup to sundown. Other things, the nonessentials, are put aside. Jesus had this same attitude, as we can see from Matthew 10:1-10. *W 6/1* 10-12

Monday, May 21

Keep awake, then, all the time making supplication that you may succeed in escaping all these things that are destined to occur, and in standing before the Son of man.
—*Luke 21:36.*

Jesus spoke of the need for alertness when he said this regarding the coming destruction of this present wicked system. To whom was Jesus talking? In this case he was talking to his followers. Yet he warned them that, unless they stayed awake, even some of them could be caught off guard when Jehovah's day of destruction came. What would lead to their getting caught off guard? They would become too involved with the everyday cares of this life, or with over-indulging themselves in pleasures. (Luke 21:34, 35) Those cautioning words of Jesus Christ are a real warning for us today. Because this system's end has not yet arrived, some who are serving Jehovah God may be tempted to slack off in their desire to make sacrifices for him. They may feel that they should be more concerned with leading a so-called normal life. *W 8/1* 10, 11

Tuesday, May 22

If any one of you is lacking in wisdom, let him keep on asking God.—Jas. 1:5.

How can we be assured that we will have the strength and wisdom to face a certain problem—any trial—and endure? James answers. Therefore, we can be *sure* that if we pray for the wisdom to handle any problem or trial that we face, *we will be given it.* This does not mean that the problem will always go away or that it will be solved immediately, but that we will be able to take the course that will do good, spiritually, for us and for others concerned. We will endure the trial to the end and come through it better Christians than we were when we went into it. And others who observe us, and who have a right heart, will be helped. There are many things over which we may pray that may not be answered in the way that we desire. In fact, some things that we ask for might not be for our benefit if they were granted as we ask or desire. However, *wisdom* to face a trial is absolutely promised by God. We are sure to get the necessary wisdom if we ask properly. *W 7/15 8-10a*

Wednesday, May 23

The kingdom of God does not mean eating and drinking, but means righteousness and peace and joy with holy spirit. —Rom. 14:17.

It is essential that a Christian with an overscrupulous conscience refrain from criticizing another, who is making use of his freedom, and actually doing no wrong. He is judging his brother. *He should get his view readjusted.* For otherwise he will continue to disturb the peace of the congregation. True worship and that which pertains to God's kingdom and his congrega-tion are not centered on these physical matters. (Mark 7:15) This can be said of many other things of life. Dress and grooming, entertainment, employment and other personal affairs are not the essentials "for the advancement of the good news." (Phil. 1:12) If there is no actual violation of the Scriptures and if moderation is shown by shunning extremes or involvements with worldly wrongdoing, then these matters of daily living do not come within the area where we should be judged by our brothers.—Compare Proverbs 11:2. *W 3/15 6-8a*

Thursday, May 24

Whatever it is that you do in word or in work, do everything in the name of the Lord Jesus, thanking God the Father through him.—Col. 3:17.

Never should we lose sight of the fact that we are disciples of Jesus Christ every day, yes, every hour of the day, even as the apostle Paul reminds us. So, in all matters of life, we should speak and act in the name of the Son of God, that is, as representing him, and we should be grateful to Jehovah God for the capacity he has given us to speak and to work. Really, then, it is regard for Jesus Christ as Lord that should make Christians fine husbands and fathers, good wives and mothers, obedient sons and daughters and exemplary workers and employers, even as can be seen from Paul's counsel at Colossians 3:18–4:1. So, if we profess to be Christ's disciples, our lives should demonstrate a recognition of his vital role in God's arrangement, obeying his commands and looking to his teachings and example for guidance. If we do, we can rest assured of his love and the love of his Father. *W 4/1 31-33*

Friday, May 25

Only flesh with its soul—its blood—you must not eat. —Gen. 9:4.

From the very first book of the Bible, God pointed toward the sacrificial shedding of Jesus' blood so humans could gain everlasting life. (Gen. 3:15) While that sacrifice was yet in the future, God made it clear that his worshipers should consider life and blood as sacred. But he also required that their *actions* harmonize with that divine law. Was not conduct implied in what God told Noah and his family when first permitting them to eat animal flesh? So, if they killed an animal for food, they would have to take deliberate steps to drain the blood from the animal so that blood would not be eaten. Yes, blood represented life that was from God. And it is noteworthy that he went on to say that, though an animal could be killed for food, man could not be. Hence, if animal blood representing life was to be viewed as sacred and not to be taken in to sustain life, obviously human life and blood were to be viewed and treated as even more sacred. *W 6/15 4, 5a*

Saturday, May 26

All those seeing them will recognize them, that they are the offspring whom Jehovah has blessed.—Isa. 61:9.

By his holy spirit Jehovah God energized the anointed remnant to bear testimony to all the world. While peoples and nations as such did not give Jehovah's anointed remnant this due recognition, individuals did so. Lovers of justice, righteousness and truth manifested themselves. Notably from the spring of 1935 these went lining themselves up with the remnant because they were "the ministers of our God." Since then those who are not spiritual Israelites, not "the offspring whom Jehovah has blessed," have become a "great crowd." (Rev. 7:9-17) Because of not being spiritual Israelites, they were "strangers" and "foreigners" to the anointed remnant. (Isa. 61:5) They saw that the remnant lived in a spiritual paradise, marked by "big trees of righteousness" and having citylike congregations. They too wanted to be in a spiritual paradise of that kind, to serve Jehovah God. Is that the way you feel about these things? *W 7/1 26, 27a*

Sunday, May 27

As these things start to occur, raise yourselves erect and lift your heads up, because your deliverance is getting near. —Luke 21:28.

The remnant yet on earth saw "these things" start to occur back in 1914. Their deliverance from the present wicked system of things occurs when the royal "stone" that was cut out of the mountain of God's sovereignty strikes the "image" of worldly political rulership of the earth and destroys it in the war of the great day of Jehovah God at Har-Magedon. Their "deliverance" also includes their later being taken from the earthly scene and being ushered into 'the everlasting kingdom of Jesus Christ' by the "first resurrection" from the dead. (2 Pet. 1:11; Rev. 20:6) This will enable them to rule as kings with Jesus Christ during the millennium when Satan and his demons are bound and confined in the abyss, no longer able to dominate mankind's affairs invisibly. Deliverance also nears for the "great crowd" of sheeplike people who are now taking their stand with the spirit-begotten remnant in favor of God's kingdom. *W 3/1 10, 11b*

Monday, May 28

One there is that is lawgiver and judge, he who is able to save and to destroy. But you, who are you to be judging your neighbor?—Jas. 4:12.

If we were to judge a fellow believer's actions, motives or manner of living by our own standards, making an unauthorized assessment of the person's worth, we would make ourselves guilty of a serious failure to exercise justice, even as James notes. Persons who so judge would be setting themselves above the law of love that God gives, judging that law of love as not applying to them. (Matt. 22:36-39) In so doing, they would be violating Jehovah's standard of justice, which acts in behalf of love. Furthermore, it would be unjust for a Christian to view one particular group of people as being more deserving of the "good news" than another group. Jesus Christ died for all mankind, and it is God's will that no partiality be shown in making known the message of salvation. While certain groups of people may be more inclined to listen, we need to guard against succumbing to feelings of favoritism. *W 9/15 9, 10*

Tuesday, May 29

Just as the Father has life in himself, so he has granted also to the Son to have life in himself.—John 5:26.

What does the Father's having "life in himself" really mean? Does it mean that he is self-existent, immortal? According to the line of reasoning in the immediate context the expression "life in himself" has a more forceful meaning than his self-existence. The expression means that the heavenly Father has a reservoir of life in himself, so that, like a father, he is able to impart life to others. In the face of this fact, he was able to impart life to his Son in such quantity that he also would be able to impart life to others. Why was the Son of God thus given "life in himself"? It was because he laid down his perfect human life as a ransom sacrifice for all mankind. (1 Tim. 2:5, 6) In this way he could buy back mankind from the death to which they were condemned due to inherited imperfection. With this thought in mind Jesus could open his prayer on Passover night with the words found at John 17:1, 2. *W 9/1 15-17*

Wednesday, May 30

The fruitage of the spirit is . . . joy, peace.—Gal. 5:22.

Is there not good reason to be joyful if we are walking worthily in Jehovah's name? Yes, indeed, for we are declaring "the glorious good news of the *happy* God." (1 Tim. 1:11) Moreover, we have joyful prospects, a sound hope of future blessings. Think of that when confronted with problems. Endeavor to spread joy among your Christian associates too, for are not such expected to 'serve God with rejoicing and joy of heart'? (Deut. 28:46, 47) Peace, another fruit of the spirit, is an outstanding quality of God. He is "the God of peace." (Heb. 13:20) True Christians "pursue peace with all people." (Heb. 12:14) The peace we have among us attracts lovers of peace to true Christianity. Furthermore, 'Jehovah blesses his people with peace.' (Ps. 29:11) We are not anxious over anything, but we prayerfully make our petitions known to God. As a result 'the peace of God that excels all thought guards our hearts and mental powers by means of Christ Jesus.'—Phil. 4:6, 7. *W 8/15 11, 12a*

Thursday, May 31

I am pleasing all people in all things, not seeking my own advantage but that of the many, in order that they might get saved.—1 Cor. 10:33.

Do we see such a spirit of self-sacrifice in modern times? We certainly do. In fact, the several million persons now enjoying Bible truths and Christian fellowship in association with the more than 40,000 of our congregations all over the earth are benefiting from the sacrifices made by loyal servants of God earlier in modern times. And right now, throughout the earth, many tens of thousands of devoted men and women are making unusual sacrifices to serve God. Some have literally sacrificed homes and possessions so that they could work full time in the missionary work, in Bethel homes, or as traveling representatives serving congregations. Others are making sacrifices to do special, regular or auxiliary pioneering work so they can more fully teach others about Jehovah's incoming new order. Of course, not all who are devoted to Jehovah are free to share in such work full time. *W 8/1 12-14a*

Friday, June 1

A thousand years are in your eyes but as yesterday when it is past, and as a watch during the night.—Ps. 90:4.

During the time that wickedness seems to be flourishing, we must never forget that the wicked are not really getting away with anything. Jehovah God is taking note of what is happening, and he is allowing matters to work out in harmony with his grand purpose. At times, when persons take a wrong course and experience suffering as a result, they come to their senses and turn to the Creator in sincere repentance. On the other hand, if they harden themselves in their evil ways, judgment against them is justified, completely righteous. (Rom. 9:14-24) To us, it may seem that it takes a long time for justice to be executed against those who merit punishment. But it is a very short time in the sight of the eternal God. How long does yesterday seem to you today? Perhaps it was a trying day, and it may have seemed that the day would never end. Now that it is over, it may seem as if that day hardly existed. *W 10/15 10, 11*

Saturday, June 2

Put on the Lord Jesus Christ, and do not be planning ahead for the desires of the flesh. —Rom. 13:14.

What a fine example, indeed, we have in the Lord Jesus Christ! Throughout his ministry on earth he was wide awake to the grand privilege of doing Jehovah God's will. Never did he deviate one moment from his whole-souled service in making known to others his Father's name. Even on the day that he was to die, how selfless and self-sacrificing he was in packing into every available moment of his remaining hours worthwhile, needed instruction for his disciples! (John chaps. 13 to 17) May all of us be counted in with those who "put on the Lord Jesus Christ," following his steps closely. (1 Pet. 2:21; Matt. 16:24, 25) By planning ahead for spiritual things, not the fleshly, we can keep wide awake in Jehovah's service, as did Jesus. Let us keep on the watch, therefore, filling our lives with Kingdom service right up until the hour that the "Son of man" comes to execute judgment. *W 10/1 19, 20a*

Sunday, June 3

By faith Abraham . . . the man that had gladly received the promises attempted to offer up his only-begotten son . . . But he reckoned that God was able to raise him up even from the dead; and from there he did receive him also in an illustrative way.
—Heb. 11:17-19.

In view of the foregoing, how can any of us think, on any occasion, that we must rely on our own power or ability to accomplish something in God's service? It is indeed encouraging to know that if we put implicit faith in Jehovah and obey him, just as Abraham did, we need not worry about the outcome, no matter how difficult the problem before us. It may be a matter of providing the necessities for our family. Or, a widow may have her hands full trying to bring her young children up in "the discipline and mental-regulating of Jehovah." (Eph. 6:4) Or, perhaps, the problem is finding time for field service. Some may feel trepidation about going from door to door and about teaching people from the Bible. Let all such remember Paul's words at Philippians 4:13. *W 5/1 18a*

Monday, June 4

He will certainly render judgment among the nations and set matters straight respecting many peoples. . . . Nation will not lift up sword against nation, neither will they learn war anymore.—Isa. 2:4.

Even now, in advance of its thousand-year rule over earth, the heavenly kingdom is providing many benefits for its loyal supporters, who acknowledge Jesus as their King. No longer are these divided by nationalistic pride or hatred. Tribal feuds and racial prejudices are things of the past.

Especially are Christian unity and its benefits made to stand out when the nations of earth become locked in fratricidal war. In the clergy-blessed conflicts of this twentieth century, Catholic has often slain his fellow Catholic, Protestant his fellow Protestant, and Buddhist his fellow Buddhist. But this has not happened among us. Our unity has been real, and has testified to the reality of God's kingdom as the only government that can unite peoples of all nations and races into a harmonious whole, even as foretold by Isaiah. *W 1/15 36, 37*

Tuesday, June 5

His eyes are roving about through all the earth to show his strength in behalf of those whose heart is complete toward him.—2 Chron. 16:9.

God sent Jesus to the earth so that he could taste death for every man. (Heb. 2:9) Would it, then, be logical for God's Son to be unconcerned, saying, in effect: 'I gave my lifeblood for everyone, but of what importance is this one person? Whether he loses his life or not makes no difference to me'? Never! Under his kingdom each individual to whom his ransom applies will receive attention, with opportunity for life. Note God's love for Abraham, Isaac and Jacob, who were imperfect men but who served him wholeheartedly. Centuries later, Jehovah's love was as strong as ever, even as Moses wrote. (Deut. 10:15) He put up with the nation's stubbornness for centuries because of this love. Jehovah's love is just as great and lasting for those who serve him today. He is, so to speak, watching for an opportunity to show his strength toward those who call on him in sincerity and truth. *W 2/1 3-5a*

Wednesday, June 6

And they keep on crying with a loud voice, saying: "Salvation we owe to our God, who is seated on the throne, and to the Lamb."—Rev. 7:10.

Divine world government for the relief and blessing of oppressed dying mankind is certain. Do we believe that fact? Our belief in this joy-inspiring fact calls for us to do something now! Do what? Do like the dedicated, baptized "great crowd," which began forming 20 years after the birth of God's kingdom in 1914. They are hailing the kingdom of our God and of his Christ as the only hope for everlasting deliverance! According to the prophetic vision given in Revelation 7: 9-17, the "great crowd" clean up their lives and serve Jehovah God at his spiritual temple *now!* Our following this same course will ensure our being on the winning side during "the war of the great day of God the Almighty" at Har-Magedon. (Rev. 16:14, 16) Before us will open the way to Paradise on earth under the best government that humankind will ever have had. Our desire for the best moves us to prepare for its coming now! *W 3/1* 17b

Thursday, June 7

This is my Son, the beloved, whom I have approved. —Matt. 3:17.

In the autumn of 29 C.E., Jesus left Nazareth and went to the Jordan River to be baptized by John the son of Zechariah the priest. Immediately after Jesus came up out of the baptismal waters John the Baptizer saw the holy spirit descending upon him under manifestation of a dove. At the same time he heard Jehovah's voice from heaven saying the above. That same spirit impelled Jesus to retire into the wilderness of Judea for 40 days. After those 40 days of fasting and communing with his Father Jehovah, Satan the Devil set before him three temptations. If Jesus had succumbed to those temptations, he would have lost the spirit of anointing. But, by resisting the Tempter, he retained the spiritual anointing. So he still had it when he gave his talk in the synagogue of Nazareth. (Matt. 4:1-13; Luke 4:1-21) Whether we profess to be of the remnant or are of the "other sheep," we likewise must resist Satan's temptations lest we lose Jehovah's holy spirit. *W 7/1* 10, 11

Friday, June 8

But know this, that in the last days critical times hard to deal with will be here. For men will be lovers of themselves, . . . without self-control.—2 Tim. 3:1-3.

For many people in the world today, the thought of making personal sacrifices for someone else, or for a cause, does not have much appeal. Indeed, the attitude of increasing numbers of persons is to want more material things, more pleasures and more freedom to do whatever they desire, with little regard for God or man. Even the willingness to sacrifice for the sake of one's own family has diminished in recent years, as family breakdowns and divorces have reached record highs in nation after nation. This self-indulgent trend does not come as a surprise to those who have kept alert to God's inspired Word. Accurately it foretold what these "last days" would be like, with people so intent on pursuing their self-indulgent ways that they are "without self-control." This can also be seen in the huge increase of alcoholism, drug abuse and sexual immorality in recent years. *W 8/1* 1, 2

Saturday, June 9

"Abraham put faith in Jehovah, and it was counted to him as righteousness," and he came to be called "Jehovah's friend."—Jas. 2:23.

Jehovah God is the best friend anyone can have. Because of his faith, Abraham came to be known as Jehovah's friend. What a splendid relationship! But Jehovah desires that all persons possessing such faith walk in his name as his friends. Of course, if we are to please God and enjoy a friendly relationship with him, we must heed the words of the Congregator, who declared: "Fear the true God and keep his commandments. For this is the whole obligation of man." (Eccl. 12:13) Accurate knowledge is vital in order to be God's friend, to keep his commandments and to walk in his name, even as indicated by the apostle Paul. (Col. 1:9, 10) Friendship with another human cannot be maintained if we misrepresent that person in some way. Accordingly, if we wish to have Jehovah as our friend, we must realize that walking worthily in his name involves living in harmony with all that it represents. *W 8/15* 1-3a

Sunday, June 10

He that feeds on my flesh and drinks my blood remains in union with me, and I in union with him.—John 6:56.

In John 6:53 Jesus said: "Unless you eat the flesh of the Son of man and drink his blood, you have no life in yourselves." This is similar to the expression that appears in John 5:26. So Jesus here meant "life" with a specific capacity when he went on to say: "He that feeds on my flesh and drinks my blood has everlasting life." (John 6:54) That everlasting life is to be enjoyed in the heavenly kingdom. Such a person will enter into such life when he is resurrected at the last day. Those who, with Christ in the heavens, have such 'life in themselves,' will be able to impart to others the benefits of Christ's sacrifice. When we contemplate the quality of the "everlasting life" that is to be gained in heaven, we appreciate why Jesus said: "My flesh is true food, and my blood is true drink." (John 6:55) After that remark Jesus showed the special relationship into which his obedient disciples would enter by adding the above words. *W 9/1* 20, 21b

Monday, June 11

Love is not jealous, it does not brag, does not get puffed up.—1 Cor. 13:4.

If we really love our Christian brothers, how could we possibly be jealous or envious of their accomplishments, blessings or abilities? Rather, we would rejoice with them and be happy for the part that they are able to play in building up the congregation. Similarly, how could we constantly put ourselves forward and highlight our own accomplishments and experiences? This could be discouraging to those listening to us. They might begin to feel that they have done very little in comparison. Our bragging would only tear others down and distract from the glory that should be given to Jehovah God. How unloving that would be! It would be far better to minimize our own role. We are merely slaves of God, and to him should go all the credit and praise for growth in the Christian congregation. Humility will prevent us from having an inflated opinion of ourselves and will restrain us from trying to impress others with supposed importance. *W 9/15* 8a

Tuesday, June 12

The night is well along; the day has drawn near. Let us therefore put off the works belonging to darkness and let us put on the weapons of the light.—Rom. 13:12.

The ride of the horsemen is clearly in evidence today. (Rev. 6:2-8) Total warfare, food shortages, epidemics and wholesale death are now the ominous experience of all mankind. But it is only those who see with the eye of faith that perceive the white horse, with the all-conquering "King of kings," the crowned Bowman. How grateful we should be for this faith-strengthening vision! It should stimulate us to be very active in witnessing concerning these things. In this, we can be loyal to our commission from Jehovah after the example of Jesus, who came to be called "Faithful and True"—"the faithful and true witness." (Rev. 3:14; 19:11) The apostle Paul extends fine counsel to any who may have become drowsy. The weapons of the light are well known to us, for it has been our grand privilege to use them in proclaiming "this good news of the kingdom." *W 10/1 14, 16a*

Wednesday, June 13

We have finished our years just like a whisper.—Ps. 90:9.

To the Creator, Jehovah God, a thousand years are as brief as a four-hour watch during the night. (Ps. 90:4) Hence, the human life-span of but 70 or 80 years is virtually nonexistent in God's sight. Yes, our brief life-span may be compared to a breath that passes our lips in a whisper. When we consider that Jehovah God promises to give his loyal servants an eternity of happy living in peace and security, even a lifetime of extreme suffering is nothing at all. This viewpoint can help us to be patient when we are troubled by having to face injustice, oppression and favoritism. There is yet another factor that comes into the picture. The great adversary of mankind, Satan, maintains that those who serve God are motivated by selfishness. This is evident from the charge Satan leveled against Job. (Job 2:4, 5) Hence, by our maintaining loyalty to Jehovah God in the face of injustices, we can demonstrate our proper heart motivation, even as Job did. *W 10/15 11, 12*

Thursday, June 14

He that does not love has not come to know God, because God is love.—1 John 4:8.

In order to serve properly in behalf of God's sovereignty, or under it, a person must come to know Jehovah God and his Son Jesus, the King of the kingdom of God. (John 17:3) To know God is to establish a close relationship with him, to become an intimate of him and his Son, who said: "No one fully knows the Son but the Father, neither does anyone fully know the Father but the Son and anyone to whom the Son is willing to reveal him." (Matt. 11:27) One who knows God knows his wonderful qualities, and by the help of God's spirit develops these qualities, so that he comes to be more and more a true reflector of the image of God. (2 Cor. 3:18) If a person does not develop the fruits of the spirit, he has not come to know God. How does the person act who recognizes God's sovereignty? His dominant qualities will be love, mercy, sympathy, kindness and the doing of good to his fellowman. If supervising any activity, he will not be demanding. *W 7/15 10, 11*

Friday, June 15

Hold a good conscience, so that in the particular in which you are spoken against they may get ashamed who are speaking slightingly of your good conduct in connection with Christ.—1 Pet. 3:16.

Having been so careful to heed this counsel of Peter, what a shame it would be to destroy this good influence for true worship by insisting on doing something that is in itself entirely right but which looks wrong in the eyes of an overly sensitive Christian brother. He might tend to speak disparagingly about this to others. Or, some act that the Christian might do could be misinterpreted by the whole community. Because others condemn it, they could bring injury to the Christian's good reputation. It could reflect reproachfully on the message of the "good news" that the congregation works so hard to proclaim and teach. For this reason, it would be better that the Christian restrain himself from indulging in the enjoyment or practice of certain freedoms, even right ones, on which points the conscience of another may be weak. *W 3/15 5a*

Saturday, June 16

Those slain by Jehovah will certainly come to be in that day from one end of the earth clear to the other end of the earth. They will not be bewailed, neither will they be gathered up or be buried. As manure on the surface of the ground they will become. —Jer. 25:33.

Should we fear what the enemy may do to us as we boldly proclaim this message of doom? Jeremiah feared only Jehovah. (Jer. 10:2-7) Obediently he called his people's attention to the detestable things that were being done in God's name. As Jehovah kept "getting up early and speaking" by means of his prophets in earlier times, so Jeremiah was also up early to be about his work. What a fine example for us today, that we should never slack the hand or "sleep in" when the work of Jehovah is to be done! While we declare the tearing down of the nations and kingdoms and their replacement by God's kingdom, we look forward confidently to Jehovah's settling his controversy with the nations. At his due time he will act! None of the wicked will escape. It will be a complete extermination. *W 1/1 16, 17*

Sunday, June 17

Be glad, you nations, with his people.—Deut. 32:43.

Jehovah God's government over the nation of Israel, with himself as the heavenly King, was only for a period of time. His loving purpose for the future embraced more than just that small nation. It was at Mount Sinai that Jehovah became King over the nation of Israel; but in the fortieth year thereafter his prophet Moses sang a song in the hearing of all the Israelites, in the climax of which song he said the above. Some 1,528 years later those words of Moses were caught up by the apostle Paul, who was an apostle of the "good news" to the non-Israelite nations. He was a far-ranging missionary intent on finally reaching Rome and planning to go even to Spain. He knew what God was then doing, not only for those Jews who accepted the "good news," but also for the uncircumcised non-Jews who put faith in the "good news." He knew that Jehovah God was internationally minded. For our time God purposes a world government for people of all nationalities. *W 3/1 5-8*

Monday, June 18

With men this is impossible, but with God all things are possible.—Matt. 19:26.

The kind of reasonable self-sacrifice that Jehovah requires is for us to limit our personal desires so that we can serve his cause more fully. That cause centers around God's kingdom. Thus, sacrificing for Jehovah's interests means to obey his laws and to put his kingdom first in our lives. (Matt. 6:33) Is a course of self-sacrifice an easy one? No, it is not. But it is God and Christ who invite us to this course. That means that such a course is possible since the loving Father and his Son, who created humans, know what people can accomplish. Furthermore, since Jehovah God and Jesus Christ have such great love for humans, we can be certain that they would not ask anything of us that would be damaging to our best interests. Too, when we consider the grand rewards that lie ahead, it can be said with confidence that making sacrifices to serve Jehovah is the only worthwhile course of life today. All else will sooner or later end in disappointment. *W 8/1 4, 5a*

Tuesday, June 19

Noah was a righteous man. He proved himself faultless among his contemporaries. Noah walked with the true God.—Gen. 6:9.

The faithful man Noah witnessed about God's purpose to destroy the wicked in an earth-wide deluge. Noah's faithfulness was rewarded, indeed, for it resulted in preservation for himself and seven others through the global flood. (2 Pet. 2:5) He was among the early witnesses of Jehovah. (Heb. 11:7; 12:1) They were not afraid to honor the divine name and make it known far and wide. As Jehovah's Christian witnesses of today, we have the same attitude. Fearlessly, we declare God's message of judgment. But we also preach the "good news" of a righteous new order near at hand. We yearn for the complete fulfillment of Jehovah's promise to bring about "new heavens and a new earth" wherein righteousness will dwell. (2 Pet. 3:13) What joy then will prevail! No longer will anyone be walking in the name of some other god. Rather, all intelligent creation will walk in the name of Jehovah God forever. *W 8/15 24, 25*

Wednesday, June 20

Love . . . does not behave indecently, does not look for its own interests.—1 Cor. 13:4, 5.

When we have genuine love, we hate all forms of badness. In all relations, love produces right conduct. The loving person does not look down on the poor and needy. Decent behavior also involves showing regard for proper authority. If we have true love, we will respect the person and possessions of others. That would certainly include our meeting places. How inappropriate it is for children to write on chairs or to run about, perhaps even knocking people over! Such indecent behavior has no place in the Christian congregation. It reflects unfavorably on the parents' manner of presiding over their children. Furthermore, love takes an active interest in all members of the congregation—young and old, the sick and infirm, those working hard in teaching, preaching and disciplemaking. Love is alert to the needs of fellow believers and is quick to respond, to be accommodating. It does not insist on its own way. *W 9/15 9, 10a*

Thursday, June 21

I am constantly with you; you have taken hold of my right hand. With your counsel you will lead me, and afterward you will take me even to glory.—Ps. 73:23, 24.

If we ourselves are the victims of injustice because of prejudice or because of our refusal to mix in politics, we must be careful not to react to God's permission of injustices merely on the basis of feelings, like an unreasoning animal. This could make us bitter deep within ourselves and unbalance our thinking, causing us to view things strictly from our own viewpoint and to blind ourselves to God's purpose. This is what happened to Asaph. (Ps. 73: 21, 22) Regardless of what we may personally face, we should strive hard to safeguard our relationship with Jehovah, for our exaltation will come from him. This is what Asaph came to appreciate. Yes, we should remember that under no circumstances will Jehovah abandon us if we remain faithful to him. He is always with us. The Most High will take us by the hand, to conduct and to support us. His counsel will be our guide to a happy future. *W 10/15* 13-15

Friday, June 22

We hear them speaking in our tongues about the magnificent things of God.—Acts 2:11.

From what took place on Pentecost, what do we today observe? This fact, that, in keeping with his own anointing, Jesus Christ pioneered a restoration work toward his disciples. God used him to pour out holy spirit on his baptized disciples, so that these recipients of holy spirit themselves became persons anointed with the spirit of the Sovereign Lord Jehovah. (2 Cor. 1:21) Now they also were commissioned to tell "good news" to the "meek" ones in the nation of Israel, to proclaim liberty to the captives and a release for the prisoners, and to comfort all those mourning over Zion. In this way they could help others whom they were used to comfort and liberate into exulting over "the year of goodwill on the part of Jehovah" and into praising him for restoring them to his favor and service by means of his anointed ones. (Isa. 61:2) That outpouring of the spirit made all the difference in the world for those anointed with it. *W 7/1* 23, 24

Saturday, June 23

They were eating, they were drinking, men were marrying, women were being given in marriage, until that day when Noah entered into the ark, and the flood arrived and destroyed them all.—Luke 17:27.

Noah's special work in preparing for the deluge lasted possibly through 60 years. Like Jehovah's Witnesses today, he continued to serve zealously as "a preacher of righteousness." (2 Pet. 2:5) Today, a like-minded wicked world faces the climactic global "great tribulation." Do the above-quoted words of Jesus mean that it is wrong for Christians in these final days to eat, drink and marry? No, Jesus was not saying that. It is proper to enjoy good food and drink in moderation. Likewise, marriage is God's arrangement for mankind. What Jesus was saying is that we should not regard these as the all-important activities of life, becoming absorbed in them to the point of crowding out our spiritual matters. Rather, we should plan our lives in such a way as to give first place to preaching the Kingdom good news. —Matt. 24:14. *W 10/1* 4-6

Sunday, June 24

He showed me a river of water of life, clear as crystal, flowing out from the throne of God and of the Lamb . . . And on this side of the river and on that side there were trees of life . . . yielding their fruits each month. And the leaves of the trees were for the curing of the nations.—Rev. 22:1, 2.

Now a marvelous "hour" is approaching. It is the "hour" when Jesus Christ as Jehovah's associate judge will call all those in the memorial tombs to come forth as his redeemed ones. What will these have to drink? What will they eat? John the apostle answers in the words above. Of these divine provisions, the "great crowd" and the resurrected dead will drink and eat. By taking full advantage of all this undeserved kindness of Jehovah God through Jesus Christ, the appreciative and obedient ones will make theirs "a resurrection of life." Those of the resurrectionless "great crowd" of Christ's "other sheep" will have the opportunity to live on without ever dying and returning to the dust of the ground. What a glorious prospect! *W 9/1 28, 29b*

Monday, June 25

He has told you, O earthling man, what is good. And what is Jehovah asking back from you but to exercise justice and to love kindness and to be modest in walking with your God?—Mic. 6:8.

These words remind us of faithful men who 'walked with the true God' in ancient times —Abel, Enoch and Noah. Hebrews chapter eleven shows that they pleased God well by their faith. Later, the patriarchs Abraham, Isaac and Jacob had laws on the sanctity of blood and on circumcision. But it was their faith

manifested by obedience to the commands of God that showed them to be worthy of a place as subjects of the Kingdom. No more than when they first lived on this earth, over 3,500 years ago, will these patriarchs need a host of restrictive laws for proving their faith when they are resurrected to serve as princes in a paradise earth. From all of this we can appreciate a fundamental difference between God-rule and man-rule. The rule of God is based on a moral appeal, and those who respond obey that rule because of their love for God and neighbor. *W 1/15 31, 32*

Tuesday, June 26

I will by no means leave you nor by any means forsake you. —Heb. 13:5.

Jehovah wants us to look toward the reward of life as something that he enjoys giving, knowing that we appreciate it and will use it in the right way. Jehovah wants us to know that he is the kind of God who rewards those who love him. He is not like many worldly persons who have no appreciation or consideration for those who do things out of love or loyalty. And a god without appreciation for loyalty, who never rewarded his servants, would be unworthy of worship. But Jehovah God is loyal; he is warmhearted and draws close to his friends. To those who have faith in him, he promises the above. So, in becoming an intimate friend of God, communicating and walking with him, there is great reward now. And there is a greater reward to look forward to, of things far beyond what we are able to conceive. Our maintaining faithfulness to God gives a better life *now,* with a *purpose,* and great freedom from the problems that this world experiences. *W 2/1 21, 22a*

Wednesday, June 27

In willingness I will sacrifice to you. I shall laud your name, O Jehovah, for it is good.—Ps. 54:6.

Whether you are married or single, it may be that an honest self-analysis will show that you are spending as much time as you reasonably can in serving Kingdom interests. Is there still something else that you can do? Yes, there is. You can work to make yourself a better Christian, learning to display in fuller measure the fruitage of God's spirit, which is "love, joy, peace, long-suffering, kindness, goodness, faith, mildness, self-control." (Gal. 5:22, 23) Furthermore, you can work to improve the *quality* of your service to God. In the future, in God's new order, how satisfying it will be for you to look back and know that when it really counted in this time of urgency, you put your 'shoulder to the wheel,' made the necessary sacrifices, and did your part in serving Jehovah. Yes, be willing to set aside personal interests for Jehovah's interests, keeping in view the thrilling rewards ahead. Cultivate the spirit of the psalmist David. *W 8/1* 18, 19a

Thursday, June 28

Walk worthily of Jehovah to the end of fully pleasing him.—Col. 1:10.

Walking worthily of Jehovah God requires earnest and regular study of the Holy Scriptures, as well as personal application of what they say. When people see us, they associate us with our God; and, as Jehovah's Witnesses, it is vital that we represent God properly, acting in harmony with his Word. We also realize that walking worthily in Jehovah's name involves every aspect of our lives. We have a responsibility to represent the divine name before mankind in a worthy manner. Jehovah God wants his name to be made known throughout the earth. (Ex. 9:16) And it is indeed a privilege to inform people that Jehovah is the Most High God. But our obligation involves more than merely speaking the name of God. Jehovah, our most cherished Friend, is the great King of the entire universe. His name is attached to his kingdom with Jesus Christ as Messianic Ruler under God. Surely, then, those walking worthily of Jehovah's name must advocate that kingdom. *W 8/15* 3-5a

Friday, June 29

God makes all his works co-operate together for the good of those who love God.—Rom. 8:28.

Afflictions, such as blindness or crippling deformities, may stir our emotions, but if they had not existed, we would never have come to know the grand things that Jehovah God can do for mankind. And, in view of the reward of eternal life, human suffering in this system of things will be as if there never had been any affliction. If the suffering we may yet undergo makes us kinder, more sympathetic and compassionate toward our fellow humans and results in our conforming more closely to the righteous requirements set forth in God's Word, this form of discipline will indeed have served a beneficial purpose. For this to be the case, we must have the kind of implicit trust in our heavenly Father that a young child has in its earthly father. We need unshakable faith that whatever God permits to come upon us will eventually work for our eternal welfare and happiness. May we, therefore, always keep before us the words of Romans 8:28. *W 10/15* 20, 21a

Saturday, June 30

Foreigners shall serve as shepherds of your flocks, and aliens shall till your land and tend your vines.—Isa. 61:5, The New English Bible.

Thus the figurative "aliens" or "strangers" and "foreigners" of today assist those of the remnant that they may carry out the duties devolving upon them because of being anointed with Jehovah's spirit. In Isaiah 61:5 the work of the assistants is pictured as tending to flocks, farming or plowing, and caring for vineyards. But in the Revelation vision of foreigners out of all nations, tribes, peoples and tongues, these are said to be "before the throne of God; and they are rendering him sacred service day and night in his temple." (Rev. 7:14, 15) They are thus pictured as performers of sacred service to the enthroned Sovereign Lord of the universe. Regardless of how the world views them, they are His servants! That great crowd of "strangers" and "foreigners" will survive the coming "great tribulation." How beautifully Isaiah 61:5 describes what they will do afterward, during the thousand-year reign of Christ! *W 7/1 30-33a*

Sunday, July 1

Keep on, then, seeking first the kingdom and his righteousness.—Matt. 6:33.

What does it mean to do Jehovah's work in Jehovah's way? For one thing, it means giving it priority in our lives, even as Jesus urged us to do. We have only so much time, so much physical and mental strength or energy and only so much of this world's goods. There are so many things that rightfully make demands on us. For example: a father must provide for his family, not only materially but also spiritually, and arrange for a certain amount of recreation for them. All these things are required of him. (1 Tim. 5:8) However, even in regard to such obligations there are areas where Christians may be able to choose. Thus, in order to put God's kingdom first in our lives, we may be able to take the kind of employment that will leave us the most possible time for sharing in the preaching and discipling work and in caring for the spiritual interests of our families. Some have done this to the benefit of themselves and their families. *W 11/1 4, 5a*

Monday, July 2

You are a mist appearing for a little while and then disappearing. Instead, you ought to say: "If Jehovah wills, we shall live and also do this or that."—Jas. 4:14, 15.

Christians are not immune to the danger of falling into the same state of mind as that of the rich man in Jesus' parable found at Luke 12:16-20. For example, the disciple James found it necessary to censure certain fellow believers. It was really presumptuous for them to express determination to pursue long-range material goals without any regard for God's will in the matter. The best-laid plans may fail, or death may come suddenly, unexpectedly. Human life is as frail and unstable as a mist and so is not a reliable foundation on which to build one's hopes. Hence, the person who boasts about how he will carry out his plans ignores his dependence on God and disregards the fact that divine blessing is needed for success. As James so well notes, such prideful action is wicked. It puts one in grave spiritual danger. *W 11/15 7-9*

Tuesday, July 3

When all things will have been subjected to him, then the Son himself will also subject himself to the One who subjected all things to him. —1 Cor. 15:28.

God's purpose is to restore his *original direct rule* over mankind. The Kingdom "stone" was cut out of the "mountain" of God's universal sovereignty for the purpose of vindicating his universal sovereignty and reestablishing this *original close relationship* over the earth. How will all men be again like Adam—sons of God, with direct approach to him? God's Word reveals that when the Kingdom has vindicated God's sovereignty over the earth and all the universe as righteous and just, Christ then turns this Kingdom back to Jehovah, that "God may be all things to everyone." (1 Cor. 15:28) Those on earth who thereafter pass the decisive test of their loyalty to Jehovah's Universal Sovereignty will forever honor Jesus as God's chief agent in restoring the earth to its proper place in the universe, as they serve Jehovah in pure, clean worship. What an incentive to serve Jehovah faithfully now! *W 1/15* 51, 52

Wednesday, July 4

I saw four angels standing upon the four corners of the earth, holding tight the four winds of the earth.—Rev. 7:1.

Why are these four angels "holding tight the four winds of the earth"? It can only be that Jehovah has further work for his witnesses to do here on earth. There are more of the "great crowd" to be gathered. The attendance of millions of persons at the celebration of the Memorial in recent years, together with the continued steady increase in Witnesses in many Asian lands, islands of the sea and Catholic countries of Europe, shows that the gathering work is not finished. It is urgent that all of Jehovah's people apply themselves in his service clear through to the end of this wicked system. Also, just as there was a great sifting among the anointed remnant in the decade following 1914, it seems that now there is a sifting going on among some who profess to be of the "great crowd." While the four winds will not always be 'held tight,' we can be happy that they have been up till now. *W 10/1* 16-19

Thursday, July 5

He will have subjects from sea to sea and from the River to the ends of the earth. —Ps. 72:8.

Christendom is no fulfillment of this prophecy, even though she assumes to be Christ's kingdom and today claims to have nearly 1,000 million church members, these, however, being of many sects and denominations. The nations professing to be Christian have not proved themselves to be the united subjects of the Prince of Peace, Christ. (Isa. 9:6) Till now the nations that have put their national sovereignty foremost have brushed aside what Jehovah's Christian witnesses have been proclaiming to them even in the face of cruel persecution, namely, that early in the autumn of the war-racked year of 1914 their lease on world rulership without the interference of God's kingdom expired. Then Jehovah God brought to birth the kingdom of his Christ up in heaven at his own right hand. Because this took place up in heaven, it was invisible to us. But the evidences of it are before our eyes in the things Jesus foretold for a visible "sign" to us. —Mark 13:3-37. *W 3/1* 5, 7a

Friday, July 6

What is Jehovah asking back from you but . . . to love kindness?—Mic. 6:8.

"To love kindness" means to have an active compassionate concern or regard for others. It is kindness that manifests itself in deeds. "To love kindness" would mean to find pleasure or delight in expressing kindness, cheerfully coming to the aid of others. Jesus set an excellent example in this regard. Even when he was tired and his privacy was interrupted, he gladly responded to the needs of his fellow countrymen. (Luke 9:10, 11) It brought great delight to Jesus to show such kindness. If you are a disciple of his, do you "love kindness"? Do you put personal comforts and desires in a secondary position so that you can be wholehearted in giving material and spiritual aid to those in need? Are feelings of compassion stirred within you when you see the sad spiritual plight of those lacking accurate knowledge? Are you setting aside time each month to have a reasonable share in public witnessing? Certainly this will be the case if we do indeed "love kindness." *W 9/15 11-13*

Saturday, July 7

Really, what does a man benefit himself if he gains the whole world but loses his own self or suffers damage? —Luke 9:25.

During the coming "great tribulation" there will undoubtedly be much occasion for us to demonstrate the spirit of self-sacrifice. We will need to help fellow Christians in many ways, including sharing with them material necessities. (Heb. 13:16) Due to the great upheavals that will then take place in the political, social and economic systems, God's servants may even lose some, or all, of their possessions. Hence, those who at this time put Jehovah's interests first in their lives, and who already have the spirit of self-sacrifice, will likely find it easier to make the sacrifices needed then. We cannot escape the fact that the question, "Are you self-indulgent—or self-sacrificing?" is a life or death matter when viewed from Jehovah's standpoint. If we love life, and want to live the perfect life in God's new order, then we need the spirit of self-sacrifice to serve Jehovah acceptably now. *W 8/1 19, 20*

Sunday, July 8

If this is how God loved us, then we are ourselves under obligation to love one another. —1 John 4:11.

One thing that will aid us to fix our hearts on efforts to increase our treasure in heaven is our taking time to reflect appreciatively on what Jehovah and Jesus Christ have done in our behalf. We are indebted to God for our very life. (Rev. 4:11) Despite the thankless attitude of so many, God has continued to allow all to benefit from his generous provisions for sustaining life. (Matt. 5:45) Then, in expression of his superlative love, Jehovah God did not even spare his dearest Son, Jesus Christ, from dying a shameful death on a stake. This made it possible for us to be liberated from sin and death, finally to become God's perfect children for all eternity. And Jesus Christ demonstrated his great love by willingly surrendering his life in our behalf. Should not the love that we have been shown compel us to seize every opportunity to prove ourselves thankful by aiding fellow humans spiritually and materially? *W 11/15 7a*

Monday, July 9

The fruitage of the spirit is . . . mildness, self-control.
—Gal. 5:22, 23.

Mildness might be defined as gentleness with strength behind it. Jesus said, "I am mild-tempered and lowly in heart." (Matt. 11:29) Jehovah is mild, and so, those seeking to walk worthily have no reason to be fearful of approaching him in prayer. (Heb. 4:16) True Christians display mildness in their dealings with all people. "The quiet and mild spirit" of a Christian wife may be a factor in winning her unbelieving mate over to the true faith. (1 Pet. 3:1-4) Mildness promotes pleasant relations among people even when difficulties arise, for "an answer, when mild, turns away rage." (Prov. 15:1) *Self-control* involves restraining one's person, speech and actions. Jehovah "kept exercising self-control." (Isa. 42:14, 15) As "imitators of God," Christians strive to exercise self-control in all things. Self-control is a blessing to the person practicing it and to all those associating with him. It also may attract observers to Christianity. *W 8/15* 17, 18a

Tuesday, July 10

Look! I am come (in the roll of the book it is written about me) to do your will, O God.
—Heb. 10:7.

To follow the example of Jesus Christ in this means to dedicate oneself to do God's will and to symbolize such a step by water baptism. Taking this step is the truly wise thing to do. The truly wise thing to do? Yes, Jehovah God knows what is best for us. His Word abundantly shows the folly of pursuing a selfish, unrighteous course. That is why we read that "godly devotion is beneficial for all things."

(1 Tim. 4:8) As Jehovah through his ancient prophet expressed it: "I, Jehovah, am your God, the One teaching you to benefit yourself." (Isa. 48:17) To help us to benefit ourselves we have the "holy writings," the inspired Scriptures. (2 Tim. 3:15-17) They remind us that "whatever a man is sowing, this he will also reap." (Gal. 6:7) Yes, "the blessing of Jehovah—that is what makes rich, and he adds no pain with it." (Prov. 10:22) Truly, making the choice to work with Jehovah God is the course of wisdom. *W 11/1* 10, 11

Wednesday, July 11

It is the acts of loving-kindness of Jehovah that we have not come to our finish, because his mercies will certainly not come to an end. They are new each morning. Your faithfulness is abundant.
—Lam. 3:22, 23.

No matter how desperate our situation may become, we should not allow ourselves to begin thinking that the Most High does not care about us. When we are faced with great hardships, the words of Lamentations 3:20, 21 can be of real comfort to us. In expression of his own humility, Jehovah God will "bow low" or stoop down to give us favorable attention. He will lift us up from our afflicted state, as he did the repentant Jews in the sixth century B.C.E. However, while the period of affliction is continuing, we should patiently and with unwavering faith wait for Jehovah God to act in our behalf. The very fact that we are still alive is an evidence of God's loving-kindness, his active compassionate concern. This stands as a guarantee that the Most High will show us mercy, even as noted above. *W 10/15* 14, 15a

Thursday, July 12

Jehovah has anointed me . . . to assign to those mourning over Zion, to give them a headdress instead of ashes, the oil of exultation instead of mourning.—Isa. 61:1, 3.

Whether any of Jesus' disciples had put ashes on their heads we are not told. Evidently such prophetic expressions were meant figuratively. Jesus' faith-building and comforting resurrection appearances did indeed reverse the disciples' feelings on the matter. On the day of Pentecost that followed, Jehovah used his Son to pour holy spirit upon the waiting disciples in Jerusalem. In fulfillment of the foretold "headdress," their heads were crowned with the joy of divine approval, like the joy of a priest bridegroom on a wedding day. It was as if soothing oil had been poured on their heads, refreshing them to the point of exultation. Gone was the downhearted spirit, and the praises of Jehovah God identified them as with a mantle. Observers of that Pentecostal spectacle said: "We hear them speaking in our tongues about the magnificent things of God."—Acts 2:1-11. *W 7/1 21, 22*

Friday, July 13

Consider it all joy, my brothers, when you meet with various trials.—Jas. 1:2.

In his Sermon on the Mount, Jesus had promised a heavenly reward for those who endure. (Matt. 5:11, 12) Not only is there a heavenly reward for the anointed Christians, but for all Christians there is an advantage even now, as James adds: "knowing as you do that this tested quality of your faith works out endurance." (Jas. 1:3) Faith that stands up through tests is better—it is proven faith. This kind of faith works for

stronger endurance for the next test. The Christian should not try to evade trials or feel that he has endured long enough. If we endure faithfully, not complaining against God or our own brothers, and not turning away from telling others about God's kingdom, we will be complete and sound in all respects. (Jas. 1:4) Such endurance will help us to make over our personality. We will become persons able to help others, with reasonableness, sympathy and mercy. Without having undergone trials with endurance, we cannot qualify in this way. *W 7/15 6, 7a*

Saturday, July 14

Continue in . . . that good news which you heard, and which was preached in all creation that is under heaven. —Col. 1:23.

Once again, at the climax of the age, the "good news" has been "preached in all creation that is under heaven." But today the field for preaching embraces the entire "inhabited earth," the lands in Africa, the Americas, Asia, Europe, Australasia and the islands of the sea. It could only be by Jehovah's spirit that such a globe-encircling witness could be given in the short space of 60 years. And still new ones keep flocking to God's organization! The territory has been far more extensive than in apostolic days, when it took less than 40 years to sound the final warning to the Jewish people. However, where are we in the stream of events? Revelation chapter 7 tells us. Here, John "saw four angels standing upon the four corners of the earth, holding tight the four winds of the earth." These are winds of destruction, for in due course they are to 'harm the earth and the sea and the trees.' *W 10/1 14, 15*

Sunday, July 15

This is fine and acceptable in the sight of . . . God, whose will is that all sorts of men should be saved. —1 Tim. 2:3, 4.

Jehovah God has already demonstrated his superlative love for mankind. Though he deeply loved his only-begotten Son, He arranged matters for this one to die in our behalf so that we could be reconciled with Him and eventually enjoy everlasting life in perfection. (John 3:16; Rom. 5:6-8) In view of this, could we imagine that God would regard humans as just a *mass* of "faceless" persons, or that he would select a certain group on which to bestow his favor and then simply ignore the rest? That could never happen! God sent Christ to be a ransom for all. (1 Tim. 2:6) God recognizes every person as a distinct individual. Therefore He is always willing and ready to grant his help and to show his love to anyone exercising faith in him. And the intensity and constancy of his love are far greater than what we are able to express to others. *W 2/1 1-4a*

Monday, July 16

These are the ones that come out of the great tribulation, and they have washed their robes and made them white in the blood of the Lamb. —Rev. 7:14.

As we know, since the middle of the fourth decade of our 20th century, a "great crowd" of Christ's "other sheep" has been forming. The apostle John, who had an apocalyptic vision of the "great crowd," was reminded that they also have an appreciation of the shed blood of the Lamb Jesus Christ. They appreciate it as a means of cleansing. These know that they could not serve God acceptably at his holy temple if they remained clad in filthy garments. To God and the Lamb Jesus Christ the "great crowd" ascribe, not a resurrection out of the memorial tombs, but "salvation" out of the "great tribulation." They are preserved alive through that "great tribulation." So they do not need to be resurrected at the last day. (John 6:54) However, they will need the benefit of the services of the High Priest Jesus Christ and his 144,000 underpriests during the millennium. *W 9/1 26, 27b*

Tuesday, July 17

As for me, in righteousness I shall behold your face; I will be satisfied when awakening to see your form.—Ps. 17:15.

Throughout human history, many have centered their lives around the acquiring of material possessions. But are material possessions rightly the treasure that should get the prime attention from God's servants? If a Christian were to devote himself mainly to the pursuit of material goals, would he not be at variance with persons who are serving God? (Ps. 17:14) "Men of this system of things" give no thought to their obligation to Jehovah God. How different was David's outlook on life! His chief interest was in remaining righteous so that he might see God's face, that is, experience divine favor and blessing as if standing before his Maker. On awakening to an assurance from God, David would rejoice in Jehovah's presence with him. Truly, his heart had set its affections on spiritual treasures that endure. Where is our treasure? Is it here on earth or is it in the heavens? That depends upon our heart.—Luke 12:34. *W 11/15 1-4*

Wednesday, July 18

For if you publicly declare that . . . Jesus is Lord, and exercise faith in your heart that God raised him up from the dead, you will be saved. For with the heart one exercises faith for righteousness, but with the mouth one makes public declaration for salvation.—Rom. 10:9, 10.

These words do not apply to just any public declaration, but have particular application to a formal public declaration such as that made at the time one who has dedicated himself to do God's will gets baptized. Such declaration gives notice to all that a person has made the choice to work with Jehovah. Yes, we cannot expect God to reward us with everlasting life if we do not make such a public declaration. A person may profess that he loves God and that he appreciates all that God has done for him. But if within a reasonable period of time he does not dedicate himself to do God's will, following in Jesus' footsteps, his professions have a hollow ring, betray a lack of love, trust and faith in Jehovah God and may actually be insincere. *W 11/1 16, 17*

Thursday, July 19

Maintain your conduct fine among the nations, that, in the thing in which they are speaking against you as evildoers, they may as a result of your fine works of which they are eyewitnesses glorify God in the day for his inspection. —1 Pet. 2:12.

Because we stand in the same position as that of Jesus Christ, who declared, "My kingdom is no part of this world," we do not have any part in the political affairs of this world. (John 18:36) The world is steeped in unrighteousness. Therefore, if we would walk worthily in Jehovah's name as his friends, we must shun the world and everything that is evil in it. We must have the same view of sin as that possessed by Jehovah God, who "is righteous in all his ways and loyal in all his works." (Ps. 145:17) As Christians, we know that if we were to steal, to commit adultery or otherwise violate God's law, the name of Jehovah would be reproached on that account. Never would we want that to happen! Rather, we desire that our conduct bring glory to Jehovah God, even as the apostle Peter wrote. *W 8/15 5, 6a*

Friday, July 20

Truly I tell you today, You will be with me in Paradise. —Luke 23:43.

During Christ's thousand-year reign the "priests of Jehovah" who are "the ministers of our God" will be exalted in the heavens where they will occupy themselves with priestly service for all mankind. (Rev. 20:6) But the "great crowd" will be left here on the cleansed earth. Who then will be the pioneers in rehabilitating and beautifying God's earthly footstool? Why, the "great crowd" of tribulation survivors who have stuck to the spiritual paradise with the anointed remnant. The wool from the flocks that the "great crowd" will tend will be ample for clothing. The "farmers" will see to satisfying hearty appetites. The vinedressers will be able to furnish the best of wines to gladden the hearts of men. Despite all of this, the "great crowd" will not neglect rendering sacred service to Jehovah God regularly in the earthly courtyard of God's spiritual temple. In this they will take the lead and set an excellent example for all those resurrected from the dead. *W 7/1 32, 33a*

Saturday, July 21

For if the readiness is there first, it is especially acceptable according to what a person has, not according to what a person does not have.
—2 Cor. 8:12.

Family heads appreciate that they must provide for their own households. (1 Tim. 5:8) Christian parents also have the responsibilities that come with having children. They understand that they must sacrifice some of what *they* might prefer to do so that they can spend time bringing up their children "in the discipline and mental-regulating of Jehovah." (Eph. 6:4) Too, there are some who, because of poor health, advanced age or other limitations, can offer little in direct service to Jehovah. In this, they are like the needy widow who could offer at God's temple only "two small coins of very little value." (Luke 21: 1-4) Yet all such persons who do what they can to help others to learn of Jehovah are surely making sacrifices that please him. He loves them for their willingness to endure difficult conditions and yet make some offering of service to him, as their situation permits. *W 8/1 14a*

Sunday, July 22

[Love] does not rejoice over unrighteousness, but rejoices with the truth.—1 Cor. 13:6.

Yes, love would not rejoice when others get ensnared by wrongdoing, disgrace themselves and come to ruin. True Christians do not rejoice, saying that the individual deserved to have trouble come upon him. (Prov. 17:5; 24:17, 18) Even our seeing unrighteous things depicted in movies or television programs should bring us no pleasure. Then, too, it would be improper to side with unruly members of the congregation, finding fault with the reproof given to them. This would not help the wrongdoer to take positive steps to recover fully from the spiritual weakness that led to his misconduct. Rather, we should rejoice with the truth. Yes, we should rejoice to see the powerful influence for righteousness that the truth has on people's lives. We should find pleasure in all things that lead to blessings, that have a wholesome, up-building effect on others and that serve to advance the cause of truth and righteousness. *W 9/15 13, 14a*

Monday, July 23

God has become king over the nations.—Ps. 47:8.

Today in the year of 1979 the "war of the great day of God the Almighty" at Har-Magedon approaches. Now, long since the Gentile Times ended in 1914, "Jehovah of armies" is especially "the glorious King." Why so? Because, as noted above, he again is acting as the Universal Sovereign toward this earth. He will display his mightiness in further maintaining at Har-Magedon "the kingdom of our Lord and of his Christ." (Rev. 11:15-18) Jehovah's Christ, the Son greater than King David, is the one whom he has enthroned to represent Him in the world government. First, Jehovah of armies, attended by his Son Jesus Christ and armies of heavenly angels, will rid the universe of today's wicked system of things. Then he will bless mankind with righteous world rulership through his Son, Jesus Christ. This grand prospect gets nearer to its realization! Does not this "glorious King," Jehovah of armies, deserve now a heartfelt welcome from us? Most certainly, Yes! Come in, then, O our glorious King! *W 3/1 23, 24b*

Tuesday, July 24

*In carrying on your contest against that sin you have never yet resisted as far as blood, but you have entirely forgotten the exhortation which addresses you as sons: "My son, do not belittle the discipline from Jehovah, . . . for whom Jehovah loves he disciplines."
—Heb. 12:4-6.*

Early Christians were beaten and imprisoned. Their homes were invaded and their possessions plundered. Some of their loyal friends and relatives perished at the hands of angry mobs or were sentenced to death by judicial decree. They had committed no crime to justify such treatment. They lived in an exemplary way and had real love for fellow humans. But they incurred the hatred of many. Why? Because they were disciples of Christ. Was the terrible suffering that Christians underwent beneficial? One might be quick to answer, No. God's Word, however, presents the matter of a person's being forced to undergo mistreatment as something highly profitable, even as Paul told those Christianized Jews of the first century. We can truly profit from his words today. *W 10/15* 1, 2a

Wednesday, July 25

*Jehovah knows how to deliver people of godly devotion out of trial, but to reserve unrighteous people for the day of judgment to be cut off.
—2 Pet. 2:9.*

At the time when Abraham and Lot were serving as God's witnesses on earth, Jehovah warned of his judgment against the two cities of Sodom and Gomorrah. Not even 10 righteous men could be found in them! As Jehovah's angels prepared to bring the foretold destruction, Lot repeatedly urged the men who were engaged to his daughters

to "get out of this place." (Gen. 19:14) However, those prospective sons-in-law, much like persons of this immoral world today, passed the divine warning off as a mere joke. May we be like righteous Lot in giving urgency to Jehovah's judgment message for *our* day. And let us not be like Lot's wife, but, rather, guard against looking back with desire for the material advantages of this doomed world. Our becoming completely absorbed in doing God's will for this day will serve as our protection. Remember what Peter said in connection with Lot's deliverance. *W 10/1* 7, 9

Thursday, July 26

Keep yourselves clean, you who are carrying the utensils of Jehovah.—Isa. 52:11.

While this command may have had primary reference to religious cleanness, the principle also applies to moral cleanness. Yes, to do Jehovah's work in his way we must do it with clean hands, that is, virtuously. We may be as busy as possible in Jehovah's work, but unless we live by the Bible's moral principles it is all in vain. God made that point in connection with his ancient people Israel. Because of their uncleanness he found their various kinds of formal worship detestable. (Isa. 1:13-16) Jehovah is holy, pure and righteous, and he commands that we be likewise holy and pure. (1 Pet. 1:16) At times we may feel as did Paul when he wrote that the things he wanted to do he did not do, and the things he did not want to do he did. (Rom. 7: 19) But he never quit striving against inherited weaknesses. (1 Cor. 9:27) We must also keep clean, not only so as to keep from bringing reproach upon Jehovah, but also so as not to stumble others.—Luke 17:1, 2. *W 11/1* 13-15a

Friday, July 27

Your Father knows you need these things. . . . seek continually his kingdom, and these things will be added to you. —Luke 12:30, 31.

In view of Jehovah's matchless record as a Provider, there is no reason for us to give in to a lack of faith. As Jesus pointed out, ravens, by looking for food, find enough to sustain them, and the lilies simply grow and put on a display of color. Yes, Jehovah God has arranged matters so that the ravens are able to find the needed food and the vegetation can be adorned with blossoms. Could we, therefore, imagine that he would callously allow his servants to starve to death or to walk about without essential clothing? Certainly not. Hence, as a general rule, true Christians can rest assured that, when they do not let the cares of life hinder their service to God, they will have the basic essentials. In fact, they will be better off than worldlings in like economic circumstances. Christians fare better because of not wasting their assets in gambling, smoking, heavy drinking or the like. *W 11/15 13*

Saturday, July 28

Keep on the watch, for you do not know when the master of the house is coming, . . . in order that when he arrives suddenly, he does not find you sleeping. But what I say to you I say to all, Keep on the watch.—Mark 13:35-37.

The way was hard for Jeremiah. But his confidence in Jehovah and his loyalty to his commission carried him through. He was able also to encourage his faithful companion, the scribe Baruch. (Jer. 45:1-5) Like Jeremiah, we should have unshakable confidence in Jehovah's prophetic word. As a token of such confidence, Jeremiah obeyed God's word in buying a hereditary field in Anathoth, and that just one year before the Babylonian armies moved in to devastate the land! In these final days, we should likewise be confident that Jehovah will fulfill every word of his promise to protect and establish his people. The time for the heavenly assault forces under Christ Jesus to strike is perilously close! It is therefore urgent that we keep ever on the watch, proclaiming this good news of the Kingdom. —Mark 13:10. *W 1/1 15, 14a*

Sunday, July 29

Let us pursue the things making for peace and the things that are upbuilding to one another.—Rom. 14:19.

Each one of us should strive to become mature and firmly established, making our faith on all points strong, so that we will not be prone to stumble or to condemn others. To this end, Paul advises us to set aside all causes of contention and to live in harmony with one another. His appeal is for us to do the things that build up one another spiritually, instead of finding fault or, on the other hand, stubbornly insisting on a personal right—the things that tear down others. Paul, at Ephesians 4:13, 15, recommends that we work so that all can "attain to the oneness in the faith and in the accurate knowledge of the Son of God, to a full-grown man, to the measure of stature that belongs to the fullness of the Christ," and "by love grow up in all things into him who is the head, Christ." Then we can join together unitedly and, with zeal, force and effectiveness, bring the message of salvation to mankind. *W 3/15 6, 11a*

Monday, July 30

God lifted him up to his right hand as our pioneer and saviour, in order to grant repentance and remission of sins to Israel.—Acts 5:31, Moffatt.

Jesus met the needs of those described at Isaiah 61:1, 2. He comforted those mourners by preaching the good news of "the kingdom of the heavens," besides curing the sick and even raising the dead. (Matt. 4:17; 11:4-6) But still greater comfort and liberty were ahead for those mourners over Zion. This came by Jesus' death and resurrection and his ascension into heaven to present the value of his sacrifice to God. By thus fulfilling the Bible prophecies concerning him, Jesus Christ became a pioneer of life and salvation for those who accepted his life-giving ministry. John the Baptizer had gone in advance of Jehovah's Messiah and had prepared the way, and so John could also be called a pioneer. Jesus, however, did more than John in order to pioneer the way to life and salvation. Before the bloodguilty Sanhedrin at Jerusalem the 12 apostles of Jesus Christ testified to this effect. *W 7/1* 15, 17

Tuesday, July 31

[Adam and Eve] heard the voice of Jehovah God walking in the garden about the breezy part of the day.—Gen. 3:8.

By what means can God provide the things every human needs? He can do this by means of the Kingdom under his Messiah, Jesus Christ. In the beginning, God was Ruler directly over mankind. Adam worshiped God in a Father-son relationship. He needed no temple on earth in order to worship God. Neither did he need an intermediary through whom to make an approach to God. As a son of God he had intimacy with Him, evidently receiving daily communication. But this man rebelled and became unclean and unfit to stay a member of God's family and was expelled from his garden home as a rebel. This alienated mankind from God. God, however, was not limited in his means to correct this. He chose to set up a special Kingdom arrangement to act for him. That kingdom would reestablish his relations with humankind and bring them back into proper orbit in his government. *W 1/15* 14, 15

Wednesday, August 1

Lord, whom shall we go away to? You have sayings of everlasting life; and we have believed and come to know that you are the Holy One of God. —John 6:68, 69.

The eleven faithful apostles had wholeheartedly accepted Jesus' word or Messianic message, and for that reason he pronounced them "clean." (John 15:3) For instance, when Jesus asked them, "You do not want to go also, do you?" Simon Peter answered as above. (John 6:67) So there were no dead twigs of fruitless unbelief about those loyal apostles. They were undividedly giving their attention to the cause of "the Holy One of God." They believed him to be "the Christ, the Son of the living God." (Matt. 16:16) In the face of such decisions, Jesus' words, especially spoken to the apostles privately, must have had a purging effect, leaving them in a spiritual condition that was "clean." All the "branches" that remain in such a "clean" condition could devote themselves in full commitment to the unique purpose of Jehovah's "true vine." This would work out in gladness for both God and men. *W 12/15* 20, 21

Thursday, August 2

Not many of you should become teachers, my brothers, knowing that we shall receive heavier judgment.—Jas. 3:1.

Because sound doctrine has a bearing on a person's salvation, teaching is a responsibility that should be entrusted *only to men who are qualified.* The above inspired admonition was not given to discourage qualified men from becoming teachers, for the Scriptures also say: "If any man is reaching out for an office of overseer, he is desirous of a fine work." (1 Tim. 3:1) James evidently was directing his words to men who were setting themselves up as teachers even though they were not appointed or qualified to teach. These unqualified men wanted the prominence and authority that was associated with being teachers, without regard for the qualifications. Such would-be teachers needed to have impressed on them the serious position in which a teacher finds himself. Because a teacher stands before others as instructing or leading them, more is expected from him than from other members of the congregation. *W 12/1 4, 5a*

Friday, August 3

Surely on slippery ground is where you place them. You have made them fall to ruins. O how they have become an object of astonishment as in a moment!—Ps. 73:18, 19.

These words reveal a vital point that can help us to bear the injustices of an ungodly system. The seeming prosperity of the wicked is but temporary. Because their life centers around corruptible possessions, they are standing on "slippery ground" and are in constant danger of experiencing a terrible crash, suddenly and without warning. At the latest, death will overtake them in old age, and their ill-gotten gain will be of no value in securing for them a longer life. (Ps. 49:6-12) It may even be that justice will catch up with them long before they reach old age. The unchangeable law of God may go into effect against them: "Whatever a man is sowing, this he will also reap." (Gal. 6:7) Since they have turned their backs on the Most High, the full impact of the disaster comes crashing down on them. They are left completely helpless, without hope and comfort. *W 10/15 9*

Saturday, August 4

*Then people will deliver you up to tribulation and will kill you, and you will be objects of hatred by all the nations on account of my name.
—Matt. 24:9.*

Toward what one people have these words been fulfilled in modern times? Why, toward the Christian witnesses of Jehovah! Of all religious groups, they stand alone as the ones who have been set upon by the Nazis, the Communists, the military dictatorships and even the so-called democratic countries. Today, not only many African lands but also many other countries on earth have been closing in on Jehovah's Witnesses, so that regular preaching activity and the arranging of Christian assemblies have become more difficult. Missionaries have been expelled from a number of countries, and it becomes harder to send missionaries into new fields. It is exactly as Jehovah God foretold: "They will be certain to fight against you." They are doing just that! But in the face of bitter propaganda and persecution, Jehovah's people continue to give a thorough witness.—Jer. 1:19. *W 10/1 1, 3*

Sunday, August 5

[Jesus] went journeying from city to city and from village to village, preaching and declaring the good news of the kingdom of God.—Luke 8:1.

Jesus followed closely the direction given him by his Father. (John 14:10) So, we do well to carry on the preaching of the "good news" in the ways that he did. He did not wait for people to come to him but he went to them. His disciples did the same. (Acts 16: 13-15; 17:17-21) We today should do likewise, taking the initiative in sharing the "good news" with others. As we go about our affairs of daily life, we have various contacts and we should try to use these to share Bible truths in appropriate ways. But not everyone would hear the "good news" if we limited our activity to this. There are some who would never be met if we did not call personally at their homes. Having the kind of love that reaches out to include all sorts of persons, we will put forth the effort to reach everyone with the Kingdom message. Does your personal share in this activity reflect this balanced Christian outlook? *W 11/1 7a*

Monday, August 6

*The love of money is a root of all sorts of injurious things, and by reaching out for this love some have been led astray from the faith and have stabbed themselves all over with many pains.
—1 Tim. 6:10.*

If our hearts are motivating us aright, we will not lose sight of the uncertainty of life and our total dependence upon Jehovah God. Then, whenever we make plans for the future, we will prayerfully consider how these plans fit in with God's purpose. This will prevent our getting so wrapped up in materialistic pursuits that we have less and less time for building a strong faith. Such prayerful consideration will also help us to see that material assets are not to be simply piled up for the satisfying of personal pleasures but should be used to benefit needy fellow humans. This unselfish use of money is basic to a person's being a true Christian. The Scriptures tell us: "Let the stealer steal no more, but rather let him do . . . good work, that he may have something to distribute to someone in need."—Eph. 4:28. *W 11/15 10*

Tuesday, August 7

*With the sleeveless coat of righteousness he has enwrapped me, like the bridegroom who, in a priestly way, puts on a headdress.
—Isa. 61:10.*

A "sleeveless coat of righteousness" is something added to "the garments of salvation" with which Jehovah has arrayed his restored remnant. In the eyes of the world, especially due to misrepresentation by Christendom's clergy, the remnant of spiritual Israelites appeared to be unrighteous in a religious way. They were branded as children of the Devil. Their being made the target of worldwide persecution seemed to confirm such charges against them, particularly so in Christendom. But how did Jehovah view them? The great Judge of all the earth did not condemn them. Because of their seeking him and his Word, he received the repentant remnant back into his favor. He accorded to them the honorable privilege of being his witnesses. He caused his name, Jehovah, to be called upon them and used them mightily to make his name and purposes known world wide. *W 7/1 3, 4b*

Wednesday, August 8

[Do] nothing out of contentiousness or out of egotism, but with lowliness of mind considering that the others are superior to you, keeping an eye, not in personal interest upon just your own matters, but also in personal interest upon those of the others.—Phil. 2:3, 4.

As part of their sacrifices to Jehovah God, must all Christians today give up homes and other material possessions, as did the first-century Christians in 66 C.E.? No, that is not the point, although there must be the willingness to put God's interests first in one's life, making whatever sacrifices might be necessary to do that. It is not so much what we have or do not have, but where our heart is. Is it toward Jehovah's interests first, or is it toward personal interests first? And part of Jehovah's interests includes doing things for other people, as God's Word says above and as we read at Romans 15:2: "Let each of us please his neighbor in what is good for his upbuilding." *W 8/1* 11a

Thursday, August 9

All the peoples, for their part, will walk each one in the name of its god.—Mic. 4:5.

Every intelligent person walks in the name of some god. Yes, whether individuals realize it or not, they serve some god. True, not everyone today serves a specific god by name, as did the ancients. But some persons idolize actors, politicians, sportsmen, even themselves. Why, their god may be their own belly! (Phil. 3:18, 19) Some directly worship Satan the Devil, whereas others serve him unwittingly, for "the whole world is lying in the power of the wicked one." (1 John 5:19) How true

are the words recorded under inspiration by the Hebrew prophet Micah during the eighth century before the Common Era! Just prior to these words, reference had been made to what would occur "in the final part of the days." Then the mountain of Jehovah God's house would be firmly established above all other mountains (denoting the exalted position of true worship). Many are now streaming to it. It is our blessed privilege to be among those doing so. *W 8/15* 1, 2

Friday, August 10

Keep zealously seeking the greater gifts. And yet I show you a surpassing way. —1 Cor. 12:31.

In First Corinthians chapter 13, we find a masterful description of the love that Christians should have. The emphasis in this chapter is not on the expression of God's love for us nor on our love for God. But the main import of the material is on how love should be shown to fellow humans. This is what the Christians at Corinth needed, for they were not enjoying the best of relationships with one another. As is evident from an examination of the entire letter of First Corinthians, the congregation there had problems with jealousies, strife, divisions, boasting, immorality, dishonesty and the taking of undue liberties. Some in the congregation were desirous of having prestige. They wanted to outshine one another as to abilities and gifts or endowments. It was not wrong for one to view the greater gifts of the spirit as desirable. But there was something even more outstanding than the pursuit of the "greater gifts." *W 9/15* 2-4a

Saturday, August 11

That which corresponds to this is also now saving you, namely, baptism.—1 Pet. 3:21.

Baptism is a most fitting symbol of our having made a dedication to do God's will as followers of Christ. By going down into the water, being covered by it, we are, as it were, buried. We die as to our former course of action; it marks the death of our selfish course, our choosing to do as WE please. Being raised up out of the water well pictures our being made alive to the doing of God's will. Water baptism might also be said to have a very practical aspect, as a person might easily forget that he orally agreed to do God's will, or even forget that he once signed a paper to that effect; for how many things we forget that we have said or even written down! But can we forget that once, after having heard a discourse on baptism and joining in prayer, we changed our clothes to a bathing suit and got baptized in the presence of witnesses? Hardly! Having taken such a step, we have the obligation of following through by being co-workers with God. *W 11/1 19*

Sunday, August 12

To the extent that you did it to one of the least of these my brothers, you did it to me. —Matt. 25:40.

Since 1935 the foretold "great crowd" began to form of men and women who were made glad by the Kingdom fruit that was held forth by the branches of "the true vine." The cruel hardships and trials imposed upon them during World War II because of their association with the remnant did not force them to dissociate themselves from those bearers of Kingdom "fruit." They knew that, to be loyal to the enthroned King who is "the true vine," they had to be loyal to the "branches," his spiritual brothers. When it comes to dwelling safely on earth under one's own vine and fig tree in a figurative way, what does the "great crowd" prefer? They prefer to dwell under "the true vine" and its "branches" because these represent God's kingdom by Christ. And so, instead of advocating the United Nations, these, along with Christ's brothers, keep on preaching the good news of God's kingdom. Are you having a full share in that grand work? *W 12/15 16, 17a*

Monday, August 13

I am longing to see you, that I may impart some spiritual gift to you in order for you to be made firm; or, rather, that there may be an interchange of encouragement among you, by each one through the other's faith, both yours and mine.—Rom. 1:11, 12.

One of the things that people most need in our times is *encouragement.* Everyone feels discouraged now and then because of the pressures of this world and on account of his own weaknesses. Christians are no exception. Paul described the purpose of his visit to a congregation as above. When Christian men from Jerusalem traveled to other cities, they "encouraged the brothers with many a discourse and strengthened them." (Acts 15:32; 20:1) This is a fine pattern for elders today. Sometimes you may have a problem or a job that seems like a mountain. Or, you may encounter some very unfavorable circumstance in life. What should you do? Instead of being discouraged or giving up, you should turn to "the God of all comfort."—2 Cor. 1:3, 4. *W 5/1 1, 2a*

Tuesday, August 14

The wisdom from above is first of all chaste, then peaceable, reasonable, ready to obey, full of mercy and good fruits, not making partial distinctions, not hypocritical.—Jas. 3:17.

Yes, heavenly wisdom never makes a person "hypocritical." A hypocrite pretends to be what he is not. His actions are out of harmony with his words. The man who displays heavenly wisdom, however, does not wear a mask, so to speak. In all his relations, he is upright and trustworthy. Are we giving evidence that we want to live in harmony with heavenly wisdom? All of us have the responsibility as Christ's disciples to teach the truth to others. It is, therefore, vital that our attitudes, words and actions are in agreement with what we profess to be. (Rom. 2:21, 22) None of us, including congregation elders, should feel that we have made sufficient advancement in Christian living and can now take it easy. Rather, may we keep on striving to be better servants of our heavenly Father and rejoice in the blessings he has bestowed on us, always displaying heavenly wisdom. *W 12/1 20, 21a*

Wednesday, August 15

Jehovah will not forsake his people.—Ps. 94:14.

Truly, all who seek God's kingdom and his righteousness first will experience his loving care. (Matt. 6:31-33) Though they may find themselves in seemingly hopeless circumstances, the expressions of Jehovah's mouth will sustain them. As the manna was a tangible expression from Jehovah's mouth and kept the Israelites alive in the wilderness, so today Jehovah's promise to sustain his servants will take a tangible form. For ex-ample, Jehovah has at times moved fellow believers or even unbelievers to come to the aid of his needy servants. Since undue worry about daily cares of life can be destructive to our spiritual outlook, we do well to keep strong our faith in Jehovah's ability to provide for us. So, let each one examine himself and ask: Do I manifest faith in the promise uttered by the psalmist? Am I using my time, energies and assets in a way that results in praise to God's name and in benefit to my fellow humans? Does my greatest joy come from serving Jehovah God? *W 11/15 16-18*

Thursday, August 16

It is for discipline you are enduring. God is dealing with you as with sons. For what son is he that a father does not discipline?—Heb. 12:7.

The opposition directed against Christianized Jews was indeed severe. But their struggling against the easily entangling sin—loss of faith —had not come to the point of their having their blood spilled. Many of them possibly were halfhearted in the race for life and so were not carrying on the contest against this sin in a way that would be needed for them to succeed in 'resisting it as far as blood.' They were getting tired of having to face the reproaches of godless people. (Heb. 12:3, 4) They failed to realize that the harsh treatment from opposers served as discipline from Jehovah and confirmed that he loved them deeply as his sons. (Prov. 3:11, 12) In harmony with this inspired counsel, how should we view the suffering that God permits to befall us? We should regard it as a form of discipline or training given to us by a Father who has deep love for us and is interested in our eternal welfare. *W 10/15 3, 4a*

Friday, August 17

By this all will know that you are my disciples, if you have love among yourselves. —John 13:35.

Will God's kingdom rob its subjects of the joys of life? Or, rather, will they find genuine happiness in submitting to its rule? Jesus Christ showed by his words and his actions that the law of the Kingdom would be a law of love. He proved that he had, in perfect measure, the qualities needed for one who could be entrusted with full authority. He made it plain that it was because of God's love for us that he sent his Son to earth. (John 3:16) And Jesus, speaking of his own sacrifice on behalf of mankind, said the words recorded at John 15:13. He encouraged his disciples to cultivate the same quality of self-sacrificing love. Are the two great commandments restrictive? Absolutely not! (Matt. 22:37-39) The spirit of self-sacrificing love already abounds among true Christians, marking them as Jesus' disciples. It makes unnecessary a law code with a long list of rules. The law of love is upbuilding, beneficial. *W 1/15 27-29*

Saturday, August 18

The kingdom of God will be taken from you and be given to a nation producing its fruits. —Matt. 21:43.

Keeping separate from the world is the fruit that must characterize those who belong to Jehovah's organization as represented by his Son. They must demonstrate unqualified attachment to God's kingdom in the hands of Jesus Christ. This calls for their open acknowledgment and acceptance of the Son of God as the long-promised Messiah. Fruit of this kind was not presented to Jesus by the typical "vine" of natural Israel. It failed to produce the "fruits" of the kingdom of God. This resulted in tremendous loss to them, for the kingdom of God was taken away from them and was given to the nation that would produce the required fruit, spiritual Israel. This new nation is made up of the "branches" that prove their union with the "true vine" by openly accepting Jesus Christ and walking in his footsteps, personally taking part in preaching "this good news of the kingdom," in which work the "other sheep" are happy to share. —Matt. 24:14. *W 12/15 10, 11a*

Sunday, August 19

The foreigners that have joined themselves to Jehovah to minister to him . . . I will also bring them to my holy mountain and make them rejoice. —Isa. 56:6, 7.

We certainly have every reason to be *joyful workers.* We have Jehovah's spirit, and "joy" is a part of the fruitage of that spirit. (Gal. 5:22) We also have the "sword of the spirit, that is, God's word." (Eph. 6:17) What a joy it is to use this in preaching the "good news" to others! As regards God's holy spirit, Jesus told of his heavenly Father's willingness to "give holy spirit to those asking him," and it is that spirit that keeps us going as joyful workers. (Luke 11:13) Cooperate with God's spirit and trust in it. It gave Paul strength for all things. (Phil. 4:13) While it is true that the prophecy at Isaiah 65:13-18 applies particularly to those with the heavenly hope, the spiritual Israelites, God's Word also speaks of a "great crowd" of others, referring to them as "foreigners" in comparison, yet it also invites them to be joyful workers, as at Isaiah 56:6, 7. *W 6/1 4, 12, 13a*

Monday, August 20

I am grateful to Christ Jesus our Lord, who imparted power to me, because he considered me faithful by assigning me to a ministry.—1 Tim. 1:12.

The apostle Paul wrote to Philemon, urging him to forgive Onesimus, accepting him now as a brother. (Philemon 8, 9, 21) Certainly Philemon would not feel that he was acting under compulsion, and so he would be happy to comply. He would feel genuinely ready to respond to Paul's appeal and also would be more obligated to do so, because Paul put such trust in him. Likewise, the overseer who encourages others and trusts his brother when he gives him a job will get more accomplished than the overseer who dictates, or who feels that no one can do a job as well as he does. Trusting in a brother and showing confidence in him contribute to greater exercise of initiative as well as effort on the part of the brother. Such an overseer is properly representing God's sovereignty and is following Christ's pattern. Christ treated Paul in this way, even as can be seen by what Paul appreciatively said. *W 7/15 11, 12*

Tuesday, August 21

Why is it that this people ... is unfaithful with an enduring unfaithfulness?—Jer. 8:5.

Thus Jehovah asked concerning ancient Jerusalem. It was because they followed a stubborn course, "like a horse that is dashing into the battle." And their fleshly way of viewing things brought calamity, for they 'did not come to know the judgment of Jehovah.' (Jer. 8:6, 7) In striking contrast Jeremiah endured in faithfulness. For 40 years, until the destruction of Jerusalem, and beyond that time, he continued to fulfill his commission in proclaiming Jehovah's judgments. It appears that Jeremiah did not know in advance the day or hour that Jerusalem's destruction would come. But he was aware of the "great pounding from the land of the north"—Babylon. He knew that the executional forces were drawing near, and that God's judgments were sure. Likewise, Jehovah's people today see clearly the "sign" of the approach of "a tribulation such as has not occurred from the beginning of the creation." —Jer. 10:22; Mark 13:4, 19. *W 1/1 1, 2a*

Wednesday, August 22

Who is wise and understanding among you? Let him show out of his fine conduct his works.—Jas. 3:13.

It is noteworthy that James did not merely ask: 'Who has fine speaking ability?' To be a good teacher, a man needs more than the ability to express himself well. Wisdom and understanding are essential. A wise person has a proper fear of Jehovah God and knows how to apply knowledge in a manner that will bring good results. (Prov. 9: 10) One who possesses understanding is able to see into a matter, to get the sense of it and to discern the relationships of various aspects of a situation or circumstance. The person grasps the full significance of what he is considering. This means that he must be a mature Christian whose 'perceptive powers have been trained through use to distinguish both right and wrong.' (Heb. 5:14) How is it evident that a man has the needed wisdom and understanding to teach his fellow believers? His life should demonstrate that he does have the wisdom and understanding associated with the fear of God. *W 12/1 7, 8a*

Thursday, August 23

You are worthy, Jehovah, even our God, to receive the glory and the honor and the power, because you created all things. —Rev. 4:11.

To choose to dedicate ourselves to do Jehovah's will is the just, the right thing to do. In fact, we owe it to God to do his will. Why? Because by reason of his having created all things, Jehovah owns the earth and all on it. He made us not merely to enjoy our own pleasure but also to serve his purpose, to do his will. Moreover, he also keeps sustaining us, for example, by providing the sunshine and the rain. Additionally, to dedicate ourselves is the loving, the grateful thing to do. When we think of all the love that Jehovah has showered upon mankind to make life possible and a joy, when we think of his patience in dealing with mankind for 6,000 years, and when we think of his loving us so much as to give his only-begotten Son to be our Savior, what must we conclude? The least that we can do to keep self-respect is to dedicate ourselves to our heavenly Father to do his will, and then symbolize this by water baptism. *W 11/1 12, 13*

Friday, August 24

Where your treasure is, there your hearts will be also. —Luke 12:34.

Yes, just where our treasure is depends on the way in which our hearts are motivating us. As we examine the context of Jesus' words, we note that a large crowd had been listening to the Son of God. One of them apparently wanted more than his legal share of an inheritance and so asked Jesus to intervene. Seeing the issue, Jesus refused to get involved but warned the crowd against wrongly desiring what others have. (Luke 12:15) No matter how wealthy a person might be, he simply cannot keep himself alive indefinitely. He will die just like any other man and leave all his piled-up wealth behind. Jesus further emphasized this point by giving the illustration recorded at Luke 12:16-20. The rich man in this illustration gave no thought as to how he could use his riches to help others. He lost sight of the fact that his life could end very quickly and so failed to use his assets in building up a record of fine works with God. May we never make that mistake! *W 11/15 4-6*

Saturday, August 25

Since, in the wisdom of God, the world through its wisdom did not get to know God, God saw good through the foolishness of what is preached to save those believing. —1 Cor. 1:21.

The wisdom of both the Jewish scribes and the Greek philosophers blinded them to the wisdom of God, even as Paul notes. This preaching was foolishness to the Jews. Their wisdom taught them that they would be saved by works of the Law. Moreover, they wanted no weak Messiah allowing himself to be nailed to a stake! The preaching was foolishness also to the Greeks. They needed no Jew dying like a despised criminal to save them —they had immortal souls that were never going to die! So Paul wrote his warning to the Christian congregation in Corinth. Human wisdom, whether that of the Jewish scribes or that of the Greek philosophers would make the torture stake of Christ useless to them if they were persuaded by such wisdom. Paul would not adulterate God's Word to make it more palatable, and neither should we in our witnessing. *W 5/15 8, 9a*

Sunday, August 26

What is Jehovah your God asking of you but to fear Jehovah your God, so as to walk in all his ways and to love him and to serve Jehovah your God with all your heart and all your soul?—Deut. 10:12.

It was in Israel's best interests to show deep love for Jehovah God and to adhere loyally to his commands. Obedience to divine law assured them of his protection and continued blessing in every undertaking of theirs. On the other hand, disregard for divine law would result in insecurity and ruin. Similarly, persons today who have genuine love for God and who seek to follow his guidelines are pursuing a course that promotes their greatest good. Why is this? Since Jehovah is an all-wise and a loving God, he has given only such commands as would promote man's welfare. Love is the very basis for all divine laws governing human relations. Paul emphasized this point when he wrote: "Love is the law's fulfillment." (Rom. 13:8-10) Clearly, if humans everywhere would display true neighbor love, this would result in happiness, peace and security. *W 9/15 4, 5*

Monday, August 27

As in the daytime let us walk decently, not in revelries and drunken bouts, not in illicit intercourse and loose conduct, not in strife and jealousy.
—Rom. 13:13.

These are the worldly things that would creep into our Christian lives and into the congregation if we did not guard against them. In more prosperous lands, people generally attach great importance to leisure and material things. In many places, pressure is exerted on God's people to become like the world. Will we meet this challenge in the Christian spirit of self-sacrifice? If we keep awake, alert and active in God's service, then we will have no time to get tangled up with "revelries and drunken bouts," with "illicit intercourse and loose conduct." Our love for Jehovah and his service, and placing these first, will act as a protection. With our minds on spiritual matters, and on developing the fruitage of the spirit, we will be humble and understanding in our relations with our families and with our brothers. We will avoid "strife and jealousy." *W 10/1 17, 18a*

Tuesday, August 28

Discipline always seems for the time to be a thing of pain, not of joy; but those who are trained by it reap the fruit of it afterwards in the peace of an upright life.—Heb. 12:11, Moffatt.

There certainly can be no feeling of exhilarating pleasure about having to undergo painful mistreatment. The experience is a grievous one. However, if we submit to it and let it help us to see wherein we must make improvements, the trial can be good training for us. The final result of that training then will be as noted above. It may be that we have come to appreciate the good effect that such discipline can have from association with faithful Christians who may have undergone years of trial under oppressive dictators or in concentration camps and in prisons. Often, however, their integrity shines through their entire personality. A person realizes that he is in the presence of those whose faith has been molded by discipline, and the calm, joyous expression of that faith can be an inspiration to others to walk likewise in integrity. *W 10/15 8, 9a*

Wednesday, August 29

The priests of Jehovah you will be called; the ministers of our God you will be said to be.—Isa. 61:6.

Jehovah God's work of spiritual restoration and rehabilitation is the greatest public service that is being rendered to mankind today. Those whom he is using as his public servants in this work are prophetically designated as "the ministers of our God." Their Leader, Jesus Christ, in his days on earth, 19 centuries ago, performed an astounding work of rehabilitation on poor mankind. Back there the public ministry of Jesus and his apostles did not bring about the environmental restoration of the land of Palestine in which they preached the good news of God's kingdom. To work for such a thing would have been in vain in view of the destruction that was to come in 70-73 C.E. But the spiritual rehabilitation work pioneered by Jesus and carried forward by his disciples continued advancing onward through all that trialsome period and beyond, until the foretold "apostasy" set in after the death of the apostles. —2 Thess. 2:3. *W 7/1 1, 2a*

Thursday, August 30

Because you are no part of the world, but I have chosen you out of the world, on this account the world hates you. —John 15:19.

Instead of worshiping Jehovah exclusively as their covenant God, Israel was idolatrously running after the Baal images and worshiping them. (Deut. 32:32) The undesirable fruit stands in contrast with what God wants. The unchanging God does not want such kind of fruit on the "branches" of his "true vine," Jesus Christ. So the spiritual Israelites of the Kingdom class must keep themselves morally clean. They must not commit spiritual adultery by making friends with the world. Nothing less than exclusive devotion to Jehovah as God is what is absolutely required of them. What do they care if the world hates them for bearing such fruit? Their being no part of this world by keeping away from its politics and conflicts is the expression of the fruit of cleanness and stainlessness from this world. The same is required of the "great crowd" of "other sheep" associated with the Kingdom class. *W 12/15 8-10a*

Friday, August 31

How long shall I call to you for aid from violence, and you do not save? Why is it that you make me see what is hurtful, and you keep looking upon mere trouble?—Hab. 1:2, 3.

Oppression, injustice and favoritism are very common in this world. A multitude of defective things simply cannot be straightened out, and the flaws in human affairs are without number. The wisest ruler of ancient times, King Solomon, said: "That which is made crooked cannot be made straight, and that which is wanting cannot possibly be counted." (Eccl. 1:15) On account of their sense of justice, many people find it distressing to witness the seeming success of those who are dishonest and have no regard for God or for fellowmen. Like the Hebrew prophet Habakkuk, other lovers of righteousness have asked the above questions. So disturbing has it been for them to face injustice that some of God's servants have found themselves giving way to serious doubts about the value of an upright life. But scriptures such as 1 Timothy 4:8 leave no doubt about the value of godly devotion. *W 10/15 1-3*

Saturday, September 1

Ponder over these things; be absorbed in them, that your advancement may be manifest to all persons.—1 Tim. 4:15.

The wise person does not feel that he can no longer improve. "Who is wise and understanding among you? Let him show out of his fine conduct his works with a mildness [modesty] that belongs to wisdom." (Jas. 3:13) While elders may be "equal" in their responsibility and authority to serve and work on behalf of the flock, they are not necessarily equal in other respects. Some have far greater experience, both in life and in the truth, and have made advancement in wisdom as a result of years of serious study and effort. Each has his strengths along with his weaknesses. If we appreciate and benefit from the strengths of others we, too, can 'let our advancement be manifest to all.' By means of the aid given through such humble, earnest, God-fearing shepherds possessed of knowledge and insight, God's flock today will indeed "become many and certainly bear fruit in the land," all to Jehovah's praise.—Jer. 3:16. *W 12/1 15, 16*

Sunday, September 2

You must do what is right and good in Jehovah's eyes, in order that it may go well with you.—Deut. 6:18.

What is Jehovah's work for those who have dedicated themselves to do Jehovah's will, following in the footsteps of Jesus Christ? It is a twofold work that was both foretold and commanded by Jesus, even as we read at Matthew 24:14 and 28:19, 20. Yes, Christians must both preach about God's kingdom and teach people what they themselves have been taught. They should help others to do the things Jesus commanded his apostles and early disciples to do. How is Jehovah's work to be done? Is each Christian to do this work as he feels like doing it or thinks it should be done? Not at all. Rather, God's Word also commands us *how* we should do it. This principle was illustrated as far back as the days of Moses. (Deut. 12:8) The apostle Paul shows that these principles likewise apply to Christians, that they are to speak in agreement and be united in the same line of thought. (1 Cor. 1:10) Working together harmoniously is a mark of mature Christians.—Phil. 3:15, 16. *W 11/1 1-3a*

Monday, September 3

Quit being anxious about your souls as to what you will eat or about your bodies as to what you will wear. For the soul is worth more than food and the body than clothing. —Luke 12:22, 23.

While we may realize the folly of selfishly piling up wealth, we may not realize that daily cares can also distract us from being wholesouled in our service. This was the point that Jesus once made when speaking to his own disciples. Especially in times of economic hardships or increasing inflation, we do well to meditate on these words of Jesus. All the worry and anxiety in the world will not improve our situation. Physical nourishment cannot sustain our lives everlastingly, nor can it secure for us a good name with Jehovah God. Hence, if we would make food a matter of such anxious care as to neglect our service to God, we would actually be placing a higher value on physical sustenance than on our life. Undue concern about daily needs shows lack of faith in God's ability to provide. *W 11/15 11, 12*

Tuesday, September 4

Fathers, . . . go on bringing them up in the discipline and mental-regulating of Jehovah. —Eph. 6:4.

Are you a parent? Appreciate that the best time for your young ones to begin learning a course of self-sacrifice is in childhood. Give your children some useful work around the house. Get them to see that play is not all there is to life, that it involves work, sacrifice. Giving your child everything he wants might make him think that life is easy, that doing Jehovah's will is easy, and so later he might be unwilling to make sacrifices for Jehovah. As you adults already know, life is not easy, and doing Jehovah's will is not necessarily easy. So help your children to get a balanced view of life. Teach them that while there is time for recreation, there must also be time for work, for Bible study, for sacrifice. The fruitage of this discipline could well be one of the most valuable things they will inherit from you. And your own good example will be the best reinforcement of the verbal instructions that you give. *W 8/1* 17a

Wednesday, September 5

In everything and in all circumstances I have learned the secret of both how to be full and how to hunger, both how to have an abundance and how to suffer want. For all things I have the strength by virtue of him who imparts power to me.—Phil. 4:12, 13.

Those having Jehovah's name upon them can please him if they seek his aid in cultivating the fruits of the spirit. Jehovah will answer our earnest prayer for holy spirit, to aid us in cultivating and demonstrating the spirit's fruitage in life. (Luke 11:13)

Certainly, if we truly look to God for guidance and feel deeply our responsibility before him, he will strengthen us to walk in his way, even as Paul testified regarding himself. In his loving-kindness, Jehovah aids us greatly and asks relatively little. "He has told you, O earthling man, what is good. And what is Jehovah asking back from you but to exercise justice and to love kindness and to be modest in walking with your God?" In our doing so, we know God will protect us even as he has promised. —Mic. 6:8; 1 Sam. 12:22. *W 8/15* 9, 19, 20a

Thursday, September 6

Become doers of the word, and not hearers only, deceiving yourselves with false reasoning.—Jas. 1:22.

The inspired words at Micah 6:8 leave no question about the fact that action is required on the part of all who would be pleasing to Jehovah God. The same point is made by the disciple James. It simply is not enough to pray, to read the Bible, to attend Christian meetings and there listen respectfully to what is said. Our lives must demonstrate that we are exercising justice, love kindness and are modest in walking with Jehovah. Both Enoch's and Noah's blameless walking with God included zealous activity. Surely, disciples of Jesus do not want to deceive themselves into thinking that one's having a pleasing personality and engaging in public worship are sufficient for one to be approved by God. An active concern for fellow humans must be in evidence. Is that true of you? Are you willing and eager to respond to the physical and spiritual needs of others? Is your conduct as a servant of Jehovah worthy of imitation? *W 9/15* 17-19

Friday, September 7

The ministers of our God you will be said to be.—Isa. 61:6.

Here in the Hebrew text the word translated "ministers" is *m'shareth'* (in the plural number), not *'obed,* meaning "servant," as in Isaiah 65:13. This Hebrew word and other forms of the verb *sharath'* are often used in connection with the priests of Israel, as at Joel 2: 17. The translators of the *Septuagint* recognized the difference between these two Hebrew words, and so in their rendering of Isaiah 61:6 they used the Greek word *leitourgos'* for *m'shareth'.* This word means, basically, "a public worker," that is, a public officer or minister. (Rom. 13:6) It may refer to one serving in a sacred office, as when Paul speaks of himself as "a public servant of Christ." (Rom. 15:16) Christ, as God's High Priest, is called a "public servant" at Hebrews 8:1, 2. Heavenly angels are also viewed as public servants. (Heb. 1:7, 14) All considered, the word "ministers" as used at Isaiah 61:6 refers to more than one's acting as a servant or rendering sacred service. *W 7/1 19-21a*

Saturday, September 8

*But as for me, the drawing near to God is good for me. In the Sovereign Lord Jehovah I have placed my refuge, to declare all your works.
—Ps. 73:28.*

Our being in an approved standing before Jehovah should be our greatest delight. Even if our organisms and our hearts fail, Jehovah will strengthen us. He will give stability to our hearts so that we will not lose hope and courage in the face of adversity. Truly, the privilege of enjoying an intimacy with our heavenly Father and being able to serve him is a most delightful portion, a possession of priceless value. May we never let go of it, as that would spell calamity for us, along with all those who abandon God. Like Asaph, may we draw close to Jehovah, committing all our cares to him. This is good, for it will promote our happiness and well-being. Furthermore, may we relate Jehovah's wonderful works to others, thereby strengthening any who have doubts. While injustices may be disturbing, we can bear this burden successfully if we center our life around service to God. *W 10/15 16, 17*

Sunday, September 9

My kingdom is no part of this world. If my kingdom were part of this world, my attendants would have fought that I should not be delivered up to the Jews. But, as it is, my kingdom is not from this source.—John 18:36.

Wherever they may live, true Christians give their support and lives for God's kingdom. This kingdom, about which Jesus spoke, is from a heavenly source. Therefore Christians, though they respect human efforts to bring peace, devote all their strength and resources to proclaiming that kingdom and the hope it holds out. Accordingly, loyalty to Jehovah's kingdom is the most important thing in the life of Christ's true followers. In the postapostolic period the early Christians demonstrated this belief in Jesus Christ's words. They paid their taxes and obeyed the laws of the lands in which they lived. But they took a neutral position in the midst of political factions and strifes of their day even as history shows. Today Jehovah's Christian witnesses take the same stand. *W 4/15 20-22a*

Monday, September 10

Keep on, then, seeking first the kingdom and his righteousness, and all these other things will be added to you. —Matt. 6:33.

The Kingdom has freed multitudes of honest-hearted persons from slavery to Babylonish religion and its teachings, as they have obeyed the command found at Revelation 18:4. The Kingdom also helps us to keep free from the snare of materialism. How does it do this? In his famous Sermon on the Mount, Jesus referred to "the things the nations are eagerly pursuing," such as things to eat, to drink, and to wear. But are these the all-important things? No, for Jesus added the above words. Therefore, if we make it our goal to keep seeking first the Kingdom—by giving our allegiance to it and by serving its interests—our heavenly Father will see to it that we are provided with our material necessities. Moral and physical protection are other benefits that the Kingdom can bring us. Living according to the "good news" we are also protected against dissipation and dreadful venereal diseases. *W 1/15 38-40*

Tuesday, September 11

No matter what it is that we ask according to his will, he hears us.—1 John 5:14.

A single person desiring marriage may petition God for help in finding a suitable mate or in living a balanced and useful life as a single person. Married couples may pray regarding their having children, or for wisdom in rearing their children. We have the examples of Hannah, who prayed to God for a child, and of Samson's parents, who asked for advice on bringing up their son. Also, we can pray for harmony in our marriage, asking God to bless our efforts to make our marriage a success. Even a move to another location or another job may be a subject of prayer, because one's family may be economically and, along with this, spiritually affected. Such matters, though intimately personal, definitely affect our lives and require adjustments in which we need God's wisdom. God is interested and is pleased to hear us present such prayers to him. However, it is the desire to find out and to do *God's will* that is the primary factor. *W 2/1 15, 16a*

Wednesday, September 12

Stop tearing down the work of God just for the sake of food. True, all things are clean, but it is injurious to the man who with an occasion for stumbling eats. It is well not to eat flesh or to drink wine or do anything over which your brother stumbles. —Rom. 14:20, 21.

Those who come to a knowledge of the truth are the work of Jehovah God. Much time and effort has also been spent by God's servants in teaching and assisting these, with great care and tenderness. They are "God's field under cultivation, God's building." (1 Cor. 3:9) Could any Christian be so disrespectful and destructive as to tear this work down? That is why Paul admonishes us as above. In leading another to take a course contrary to his conscience, we may tear down all the good work that Jehovah God's spirit has accomplished with that person, even though we ourselves do not realize the damage we are doing. Yes, if we do not progress in these matters, we can be a constant source of harm. *W 3/15 12, 6a*

Thursday, September 13

Let no man deprive you of the prize who takes delight in a mock humility . . . whereas he is not holding fast to the head.—Col. 2:18, 19.

Today Jehovah God's servants do not face precisely the same situations that prevailed in the first century. Nevertheless, there are vital lessons for us to draw from what Paul wrote the Colossians. For example, all Christians, especially the elders, must exercise care not to put any unscriptural personal viewpoints and philosophies on an equal footing with the truth revealed in the teachings and example of Jesus Christ. Whatever spiritual counsel or advice that a Christian may give to others should be based, not on personal preference, prejudice or on worldly principles, but on the example and teachings of Jesus Christ. Since everything he taught harmonized fully with Jehovah God's Word, the Bible can and should rightly be used for giving spiritual help. A person's failure to stick to the Scriptures would constitute a disregard for the Head of the congregation. —2 Tim. 4:1, 2. *W 4/1* 18, 19

Friday, September 14

If any man is reaching out for an office of overseer, he is desirous of a fine work. —1 Tim. 3:1.

In reality, in most cases a man who is recommended to serve as a congregation elder should be one whom the congregation members have already come to view as an 'older brother,' in the sense that he has already gained their esteem and confidence as one showing insight, balance and judgment. No one can actually "make" someone an elder, but he himself must *become* such through spiritual growth, development and ex-perience. When such a man is selected to serve in this capacity, his appointment is, in actuality, an acknowledgment and recognition of the desirable qualities of an elder that he already manifests. No man should think that this means that he can, simply by working at a certain assignment, "earn" the right to serve as an elder within God's congregation. What he can truly earn is the respect and appreciation of his brothers for his diligent and faithful service, as well as gaining a confidence toward Jehovah God. *W 12/1* 7, 8

Saturday, September 15

In the last days critical times hard to deal with will be here. For men will be . . . lovers of pleasures rather than lovers of God, having a form of godly devotion but proving false to its power.—2 Tim. 3:1, 2, 4, 5.

To keep seeking first God's kingdom and his righteousness we must watch the time we devote to leisure. (Matt. 6: 33) We all need recreation, but how much? Does it come first in our lives? Do we intensely pursue our favorite form of recreation so much that our spiritual interests suffer? Or, do we first take care of our spiritual needs and then, as time affords, engage in some recreation? Often it is a case of choosing, for usually it is not this AND that, but this OR that. Do we give God's work of spreading the "good news" the "cream," so to speak, of our lives and the other things the "skim milk"? Or, do we thoughtlessly give pleasure the "cream" of our time, energies and means, and give God's work the "skim milk"? Are we laying ourselves open to the charge of being "lovers of pleasures rather than lovers of God"? *W 11/1* 6a

Sunday, September 16

Keep ready, because at an hour that you do not think likely the Son of man is coming.—Luke 12:40.

A reason for devoted servants of Jesus Christ not to loiter in doing Jehovah's work is highlighted in the illustration recorded at Luke 12:35-40. Just as we do not know when our life might end, we do not know precisely the time when Jesus Christ will arrive for executing judgment, though we *do* know that the event is drawing ever nearer. This means that each day should find us in a state of readiness, awaiting our Master's return. In the parable, the slaves are doing just that. Over 1,900 years have passed since Jesus gave this illustration. To many, it may seem as though the second watch has already passed and that we are well along in the third watch. But are some of us getting tired? Or, are we still girded firmly for activity? Are we letting our lights shine through fine conduct and zealous witnessing as we keep ourselves fueled by yielding to the operation of Jehovah God's spirit?—Matt. 5:14-16. *W 11/15 12-14a*

Monday, September 17

The fruitage of the spirit is . . . long-suffering.—Gal. 5:22.

Long-suffering does not mean merely "suffering long." It involves slowness to anger and is the patient endurance of provocation or wrong, linked with the refusal to abandon hope for improvement in a disturbed relationship. Jehovah is "slow to anger." (Ex. 34:6) His patience allows persons time to repent and escape destruction. (2 Pet. 3:8-18) While God is exercising long-suffering, he is gathering "a people for his name," and, through them, is magnifying himself earth wide. (Acts 15: 14; Rom. 9:22-24) Jehovah's name-people strive to "be long-suffering toward all." (1 Thess. 5:14) Long-suffering not only promotes good relations with fellow believers; this fine quality also enables us patiently to help others to learn about Jehovah God, with a view to their doing his will and gaining everlasting life. (1 Tim. 4:16; Heb. 6:11-15) Also, by walking worthily of Jehovah God in this way, we have the satisfaction of pleasing him now, with eternal blessings as our prospect. *W 8/15 13a*

Tuesday, September 18

Those who did good things [will come out] to a resurrection of life, those who practiced vile things [will come out] to a resurrection of judgment.—John 5:29.

By the word "life" in this context, Jesus did not mean the measure of life that persons have on coming out of the memorial tombs. Otherwise, not only would the doers of good things have "a resurrection of life," but the practicers of vile things would likewise have such a resurrection, forasmuch as they also would have to start off by being made alive on earth. So, "life" as used in John 5:29 means perfection of life as attained by some at the end of Christ's reign through their doing good things in obedience to his kingdom and judgeship. Similarly, "judgment" represents what results to other persons either during or by the close of the millennial judgment "day." It means the opposite of "life." Hence, it means a condemnatory judgment, a sentencing of the practicers of vile things to eternal destruction. This is a destruction of soul and body in Gehenna. *W 9/1 10, 11a*

Wednesday, September 19

[Love] bears all things, believes all things.—1 Cor. 13:7.

Besides being a surpassing way, the way of love will never end or be lacking, even as can be seen from 1 Corinthians 13:8. In the sense of 'bearing all things,' true love is not quickly thrust aside, dampened or abandoned. It is not overly sensitive nor does it quickly conclude that there is no hope of seeing any improvement in others. If we are loving, we will continue to do good toward our fellowmen despite their lack of gratitude. The fact that 'love believes all things' certainly does not mean that we will be gullible, failing to discern what is truly bad. Rather, it means that love is not suspicious. Hence, even though our brothers might do and say things that hurt us, we will not immediately conclude that they wanted to injure us. When observing the conduct of others, we will not at once think the worst but strive to view it in the best light possible. We will give our Christian brothers the benefit of the doubt, not imputing evil motives to them. *W 9/15* 15-17a

Thursday, September 20

*Keep on the watch and pray continually, that you may not enter into temptation.
—Matt. 26:41.*

What was the occasion when Jesus spoke those words? It was at the time of the greatest crisis in his life on earth —on the eve of his betrayal, arrest, trial and execution. That day would prove to be the most important in human history. The events about to take place would lead to the salvation of all mankind. However, what were Jesus' apostles doing? They knew it was a very serious occasion. Yet, as he prayed, they fell asleep! Three times he found them slumbering. (Matt. 26:36-47) Today we stand on the threshold of another major event in the history of mankind—the "great tribulation," which will reach its climax in the war at Har-Magedon. It is the time of all times to stay awake! Yet the very prophecy that describes that oncoming war warns of persons who *may not* stay awake. It is Jesus Christ himself who gives the warning: "Look! I am coming as a thief. Happy is the one that stays awake."—Rev. 16:15, 16. *W 10/1* 1-3a

Friday, September 21

*James, a slave of God and of the Lord Jesus Christ, to the twelve tribes that are scattered about: Greetings!
—Jas. 1:1.*

Thus James begins his letter in a modest manner, not alluding to his family relationship to Jesus Christ, as his half brother. Those whom he addresses are not the 12 tribes of natural Israel. The content of the letter reveals this. James would not have written as he did if his readers were merely fleshly Jews. Moreover, this manner of address was common among Christians, particularly those of actual Jewish descent, as James was. Paul calls the Christian congregation "the Israel of God." (Gal. 6:16) By that time Christians were scattered into every part of the Roman Empire. The apostle Paul's exertions in the western part of the civilized world and Peter's efforts in the area of Babylon to the east contributed much toward the increase enjoyed by Christians. Most fittingly, James' letter is full of meaning to spiritual Israelites today as well as to their "alien resident" companions. *W 7/15* 5a

Saturday, September 22

So keep strict watch that how you walk is not as unwise but as wise persons, buying out the opportune time for yourselves, because the days are wicked. On this account . . . go on perceiving what the will of Jehovah is.—Eph. 5:15-17.

Do you have the spirit of self-sacrifice? Or, do you tend to be self-indulgent? Are you serving Jehovah as well as your circumstances allow? Why not examine yourself to see if your Christian service to God could be improved? Could you, for instance, devote more of your time to personal Bible reading? If you have a family, do you have regular Bible discussions with them? Could you take more time to call on people to tell them about the "good news"? Or, could you devote some time to assist the sick, the elderly, or others by performing Christian acts of kindness? Perhaps you could compare the amount of time you spend on, say, recreation, such as watching television, with the time you spend in serving Jehovah God in one sphere of his activity or another. Is it balanced? *W 8/1* 15, 16a

Sunday, September 23

If you publicly declare . . . that Jesus is Lord, and exercise faith in your heart that God raised him up from the dead, you will be saved. For with the heart one exercises faith for righteousness, but with the mouth one makes public declaration for salvation.—Rom. 10:9, 10.

Accepting Jesus and walking in his footsteps involves more than just acknowledging and accepting the Messiah in one's heart. There must be a confirming and disclosing of this by public action. There must be a personal taking part in the fulfillment of Jesus'

prophecy: "This good news of the kingdom will be preached in all the inhabited earth for a witness to all the nations." (Matt. 24:14) If a dedicated, baptized, spirit-anointed "branch" in the Christ "vine" is not taking an active part in that foretold work, how could he be producing the "fruits" of the kingdom of God? (Matt. 21:43) The obligatory feature in this regard is that they are "branches" in the one who was the first to be anointed with the spirit of Jehovah to preach the good news of the Kingdom.—Isa. 61:1-3. *W 12/15* 11a

Monday, September 24

And now, my daughter, do not be afraid. All that you say I shall do for you, for everyone in the gate of my people is aware that you are an excellent woman.—Ruth 3:11.

Ruth had uncovered slumbering Boaz at his feet and lain down there fully clad. By this symbolical act Ruth made Boaz aware of his obligation as a repurchaser, a kinsman of her late husband Mahlon and of his deceased father Elimelech. Her mother-in-law, Naomi, had been certain that this venture would be successful, and Ruth was confident that Boaz would deal with her in an honorable manner. And that he did, blessing and commending her. (Ruth 3:10) Ruth had not loudly proclaimed her virtues, and surely it was not wealth, hairstyle and expensive garb that caused others to admire her. Rather, the young woman's fear of Jehovah God, her good works, her quiet, mild spirit, her loyal love, her industriousness—acts and traits like these had caused people to view her as "an excellent woman." Is there any godly woman alive who would not desire such a fine reputation? *W 2/15* 8, 9a

Tuesday, September 25

I shall exult in Jehovah. My soul will be joyful in my God. For he has clothed me with the garments of salvation. —Isa. 61:10.

There is inexpressible joy in one's being liberated from captivity and imprisonment in Babylon the Great. There is reason for one to exult in being restored to the favor and goodwill of the God of true religion. As the anointed remnant contemplate their deliverance and restoration by Him, they overflow with joyfulness. From the postwar year of 1919 onward Jehovah has wrought salvation for the remnant by liberating them from Babylon and her worldly paramours. In spite of all the religious persecution experienced since then, the remnant still finds itself clothed with "the garments of salvation." The remnant is determined to keep on wearing these identifying garments down till Babylon and her immoral paramours are destroyed in the coming tribulation. For doing this they will never be driven out and exiled from the spiritual paradise into which Jehovah God has brought them since 1919. *W 7/1* 1, 2b

Wednesday, September 26

How they have reached their end, have been brought to their finish through sudden terrors! Like a dream after awaking, O Jehovah, so when arousing yourself you will despise their very image. —Ps. 73:19, 20.

Asaph recognized that his viewing service to Jehovah God as vain would actually mean his being disloyal to the faithful ones. Then, too, his giving way to public expression of doubt could have undermined the faith of some. Though he tried to straighten out his thinking, Asaph simply could not reconcile how the wicked could get by with their wrongdoing, while the righteous were suffering. What did he do to readjust his thinking? Asaph went to the sanctuary. There among the assembled worshipers, he came to appreciate just what was in store for the wicked. (Ps. 73:17) Similarly, if you find yourself disturbed by what you see, seek to find the answers from those who are trying to be wholehearted in their service to Jehovah God. What Asaph came to appreciate is found in verses 18 to 20 of Psalm 73. *W 10/15* 7, 8

Thursday, September 27

Always rejoice in the Lord. Once more I will say, Rejoice! Let your reasonableness become known to all men. The Lord is near. —Phil. 4:4, 5.

An important aspect of doing Jehovah's work in his way is that we do it joyfully. Even as an unhappy housewife reflects unfavorably on her husband, so would our serving Jehovah without joy reflect on him. Most fittingly, the apostle Paul commands us to rejoice. And how many reasons we have today to be joyful! The truth has indeed set us free (John 8:32); we have forgiveness of sins (Acts 13:38); we have fine association with one another (Rom. 1:11, 12); we experience the greater happiness that comes from giving (Acts 20:35); we are enjoying the blessings of a spiritual paradise (2 Cor. 12:4); and by keeping integrity we know that we make even the heart of our great God Jehovah glad. (Prov. 27:11) Moreover, doing Jehovah's work in his way also means striving to do it peaceably, calling to mind Psalm 133:1: "Look! How good and how pleasant it is for brothers to dwell together in unity!" *W 11/1* 12, 11a

Friday, September 28

I solemnly charge you before God and Christ Jesus, who is destined to judge the living and the dead.—2 Tim. 4:1.

By the expression "the dead," Paul refers to "those in the memorial tombs." (John 5:28) But who are the ones whom Paul calls "the living"? They will be those on earth who have survived the coming "great tribulation" and the binding of Satan the Devil and his demons. These will therefore be still alive on earth when the 1,000-year reign of Christ Jesus over his earthly realm begins. The ones who then become his subjects with the hope of everlasting life in an earthly paradise are the ones particularly meant. Some of the anointed remnant of prospective joint heirs of Christ will also have survived, but whether they will start judging on earth before they are transferred to the heavenly kingdom remains to be seen. However, a "great crowd" of Christ's "other sheep" will survive the "great tribulation," along with the remnant, and will enter the millennium alive. Revelation 7:9-17 proves this to be true. *W 9/1* 15, 16a

Saturday, September 29

The wisdom from above is . . . full of mercy and good fruits, not making partial distinctions.—Jas. 3:17.

A person who has heavenly wisdom has a willingness to respond to proper requests. He will yield to what the Scriptures say, not taking a position and holding to it, right or wrong. He will be quick to change when there is clear evidence that he has taken a wrong stand or has drawn erroneous conclusions. Such a one is also "full of mercy and good fruits." In dealing with others, he is compassionate. He has pity for the afflicted and distressed, and is eager and willing to do what he can to aid them. The "good fruits" include all actions that are in harmony with goodness, righteousness and truth. (Eph. 5: 9) The person who is guided by heavenly wisdom does not make "partial distinctions." He does not give preferential treatment to individuals based on their outward appearance, position, wealth, status in life or their influence in the congregation. In his dealings with his fellowmen, he strives at all times to be impartial. *W 12/1* 18, 19a

Sunday, September 30

My Father is glorified in this, that you keep bearing much fruit and prove yourselves my disciples.—John 15:8.

The bearing of the fruit of obedience to the command to preach this good news of the Kingdom has resulted in glorifying Jehovah God. It is just as Jesus said for the encouragement of his "branches." In this time for the final fulfillment of Matthew 24:14, has the remnant of such "branches" borne "much fruit"? If we check up on the records that are available for the period from the postwar year of 1919, we must say Yes! By such "fruit" production Jehovah God has been glorified. Unbreakable union of the "branches" with the Christ "vine" has been necessary for the producing of so much fruit during these turbulent times since the outbreak of World War I in 1914. To the remnant of productive "branches" the words of Jesus, as found at John 15: 4-6, have certainly applied. Loyally they have hailed the glorified Jesus Christ as God's enthroned Messianic King. To assist them to get this work done, Jehovah has provided a "great crowd" of "other sheep." *W 12/15* 13-15a

Monday, October 1

The inclination of the heart of man is bad from his youth up.—Gen. 8:21.

Many in the Corinthian congregation were glorifying ambitious men. Also, some were giving undue importance to Paul and Apollos. But Paul used himself, Apollos and Cephas as illustrations, so as to show how improper it is to look to *any* man or men. (1 Cor. 4:6; 3:5-7) Paul then pointed out that they might have been working hard to build on the right foundation, which is Jesus Christ. Nonetheless, if they failed to build properly—and so were not relying on Jehovah God to bring success—they would find, to their shame, that they had built things of no value, things that would not endure Jehovah God's test. (1 Cor. 3:10-15) The reason why we have to be very watchful of ourselves is that it is the human inclination to rely on oneself, to take credit to oneself and to act independently. That is why Jehovah God said what he did shortly after the flood of Noah's day. This inclination we have all inherited from Adam, who took an independent course. *W 5/1* 5-7a

Tuesday, October 2

Raise your eyes high up and see. Who has created these things? . . . Due to the abundance of dynamic energy, he also being vigorous in power, not one of them is missing. —Isa. 40:26.

Jehovah's spirit is dynamic in operation. Referring to himself as the Creator of all that we see when we raise our eyes heavenward, he says the above. The apostle Paul also tells of that one mighty sweep of Jehovah's power 'when he raised Christ up from the dead.' (Eph. 1:19-21) Coming down to our day, by the early summer of 1918 the political "wild beast" dealt a death-blow to the anointed remnant, bringing an end to their organized witnessing, at which time their leading members were sent off to prison for 20-year terms. In the eyes of their enemies they appeared as unburied corpses. Then what? After a short symbolic "three and a half days," *"spirit of life* from God entered into them, and they stood upon their feet." (Rev. 11:7-11) God's holy spirit or active force is with Jehovah's truly dedicated people at all times. *W 6/1* 10-12a

Wednesday, October 3

If any one of you is lacking in wisdom, let him keep on asking God, for he gives generously to all and without reproaching.—Jas. 1:5.

The wisdom we pray for will be given us in one or more of three ways: (1) Certain scriptures that provide the answer that we need will be called to our attention, either through our own study or through our brothers. (2) Circumstances and events as maneuvered through God's providence will enable us to see clearly what to do. Certain obstacles will be removed from our path. (3) God's holy angels may direct our spirit in the right course. And *God gives generously,* that is, with a wholehearted spirit, more than one asks for. (Eph. 3:20; 1 John 5:14, 15) He does this without reproaching. God never says, 'What a foolish request!' Nor does he make one feel inferior. He does not reproach you for your past conduct, as humans are prone to do. He deeply appreciates the person who has the faith and enough concern to pray repeatedly for a certain thing. *W 7/15* 10, 11a

Thursday, October 4

When you see Jerusalem surrounded by encamped armies . . . Then let those in Judea begin fleeing to the mountains.
—Luke 21:20, 21.

In the first century of our Common Era, many ordinary men and women sacrificed some of their own interests for the sake of Jehovah's interests. Yes, they worked hard and underwent difficulties, but their contentment was great in knowing that they were doing the right thing and pleasing God. Also, they had the confidence that Jehovah would remember their faith and works in his behalf and would surely give them a fine reward in the future. And what about those who were too self-indulgent, who wanted to preserve their "normal" way of life? (John 11:48) In that very generation their way of life ended anyhow. Roman armies devastated the land, with enormous loss of life and property. But self-sacrificing Christians heeded Jesus' teachings, fled the area and preserved their lives. They are counted as truly happy. We also will be truly happy if we follow Jesus' teachings and heed his warnings. *W 8/1* 10a

Friday, October 5

The fruitage of the spirit is . . . kindness, goodness.
—Gal. 5:22.

Kindness involves being actively interested in the welfare of others. Jehovah is even "kind toward the unthankful and wicked." (Luke 6:35) Accordingly we are to clothe ourselves with kindness, to "become kind to one another, tenderly compassionate, freely forgiving one another" as God by Christ forgave us. (Eph. 4:32; 5:1) Kindness begets kindness, and it has attractive force. So, it benefits the one showing it, the one receiving it and the one drawn to God's people because of seeing kindness at work among them. *Goodness,* another fruit of the spirit, denotes moral excellence or virtue. "Good and upright is Jehovah." (Ps. 25:8) As an aid in developing goodness, we do well to ask God prayerfully to teach us goodness. (Ps. 119:66) Goodness is developed by obeying God's commands. There is satisfaction in knowing that one is imitating God by practicing goodness toward fellow believers and all others. Such goodness may draw persons to true Christianity. *W 8/15* 14, 15a

Saturday, October 6

What is Jehovah asking back from you but to exercise justice?—Mic. 6:8.

Because Jehovah God "is a lover of righteousness and justice," he required that the Israelites imitate him in this respect. (Ps. 33:5) His law ruled out bribery and demanded that justice be administered impartially to the rich and the poor. Truly, Israel's responding to the urging to "exercise justice" would have improved conditions in the days of Micah. Oppression would have been kept in check. Law and order would have been restored, leading to peace, security and stability. Christians, too, are under command to "exercise justice." Elders may need to determine whether a particular Christian brother qualifies to serve as a ministerial servant or as an elder. Only by sticking loyally to God's Word and relying on the guidance of his spirit can they handle this matter impartially. Also, they may be called on to arrive at decisions concerning fellow believers who commit serious sins. How important is justice in such cases!—1 Cor. 6:1-6; 1 Tim. 5:20-22. *W 9/15* 7, 8

Sunday, October 7

Let your love be without hypocrisy.—Rom. 12:9.

All service rendered with an ulterior motive is in vain. (1 Cor. 13:1-3) Most fittingly, therefore, Paul counsels us: "Let all your affairs take place with love." (1 Cor. 16:14) But does he let it go at that? No, appreciating how treacherous our fallen hearts are, he commands as above. How easy it is to make expressions of love that do not really stem from a rightly motivated heart! That is why Paul made it a point to recommend himself as one of God's ministers by his "love free from hypocrisy." (2 Cor. 6:6) Our love needs to be "love out of a clean heart," and as Peter expresses it, ours must be an "unhypocritical brotherly love." (1 Tim. 1:5; 1 Pet. 1:22) Yes, doing Jehovah's work in Jehovah's way not only means giving it first place in our lives, doing it wisely, peacefully, joyously and with clean hands but also requires of us that we serve God with a pure heart. Doing so, we can have much joy now and win His approval and endless life in the coming new system of things. *W 11/1* 18-20a

Monday, October 8

Give orders to those who are rich . . . to be liberal, ready to share, safely treasuring up for themselves a fine foundation for the future. —1 Tim. 6:17-19.

All of us, by keeping active in helping persons in spiritual and physical need, lay up treasure in heaven that will yield rich dividends in the form of rewards from Jehovah God. A record of fine works with God is indestructible. Surely, then, while still living, we should want to do our utmost to guard against letting material possessions, daily cares or pleasures interfere with our making a fine record with God. Particularly since life is of uncertain duration, it is urgent that we do not get sidetracked from our main objective—remaining approved servants of Jehovah and loyal disciples of our Master Jesus Christ. How sad it would be for a person to be overtaken by death without his having made good use of his opportunities to store up treasure in heaven! Therefore, it is very important that we fix our hearts on efforts to increase our treasure in heaven. *W 11/15* 5-7a

Tuesday, October 9

Looking to Jesus the pioneer and perfecter of our faith, who for the joy that was set before him endured the cross, despising the shame, and is seated at the right hand of . . . God. —Heb. 12:2, Revised Standard Version.

In writing to the remnant of Hebrews who became spiritual sons of God, Paul also had said that God made "the pioneer of their salvation perfect through suffering." (Heb. 2:10, *RS*) Jesus is thus declared to be a "pioneer" for his disciples, the pioneer of life, the pioneer of salvation, the pioneer of our faith. He brought to reality hundreds of prophecies concerning the Messiah. In this way he introduced a new and essential element into our faith toward Jehovah God. So he became the pioneer of the rounded-out faith that true Christians now have. Correctly, then, he is called "the pioneer . . . of our faith." At the same time, our faith regarding Jehovah's Messiah finds its perfecting or finale in Jesus Christ. The Jews who rejected Jesus Christ and who kept holding fast to Mosaic law had their faith left incomplete. *W 7/1* 18, 20

Wednesday, October 10

"He that feeds on this bread will live forever." These things he said as he was teaching in public assembly at Capernaum.—John 6:58, 59.

Here the expression "in public assembly" is, literally in the original Greek text, "in synagogue." It is the same expression that Jesus used in John 18:20. So Jesus was addressing a Jewish audience who were in the Mosaic Law covenant. This included many disciples of Jesus. We can imagine the impact of Jesus' words when he spoke, not only of feeding on his flesh, but also of drinking his blood. "Therefore many of his disciples, when they heard this, said: 'This speech is shocking; who can listen to it?'" (John 6:60) This statement shows that not all of Jesus' disciples were shocked by his speech. Besides the shocked ones, there were more "disciples," including the 12 apostles. (John 6:61-67) Thus Jesus' words in John 6:53, 54 were directed in large part to his disciples and, by extension, to those who would become his disciples before the "last day." These became spiritual Israelites.—Rom. 2:28, 29. *W 9/1* 17b

Thursday, October 11

The wisdom from above is first of all chaste, then peaceable, reasonable, ready to obey.—Jas. 3:17.

For a person to qualify as a teacher of his fellow believers he must be free from the traits associated with the earthly, soulical and demonic wisdom. (Jas. 3:15) His life should reveal that he is governed by heavenly wisdom. Consider what this means. Those who qualify to serve as teachers are said to be "chaste," pure or undefiled in mind and heart. In being "peaceable," they are persons who promote peace. Not only do they avoid being aggressive or belligerent, but they go out of their way to establish good relations with and between others. They do not engage in or approve of anything that disrupts peace. The "reasonable" man is yielding, moderate or forbearing, not fanatical in his zeal. He will not insist on his own way or the letter of the law but will look at a matter humanely, with due consideration. Instead of being stubborn, the possessor of heavenly wisdom is "ready to obey." He has the spirit of cooperation. *W 12/1* 16-18a

Friday, October 12

I saw, and, look! a pale horse; and the one seated upon it had the name Death. And Hades was closely following him.—Rev. 6:8.

Here is the last of the riders, and a gruesome one, for he brings devastating sickness to the earth. He got away to a head start following World War I when he killed some 20 million people with the Spanish flu in 1918-1919. Now the intake of pills and other remedies is skyrocketing, but increasing heart attacks, strokes, cancer, VD and countless other afflictions keep bringing many into the clutches of Hades, the common grave of all mankind. As illness-prone humans, Jehovah's people have suffered, too, from the deadly ride of the pale horse. But they know the reason for their physical sicknesses, and are equipped to endure cheerfully in the knowledge that Jesus Christ's ransom will result soon in the removal of all such epidemics —even the horseman Death himself. Although they may fall victim to Hades (the grave), their resurrection into a righteous new order is assured.—John 5:28, 29. *W 10/1* 13a

Saturday, October 13

This good news of the kingdom will be preached in all the inhabited earth for a witness.—Matt. 24:14.

This prophecy had a partial fulfillment in the first century C.E., from the time of Jesus' ascension to heaven and appearance in God's presence to the year 70 C.E., when the Romans destroyed Jerusalem. But that fulfillment prefigured the full-scale fulfillment of the prophecy down here from 1914 onward. At the end of the Gentile Times in autumn of that year, God's Messianic kingdom was born up in the heavens. Today, more than 19 centuries after the Christ "vine" began growing its "branches," there is only a small remnant of those "branches" still alive and producing the "fruits" of the kingdom of God, inasmuch as there are to be at most 144,000 of such "branches" as joint heirs with Jesus Christ. Upon this remnant the responsibility devolves to get the Kingdom good news preached earth wide for all nations to hear. Helping them to get this work done is the privilege of all who have an earthly hope. —Rev. 7:9-14. *W 12/15 12a*

Sunday, October 14

Although he has caused grief, he will also certainly show mercy according to the abundance of his loving-kindness. For not out of his own heart has he afflicted or does he grieve the sons of men. —Lam. 3:32, 33.

Because Jehovah's faithfulness is abundant, we can rely on his mercy. The expressions of divine compassion toward us will never be ineffectual. Jehovah's mercies are "new each morning," at all times available in full strength to his loyal servants. (Lam. 3: 22, 23) For this reason, we can be certain that the Almighty sees our distresses and that he will compassionately give us the needed help. However, if he permits a yoke of discipline to be placed upon us, we should accept it uncomplainingly and not broadcast our troubles. (Lam. 3:28, 29) Meanwhile we can take comfort in the fact that the trial is but temporary and that Jehovah God finds no pleasure in our having to undergo distress. Rather, it is Jehovah's purpose that the training we get through suffering will secure our eternal welfare. *W 10/15 16-18a*

Monday, October 15

This is what Jehovah has said, "Look! I am sending you away from off the surface of the ground. This year you yourself must die, for you have spoken outright revolt against Jehovah."—Jer. 28:16.

How like Hananiah are those modern-day false prophets who try to tear down the work of Jehovah's Witnesses with evil intent! Some of these may even have walked with God's people for a time, but they became disgruntled. They preach "through envy and rivalry," certainly not "through goodwill," for they have nothing upbuilding to say. (Phil. 1:15) They hold forth expectations contrary to those of the Jeremiah class with respect to the coming of the "great tribulation." However, just as surely as Jehovah replaced the broken wooden yoke with a yoke of iron, so the "great tribulation" is certain to come at God's appointed time. And just as surely as Hananiah died under Jehovah's judgment in that same year, so these opposing prophetic groups must be executed in due time. They are without joy and do not have Jehovah's spirit to sustain them. *W 1/1 12, 13a*

Tuesday, October 16

I, Jehovah, am your God, the One teaching you to benefit yourself, the One causing you to tread in the way in which you should walk.—Isa. 48:17.

Jehovah's righteous judgments are certain of execution, and his salvation is sure. Now a great crowd recognize Jesus Christ as their King. He has shown them how to live clean lives and how to be joyful workers in the interests of his Father's kingdom. He has led them into a most precious relationship with his Father, who says the above to them. Through his prophetic Word Jehovah shows us how we may walk safely during these days just preceding the "great tribulation." There is an urgent need for all who seek God to flee out of today's wicked system of things, and to stay out of it! Though we cannot get out of it bodily, we can show our separateness by avoiding its selfish, materialistic ways of life. This is vital to our survival. Jesus warns us: "Pay attention to yourselves that your hearts never become weighed down with overeating and heavy drinking and anxieties of life." —Luke 21:34. *W 1/15 46-48*

Wednesday, October 17

The intimacy with Jehovah belongs to those fearful of him.—Ps. 25:14.

The person who prays and acts with faith in God can be assured that he will be guided so as to take the most beneficial course. He will really come to *know* God, even as He promises. God's dealings with him will be a reality, and he will discern that he is 'walking with God,' being sustained, guided and loved by God. The fear of God mentioned in the psalm is not a morbid dread, but a wholesome fear. If you love God

you will want to take your problems to him, and you will have no fear of being rebuffed or rejected. Of such inhibiting fear, the apostle John wrote: "Perfect love throws fear outside." (1 John 4:18) You should never be fearful or hesitant to take to Jehovah the most intimate matters, whatever they are, including your sins. He will not view your problem as foolish or laugh at you as humans may do. Furthermore, it is entirely proper, and not selfish, to look for God, not only to hear our prayers, but also to reward us for our faithfulness to him. *W 2/1 19-21a*

Thursday, October 18

In this way you also, when you see these things occurring, know that the kingdom of God is near.—Luke 21:31.

The 1,000-year reign of Jesus Christ with his 144,000 joint heirs did not begin in 1914 at the inauguration of the "kingdom of the world . . . the kingdom of our Lord and of his Christ." What *did* begin there for Jesus Christ was his official, royal "presence," or parousia, about which his apostles had asked, according to Matthew 24:3. His "presence" in Kingdom power did not start when God used him to pour out holy spirit at Pentecost of 33 C.E. Only since the Gentile Times ended in 1914 has the foretold "sign" become visible to prove that the Son of God is invisibly present in Kingdom power, in the "kingdom of the world." This kingdom is assigned to destroy the present wicked system of things. By carrying out this assigned work, this kingdom will deliver the faithful disciples of Christ yet on earth from further oppression by the Gentile nations. That is why Jesus gave his disciples the promise recorded at Luke 21:28. *W 3/1 8, 9b*

Friday, October 19

The faith that you have, have it in accord with yourself in the sight of God.—Rom. 14:22.

The faith here mentioned has reference to the subject Paul was discussing in this chapter. Obviously, it does not mean faith in the kingdom of Jehovah God and the important things in connection with it. (Matt. 28:19, 20) Paul refers to the faith that a Christian has that Christ's sacrifice has freed us from former restrictions, such as eating certain foods and observing certain days—things that are not the real elements of the kingdom of Jehovah God, but are now simply matters of personal preference or opinion. So the counsel is, 'Do not force your opinion on others.' If you know that there is a question in the minds of some as to the rightness of a certain thing that you know is not wrong, you should not seek to overpower them, or make a display of your own "freedom." God would then respect your considerate attitude. He would understand why you held back from exercising what really is a Christian right. *W 3/15 13a*

Saturday, October 20

I have not held back from telling you all the counsel of God.—Acts 20:27.

Paul had not withheld from the elders in Ephesus anything that was necessary for salvation. It had not been his desire to gain popularity by tickling ears or by avoiding subjects that forcefully exposed wrong attitudes, words and actions. In harmony with this example, a man who qualifies as a teacher in the Christian congregation must understand everything that is essential for salvation so that his teaching will not be seriously defective. He must also be willing to impart "all the counsel of God" regardless of the congregation's attitude. There may be times when the congregation responds well to the reproof and correction provided in God's Word. But there may also be times when many do not really want to change their wrong attitudes and ways. The Christian teacher, however, must continue to stick faithfully to God's Word in providing spiritual help. If some are wrongly inclined, he must restrain himself from becoming impatient and keep on declaring the truth. *W 12/1 2, 3a*

Sunday, October 21

Keep strict watch that how you walk is not as unwise but as wise persons, buying out the opportune time for yourselves. —Eph. 5:15, 16.

Our love for God and Christ should move us to make good use of our time. Would we be doing this if pleasures became so important as to suggest that we could not live without them? Obviously not! We should never lose sight of the fact that, for many centuries, millions upon millions of people lived without radio, television, movies, cars, sports activities, extensive pleasure trips and the like. Reasonably, then, is it not wise to let such things occupy a secondary place in our lives? Hence, if we find ourselves spending more time in the pursuit of pleasure than in matters directly related to true worship, may it not be that we have become "lovers of pleasures"? (2 Tim. 3:4) And do we not stand in danger of becoming totally unfruitful in bringing praise to God's name? (Luke 8:14) Of course, devoted servants of Jehovah God may rightly enjoy various forms of wholesome relaxation or recreation. *W 11/15 8, 9a*

Monday, October 22

Keep peace between one another.—Mark 9:50.

Well did Jesus so counsel, for, after all, is not Jehovah the "God of peace," and his Son the "Prince of Peace"? (Phil. 4:9; Isa. 9:6) And did not Jesus pronounce happy the peaceable, that is, the peacemakers? (Matt. 5:9) This means that we should be concerned and put forth efforts to have peace among ourselves. Why does working together peaceably sometimes present a problem? One reason doubtless is that we all have different personalities. So should we not be willing to make allowances for different ways of thinking and acting, being loving rather than critical? Another reason why keeping the peace at times presents a problem is that we have a strong desire to see God's work done in the best possible manner, and we naturally think our way is the best. Sometimes that may be so, but often there is more than one acceptable way to do something. When this is so, it is far more important that we work peaceably together than that something be done in absolutely the most efficient manner. *W 11/1 9, 10a*

Tuesday, October 23

[Love] . . . hopes all things, endures all things. —1 Cor. 13:7.

Love hopes that things will turn out well. So, true love is not negative. Rather, it looks for, yes, prays for the best outcome. Love is optimistic. Therefore, when calling on people in unresponsive territory, we can do so with the hope that, in time, some will turn to the truth. Also, a believing mate rightly hopes that the unbeliever will eventually accept the "good news." (1 Pet. 3:1, 2) While love helps us to hope for the best, it also enables us to endure all kinds of persecutions, trials, abuse and misrepresentation. In any given situation, our being loving will always help. We will never regret that we did the loving thing. Never has love, true self-sacrificing love, made a bad circumstance worse. Do we not have good reason, then, to imitate our heavenly Father whose dominant quality is love, even as the apostle John shows at 1 John 4:7, 8? Not just in this system of things, but for all eternity, love will continue to be the surpassing way. *W 9/15 18-20a*

Wednesday, October 24

Keep testing whether you are in the faith, keep proving what you yourselves are. —2 Cor. 13:5.

These words of Paul are particularly applicable to all of us in these critical times. Do we truly value our dedication to Jehovah—the very intimate relationship we have with him, and which has been made possible by Jesus' sacrifice? Do we appreciate our unity with the Father and the Son in the grand work that we are privileged to share in at this hour? Are we serving out of genuine love for Jehovah and for our neighbor? If we are of the "great crowd," will we continue serving God "day and night" right through to the "great tribulation"? Time is fast running out. We need to keep alive, alert, constantly moving forward with God's organization. What a joy we have in being part of the only worldwide brotherhood that is at peace, and at unity in praising Jehovah's name in these critical times! As Paul counseled: "Brothers, continue to rejoice, . . . to be comforted, to think in agreement." —2 Cor. 13:11. *W 10/1 18, 19*

Thursday, October 25

In the days of his flesh Christ offered up supplications and also petitions to the One who was able to save him out of death, with strong outcries and tears, and he was favorably heard for his godly fear. —Heb. 5:7.

It is especially important to look to Jehovah God to give us the wisdom to deal with trialsome situations. We should appeal to him for help, never doubting that he will help us by means of his holy spirit, even as James counsels us at James 1:2-8. Jesus Christ certainly set an outstanding example in leaning on his heavenly Father. Though he was perfect, Jesus prayed with great intensity while undergoing suffering. Because Jesus had a genuine fear of displeasing his Father, God gave a favorable hearing to his cries for aid. The Son of God, with the help of the holy spirit, maintained integrity and, therefore, died as one approved by his Father. He was then delivered from death's grip by a resurrection. If we likewise look to Jehovah for help in trialsome situations, we can likewise expect God's spirit to help us. *W 10/15 11, 12a*

Friday, October 26

Clothe yourselves with the tender affections of compassion, kindness, lowliness of mind, mildness, and long-suffering.—Col. 3:12.

Our continuing in an unblemished state before Jehovah God involves more than refraining from wrong conduct and unwholesome speech. (Col. 3:5-9) Positive action is also required, as can be seen by considering what Paul is here saying. As Christians, we have been cleansed by the blood of Christ and are spiritual brothers and sisters. We should therefore treat one another in a brotherly way. Being imperfect, all of us repeatedly fall short of reflecting the fine qualities of our heavenly Father and of his Son. Rightly, then, we should not be overly severe with fellow believers, treating them harshly. It would be wrong for a Christian to set himself up as a judge of his brothers, proudly asserting his claimed right to punish them for their failures. No, he should willingly put up with their shortcomings and not hold back from showing compassion, kindness, humility and long-suffering. *W 4/1 26, 27*

Saturday, October 27

I am the resurrection and the life. He that exercises faith in me, even though he dies, will come to life.—John 11:25.

True Christians need to keep in mind God's command: 'Abstain from blood.' True, when the Bible was written, blood was not being transfused. However, what God's Word says certainly covers the practice of transfusing blood. A doctor who forbids a certain antibiotic to a patient allergic to it would thus not only rule out his taking it orally but also forbid his taking it by injection. Similarly, God's command to 'abstain from blood' rules out ingesting it by the mouth as well as by transfusion into the veins. Furthermore, the Bible makes clear that God's law was not to be ignored even during an emergency that could threaten life. Many of God's approved servants have been willing to face dangers and even death rather than violate Scriptural principles and their integrity to Jehovah. They have had full confidence in God's power to restore life, and believe the words of Jesus Christ. *W 6/15 13, 14a*

Sunday, October 28

It will be given him. But let him keep on asking in faith, not doubting at all, for he who doubts is like a wave of the sea driven by the wind and blown about.—Jas. 1:5, 6.

Yes, wisdom, which we acquire under the direction of Jehovah God's spirit, is one of the things that He is very desirous of giving his servants. He is happy when we ask for wisdom. It always works for our good and helps us when we pray to understand God's Word as it applies to our situation. But as James goes on to show, we must have full faith in Jehovah God and in his Son, and in their readiness to provide what is needed, and must have no thought other than the interests of the Christian faith and the purposes of Jehovah God. We must not be praying for one thing and "halfway" wanting something else. Our prayer must be from the bottom of our heart. Otherwise we are like a sea wave, which goes back and forth and up and down. Every wind—every outside influence, every fear—would make a change in us. Surely we would not want to be like that, would we? *W 7/15 12, 13a*

Monday, October 29

In that day sing to her, you people: "A vineyard of foaming wine! I, Jehovah, am safeguarding her. Every moment I shall water her."—Isa. 27:2, 3.

Now is the time for the "great crowd" to make peace with Jehovah and to take hold on his stronghold of strength so as to be empowered to do what is pleasing to him. (Isa. 27:3-6) It is timely for them to keep in mind the words of the song that is now being sung to his "vineyard" of spiritual Israel. Now is the "day" for the remnant to show fruitfulness. Jehovah has made the land productive all around the globe, for hundreds of thousands have responded to the Kingdom witness given by the remnant and have sprung up in more than 200 lands to form a "great crowd" that hails Jehovah as Universal Sovereign and Jesus Christ as the one to rule as king over all the earth. Taking a lesson from the fruitful "vine" and its "branches," those of the "great crowd" likewise seek to be fruitful in cultivating all the qualities of godly personality and in actively expressing and displaying them to Jehovah's glory. *W 12/15 20-22a*

Tuesday, October 30

Come, you who have been blessed by my Father, inherit the kingdom prepared for you from the founding of the world.—Matt. 25:34.

The "great crowd" will be "the living" with whom the millennial day of judgment begins. The marvelous thing about this "great crowd" of "tribulation" survivors is that they never experience a resurrection. Having never died and undergone the dissolution of the human body, they will have no need for the King Jesus Christ to call them out of the memorial tombs. Because of the way they treated the anointed remnant in the past, these sheeplike ones have been put at the King's right side of favor, and to them he says the above words at the beginning of his millennial reign. Thus they will be ushered into the way toward the gaining of perfect human life on a paradise earth. Great will be their privilege to be here when the reigning "Son of man" starts calling those in the memorial tombs out in a resurrection that will afford them the opportunity to gain eternal life on earth. *W 9/1 17, 18a*

Wednesday, October 31

It must occur in the morning that if he will repurchase you, fine! Let him do the repurchasing. But if he does not . . . I will then repurchase you, I myself, as sure as Jehovah lives.—Ruth 3:13.

Naomi, upon hearing her daughter-in-law Ruth's report, was confident that Boaz would keep his word and act quickly. In the meantime the two widows waited patiently in their humble dwelling. Profitably we may consider their faith. Like Naomi, do we have confidence in our faithful fellow believers? And, like Ruth, do we readily rely upon Jehovah in times of crisis, sure that his arrangements and provisions are of the very best? Think about Ruth. She does not even know that male relative with the first right in this matter; she has no knowledge of his temperament, and yet she is willing to comply with Jehovah's law on levirate marriage. She must be certain that God will make things work out well. Comparably, are we personally confident that Jehovah "makes all his works cooperate together for the good of those who love God"?—Rom. 8:28. *W 2/15* 12, 13a

Thursday, November 1

Repent, therefore, and turn around so as to get your sins blotted out.—Acts 3:19.

Today, as a result of the preaching of "this good news of the kingdom," a choice faces all who hear. What is that? It is whether to set out on a course of righteousness and to serve Jehovah God, or to continue in a course of selfishness under the dominance of Satan the Devil. By giving heed to the preaching of the good news of God's kingdom, a person gains an accurate knowledge of God's Word and help in applying it in his life. This, in turn, can result in sincere repentance of whatever wrong course a person may have been taking, followed by a turning around or converting to take a course that is pleasing to Jehovah, even as the apostle Peter told the Jews of his day. Taking these two steps should logically lead one to making the choice to do God's will, to work with Him and to follow in the footsteps of Jesus Christ. Such a choice must be a distinct formal step, a step that Jesus himself took at the age of 30. *W 11/1* 8-10

Friday, November 2

Be modest in walking with your God.—Mic. 6:8.

Since the Hebrew term rendered "modest" at Micah 6:8 appears only here and at Proverbs 11:2, the full significance of the word is not readily discerned. Later Jewish writings indicate that this Hebrew term conveys the thought of purity and decency. The *Septuagint Version* and the Syriac present the idea of being "prepared" or "ready" to walk with God. Hence, modest walking with Jehovah evidently includes being in a fit, unassuming, not self-reliant state before God. The expression 'to walk with God,' appears much earlier in the Bible record. For instance, the prophet Enoch and the patriarch Noah are spoken of as walking with God. From Genesis 6:9 and Hebrews 11:5 we can see that walking with God involves conducting ourselves as if we were in his very presence, conforming to his will. Both Enoch and Noah enjoyed special intimacy with Jehovah God because of their faith and upright conduct. *W 9/15* 14-16

Saturday, November 3

My food is for me to do the will of him that sent me and to finish his work.—John 4:34.

Jesus did not make pleasure, including food and drink, the prime thing in his life. He found his greatest delight in doing God's will. Do we? When Jesus said the above words, he was tired and hungry. However, since an opportunity presented itself for giving a witness, he became so absorbed in it that his personal discomfort faded into the background. The joy and satisfaction that resulted from his doing God's will was as food to Jesus. Surely, we want this to be true in our case. Hence, we should keep pleasures in check so that they will not interfere with our experiencing the far greater happiness that comes from helping our fellowmen spiritually and materially. To avoid becoming selfish in our use of time, we need to keep ever before us the thought that time itself is a gift from Jehovah, to be used in harmony with his will. We are not entitled to use time simply for our own pleasure.—Isa. 58:13, 14. *W 11/15* 9-11a

Sunday, November 4

Give thanks to Jehovah, you people! . . . Make mention that his name is put on high. Make melody to Jehovah, for he has done surpassingly. This is made known in all the earth. Cry out shrilly and shout for joy.—Isa. 12:4-6.

Are you a joyful worker? Have you always been one, or have there been times when for some reason you felt tired and frustrated, sapped of all energy and initiative? You felt that you just could not do another stroke of work. Then something happened unexpectedly. You were given a different job, something more productive, yielding a fine fruitage or harvest. Instead of feeling out of favor and criticized, you now got a smile and words of commendation. What a difference it made! You felt stimulated and encouraged to press forward with enthusiasm and zeal. Nothing could hold you back. Yes, you became a *joyful worker!* Remarkably, the Bible speaks exactly in the same way about the experiences of Jehovah's people in this our day. It tells of something that happened *unexpectedly* in the year 1919. *W 6/1* 1, 2

Monday, November 5

Get wise and discreet and experienced men of your tribes, that I may set them as heads over you.—Deut. 1:13.

Thus Moses reminded his people that he had followed the counsel of Jethro. After Israel became established in the Promised Land, all the different communities were guided and aided by bodies of elders. They were to give wise counsel, help with problems, protect against apostasy and thus serve for the peace, good order and spiritual health of their respective communities. At times they were called on to fulfill judicial roles in settling disputes or in acting for the protection of the community. (Ruth 4:1-11) They were to be a source of comfort and strength in times of crisis. (Isa. 32:1, 2) But they were not the taskmasters of their fellow residents nor were they authorized or responsible to try to live the personal lives of others for them. In bearing weighty responsibilities, Christian elders serve in similar ways. Additionally, the Christian congregation has the obligation to preach this good news of the Kingdom. *W 12/1* 1, 4

Tuesday, November 6

But as for you, you keep seeking great things for yourself. Do not keep on seeking. "For here I am bringing in a calamity upon all flesh," is the utterance of Jehovah, "and I will give you your soul as a spoil in all the places to which you may go."—Jer. 45:5.

After Jeremiah had been prophesying some 20 or 30 years, his scribe Baruch became very downcast. (Jer. 45:3) Yes, this faithful servant of God had grown weary with the passage of time. But Jehovah God assured Baruch through Jeremiah that though there might be seeming delay, that calamity was certain! Jehovah warned Baruch not to return to the worldly, materialistic ways of the Judeans, seeking his own personal advantage. No, his place was to keep serving faithfully beside Jehovah's prophet. Likewise, in these twentieth-century final days, it is no time for any of us to return to this doomed materialistic world. Our proper place is to serve with endurance until at last we receive our soul as a spoil in the realm of God's kingdom by Christ Jesus, beyond the storm of Har–Magedon. *W 1/1 15, 16a*

Wednesday, November 7

Bodily training is beneficial for a little; but godly devotion is beneficial for all things, as it holds promise of the life now and that which is to come.—1 Tim. 4:8.

By letting the Kingdom's principles operate in our lives, we are spared many of the sorrows that accompany the breakdown of the family in this modern world. The Bible encourages families to stay together, to communicate together, to enjoy life as a family, to serve God as a family. (Col. 3:14, 18-21) It shows us in a practical way just how we can do this. While the United States alone was registering a record one million divorces in 1976, and while child delinquency and other family problems were mushrooming, families of Jehovah's Witnesses, by and large, were able to keep clear of these problems. And why? Because they apply the law of the Kingdom in their lives. New ones coming to a knowledge of Kingdom truths have often been benefited, too, in finding proper guidance on how to solve life's problems. In the words of Paul they have found the benefits of godly devotion. *W 1/15 41, 42*

Thursday, November 8

But if he has doubts, he is already condemned if he eats, because he does not eat out of faith. Indeed, everything that is not out of faith is sin.—Rom. 14:23.

What a person who professes to be a true Christian does should be something that in no way makes his conscience uncomfortable. If his conscience is bothered, he is self-condemned. And he should constantly strive for a clear picture of the Christian faith, so as to achieve a more balanced conscience. While not all things that a Christian does have a direct bearing on the proclamation of the "good news," what he does, even in recreation and relaxation, he does with the view of upbuilding himself and others. So, "do all things for God's glory." (1 Cor. 10:31) Before taking any step, ask, 'Will this work for the peace of the congregation, so that God's spirit will operate freely among all?' Happy, indeed, are we if we can keep our lives in full harmony with a right, balanced, clean conscience before Jehovah God. Doing so, we will be a blessing to our congregations. *W 3/15 15, 16a*

Friday, November 9

Ask of me, that I may give nations as your inheritance and the ends of the earth as your own possession. You will break them with an iron scepter, as though a potter's vessel you will dash them to pieces.—Ps. 2:8, 9.

Well might an earthworm try to prevent a farm tractor from running over it as for Satan and all the earthly nations of which he is the invisible ruler to succeed in crippling and halting God's incoming world government! Besides having suffered defeat in the earlier war in heaven, Satan will see the defeat of his misled nations at Har-Magedon. He will see Christ irresistibly use his "iron scepter" in dashing all the assembled nations to pieces as if they were earthenware vessels fashioned by a potter. Then Satan and his demons will be seized by the victorious Christ and be chained and hurled into the abysmal dungeon. This will be sealed tight shut for 1,000 years. During that demon-free millennium God's world government by Christ will rule as an expression of his rightful universal sovereignty. *W 3/1* 16b

Saturday, November 10

The vision is yet for the appointed time, and it keeps panting on to the end, and it will not tell a lie. Even if it should delay, keep in expectation of it; for it will without fail come true. It will not be late.—Hab. 2:3.

Should we not be glad that Jehovah has held off the "great tribulation" to this hour so that more precious "sheep" might be gathered? But make no mistake! That day of reckoning with the nations is hastening ever closer! Jehovah has given us every indication that the work has not yet been brought to a completion. We must continue at it, not until *we* decide that it is done, but until *Jehovah* finishes it according to his good pleasure. Indeed, Jehovah keeps showing us that the work has not yet come to its finale. This is seen in the fact that he keeps bringing in the harvest. We should never lose sight of the principle that Paul so clearly expressed at 1 Corinthians 3:7: "Neither is he that plants anything nor is he that waters, but *God* who *makes it grow.*" So all the credit for the harvest goes to him. *W 6/1* 17, 18

Sunday, November 11

Rejoicing to time indefinite is what will come to be theirs.—Isa. 61:7.

Jehovah's vindication of the remnant has proved to be a declaring of them righteous before all the world. Their joy at this has been like that of a bridegroom and his bride on their wedding day! As regards rejoicing, well, what Isaiah's prophecy says has proved to be true. Today the vindicated remnant continue to rejoice, indeed, but more than that, the "great crowd" of their assistants join in the rejoicing. Taking the Bible's viewpoint, they have come to view the anointed remnant as "priests of Jehovah" and "the ministers of our God." They express their own joy at this by serving Jehovah God alongside this approved remnant of priestly, public servants. Even though the "great crowd" are classed as "strangers" and "foreigners" and are likened to shepherds, farmers and vinedressers, the amount of relief and assistance that they have brought to the remnant has been tremendous. The spiritual paradise has indeed benefited from their presence. *W 7/1* 5, 6b

Monday, November 12

For everything there is an appointed time, even a time for every affair under the heavens: . . . a time to keep quiet and a time to speak.
—Eccl. 3:1, 7.

Christians not only need to be balanced in their service to Jehovah God but also need to give thought to the matter of timing. There is indeed 'an appointed time for every affair under heaven.' In keeping with this principle, when we are at a congregation meeting and a Christian minister is giving a talk, that is not the time to be dozing, whispering or reading something not related to the subject being discussed. Also, the evenings when congregation meetings are being held are not the time to make return visits or to engage in other Christian activities that could just as well be taken care of at some other time. It seems that elders especially need to exercise care in this matter of timing. Often they may be tempted to take care of congregation matters right during meetings. With a little better planning, however, these things could well be cared for at some other time. *W 11/1* 8a

Tuesday, November 13

If you have bitter jealousy and contentiousness in your hearts, do not be bragging and lying against the truth.—Jas. 3:14.

These words call for self-examination. A man might ask himself: 'Do I harbor bitter jealousy? Am I contentious?' Bitter jealousy would include a person's having a desire to glorify himself and his opinions. It could manifest itself in a fanatical and stubborn zeal for his own views while loudly decrying opinions different from his, or failing to acknowledge that others possess wisdom and understanding equal to or superior to his own. As for contentiousness, this refers to a person's having a spirit of quarreling or strife. A man may be inclined to use means that give rise to disturbance in order to confuse others and to further his own ends. Such contentiousness would be a product of pride and selfish ambition. A bitterly jealous and contentious man, by calling attention to his qualifications as a teacher, would indeed be bragging. Such would disqualify him as a Christian teacher. *W 12/1* 10, 11a

Wednesday, November 14

Noah proceeded to do according to all that God had commanded him. He did just so.
—Gen. 6:22.

We can be greatly encouraged in our course of self-sacrifice when we examine Bible history and see how other ordinary people successfully pursued such a course, and the blessings they received for doing so. For example, Jehovah asked Noah to sacrifice things so that he could do a work that the world of his day considered foolish. He was instructed to make a huge vessel, an ark. Yet there never had been any pouring rains or floods. Furthermore, Noah was not a shipbuilder, and he had family responsibilities as well. Building such a huge ark would require Noah to take time from things that he may have preferred to do. Indeed, had he put that same time and energy into increasing his material wealth, he no doubt could have been more comfortable. But Noah patiently continued his course of self-sacrifice. He understood that he did not live in a "normal" world, but one that was 'ruined in the sight of God' and 'filled with violence,' one that would eventually be destroyed. *W 8/1* 6, 7a

Thursday, November 15

Blessed be Jehovah, who has given a resting-place to his people Israel according to all that he has promised. There has not failed one word of all his good promise that he has promised by means of Moses his servant.—1 Ki. 8:56.

Those who walk in Jehovah's name recognize him as the God of reliable prophecies. Jehovah's forecasts of future events are recorded over his own name. It is as though he has put his signature to them as a guarantee of their authenticity. We can depend on such prophecies. For instance, Jehovah promised to deliver his people from Egyptian bondage and to give them a particular land. This was accomplished. (Ex. 3:6-17; 14:19-31) Many years later, King Solomon could well say the above. (See also Joshua 21:45.) Furthermore, those walking in Jehovah's name have learned about God's purpose to cleanse the whole human family of sin by means of the expiatory power of the sacrifice of his dear Son, Jesus Christ. They are happy to see that justice is associated with the divine name, as is love for mankind.—John 3:16. *W 8/15 15, 16*

Friday, November 16

True, no discipline seems for the present to be joyous, but grievous; yet afterward to those who have been trained by it it yields peaceable fruit, namely, righteousness. —Heb. 12:11.

Since Jehovah God permits us to experience this severe treatment, we should humbly submit to it. (1 Pet. 5:6, 7) It is only right that we accept this discipline without rebelling against it, without seeking to get out from under the hand of God. A man who has love for his children will discipline them when he deems it necessary to do so. Being imperfect, he may misjudge matters. Hence, in administering 'discipline according to what seems good to him,' he may not always do what is right and beneficial. (Heb. 12:9, 10) Yet such a father is shown respect by children who love him. On the other hand, Jehovah God never makes a mistake, and he is responsible for our spiritual as well as our eternal life. Surely, then, there is even stronger reason to submit to the heavenly Father's discipline than there is to respect an imperfect earthly father. *W 10/15 4, 5a*

Saturday, November 17

He humbled you and let you go hungry and fed you with the manna, which neither you had known nor your fathers had known; in order to make you know that not by bread alone does man live but by every expression of Jehovah's mouth.—Deut. 8:3.

In the uncultivated wilderness Jehovah God allowed the some three million Israelites to come into a situation where they thought they would actually starve to death. (Ex. 16:3) Without the ordinary means for sustaining life—bread—the Israelites felt that they were doomed. Jehovah God indeed humbled them by letting them experience such helplessness. His purpose in doing so was to teach them that, when the common supply of food failed, the expressions of Jehovah's mouth could sustain man. The miraculous manna was such an expression, for Jehovah God gave the command and the manna came to be. Since Jehovah God kept a whole nation alive in a wilderness for 40 years, we can have every confidence that the expressions of his mouth can sustain us. *W 11/15 14, 15*

Sunday, November 18

What, then, is Apollos? Yes, what is Paul? Ministers through whom you became believers, even as the Lord granted each one. I planted, Apollos watered, but God kept making it grow; so that neither is he that plants anything nor is he that waters, but God who makes it grow.
—1 Cor. 3:5-7.

Truly this is also our privilege today, to make believers, gathering still others into God's storehouse. In the 1978 service year 95,052 new ones took the step of water immersion, signifying their whole-souled dedication to God to do his will. Why should we not expect the harvest to keep growing? It is not yet over. It is time to keep *harvest-minded* until all are gathered in. The time continues for harvest joys! Of course, harvesting is not always done under favorable conditions but with perseverance. Stiff opposition rises up in some places, but the point is made that the ingathering continues. Experience shows that it is often because of opposition that some, who otherwise were not interested, are prompted to take a fresh look at the situation. *W 6/1* 19; 1a

Monday, November 19

Look! I am coming as a thief. Happy is the one that stays awake and keeps his outer garments, that he may not walk naked and people look upon his shamefulness.
—Rev. 16:15.

Those in the priestly service of God today, and also the "great crowd," must be careful not to lose their garments of identification. And what is it that identifies them as God's servants? Why, it is their zealous works, as they talk with people at their homes and in public places, and their prac-ticing in their lives the same fine Christian principles that they recommend to others. For a servant of God to fall asleep spiritually would bring him great shame. He would be stripped of his identity as a witness of the true God, Jehovah. This would be disastrous on the eve of "the war of the great day of God the Almighty." (Rev. 16:14) Conditions on earth have never been more dangerous. Jesus Christ prophesied plainly concerning our day. Repeatedly in his prophecies, he emphasized the need for our keeping awake, as in the text above. *W 10/1* 3-5a

Tuesday, November 20

Do not be anxious over anything, but in everything by prayer and supplication along with thanksgiving let your petitions be made known to God; and the peace of God that excels all thought will guard your hearts and your mental powers by means of Christ Jesus.—Phil. 4:6, 7.

Keep in mind that Jehovah God and Jesus Christ are by your side. You can endure "as seeing the One who is invisible," just as Moses did when he was faced with the great task of leading all those Israelite slaves out of Egypt, through a wilderness—a task entirely beyond human capability. (Heb. 11:27-29) Moses had to cast his entire burden upon Jehovah. Certainly our problems are no harder than the ones Moses faced. That is why Paul counsels as above. In this way we can cast our burden upon Jehovah, continuing to look to him to cause our plans to be firmly established. (Ps. 55:22) As Jesus did, we will then sanctify Jehovah's name and acknowledge him as actually bringing the results, giving him the credit and praise for what is accomplished. *W 5/1* 18, 19a

Wednesday, November 21

Woe to you . . . because you took away the key of knowledge; you yourselves did not go in, and those going in you hindered!—Luke 11:52.

Jehovah God had executed a "day of vengeance" on the Babylonian Empire, whose rulers had refused to 'open the way homeward to the prisoners.' (Isa. 14:17; 61:2; Jer. 50: 15, 28; 51:6, 11, 36) When restored thereafter to their homeland those Jewish "prisoners" did not come into bondage to idolatry with literal graven images. Yet they came into a greater bondage, that to the religious system of Judaism. This was a system dominated by precepts and traditions of men, things that made invalid the Law and the commandments of Jehovah God. The official scribes and Pharisees became prominent in this religious system. They blinded the people to the truth by taking away "the key of knowledge," hindering them from entering into the kingdom of God, and binding heavy loads on the common people that they themselves would not touch. Today the religious leaders treat their flocks in the same way. *W 7/1 13*

Thursday, November 22

Keep your senses, be watchful. Your adversary, the Devil, walks about like a roaring lion, seeking to devour someone. —1 Pet. 5:8.

As we progress deep into the "last days" there is an ever greater need to keep wide awake spiritually and to intensify our willingness to make sacrifices to serve God acceptably. One reason for this is that Satan knows that he has only "a short period of time" left before he is put out of the way. (Rev. 12:12; 20:1-3) Since his time by now is very short, we can expect him to intensify his insane efforts to corrupt and destroy. He would like nothing better than to influence us to dull our spiritual perception and to lose our sense of urgency regarding these critical times. And he would certainly be pleased if we would diminish, or abandon altogether, our telling of the "good news of the kingdom" of God to others. (Matt. 24:14) We should never underestimate Satan's power for deception and harm. We do well to heed the warning that God's Word gives regarding Satan the Devil. *W 8/1 8, 9*

Friday, November 23

I had planted you as a choice red vine, all of it a true seed. So how have you been changed toward me into the degenerate shoots of a foreign vine? —Jer. 2:21.

Justice, mercy, faithfulness, righteousness, the keeping and not a twisting of God's Law were part of the fruit that Jehovah looked for from the typical "vineyard," Israel. To be consistent, should he look for fruit different from all that to be on the "branches" of his "true vine"? Not at all! The fruit that He desires as an adornment of these "branches" is Christlike qualities of personality. But there is more to the fruit than an idle personality. The active expression of traits of personality is also required! For example, in the prophet Jeremiah's day Jehovah voiced his disappointment at the fruit offered to him by the typical "vineyard" of Israel. (Jer. 2: 20-23) So another part of the fruit for which Jehovah looked from the "vine" of typical Israel was moral cleanness and the exclusive worship of Him. Jehovah looks for this same fruit from all who serve him today. *W 12/15 6, 7a*

Saturday, November 24

We, for our part, shall walk in the name of Jehovah our God to time indefinite, even forever.—Mic. 4:5.

These words well express the attitude of true Christians. What do they mean to us? Are we walking in God's name? A name is a designation by which a person or thing is identified. The word "god" is a common title. On the other hand, a proper name distinguishes a person from all other individuals. "Jehovah" is a proper name. But the term "name" also means reputation or fame. So the 'name of our God' is the proper or personal name by which he is known, and there is a certain reputation associated with it. To "walk in the name" of a certain god means doing things approved or done by that god. It means acting in harmony with the reputation of that god and also recognizing the authority of that divinity. Actually, 'walking in the name of a god' means being dedicated to that god, having his name called on one and representing that god on earth. It means living in harmony with the traits of that god. For us that God is Jehovah. *W 8/15 3, 4, 6*

Sunday, November 25

Show yourselves thankful. —Col. 3:15.

Letting the peace of the Christ control our hearts will further the peace in the congregation and prevent us from becoming agitated to the point of sinning against our brothers. Also, a spirit of gratitude contributes much toward the preservation of the peace that we enjoy as Christians. Persons who genuinely recognize God's undeserved kindness toward them and fellow believers are happy and content. Because they deeply appreci-ate what Jehovah God and Jesus Christ have done in making it possible for them to be cleansed from sin with everlasting life in view, they do not quickly take offense when others fail in some way but forgive them freely, from the heart. How different it is with thankless persons! They often voice complaints, are never satisfied and are most unhappy. Their selfish, unloving attitude is discouraging to those who are brought into association with them and gives rise to quarrels and strife. So, we do well to cultivate the spirit of gratitude. *W 4/1 28, 29*

Monday, November 26

By means of him we have the release by ransom through the blood of that one [Christ], yes, the forgiveness of our trespasses, according to the riches of his undeserved kindness.—Eph. 1:7.

All of us must admit that we are imperfect and sinful. The apostle Paul confirmed this and, at Romans 5:12, explained how it came about. This fact has a direct bearing on our appreciation of life and blood, even as can be seen by Paul's words above. Do these words not help us to understand more fully why it is so vital to have God's view of blood, representing life? One of the central themes of the Bible is that Jesus came to earth to give his life as a ransom sacrifice. Only by that ransom can we have the prospect of forgiveness of sin and the hope of "everlasting life." (Matt. 20:28; Rom. 3:23, 24; 6:22, 23; 1 Tim. 1:15, 16) To receive those blessings, we must exercise faith in Jesus' ransom, which involves having accurate knowledge of and appreciation for his giving up his life represented by his blood.—1 Tim. 2:3, 4. *W 6/15 13, 15*

Tuesday, November 27

I shall make you have insight and instruct you in the way you should go. I will give advice with my eye upon you. —Ps. 32:8.

Of course, each person has his own circumstances, differing from those of others, and this will affect the subjects of his prayers. The answer from God can be confidently expected in the form of wise guidance suited to the person's own individual case, even as God promises. Having prayed, we should then be consistent and act in harmony with our prayers. We should seek counsel on the problem, first, from the Bible. God, knowing our problems in advance, saw to it that counsel on all human problems was written in his inspired Word. A person may also consult others who can help him to see what the Bible says on the matter, even seeking their prayers in his behalf. He should persist in praying until he gets a clear understanding on what is the wise course to take. If he does not do so, he will not be showing God that he is really concerned about getting God's answer. *W 2/1 16-18a*

Wednesday, November 28

Sell the things belonging to you and give gifts of mercy. . . . For where your treasure is, there your hearts will be also.—Luke 12:33, 34.

All who are serving Jehovah God as loyal disciples of Jesus Christ have a precious treasure. They have in their possession vital knowledge that can mean life to those who act in harmony with it. Logically, then, they should be exerting themselves in efforts to aid fellow humans spiritually. Also, they should be willing to give material aid to those in need. Such material giving goes hand in hand with spiritual giving. This is because food, clothing and shelter are essential for life, and, without life, a person cannot praise Jehovah God. In view of Jesus' words, there should be a willingness to use one's time and assets to benefit others. Manifestly, Jesus did not mean that his disciples reduce themselves to poverty and thereafter depend on the charity of others. But these disciples were to be willing to part with possessions to aid persons in real physical or spiritual need. *W 11/15 1, 2a*

Thursday, November 29

The things you heard from me with the support of many witnesses, these things commit to faithful men, who, in turn, will be adequately qualified to teach others.—2 Tim. 2:2.

The years that Timothy spent with Paul and others contributed a wealth of valuable experience and knowledge that few persons would gain at his age. Paul encouraged Timothy to aid other elders to benefit from what he had learned. In a similar way, elders can help other brothers in the congregation to develop spiritually, endeavoring to pass on to them the benefit of their experience and knowledge. It is not simply a matter of helping them to learn some clerical duty within the congregation but of aiding them to develop in judgment, insight and ability to communicate the sound principles of God's Word to others. As Paul had Timothy accompany him while he carried out his commission as an apostle to the nations and as he served as a shepherd in God's flock, so elders can invite other developing men in the congregation to accompany them as they serve in a similar way. *W 12/1 10, 11*

Friday, November 30

Instruct me, O Jehovah, about your way. I shall walk in your truth. Unify my heart to fear your name.—Ps. 86:11.

In particular does doing Jehovah's work in Jehovah's way mean doing it out of love, unselfishly, out of a pure and undivided heart. King David appreciated the importance of this, and that is why he prayed as he did. To serve with a divided heart would mean to let selfishness enter. It would indicate an ulterior motive. That is why we are commanded to love Jehovah with our *whole* heart, soul, mind and strength. (Mark 12: 29-31) This is not an easy thing to do. The Israelites continually were falling short in this regard. Why? Because imperfect human hearts are exceedingly deceitful, treacherous, even as we read at Jeremiah 17:9. And, as Jeremiah goes on to show, only Jehovah God can fully understand the heart. That is why a study of his Word will help us to discern our selfish tendencies or schemings, and to war against them successfully. Yes, our fallen inclinations are ever out to spoil our good works. *W 11/1 16, 17a*

Saturday, December 1

For as the earth itself brings forth its sprout, . . . in like manner Jehovah himself will cause the sprouting of righteousness and of praise in front of all the nations. —Isa. 61:11.

How true to his own word Jehovah God has acted! He could never leave things unrectified. He is the God "loving justice, hating robbery along with unrighteousness." (Isa. 61:8) He concluded the promised "new covenant" toward his anointed servants, and from this the "great crowd" has also benefited. (Jer. 31: 31-34) He has already vindicated his Christian witnesses as his approved servants and will make his own righteousness spring forth for all the universe to see. It will also redound to Jehovah God's everlasting praise from the lips of all lovers of truth, righteousness and pure worship. Away, then, with "the downhearted spirit"! Let us ever identify ourselves with "the mantle of praise" and exult in Jehovah God through his anointed High Priest, Jesus Christ.—Isa. 61:1-3. *W 7/1 8, 9b*

Sunday, December 2

Throw your burden upon Jehovah himself, and he himself will sustain you.—Ps. 55:22.

What does it mean to "throw your burden upon Jehovah"? It means to take the burden off your shoulders, as it were, and put it on his. Of course, the plans or desires you have must be right, good, in harmony with God's Word of truth, not for selfish satisfaction, revenge, and so forth. But instead of feeling that the burden is on you, lay everything before Jehovah, fully putting the issue in his hands. Then, through prayer and by following the Bible's counsel to the best of your ability, look to him to accomplish what you ask. (Jas. 1:2, 5; Matt. 7:7, 8) This is a very serious matter. If a Christian does not do this, he may begin relying too much on himself, thinking, perhaps not even consciously, of his own importance or ability. If his plans appear to succeed, he may take credit to himself, only to find out later that his "success" was only temporary or superficial. Such success does not bring glory to Jehovah God. *W 5/1 3, 4a*

Monday, December 3

In fact, let not that man suppose that he will receive anything from Jehovah; he is an indecisive [Greek, "two-souled"] man, unsteady in all his ways.—Jas. 1:7, 8.

In view of what Jesus said at Luke 11:13, there is no need for us to doubt. But about the person who doubts, James says the above. Such a one is double-minded, trying to go in two directions at once, torn between something of the world and the things of God; or influenced by things other than God's Word, being of one opinion and then another. (Compare Matthew 6:24.) He may even hesitate about taking the matter to God. He has enthusiasm at one moment and discouragement at the next. He is that way not only in the matter of prayer but also as to other things in connection with faith. He is not a steady, reliable witness of Jehovah God. To the contrary, the Scriptures say: "Without faith it is impossible to please him well, for he that approaches God must believe that he is and that he becomes the rewarder of those earnestly seeking him."—Heb. 11:6. *W 7/15 12, 14a*

Tuesday, December 4

Even if it should delay, keep in expectation of it; for it will without fail come true. It will not be late.—Hab. 2:3.

The day of Jehovah's wrath against wickedness will come exactly as he has scheduled it. It will not be delayed an instant. Therefore, no person who loves Jehovah should ever get into a frame of mind or into a pattern of life that suggests disbelief in Jehovah's purpose to rid this earth of wickedness and establish a righteous new order. If a person were to adopt such a negative attitude, he would be much like those described at 2 Peter 3:3, 4. True, the original processes of life have gone on till now. However, in this century, all the evidence of the "last days" is on us in full measure. Most of the greatest calamities in history have been concentrated in this century. And now man has the capability of destroying all life on this earth. Surely, all the evidence in fulfillment of Bible prophecy shows that this world is moving relentlessly toward its end, in the "great tribulation."—Matt. 24:21. *W 8/1 17, 18*

Wednesday, December 5

The fruitage of the spirit is . . . faith.—Gal. 5:22.

Faith, the seventh-listed fruit of the spirit, is vitally important to those desiring to "walk worthily of Jehovah." (Col. 1:10) It is impossible to maintain friendship with Jehovah and to please him without this quality. (Heb. 11:6) "Faith is the assured expectation of things hoped for, the evident demonstration of realities though not beheld." (Heb. 11:1) It is not just a baseless hope, but is a well-founded expectation. Furthermore, faith is the evidence needed for conviction regarding unseen realities. For instance, created things such as the sun, the moon and the stars prove to the thinking person that God the Creator exists. (Rom. 1:20-23; Heb. 11:3) When an individual displays faith in Jehovah, he is setting a fine example for fellow Christians. Their faith may be strengthened by observing his implicit faith in Jehovah. And such active faith may also move unbelievers to begin placing confidence in Jehovah God. Do you do all you can to strengthen your faith? *W 8/15 16a*

Thursday, December 6

"Keep yourselves in expectation of me," is the utterance of Jehovah, "till the day of my rising up . . . for by the fire of my zeal all the earth will be devoured."—Zeph. 3:8.

Make no mistake! This world is fast moving toward its foretold end. It is in its death throes. It is openly stated that many of the great cities are dying. But Jehovah will put them out of their misery before they can die their natural death. We must remain alert, ready for the great day that so many of Jehovah's prophets have described. The day of Jehovah's "burning anger" foretold by the prophet Zephaniah is drawing perilously close. Jesus' own great prophecy concerning "the conclusion of the system of things" has now reached its remarkable fulfillment in our 20th century since 1914. We clearly see the militaristic elements of that "disgusting thing," the UN organization, poised to wreak havoc on the realm of Christendom. (Matt. 24:15) The "great tribulation" will no doubt be a faith-testing time for God's own people here on earth. *W 10/1* 7-9a

Friday, December 7

Without fail [Jehovah] will remember and bow low over me. This is what I shall bring back to my heart. That is why I shall show a waiting attitude. —Lam. 3:20, 21.

Those who make life hard for God's servants are not excused for their hateful course. Also, God's permission of this treatment does not reflect unfavorably on him. Why not? Because, although he permits it so that it might have a beneficial effect on his people, he does not countenance man's inhumanity to man. His Word condemns such mistreatment: "To deprive a man of his rights in defiance of the Most High, to pervert justice in the courts—such things the Lord has never approved." (Lam. 3:35, 36, *The New English Bible*) Men who mistreat fellow humans will have to render an account to Jehovah God. "Vengeance is mine; I will repay, says Jehovah." (Rom. 12:19) Therefore, we must be careful not to become embittered against the Almighty God Jehovah for the badness that is practiced by men who disregard divine law, but we must adopt a waiting attitude. *W 10/15* 19a

Saturday, December 8

By this we have come to know love, because that one surrendered his soul for us; and we are under obligation to surrender our souls for our brothers.—1 John 3:16.

In this world, we repeatedly see and hear the word "love." Yet we find ourselves living in a world where self-sacrificing love is indeed rare. This should not be surprising, for many people mistakenly refer to passion and sentimentality as love. They are unacquainted with the love that distinguishes true disciples of Jesus Christ. This love goes beyond a person's loving his neighbor as himself. It includes, if necessary, a willingness to surrender one's life for one's Christian brothers. Thus a person would be imitating Jesus Christ, who voluntarily laid down his life for mankind. Clearly, Christian love is active, manifesting itself in the positive good it does for others. Being a feeling or an emotion, this love is not easily defined. The way in which it expresses itself, however, can be described. In First Corinthians chapter 13, we find a masterful description. *W 9/15* 1, 2a

Sunday, December 9

You will certainly come to have your soul as a spoil, because you have trusted in me. —Jer. 39:18.

Jeremiah was thrown into a cistern, where he seemed doomed to a miserable death. But an Ethiopian eunuch, Ebed-melech, was instrumental in having Jeremiah drawn out of this cistern and restored to a place in the Courtyard of the Guard. When Jerusalem was destroyed he was set free. But what of Ebed-melech? While Jeremiah was still in the courtyard, the word of Jehovah came to him in regard to Ebed-melech. Thus, when the armies of Babylon came crashing in from the north, Ebed-melech escaped with his life. In modern times, too, there have been many, including even government and prison officials, who have shown kindness to the persecuted witnesses of Jehovah. Later some of these have become Witnesses in line for salvation when the heavenly executional forces of Christ Jesus go into action at Har-Magedon. Yes, great will be the reward of all who diligently exercise faith in Jehovah's promises, and who endure to the end! *W 1/1 20, 21a*

Monday, December 10

Give orders to those who are rich in the present system of things not to be high-minded, . . . [but] to be rich in fine works.—1 Tim. 6:17, 18.

What does this admonition mean? Rich Christians were not to view themselves as superior persons nor were they to put their confidence in riches. Jehovah merits our absolute confidence. Were it not for the provisions that He made for sustaining life on earth, no one could keep himself alive. How foolish, then, it would be to ignore the Cre-

ator and to center one's life around material things! By reason of his Creatorship, Jehovah is the Owner of all things. Hence, it is only right that we worship him and use whatever assets that we may have in a way that is pleasing to him. This means our using these assets to help others spiritually and materially. In the case of wealthy Christians, they were urged to make their fine works that went on record just as abundant as their possessions. By using what they had in relieving the distress of others, they would be laying up treasure in heaven. *W 11/15 3-5a*

Tuesday, December 11

Day after day they were in constant attendance at the temple with one accord . . . and partook of food with great rejoicing and sincerity of heart.—Acts 2:46.

Keeping together as a family and as a Christian congregation can bring benefits in many ways. Before the flood, Noah and his family worked together, then survived the flood and gave thanks together as a family. (Gen. 8:18, 20) When Moses parted the waters of the Red Sea, the entire congregation of Israel was journeying with him, and as a congregation they passed through under Jehovah's protection. Similar benefits may be enjoyed today as families and congregations keep together in the loving association that God's Word encourages. In crisis periods, such togetherness has at times brought special benefits. But be that as it may, the fact remains that our prayerful reliance on God, our togetherness as a congregation and our calmness under pressure have worked to our benefit, a foretaste of the protection God assures us during the "great tribulation." *W 1/15 43-45*

Wednesday, December 12

Whoever gives one of these little ones only a cup of cold water to drink because he is a disciple, I tell you truly, he will by no means lose his reward.—Matt. 10:42.

When Jehovah God responds to your effort to get understanding, He is displaying another fine quality toward you. That quality is *appreciation*. You no doubt have and express appreciation for most things that others do for you, and you may say, Thank you, or make some other gesture. But the appreciation that humans feel is far less deep and heartfelt than is God's appreciation of those who show faith in him and who have respect for his Word. He *rejoices* in them. Jesus even spoke about *joy in heaven* over one sinner that repents or forsakes wrong things in order to please Jehovah God. (Luke 15:10) And Jehovah's reward always far exceeds the value of worship or service that one renders to him. Jehovah observes and appreciates each one who respects his name and treats his people kindly. So his heart and his help go out to that person, even as Jesus said. *W 2/1* 10a

Thursday, December 13

Happy is the man that does not put himself on judgment by what he approves. —Rom. 14:22.

If you knew that your doing a certain thing would not cause qualms of conscience in others, you could go ahead. God would appreciate that you have a well-trained conscience and exhibit good judgment. Either way, God would see the sincerity of your faith. His judgment is what counts. But as for the one who is conscientiously hesitant about taking a certain step, the apostle Paul says the above. By never going contrary to his conscience, the Christian will have peace of mind. But if he has doubts about a certain course, then without hesitation he should reject or abandon it. Whatever a person approves, it should not violate his conscience, however appealing it may be, or whatever argument someone else might make. On the other hand, if he finds that argument to be based on the Scriptures and becomes thoroughly convinced of its correctness, then he may adjust his conscientious view accordingly.—Rom. 14:5. *W 3/15* 13, 14a

Friday, December 14

Let the peace of the Christ control in your hearts. —Col. 3:15.

A person may have a valid complaint against a brother. But he does well to ask himself, Is my brother's failing really so grave that I cannot forgive him? Then, when the one having the complaint views his own shortcomings, he will be far more inclined to be forgiving, just as Jehovah has been forgiving toward him. (Matt. 18:21-35) But what if the failings of others put our heart in a state of agitation? How can we calm it? Paul provides this inspired counsel. This "peace" is the tranquillity, the calmness, that we gain upon becoming disciples of the Son of God. It results from our knowing that we are loved and approved by Jehovah God and by his Son. When this peace is the controlling force in our hearts, we will do our utmost to speak and act in a way that will preserve it. We will safeguard our precious relationship with God and Christ by treating fellow believers in a kind, loving manner. This will lead to the furtherance of peace in the congregation. *W 4/1* 27, 28

Saturday, December 15

*If you keep on doing these things you will by no means ever fail. In fact, thus there will be richly supplied to you the entrance into the everlasting kingdom of our Lord and Savior Jesus Christ.
—2 Pet. 1:10, 11.*

The Kingdom of which the spirit-begotten disciples on earth were "joint heirs with Christ" is not something in which they had been since the outpouring of holy spirit at Pentecost of 33 C.E. In God's due time the 144,000 joint heirs with Christ are richly supplied that entrance into the heavenly kingdom by means of the "first resurrection." Then they will no longer be the spirit-begotten subjects on earth under 'the Son of God's love.' That temporary relationship with the glorified Jesus Christ will be gone forever. They will be the heavenly, immortal, incorruptible kings with him. For having lived clean and faithful lives on earth, they inherit "the kingdom of the Christ and of God." (Eph. 5:5) By similarly leading clean and faithful lives the "great crowd" can hope to become earthly subjects of that kingdom. *W 3/1 6, 7b*

Sunday, December 16

*Jehovah will not desert his people for the sake of his great name, because Jehovah has taken it upon himself to make you his people.
—1 Sam. 12:22.*

We are not left unprotected in this hostile system of things. No, for we can be confident that Jehovah will protect and aid us and will deliver us as his people into the promised new order, if we continue walking worthily of him, even as he once declared by his prophet Samuel. If we take seriously our responsibility before God, truly walking worthily in his name, he will be with us as our friend. Surely, if we continue to acquire and apply knowledge of his inspired Word, Jehovah will not abandon us. As his Witnesses, we have declared that whereas "all the peoples, for their part, will walk each one in the name of its god; . . . we, for our part, shall walk in the name of Jehovah our God to time indefinite, even forever." (Mic. 4:5) May we live up to that decision. By doing so, we will have the marvelous prospect of walking worthily of Jehovah throughout eternity. *W 8/15 20, 21a*

Monday, December 17

Because you did not show faith in me to sanctify me before the eyes of the sons of Israel, therefore you will not bring this congregation into the land that I shall certainly give them.—Num. 20:12.

With regard to those not in the truth, just as with our Christian brothers, we must always think first: Is what I am doing or about to do putting God's sanctification first? It is easy to become impatient or to become a little self-righteous, forgetting to rely wholly on Jehovah. This is a course of unwisdom. Moses made this very sad mistake once. The Israelites were very rebellious and troublesome to Moses. In the wilderness of Zin they began quarreling with Moses because there was no water. Jehovah told Moses to speak to the mountain crag to bring out water. But Moses said to the people: "Hear, now, you rebels! Is it from this crag that we shall bring out water for you?" (Num. 20:10) Instead of speaking to the crag, he struck it twice, after which water came out. Moses succeeded in getting water for the people. But what did Jehovah say? The above. *W 5/1 15, 16*

Tuesday, December 18

Like a flower of the vegetation he will pass away. . . . So, too, the rich man will fade away in his ways of life.—Jas. 1:10, 11.

The rich man can rejoice over his humiliation because he realizes that spending time and effort to amass worldly riches is a waste and tends to destroy spirituality and often the health of a person. James gives the reasons why. Yes, vegetation withers and its beauty fades away. Just so, when the rich man grows old and dies, the splendor of the wealth that surrounds and 'beautifies' him is gone. This "beauty" of the rich man is taken by his heirs and others, and often the "empire" that he was building is dissolved, or his goals are discarded. But the rich man who becomes a Christian can even enjoy his material riches if he uses them to further the interests of God's kingdom. Thus he may be able to arrange to devote more time to proclaiming the "good news" and can contribute to the maintaining of meeting places and to the promotion of the Kingdom work as it is done world wide. *W 7/15 16, 17a*

Wednesday, December 19

For you know that it was not with corruptible things, with silver or gold, that you were delivered from your fruitless form of conduct . . . But it was with precious blood, . . . even Christ's.—1 Pet. 1:18, 19.

How meaningful, how full of blessed implications for us, are many of the Bible passages mentioning Jesus' blood! By means of it our sins can be forgiven. (Rev. 1:5; Heb. 10:29) It is possible to be delivered from fruitless conduct. (1 Pet. 1:18, 19) We can be among a congregation of people whom God approves of and guides. (Acts 20:28) And there is the hope of perfection and everlasting life under the rule of a kingdom incorporating persons bought with that blood. (Rev. 5:9, 10; 12:10, 11; Col. 1:20) All who have an appreciation of the value of their own life thus need to appreciate what God says about blood. He views it as sacred. He determined its exclusive usefulness and acceptability for sacrifice on the altar. And he clearly showed in his Word that all our hopes for a lasting future rest on the sacrificial blood of his Son. *W 6/15 22, 23*

Thursday, December 20

I am being poured out like a drink offering upon the sacrifice and public service to which faith has led you.—Phil. 2:17.

Hebrews 10:11 speaks of each and every priest of ancient Israel as taking his stand daily "to render public service and to offer the same sacrifices often." Of God's Son, Hebrews 8:6 says: "Now Jesus has obtained a more excellent public service." In the congregation at Antioch, Syria, certain Christian prophets and teachers, including Paul and Barnabas, were said to be "publicly ministering to Jehovah." (Acts 13:1, 2) Paul, who founded the congregation at Philippi, speaks of their special ministry, saying the above. So all those anointed Christians acted as God's public servants. Likewise the anointed remnant of spiritual Israelites today render to God "public service" as the "faithful and discreet slave" class. (Matt. 24:45-47) So all the anointed remnant of the spiritual body of Christ are properly viewed and spoken of as "ministers of our God."—Isa. 61:6. *W 7/1 22, 23a*

Friday, December 21

At that Abram went just as Jehovah had spoken to him. —Gen. 12:4.

Abraham set a fine example for us. He appreciated the need to make sacrifices for Jehovah God. Jehovah instructed him: "Go your way out of your country and from your relatives . . . to the country that I shall show you." (Gen. 12:1) Abraham did not hold back because Jehovah was asking him to leave a secure way of life for something so uncertain. He had confidence that whatever God required of him was right and for his own good. True, that meant considerable sacrifices for many years. But Jehovah greatly blessed his willingness to serve: Abraham saw many of Jehovah's marvelous acts in behalf of himself and his family; he did not lack material necessities; he came to be called "Jehovah's friend." (Jas. 2:23) Also, God promised Abraham that an entire nation would come from him. Significantly, the Bible says of this: "After Abraham had shown *patience,* he obtained this promise." (Heb. 6:15) Further, he was privileged to be an ancestor of Jesus Christ. *W 8/1 9a*

Saturday, December 22

Whether there are gifts of prophesying, they will be done away with; whether there are tongues, they will cease; . . . Now, however, there remain faith, hope, love, these three; but the greatest of these is love.—1 Cor. 13:8, 13.

Love will never "fail" or come to an end. Paul pointed this out when he wrote the above. History confirms that the miraculous gifts did pass away, evidently by the second century C.E. Nevertheless, true disciples of Jesus Christ can, to this very day, be identified by the love that they have among themselves. What about us individually? Are we widening out in our love for our Christian brothers? Are we making improvement in displaying love in the manner described by Paul? Surely, this is what we want to do. Since love is a fruit of God's spirit, do we pray for more of that spirit so that we might let love have a fuller expression in our lives? May love continue to be in action in our lives so that we may keep on living, yes, keep on loving for all eternity as loyal servants of the God of love, Jehovah. *W 9/15 20, 21a*

Sunday, December 23

We must all be made manifest before the judgment seat of the Christ, that each one may get his award for the things done through the body, according to the things he has practiced, whether it is good or vile.—2 Cor. 5:10.

All of us should think seriously about our standing before God and Christ now. We do not have endless time to build up a record of fine works. Either death or our Master's return will overtake us. If we are negligent about our Christian responsibilities, then, as a thief, either event could catch us in an unprepared state. May we, therefore, do our utmost each day to live as if it were our last, not allowing personal desires or pleasures to interfere with our faithfully serving God and our Master Jesus Christ. In that case, we will never regret the way in which we have used our time, our energies and our material assets. We will have nothing to fear when standing before the judgment seat of Christ as he renders decisions for his Father. May we then be found as persons with abundant treasure in heaven. *W 11/15 16a*

Monday, December 24

Do not marvel at this, because the hour is coming in which all those in the memorial tombs will hear his voice and come out.—John 5:28, 29.

This "hour" will come during the 1,000-year reign of Jesus Christ with his 144,000 glorified joint heirs. During that reign Ha'des, or the common grave of mankind, is to be destroyed by its being emptied of all the redeemed dead humans. (John 5:28-30) During their sleep of death there comes no change in their personality. Hence, what they did or how they lived during the current wicked system of things will affect them as to their inclinations or attitudes toward Christ's kingdom. Yes, the former life pattern will affect the problem of the resurrected ones as to their conforming to Kingdom requirements for righteousness and their progress toward attaining perfect human life on earth. There will be two outcomes possible. As Jesus indicated, they will either turn to the course of doing good things or turn to the practicing of vile things, with the respective consequences of life or death. *W 9/1 6, 8, 9a*

Tuesday, December 25

Look! a black horse; and the one seated upon it had a pair of scales in his hand. And I heard a voice . . . say: "A quart of wheat for a denarius, and three quarts of barley for a denarius; and do not harm the olive oil and the wine."—Rev. 6:5, 6.

Thus John describes what he further saw in vision. This third horseman symbolizes famine, and with famine there goes food rationing, as in a time of total warfare. Even the very essentials, the wheat and the barley, are in short supply. The wealthy get jittery, lest their luxuries, such as 'oil and wine,' be taken away. This horseman has ridden devastatingly through the earth since 1914. Inflation, spiraling prices, the shaky monetary system and the energy crisis all have to do with his headlong gallop. Nevertheless, we should not be discouraged by any short rations or economic hardships that we are compelled to endure temporarily. We can draw comfort from obeying Matthew 6:33. Also, remember, the rider of the white horse is out in front, and he will bring an end to food shortage and its attendant problems. *W 10/1 12a*

Wednesday, December 26

They for a few days used to discipline us according to what seemed good to them, but he does so for our profit that we may partake of his holiness.—Heb. 12:10.

The discipline that comes in the form of suffering is always profitable. It can have a refining effect, revealing personality flaws that must be corrected. These might include pride, stubbornness, impatience, selfishness and worldliness. When we make the needed improvements, we become purer or more holy in our conduct. By 'becoming holy as Jehovah is holy,' we become 'partakers of God's holiness.' (1 Pet. 1:14-16) From affliction we may also learn things that can better equip us for God's service. Thus Jesus, by having to undergo extreme suffering in the flesh, gained the needed experience to be a compassionate and sympathetic high priest. This has made it possible for us to make our approach to God through Christ with the greatest freeness of speech, confident that Jesus understands our situation and will plead in our behalf. *W 10/15 6, 7a*

Thursday, December 27

All the people answered unanimously and said: "All that Jehovah has spoken we are willing to do."—Ex. 19:8.

Could we not please God and gain the reward of everlasting life by merely leading a clean life? believing in God and Christ? associating with God's people? telling others about the "good news"? without formally dedicating ourselves to do God's will and getting baptized? Apparently there are some who think so. But in this they are mistaken. For God to reward us we must exercise faith in him and love him to the extent of dedicating ourselves to do God's will, following in the footsteps of Jesus Christ. For example: At Mount Sinai, God set before the Israelites his laws and the rewards that they would get from obeying his laws. The Israelites formally agreed to do God's will so that they might receive his guidance, protection and blessing. Likewise, his servants today must make such a commitment. They must heed Jesus' command that those who would observe his commandments must begin by getting baptized.—Matt. 28:19, 20. *W 11/1 14, 15*

Friday, December 28

Is there not wisdom among the aged and understanding in length of days?—Job 12:12.

No age limit is specified in the Bible for those serving as elders. The term "elder" of itself implies age, though it must be recognized that the emphasis is on spiritual, rather than physical, qualities. Age alone is not the determining factor, even as Moses recognized; yet experience is certainly a valuable asset for men caring for responsibilities. (Deut. 1:13) While youth may manifest much energy and enthusiasm, this is not proof of wisdom. But the years of life represented by gray hairs generally give reason for expecting an increased measure of wisdom, even as Job said. (Compare Job 12:20; 32:6, 7.) A young person may be willing, even eager, to serve and show promise for the future. But lack of experience in life can put him at a severe disadvantage when it comes to helping those older than himself with the serious problems of life. His words, however sincere, cannot be expected to carry the same weight as those of one with more years behind him. *W 12/1 9*

Saturday, December 29

We preach Christ impaled . . . Christ the power of God and the wisdom of God. Because a foolish thing of God is wiser than men, and a weak thing of God is stronger than men. —1 Cor. 1:23-25.

The Greeks acquired their teachings from older cultures, for they go all the way back to Egyptian and Babylonian religions. Many religions today are also teaching that God created by means of evolution, thinking to modernize their doctrines, but in fact embracing the error of Greek philosophy. They set aside the Bible truth that Jehovah created life on the earth, that life reproduces "after its kind," that Jehovah is from everlasting and is all-powerful and that Jesus Christ is his Son having a beginning and being subject to him. Happily, for millions on earth today, this religious and philosophical wisdom that views Christ impaled as foolish and weak is itself empty foolishness. They respond to Paul's declaration above to the Corinthian Christians. They raise this cry in all the earth for all who seek the wisdom that gives life. *W 5/15 11, 12a*

Sunday, December 30

Each tree is known by its own fruit. For example, people do not gather figs from thorns, nor do they cut grapes off a thornbush.—Luke 6:44.

The "winepress" of God's "anger" is reserved for the anti-Christian "vine of the earth." On the other hand, ever since God restored the remnant of spiritual Israelites to his favor in the postwar year of 1919, there is no "rage" that he has against this symbolic "vineyard." He has watched over this "vineyard" of spiritual Israel to make it productive to his glory. There is no proper place in it for things similar to thornbushes and weeds that hinder and take away from the fruitfulness of this "vineyard." Hence, the "great crowd" now associating itself with Jehovah's "vineyard" should not want to bring improper things like thornbushes and weeds into the fruitful "vineyard." This would result in hurt to the "great crowd," for Jehovah, in his unchangeable purpose to make his spiritual "vineyard" productive to the full, would war against such weeds. *W 12/15 19a*

Monday, December 31

If anyone is not obedient to our word through this letter, keep this one marked, stop associating with him, that he may become ashamed. And yet do not be considering him as an enemy, but continue admonishing him as a brother. —2 Thess. 3:14, 15.

Individual Christians may have to determine whether the unruly conduct of certain persons associated with the congregation makes them undesirable companions. Here, too, the proper exercise of justice would require that such a decision be based on God's Word and not on personal prejudice or on unscriptural opinions. The motive for stopping association with certain fellow believers in a social way should be a desire to help to bring home to them the need to change their ways. It would not mean being unkind to such persons, 'treating them as enemies.' These individuals should continue to be 'admonished as brothers.' Of course, this also serves to protect those who follow the Bible's advice in this matter from coming under unwholesome influence. *W 9/15 8*

1979

	S	M	T	W	T	F	S
JAN	..	1	2	3	4	5	6
	7	8	9	10	11	12	13
	14	15	16	17	18	19	20
	21	22	23	24	25	26	27
	28	29	30	31	..	..	..
FEB	..	..	..	..	1	2	3
	4	5	6	7	8	9	10
	11	12	13	14	15	16	17
	18	19	20	21	22	23	24
	25	26	27	28	..	..	..
MAR	..	..	..	..	1	2	3
	4	5	6	7	8	9	10
	11	12	13	14	15	16	17
	18	19	20	21	22	23	24
	25	26	27	28	29	30	31
APR	1	2	3	4	5	6	7
	8	9	10	11	12	13	14
	15	16	17	18	19	20	21
	22	23	24	25	26	27	28
	29	30	..	..	..	..	..

	S	M	T	W	T	F	S
MAY	..	..	1	2	3	4	5
	6	7	8	9	10	11	12
	13	14	15	16	17	18	19
	20	21	22	23	24	25	26
	27	28	29	30	31	..	..
JUN	..	..	..	..	..	1	2
	3	4	5	6	7	8	9
	10	11	12	13	14	15	16
	17	18	19	20	21	22	23
	24	25	26	27	28	29	30
JUL	1	2	3	4	5	6	7
	8	9	10	11	12	13	14
	15	16	17	18	19	20	21
	22	23	24	25	26	27	28
	29	30	31	..	..	..	..
AUG	..	..	..	1	2	3	4
	5	6	7	8	9	10	11
	12	13	14	15	16	17	18
	19	20	21	22	23	24	25
	26	27	28	29	30	31	..

	S	M	T	W	T	F	S
SEP	..	..	..	..	..	..	1
	2	3	4	5	6	7	8
	9	10	11	12	13	14	15
	16	17	18	19	20	21	22
	23	24	25	26	27	28	29
	30	..	..	..	..	..	..
OCT	..	1	2	3	4	5	6
	7	8	9	10	11	12	13
	14	15	16	17	18	19	20
	21	22	23	24	25	26	27
	28	29	30	31	..	..	..
NOV	..	..	..	..	1	2	3
	4	5	6	7	8	9	10
	11	12	13	14	15	16	17
	18	19	20	21	22	23	24
	25	26	27	28	29	30	..
DEC	..	..	..	..	..	..	1
	2	3	4	5	6	7	8
	9	10	11	12	13	14	15
	16	17	18	19	20	21	22
	23	24	25	26	27	28	29
	30	31	..	..	..	..	..

CHIEF OFFICE AND OFFICIAL ADDRESS OF
Watch Tower Bible and Tract Society of Pennsylvania
Watchtower Bible and Tract Society of New York, Inc.
International Bible Students Association
124 Columbia Heights, Brooklyn, New York 11201, U.S.A.

ADDRESSES OF BRANCH OFFICES:

ALASKA 99507: 2552 East 48th Ave., Anchorage. **AUSTRALIA:** 11 Beresford Road, Strathfield, N.S.W. 2135. **AUSTRIA:** Gallgasse 44, A-1130 Vienna. **BAHAMAS:** Box N-1247, Nassau, N.P. **BARBADOS:** Fontabelle Rd., Bridgetown. **BELGIUM:** rue d'Argile 60, B-1950 Kraainem. **BELIZE:** Box 257, Belize City. **BOLIVIA:** Casilla No. 1440, La Paz. **BRAZIL:** Rua Guaíra, 216, Bosque da Saúde, 04142 São Paulo, SP; Caixa Postal 12.896, 01000 São Paulo, SP. **BURMA:** P.O. Box 62, Rangoon. **CANADA M6A 1Z5:** 150 Bridgeland Ave., Toronto, Ontario. **CHILE:** Clorinda Wilshaw 501, Ñuñoa; Casilla 261-V, Santiago 21. **COLOMBIA:** Apartado Aereo 91346, Bogotá 8, D.E. **COSTA RICA:** Apartado 10043, San José. **CYPRUS:** P.O. Box 288, Limassol. **DENMARK:** Kongevejen 207, DK-2830 Virum. **DOMINICAN REPUBLIC:** Avenida Francia 33 (Apartado 1742), Santo Domingo. **ECUADOR:** Casilla 4512, Guayaquil. **EL SALVADOR:** Apartado 401, San Salvador. **ENGLAND:** Watch Tower House, The Ridgeway, London NW7 1RN. **FIJI:** Box 23, Suva. **FINLAND:** Postbox 68, SF-01301 Vantaa 30. **FRANCE:** 81 rue du Point-du-Jour, 92100 Boulogne-Billancourt. **GERMANY, FEDERAL REPUBLIC OF:** Postfach 5920, D-6200 Wiesbaden 1. **GHANA:** Box 760, Accra. **GREECE:** 4 Kartali St., Athens 611. **GUADELOUPE:** B.P. 239, 97156 Pointe-à-Pitre Cedex. **GUATEMALA:** 11 Avenida 5-67, Guatemala 1. **GUYANA:** 50 Brickdam, Georgetown 16. **HAITI:** Post Box 185, Port-au-Prince. **HAWAII 96814:** 1228 Pensacola St., Honolulu. **HONDURAS:** Apartado 147, Tegucigalpa. **HONG KONG:** 312 Prince Edward Rd., Second Floor, Kowloon. **ICELAND:** Vardturninn Box 251, 121 Reykjavik. **INDIA:** Post Bag 10, Lonavla, Pune Dis., Mah. 410 401. **IRAN:** P.O. Box 11-1797, Tehran. **IRELAND:** 86 Lindsay Rd., Glasnevin, Dublin 9. **ISRAEL:** P.O. Box 44520, Haifa 31 040. **ITALY:** Via della Bufalotta 1281, 00138 Rome. **IVORY COAST:** B.P. 10250 Koumassi, Abidjan. **JAMAICA:** 41 Trafalgar Rd., Kingston 10. **JAPAN:** 5-5-8 Mita Minato-Ku, Tokyo, 108. **KENYA:** Box 47788, Nairobi. **KOREA:** Box 7 Sodaemun P.O., Seoul, 120. **LEEWARD ISLANDS:** Box 119, St. Johns, Antigua. **LIBERIA:** P.O. Box 171, Monrovia. **LUXEMBOURG:** 15, rue de l'Egalite, Luxembourg-Bonnevoie, G.D. **MALAYSIA:** 20 Scotland Close, Penang. **MARTINIQUE:** Alize 4, B-7 Floreal, 97200 Fort de France. **MAURITIUS:** 42 Vandermeersch St., Rose Hill. **MEXICO:** Apartado Postal 42-048, Mexico 4, D.F. **NETHERLANDS:** Voorburgstraat 250, 1059 VD Amsterdam. **NETHERLANDS ANTILLES:** Oosterbeekstraat 11, Willemstad, Curaçao. **NEW CALEDONIA:** B.P. 787, Nouméa. **NEWFOUNDLAND, CANADA A1C 2M1:** 239 Pennywell Rd., St. John's. **NEW ZEALAND:** 6-A Western Springs Road, Auckland 3. **NICARAGUA:** Apartado 183, Managua, D.N. **NIGERIA:** P.O. Box 194, Yaba, Lagos State. **NORWAY:** Inkognitogaten 28 B., Oslo 2. **OKINAWA JAPAN, 901-13:** 546 Itarashiki-ku, Yonabaru-Cho. **PAKISTAN:** 8-E Habibullah Rd., Lahore 3. **PANAMA:** Apartado 1386, Panama 1. **PAPUA NEW GUINEA:** Box 113, Port Moresby. **PARAGUAY:** Casilla de Correo 482, Asunción. **PERU:** Gervasio Santillana 370; Casilla 5178, Miraflores, Lima 18. **PHILIPPINES, REPUBLIC OF:** P.O. Box 2044, Manila 2800; 186 Roosevelt Ave., San Francisco del Monte, Quezon City 3010. **PORTUGAL:** Apartado 21.022, Lisbon 2. **PUERTO RICO 00927:** Calle Onix 23, Urb. Bucaré, Río Piedras. **RHODESIA:** 35 Fife Avenue, Salisbury. **SENEGAL:** B.P. 3107, Dakar. **SIERRA LEONE:** Box 136, Freetown. **SOLOMON ISLANDS:** P.O. Box 166, Honiara. **SOUTH AFRICA:** Private Bag 2, Elandsfontein, 1406. **SPAIN:** Calle Pardo 65, Barcelona 16. **SRI LANKA, REP. OF:** 62 Layard's Road, Colombo 5. **SURINAM:** Wicherstraat 8-10; Box 49, Paramaribo. **SWEDEN:** Box 8, S-175 21 Järfälla 1. **SWITZERLAND:** Ulmenweg 45; P.O. Box 477, CH-3601 Thun. **TAHITI:** B. P. 518, Papeete. **TAIWAN 106 (REPUBLIC OF CHINA):** 5 Lane 99, Yun-Ho St., Taipei. **THAILAND:** 69/1 Soi 2, Sukhumwit Rd., Bangkok 11. **TRINIDAD:** 2 La Seiva Road, Maraval, Port of Spain. **UNITED STATES OF AMERICA:** 117 Adams St., Brooklyn, N.Y. 11201. **URUGUAY:** Francisco Bauzá 3372, Montevideo. **VENEZUELA:** Apartado 116, La Victoria, Edo. Aragua. **ZAÏRE, REP. OF:** B.P. 634, Limete, Kinshasa. **ZAMBIA, REP. OF:** Box 1598, Kitwe.

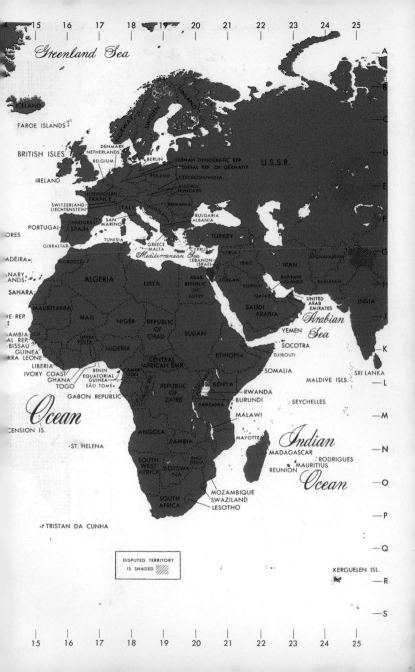